The Routledge Co[mpanion]
to Social The[ory]

)nd
all

)an

:his
ing
ng,
ink

UK

The Rou
and prov
ground-b
emergent
contemp

ive
'his
and
the

- the ti
- symt
- psycl
- struc
- ident
- theor
- globi

The Rou
ities of b
terms ar
sionals ii
politics.

ex-
key
fes-
and

Anthony Elliott is Professor of Sociology at Flinders University, Australia, and Visiting Research Professor in Sociology at The Open University, UK. His publications for Routledge include *Contemporary Social Theory: An Introduction* (2009), *The New Individualism: The Emotional Costs of Globalization* with Charles Lemert (revised edition, 2009), and the co-edited volume *Globalization: A Reader* (2010).

Also available from Routledge

Sociology: the Basics
Martin Albrow
978–0–415–17264–6

Sociology: the Key Concepts
John Scott
978–0–415–34406–7

Fifty Key Sociologists: the Formative Theorists
John Scott
978–0–415–35260–4

Fifty Key Sociologists: the Contemporary Theorists
John Scott
978–0–415–35259–8

Cultural Theory: the Key Thinkers
Andrew Edgar and Peter Sedgwick
978–0–415–23281–4

Cultural Theory: the Key Concepts (second edition)
Edited by Andrew Edgar and Peter Sedgwick
978–0–415–39939–5

Social and Cultural Anthropology: the Key Concepts (second edition)
Nigel Rapport and Joanna Overing
978–0–415–36751–6

Habermas: the Key Concepts
Andrew Edgar
978–0–415–30379–8

The Routledge Companion to Feminism and Postfeminism (second edition)
Edited by Sarah Gamble
978–0–415–24310–0

The Routledge Companion to Postmodernism (second edition)
Edited by Stuart Sim
978–0–415–33359–7

THE ROUTLEDGE COMPANION
TO SOCIAL THEORY

Edited by
Anthony Elliott

With the assistance of Daniel Mendelson

Routledge
Taylor & Francis Group

LONDON AND NEW YORK

First published 2010
by Routledge
2 Park Square, Milton Park, Abingdon, Oxon OX14 4RN

Simultaneously published in the USA and Canada
by Routledge
270 Madison Avenue, New York, NY 10016

Routledge is an imprint of the Taylor & Francis Group, an informa business

© 2010 Anthony Elliott for selection and editorial matter; individual
contributors their contribution

Typeset in Times New Roman by Book Now Ltd, London
Printed and bound in Great Britain by CPI Antony Rowe, Chippenham, Wiltshire

British Library Cataloguing in Publication Data
A catalogue record for this book is available from the British Library

Library of Congress Cataloging in Publication Data
The Routledge companion to social theory / edited by Anthony Elliott.
p. cm.
Includes bibliographical references and index.
1. Sociology—Philosophy. 2. Social sciences—Philosophy. I. Elliott, Anthony.
HM585.R68 2009
301—dc22
2009023514

ISBN10: 0–415–47015–3 (hbk)
ISBN10: 0–415–47016–1 (pbk)
ISBN10: 0–203–86401–8 (ebk)

ISBN13: 978–0–415–47015–5 (hbk)
ISBN13: 978–0–415–47016–2 (pbk)
ISBN13: 978–0–203–86401–2 (ebk)

Contents

Preface   vii
Contributors   ix

Editor's introduction   xi
Anthony Elliott

Part I Traditions and riddles of social theory   1

1   What is social theory?   3
    Charles Lemert

2   Classical social theory   19
    Larry Ray

3   Symbolic interactionism   37
    Philip Manning and Greg Smith

4   Social theory and psychoanalysis   56
    Anthony Elliott

5   Structuralist and post-structuralist social theory   73
    Daniel Chaffee

6   Theories of structuration   86
    Anthony Elliott

7   Social theory of the body   102
    Mary Holmes

8   Postmodern social theory   117
    Sam Han

9   Identity and social theory   135
    Ann Branaman

CONTENTS

10 New media, popular culture and social theory   156
    Nick Stevenson

11 Citizenship, cosmopolitanism and human rights   173
    Engin F. Isin and Bryan S. Turner

12 Cultural social theory   188
    Brad West

13 Social theory and globalization   203
    Eric L. Hsu

Part II Central terms and thinkers   **219**
Daniel Mendelson

    Bibliography   304
    Index   320

PREFACE

This book seeks to provide a reasonably comprehensive, accessible and provocative introduction to some of the key traditions of thought in social theory. In certain respects, the book is a companion volume to my recent book, *Contemporary Social Theory: An Introduction* (London and New York: Routledge, 2009). There I put forward the view that social theory is essential to our practical and political engagement with the self, with others and the wider world in these troubled and troubling times. In this book, *The Routledge Companion to Social Theory*, I have commissioned important social theorists (both world-acclaimed and emergent new voices) to reflect on the complex, contradictory ways in which social theory sheds light on our practical and political engagement with the contemporary world.

I owe a substantial debt to numerous colleagues and friends who have assisted with the preparation of this book. The idea for the book came from David Avital at Routledge, and I thank him for his early input into the conceptual architecture of the project. As with everything I publish with Routledge, I must thank Gerhard Boomgaarden: he gave me many helpful suggestions and has been a huge source of encouragement and support. Nicola Geraghty, Fiore Inglese, Nick Stevenson, Paul du Gay, John Urry, Bryan Turner, Charles Lemert, Anthony Moran, Conrad Meyer and Deborah Maxwell were generous with their time and provided much-needed support. As always, colleagues at Flinders Sociology were especially wonderful. I am particularly grateful to Daniel Mendelson, who was marvellously helpful in providing editorial assistance and was a pleasure to work with on the project. Thanks also to Daniel Chaffee, Eric Hsu, Atsushi Sawai and Jordan McKenzie. Thank you to Richard Cook and his colleagues at Book Now. Finally, I should like to thank Katherine Ong at Routledge for preparing this book for publication.

Anthony Elliott

Contributors

Ann Branaman is Associate Professor of Sociology at Florida Atlantic University, USA. Publications include *The Goffman Reader* (co-edited with Charles Lemert, 1997) and *Self and Society* (2001).

Daniel Chaffee is Associate Lecturer of Sociology at Flinders University, Australia. Publications include *The Race of Time: A Charles Lemert Reader* (with Sam Han, 2009) and *Globalization: A Reader* (with Charles Lemert, Anthony Elliott and Eric Hsu, forthcoming).

Anthony Elliott is Head of the Department of Sociology at Flinders University, Australia, and Visiting Research Chair at The Open University, UK. Publications include *Making the Cut: How Cosmetic Surgery Is Transforming our Lives* (2008) and *Contemporary Social Theory: An Introduction* (2009).

Sam Han is Visiting Instructor of Sociology at the College of Staten Island, City University of New York, USA. Publications include *Navigating Technomedia: Caught in the Web* (2007) and *The Race of Time: A Charles Lemert Reader* (with Daniel Chaffee, 2009).

Mary Holmes is Senior Lecturer of Sociology at Flinders University, Australia. Publications include *The Representation of What is Gender* (2007) and *Feminists as Political Actors* (2008).

Eric L. Hsu is Associate Lecturer of Sociology at Flinders University, Australia. Publications include *Globalization: A Reader* (with Charles Lemert, Anthony Elliott and Daniel Chaffee, forthcoming).

Engin F. Isin is Professor of Citizenship at the Open University, UK. Publications include *Being Political* (2002) and *Recasting the Social in Citizenship* (2008).

Charles Lemert regularly teaches sociology at Wesleyan University in Connecticut, the American University of Central Asia, the Boston Graduate School of Psychoanalysis, and at Flinders University. Publications include *The New Individualism* (with Anthony Elliott, 2005) and *Thinking the Unthinkable: An Introduction to Social Theories* (2007).

CONTRIBUTORS

Phil Manning is Professor of Sociology at Cleveland State University, USA. Publications include *Erving Goffman and Modern Sociology* (1992) and *Freud and American Sociology* (2005).

Larry Ray is Professor of Sociology at the University of Kent, UK. Publications include *Social Theory and Postcommunism* (with William Outhwaite, 2005) and *Globalization and Everyday Life* (2007).

Greg Smith is Professor of Sociology at the University of Salford, UK. Publications include *Erving Goffman* (2006) and *Introducing Cultural Studies* (2nd edition, 2008).

Nick Stevenson is Reader in Cultural Sociology at the University of Nottingham, UK. Publications include *Understanding Media Cultures* (2002) and *Cultural Citizenship* (2003).

Bryan S. Turner is Alona Evans Distinguished Professor of Sociology at Wellesley College, USA. Publications include *Rights and Virtues* (2006) and *The Body and Society* (3rd edition, 2008).

Brad West is Senior Lecturer of Sociology at Flinders University, Australia. He is editor of *Down the Road: Exploring Backpackers and Independent Travel* (2005).

EDITOR'S INTRODUCTION

ANTHONY ELLIOTT

It is customary to begin reference works, such as this one, with a definition. As it happens, I am going to suggest in these opening remarks that it is not necessarily helpful – and certainly not necessarily more truthful – to think that a definition of a field as complex and contradictory as social theory is a way of being serious. But before I make that argument, let's try out a definition at any rate. Here's what I often tell my students, or, at least, what I used to tell my students:

> Social theory is the systematic analysis of the broad developmental contours of modernity, involving the multidisciplinary reconstruction of terms, issues and problems in the social sciences such as human agency, intersubjectivity, social structure and society. Unlike philosophy, social theory is more directly concerned with the immediate experience of our lives and especially of our lives in the troubled times in which we live. That is to say, social theory is more concerned with ontological than epistemological issues. Moreover, social theory is not the province of any one discipline in the social sciences, although it has certainly been institutionalized and professionalized in some disciplines – such as sociology, political science and anthropology, for example.

Such a rough definition of social theory, I would suggest, goes to the heart of the problem of the production and reproduction of society, as well as of the relation between human agency and social structure, all of which can be traced out in social-theoretical debates in the social sciences throughout the nineteenth, twentieth and, now, twenty-first centuries. But whether one agrees or disagrees with this underscoring of the main themes of social theory, even the most cursory glance at this book suggests that it does not take too much questioning to burst the bounds of the sort of definition I have provided above. For whether sympathetic or critical of social theory, it would appear that a multidisciplinary enterprise that has as its subject-matter a topic as broad as 'human social activity' is bound to always elude precise definitions, designations, categories and analytical expectancies. In this connection, while a neat, tidy definition of social theory may appear 'serious' enough for analytical purposes from one angle, it might still fall short – or, miss the mark – of capturing other aspects of 'human social activity' from another angle. Consider any the following themes and thematics, for example, in respect of the working definition of social theory I have provided: What about the role of culture? What of our private worlds of sexuality, intimacy, eroticism and affect? What of unconscious forms of knowledge, or the only half-conscious manner in which much of human social activity in performed? Indeed, what of performance itself – both the performativity of everyday social life and of the critical engagement of ideas performed by social theorists? And still there is more. What impact does nineteenth-century social theory have (and how might we assess its likely impact for social thought in the future) for theorizing the world today, for confronting its novelties and dangers? Is social theory only about 'conceptual perspectives' on the world – functionalism, structuralism, postmodernism – or can it also be a way to 'translate' the world? Most pressing of all, is social theory capable of changing the world?

All of these conceptual and political concerns – and a good deal more besides – are charted in *The Routledge Companion to Social Theory*. At one level, this reference work seeks to provide a reasonably comprehensive, but concise, set of appraisals of the most influential traditions of thought in the social sciences in general and social theory in particular. Commencing with such fundamental topics as the transdisciplinary nature of social theory (expertly navigated by Charles Lemert in Chapter 1) and the legacy of classical social thought (as accessibly retold by Larry Ray in Chapter 2), the book covers a remarkably broad range of social-theoretical traditions – from neo-Marxism to structuralism, from symbolic interactionism to postmodernism, from psychoanalysis to feminisms, and from theories of structuration to globalization. In doing so, the book offers detailed appraisals of some of the core contributions to the critique of social life in contemporary social science. As editor, my hope is that readers will come away from engaging with the book with a better sense of why social theory must incorporate – among other topics – a treatment of human subjectivity (both consciousness and the unconscious) as embroiled in the structural conditions of everyday life, and also critically grasp the significance of language, reflexivity and critical self-reflection as core mediums for the production and reproduction of society. There are, as we shall see, different suggestions for how these problems are best handled in current forms of social theory. Whether one finds the most convincing answers in the writings of, among others, Anthony Giddens, Jürgen Habermas, Julia Kristeva, Jean Baudrillard, Judith Butler, Michel Foucault, Jacques Derrida, Pierre Bourdieu or Luce Irigaray is, perhaps, a matter of individual preference or political disposition. Yet, whatever the internal dialogues that readers of this book fashion with these leading intellectuals of our age, one central point emerges most forcefully: the problem of the relation between self and society, or the individual and culture, is the very life-blood of fertile conceptual development in social theory.

The Routledge Companion to Social Theory differs significantly from other reference books in the field, I hope, for one key reason: it is not, in fact, a 'standard' reference work at all! For too many years now, social science publishers have churned out dull, dry and turgid reference books that few could read beyond the academy, and even then only with considerable difficulty in the classroom itself. In the case of social theory, this was especially perverse – given that the field always was, and hopefully shall remain, a public political enterprise. Just consider public political debate today in, say, the UK and Europe and one would surely recognize the immense contribution of social theorists to the politics of our time. Indeed, many of the most vocal social-theoretical contributors to today's public sphere – Jürgen Habermas, Julia Kristeva, Anthony Giddens, Ulrich Beck, Slavoj Žižek and Zygmunt Bauman – are read well beyond the classroom precisely because they write with an alert speculative intelligence on the most pressing issues of the day. The same is surely true of public political debate in the United States, where the contributions of social theorists – among others, Judith Butler, Fredric Jameson, Charles Lemert and Manual Castells – loom large. Accordingly, and against this backdrop, I have endeavoured, as editor, to solicit contributions to this book that would similarly provide theoretical insights into the fabric of everyday living.

If this focus on the practical and political relevance of social theory is underscored in Part I of *The Routledge Companion to Social Theory*, such themes are equally pertinent to Part II of the book, written by Daniel Mendelson. 'Practical' and 'political' in the sense that this is not so much a short dictionary of theorists and terms to be consulted as 'facts'; it is rather a work that calls for the active engagement of the reader. Again, I believe that *The Routledge Companion to Social Theory* breaks new ground in Part II in its detailed treatment of the theories, criticisms and the lives of both classical and contemporary social theorists, as well as key terms and concepts. It is, of course, standard fare for the dictionary component of reference works to be somewhat tedious. Yet, by contrast, Mendelson promotes an understanding of social theory with a light touch – in a dictionary for curiosity and engagement. My own sense is that readers might use Part II with profit by consulting entries as they navigate the wider theoretical arguments in developed in Part I. But the point is that chapters can be read in any order, and Part II similarly mined for information according to the reader's interests.

It is also important to emphasize that, in trying to provide a reasonably comprehensive overview of some of the main lines of development in classical and contemporary social theory, as editor, I have refrained from organizing chapters in terms of strict disciplinary boundaries and concerns. Such an approach derives from the transdisciplinary concerns of social theory itself, but it is worth underscoring this point here because – due to limitations of space – it has not been possible to provide chapters covering every emerging trend or trajectory in contemporary social thought. One area of massive social change where this point is especially relevant concerns gender, and especially the rapidly developing areas of feminist and post-feminist social theory. Rather than devote a separate chapter to gender and feminism, however, this book integrates the feminist and post-feminist problematization of gender throughout many of the chapters which follow. As such, the diversity characteristic of feminist social thought becomes evident when comparing, say, the contributions of feminism to psychoanalytic social theory (traced by the editor in Chapter 4) to the importance of gender systems in the constitution of human bodies (as critiqued by Mary Holmes in Chapter 7).

What this highlights, perhaps above all, is that social theory is an amazingly diverse and varied enterprise. The contributors to this volume, whilst not always (and in some cases rarely) agreeing on the political ends of this enterprise, certainly outline powerful arguments for the ongoing relevance of the leading traditions of social thought to the analysis and critique of today's globalized world. It is my hope that readers will find *The Routledge Companion to Social Theory* a wide-ranging, accessible and provocative introduction to the present state of social theory.

Part I

TRADITIONS AND RIDDLES OF SOCIAL THEORY

1

WHAT IS SOCIAL THEORY?

CHARLES LEMERT

WORDS AND THINGS

What is social theory? The question does not abide a ready answer. It is easier to answer other questions of the kind. What is music? What is biology? What is poetry? What is a cow? What is shit? But, what is social theory? This, latter, is far the more complicated question as becomes evident when it is put side by side the others.

What is *music*? Most people, whether good at it or not, know what music is or, at least, having heard a lot of that sort of thing, they think they do. When it comes to *biology*, it may to most sound familiar, but saying what biology actually is might be difficult for those without a long history in schools. Biologists and associates of other groups that similarly demand a high degree of technical expertise tend to keep to themselves the right to define their fields. I was a zoology major in college but, soon enough, zoology was absorbed into biology, after which biology split into several fields, including microbiology which, so far as I can tell, is a kind of biochemistry of life, and then came neuroscience, and so on. Who knows where it will end?

Then, continuing, we come to: What is *poetry*? One would think that poetry is much like music in that people without technical qualification in the subject think they know what it is. Yet it is fair to ask, for example, whether rap is poetry or music of the same order as, say, the Davidic Psalms or Shakespeare's sonnets? For which the sensible answer is that they are not because there is little evidence that a natural acquaintance with poetry is as common as a native appreciation of music – if only because low-brow musics have qualities of their own, but bad poetry is, well, obviously bad. Then we come to *cows*. As any parent or minder of small children knows, a cow exists only in certain cultures where the English language is widely practiced. In rural France, where there are many creatures of the kind English speakers refer to as cows, in the fields there are not cows, but *vaches*. The same critter can be found in both places, but what children learn to call them is different enough that it would be right to wonder what the hell that animal is, when all is said and done.

Finally, what is *shit*? You might think that the word refers to a thing of the same sort as does 'cow'. Indeed, it is true that various languages have different slang expressions for this more or less daily excretion from the rearmost

3

orifice of the nether regions of the human body. The difference is that, though cows unembarrassedly will shit in public as human normally do not, 'shit' is a word the shock value of which derives from the manners of certain groups that think talk of this common, if malodorous, bodily produce is uncouth. Both cows and the feces they produce have commodity value, yet the one is couth, even when it shits, while the shit itself is unspeakable. Mannered persons may teach their children that a cow is pooping but not, as a rule, that it is shitting.

POETRY AND SHIT

Thus, after *music, cows, poetry, biology, cows* and *shit*, we come to the subject with which we are meant to occupy ourselves. What is *social theory*? There are those, we should say right off, who think it is shit. And some, being of a more generous disposition, would say that 'social theory', whatever it is, is like 'cow' in that it refers, not to a real thing in the world, but to an activity that requires very different words, depending on local habits.

At the other extreme, there are those (I would be among them) who think of social theory as more like poetry than anything else – as, that is, a song arising from the heart of ordinary life that, when well composed, can tell the story of human good and evil. Yet, in defense of this idea, I should say that to think of social theory as poetry runs up against the fact that some who are professional practitioners of it write, if not like shit, at least like the most egregious bars of experimental music including some popular hip-hop lyrics that make no sense whatsoever outside the community to which the words are addressed. In this respect, what poetry social theory might be is always at risk of degradation by the tin ears of those who do it. Still, even in its earliest days, social theorists sang with an ear to the ground of human feeling and need.

> A commodity is a queer thing abounding
> In metaphysical subtleties and theological niceties
>
> (Karl Marx, 1867)

> No one knows who will live in this cage of the future
> Or whether at the end of this tremendous development,
> Entirely new prophets will arise,
> Or there will be a great rebirth of old ideas and ideals,
> Or, if neither, mechanized petrifaction,
> Embellished with a sort of convulsive self-importance
>
> (Max Weber, 1905)

> The stranger is near and far at the same time,
> As in any relationship based on merely human similarities
>
> (Georg Simmel, 1908)

It is a peculiar sensation, this double-consciousness,
This sense of always looking at one's self through the eyes of others,
Of measuring one's soul by the tape of a world
That looks on in amused contempt

(W.E.B. Du Bois, 1903)

What a responsibility it is to have the sole management
Of the primal lights and shadows!
Such is the colored woman's office

(Anna Julia Cooper, 1892)

All fixed, fast-frozen relations,
With their train of ancient and venerable prejudices and opinions,
Are swept away […]
All that is solid melts into air,
All that is holy is profaned,
And man is at last
Compelled to face,
With sober senses,
His real conditions of life,
And his relations with his kind

(Marx and Engels, 1848)

One might say that none of these lines is true poetry. The meter is odd or lacking. The tone can be arrhythmic. The phrasing is out of proportion. Yet, there is poetry here in the beat of longings for a purpose higher than the mundane. Social theory can be poetic, if not poetry outright. But when it is, it is because, at its best, it is willing to venture beyond the obvious and factual to the farther reaches of life's unfathomable shores.

To speak of poetry and shit in one breath may seem an odd way to introduce a book on (and of) a third subject, social theory. Odd or not, the elegant crudity of the allusion has at least the virtue of honesty in respect to the possibilities and limitations of the subject at hand. Like so many creative aspects of human life, much social theory has been known for lacking modesty – a failure that is baggage to all attempts to explore unknown or unspeakable territories. To sail into the seas, long from land, the adventurer comes to terms with the risks she takes. Sailing where no one else has can instill a righteous self-confidence – this being the only true compass she can count on. One sets the trim into the bad winds, ignores the worst that could happen, tolerates the burning sun, the rotting rations, the odors rising up from the hold.

The important virtue in the venture is to keep both aspects in proportion. One never sails alone. Others foul the air. This is the honest truth of creative attempts to imagine the meaning of social things – which is what social theory does.

CHARLES LEMERT

Imagination and Arrogance

Social theorists, at their best, do something rare among imaginative artists of the species. As persons they are not special, but their labors may be unique. There are, of course, poets and biologists and many others of all walks who come to think of themselves as telling the stories or enunciating the facts of life. When they do it well, one can only stand back in awe.

> To see in death a sleep, and in the sunset
> A sad gold, of such is Poetry
>
> (Jorge Luis Borges, 1964)

> It may metaphorically be said
> That natural selection is daily and hourly
> Scrutinizing, throughout the world,
> The slightest variations;
> Rejecting those that are bad,
> Preserving and adding up all that are good
>
> (Charles Darwin, 1859)

Humility is not a natural aptitude of the human mind. The mind tempts those who use it to imagine so much more than they can understand. Arrogance in the breed occurs when it is forgotten that the ability to imagine or explain a possible state of affairs is far – very far – from the ability to understand it.

Still, there are those like Borges and Darwin who kept their imaginations within the limits. This is the exceptional genius of the best poets and scientists. Borges grew blind. He labored alone in the basement of a library. Darwin was cautious. He labored for 20 years after the voyage of the *Beagle* before offering his ideas in public. Composition and scientific work have in common the hard reality that notes and words, like facts, occur to us (as Max **Weber** once put it) only when *they* please. All the hard work in the world cannot call forth beauty or truth. In this respect, social theory also must face the hard necessities of its limitations.

Social theorists, like others, can be cautiously daring. Like others they too, being human, can be arrogant. Social theory is at once poetry and science, but it is, in its way, different from both. This difference is what marks social theory off from other acts of the imagination. Still, it must contend with problems inherent in the nature of theory.

Any human endeavor that calls itself 'theory' suffers the danger that the one who theorizes will succumb to his humanity. Theories, by nature, are attempts to reach freely for horizons beyond the edge of seas and lands. This is what it is meant to do. Poetry, notwithstanding poetics (the theory of poetry), does not in and off itself claim to be a theory. Yet, it reaches very far beyond the evidence to make statements that may refer to the more universal of human things, but the reach can result in creating a foreboding abstraction.

6

Those who wait on the Lord will renew their strength/ they shall mount up with wings like eagles/ they shall run and not be weary/ they shall walk and not faint.

This most ancient of verses by the Hebrew prophet Isaiah proclaims not a fact or a logic of human life, but a belief that, over the centuries, has been powerful beyond its ability to document or prove a general idea. When one lives without grasping for power, she is refreshed in ways not available to those who spend their energy seeking to control the things of this world.

Still, poetry may, and probably does, contain a theory of itself. 'To see in death a sleep, and in the sunset, a sad gold, of such is Poetry.' This is a theory of poetry. But it is a theory that has an anchor to leeward – death in sleep, gold in sunset's sadness. Borges, thus, feels his way to the fantastic by touching the daily cycles of human experience. Likewise, by explaining natural selection as a 'daily and hourly scrutinizing', Darwin sets his grand theory of natural life in the soil of what he observed in his voyages years before.

But social theory faces a series of problems that may not be as disruptive in the literary arts or the natural sciences. When it comes to social theory, as it has come to be understood it modern times, the drift of popular opinion is that theories of social things are impossibly abstract. Of course, the better ones are not any more abstract than are the best theories of metaphor or nature. Plus which, it needs saying (but should not) that abstractions are part of life. Were we to shut ourselves up in the sunsets and deaths or the daily scrutiny of events that pass before our local ecologies, we would be truly dead, selected out of the higher truths of human meaning and life. Abstractions, in the sense of reaching as far beyond the ordinary as we can, are zest to the humdrum. That this may be true, or even a truism, does not mean that some cooks season their meat to death – reduce, that is, the ordinary to the commonplace.

In the modern world, abstractions are an acquired taste. When it comes to social theory one ought not to ignore the implications of this observation.

SOCIAL THEORY AND THE MODERN

When one speaks of such a thing as 'the **modern** world', he is speaking irrevocably not of life itself, or humankind as such, but of a real and quite specific social arrangement. To the young, the so-called 'modern world' may seem impossibly abstract. But, historically, the structures, accords, and patterns of life associated with 'the modern' are utterly different from each and every social form that came before and, it seems, different too from what is coming after as a new millennium comes into its surprising own. In fact, social theories might best be defined as those theories of human society unique to the modern era. We can wonder whether some other social assemblage will dominate in the after of the modern. We know, however, that there was nothing like the modern before. Some consider theories of the **postmodern** helpful in tracing the history of modern. On the other hand, almost no one who attempts a social theory of the modern fails to use a theory of what came before. It is in the nature of the modern to think of itself as different from and better than the past.

There are, of course, many different kinds of theory that think of themselves as having a modern stage. Among physicists, for example, mathematically formulated theories are at the very essence of the work. No field is more serious about formal theory. Modern physics after Newton and since Einstein is a terribly unsettled but powerful theory of the way the small and large in the universe behave. Ancient and traditional cultures had their sciences, much of which still contributes to modern thinking, but physics in the sense we think of it today is entirely modern.

And in none of the sciences is this more true than among the social and cultural sciences. Literature and culture studies, musicology, economics, and politics have long embraced theories appropriate to their domain interests; psychology and history less so, unless you mean psychoanalysis and historiography. In all these cases, however, the best theories, whether grand or tiny, can be called theories to the degree that they concern *modern times*. And modern things are irrevocably social things. Whether one speaks of modernity, the modern world-system, modern science or culture, modernism, or any of the variants of the ideal of the modern, one is speaking of a particular occurrence in the social history of the species. Social theory itself, if we grant that it came into its own in the nineteenth century, came to be precisely *social* theory because it aimed to generate theories of this very specific social form.

When exactly the modern emerged or began to emerge from the past is subject to much debate, as are most topics social theorists worry about. Some would say that the modern began in the aftermath of the Renaissance which broke the hold of traditional beliefs and inspired, among other things, the world explorations on either side of 1500. This, of course, identifies the beginnings of the modern with a number of specific advances in European culture and science which made scientific navigation and global thinking rational.

The modern thereby is considered a uniquely Western development that spread over time around the world through a long, sad history of colonizing adventures that exploited the indigenous people and natural resources of Africa and the Americas first; then of the East Indies, ultimately most of the Asias. Yet, it would be another century before, in the 1600s, early modern ideas of consciousness, science, and political rights would emerge – a movement that would come into its own in the revolutions in England and the Netherlands in the 1600s and in France and the Americas in the 1700s. Yet, the Enlightenment, itself a variety of differing philosophies sharply enunciated by English, Scottish, Dutch, German, French and American political thinkers, came to assume the appearance, if not the reality, of a universal culture of human nature.

The Enlightenment is, by its historical nature, a movement of many variants that, oddly, is understood by adherents as a universally true philosophy of humanity. But on the surface this does not make complete sense. To the French in 1789, Enlightenment entailed: *liberty, equality, fraternity*. A few years before, in 1776, American revolutionaries (who had learned quite a lot from the French) defined their Enlightenment as an inalienable right to *life, liberty, and the pursuit of happiness*. As is evident in the comparison, these famous Enlightenment slogans are similar, but different. Both wanted liberty; the French, however, emphasized equality, while the Americans insisted on 'life' (without ever saying what this meant) and the pursuit of happiness. Of course, both doctrines are marked, as are all ideals, by their common failure to achieve what they professed. France is no more equal than is America; nor do the French enjoy high degrees of brotherly love, anymore than Americans can be said to be more happy than, say, the French. The principles they share, like the comparable principles of other modern nation-states, are, as principles, similar, but as national practices they can be quite different. The English and the Scottish, both founders of the Enlightenment are still, after many centuries, at some odds with each other, as they both are with Germans and Americans (who in turn are still divided by Confederate and Yankee values), not to mention the Japanese (who are famous for being modern but in a very Japanese sort of way) and the people of the Kyrgyz Republic (which is not technically a modern state, but actually a wild mixture of ethnic groups the Russians would like to keep in check, if only they knew how).

What different modern nations have in common is rationality, in the phrase Max Weber made famous; which is much more, Weber pointed out, than simply being reasonable. Rationality is, in fact, a practical ethic – a very common, not always well thought through, set of rules by which ordinary people orient themselves to life. In this sense, rationality is a calculating attitude, which is to say that modern people tend to ignore their pasts (for the most part) in order to focus on the time and energy and costs necessary to achieve a better life in the future. Modern is action oriented, thus future oriented. The traditional past is usually thought to be bogged down in the past and oriented to preserving the lives passed down to them.

The essence of the modern, therefore, is to calculate the odds that the future can be better, thus to act in ways that increase one's chances of doing better in this future. As an essence, however, rationality is far from being easily attainable or even widely understood. Still, if we think of rationality as an ethic that guides daily lives (and not as an abstract principle of economic investment or legal theory), it is possible to see what it might mean. Of course, rationality works itself out differently in different places. If it is an ethic of calculating odds, the odds differ according to social and cultural differences, so the application of the ethic will differ; hence, the variations in the original Enlightenment ideals. Still, there is a detectable thread that appears as much in different lives of moderns as in the differing rules of modern societies, and much else. What is common to the modern individuals as to modern social structures is an ethic of living for the future, not the past – and organizing life and behavior in ways that make this possible.

Unfortunately, rationality as a moral ideal is as fallible as all moral ideas. But it turns out that it is also deceptive, if not downright evil. By this, I do not mean to suggest that people, as individuals or nations, who profess and aspire to rational ways of organizing their lives to achieve a better outcome (than, say, their parents or ancestors) are somehow foolish, or ill-intended.

The problem is not in the ideal (as it hardly ever is). The problem with the practical ethic of rationality (as with all others) is in the particular applications of the ideal. For example, it is very difficult to teach schoolchildren to 'be rational'. What would that mean, as a teaching? Yet, it happens that children who advance through many years of school or upon leaving school work hard at a good job actually exhibit the rationality that the ethic calls for. They attend school regularly, more or less on time. They pay attention under no more than the threat of usually mild punishment. They, if they are to stay in school, do their lessons, often when they'd rather do something else, like go to bed early. I personally do not know anyone who enjoys getting up early to go to school or job at the same hour each work day; nor anyone who finds paying attention a great pleasure. I know a few who enjoy studying but even they have evenings when they would rather watch a show or generally fool around, not to mention go to bed early. Yet, schoolchildren do it more or less well, even when they go to terrible schools with cruel teachers who impose stupid rules. Why? Because somehow they learn the ethical ideal that one must do these things in order to get ahead. Children are not stupid, of course. They realize that some kids work hard and will not get anywhere in the long run; and, even if they are excellent students, they fear some things about the process – exams, grades, standardized tests, admissions applications, job interviews. They do so because, in a culture of rationality, everything depends on the ability of the individual to organize daily life in order to do the rational things that will secure their futures. They know it does not necessarily work out, but they also believe that one must try.

So the problem with modern culture is not in the ideals, but in the terrible burden the ideals put on people, not to mention on the national cultures that advertize their modernity. France professes equality, but French society is fair only when it is compared to societies like that of America that do not provide the social benefits the French have. Americans still believe that theirs is the best place on the earth, yet there is no hard evidence that, on average, Americans are more happy with their freedoms than are, say, the Finns or the Swedes. On it goes.

And this is where social theory as a theory of the modern comes in.

SOCIAL THEORY AND CONTRADICTIONS

The modern is, in effect, a contradiction. No traces of civilization which endure down into our time have left behind so much that is good as has the modern. Yet, at the same time, for all the good, it also has done more than its share of evil.

On the good side, the modern wrought by early science and art in the Renaissance has, over the centuries, come to remake the world. Modern science and technology have made life better for millions upon millions who have had access to their miracles. Modern music and the arts have reinvented classical forms and enriched the cultures of the world with new aesthetic wonders that have opened the hearts and minds of people exposed to them. Modern education and schools, where they are established and made to work as they should, have taught countless children to delight in literature and mathematics, in science and the written word.

By contrast, in pre-modern times, what is known today in nearly every field of human endeavor had its forerunners. But in premodern times where there were poets and philosophers, sciences and inventions, the pleasures and advantages they bestowed were bestowed on no more than a fraction of the people, while the majority lived under oppressive, often tyrannical, regimes. There can be no doubt that what good the modern has achieved has been available to a great many more of the people in the world than the number to which ancient civilizations made available the benefits of their achievements.

At the same time, on the evil side of the ledger, the failures of the modern have betrayed its brilliance. Today, early in the twenty-first century, there are more people on the planet than ever before but, as a percentage of the whole, more of them live in economic and social misery. Today, under the sway of modern rational cultures of progress, there is more, not less, violence the world over – the real violence of senseless war or civil strife, of starvation and disease, and the symbolic violence of exclusion from even the most elementary of the rights professed by modern cultures. Today, however wonderful some neighborhoods are, there are as many as a billion people (and perhaps twice that number – nearly a third of the global population) who are homeless and with scant hope of a shelter better than a cardboard shack or dangerous refuges in abandoned buildings, empty lots, or some by-way of human traffic.

The modern promises a better life. In reality, it has not delivered except for the people of relative privilege. I live in a nice home, one bigger than my family needs, and in a very nice neighborhood. But on my daily walks with the family dog I can come upon a place just a few blocks from my home which is strewn with sorry and soiled blankets and boxes, clothes and other leavings of the homeless who are, in effect, my neighbors. Nights, they sleep under a highway bridge. Days, they troll the city looking for food and shelter. They harvest the junk left on my street for the trash pick up. They survive – until, that is, they do not. My home town is a modest one in a wealthy nation. But no where in particular in that nation can it be assumed that there are no uprooted and excluded people; or I should say, no where *should* it be assumed, as it too often is by the well-off who have no interest in regarding those excluded by the system that provides them their wealth. Knowing the truth of these things is unsettling. These men and women in my town who sleep beside the highways are – and this could sound crude – better off by far than their brothers and sisters and the babies and aged parents consigned to the impoverished corners of the world. In Congo and Darfur, in Haiti and parts of Mexico, in North Jakarta and Douala, people congregate around once major and proud cities in the vain search for work or enterprise, for shelter of some kind, for freedom from the militia. In an American city like mine, in most European Cities, and those in Japan and Korea, certainly Australia and New Zealand, in even Mumbai and Shenzhen, the mostly invisible poor have at least the possibility of begging from the wealthy or working at subsistence wage for the corporations; or, as in the circumstance of my neighbors who sleep by the highway they can at least forage the leavings of the well-off not far away.

How do they, the miserable of the world, survive? Could it be that they have no idea what others have? Perhaps, in a few remote villages, some may not. But with rare exception, the technological genius of the modern era has made information as to the realities of distant places available – if only by the one cell phone in the village, or a television strung up in a shanty-town, or by word of mouth, or by the media people who come from time to time to visit, to gawk, to take note of their misery. Their exclusions are many and overwhelming but, in this world, information travels even into the caves and barren corners where the excluded survive as best they can, until they no longer can.

This is but one of the contradictions social theory is meant to understand. **Marx**, in the earliest of his many social theoretical writings, asked the question that would be at the heart of all he wrote in the years to follow: Why is it that the more wealth there is, the more the poor grow poor? For him this is was a question in the 1840s when in Europe there were already the strong beginnings of modern capitalism with its promises of fairness, progress, and rational outcomes for all men (as the expression went). Marx knew better, and he said so. He knew because he dared examine the facts behind the promises of a better world. So too Weber, born to the affluent class, educated in the finest universities; yet he too was a man able to look behind the glories of the rational modern, to see the grave damages the modern could do to the human spirit. So too it was for all the early social theorists; so too it is today.

The modern age promises progress and rational outcomes, pledges that hard work will produce good results, makes commitments to fairness and the protection of the rights of man. But, like most other social arrangements, the modern nations have paid out the promised goods only for those closest to home, if then. Others outside the spheres of their alleged responsibilities have been subjected to colonization and slave trading, to modern economic greed and the belligerence of modern foreign policies; to ruthless corporations and worse, and more. It is not that the modern world has done worse than other civilizations. It likely has done better by far – therein lies the contradiction.

The contradiction of the modern is that it promises so much that it cannot possibly deliver. To begin, as in the Enlightenment, with the promises that modern rationality *is* the universal truth of humanity, is to begin from a premise that cannot be proven. Such a faith that the future is always better endures only to the extent that modern wonders and riches are widely and visibly shared, which they are not. Those in the better position have not ever been known to give up their advantages to help those less well off – at least not to the extent that would be required to make the world as a whole a better place for most, if not all. Many people the world over have, of course, trusted in the promise of the West – and some have gotten what they hoped for. Yet, what are they to say to those left behind? How do the left behind figure in the calculus of hard work and the good life?

There is no easy answer to these questions. Surely there is little cause to reject the ideals in the long run because they do not work in the short run. What then are we to think, if we are to think as social theorists? The answer is not satisfying, but it is one that social theorists, when wise and patient, have tried to work through.

The basic facts of the modern world are, in a word, unthinkable and thus unspeakable. They are because the modern has held itself to such a high standard before which it has failed. Is it possible to think the unthinkable? Not in so many words. But it is possible to give it a go – to try to formulate the possible causes of the misery, then to suggest the way beyond them. Marx thought that the cause was the exploitative structure of capitalism. Not a bad explanation, but as time went by his idea that a post-capitalist revolution would heal all wounds has proven a failure. Émile Durkheim, the great French contemporary of Weber, believed that the problem with the modern age was that there remained nothing like religion to guide the members of a society. He thought that cultural education would fill the gap and guide the modern man of the future. Yet, hopes aside, his answer has nowhere proven itself effective.

Social theory is modern because it thrives in a state of affairs where there are palpable contradictions in need of sorting out. Social theory, thus, is thinking these unthinkables that are most acute in the modern age. All cultures have insolvable problems. Culture itself is probably a shared illusion that things are not as bad as they seem to be. The modern age has solved many of the problems of former ages. Where it got itself into trouble was in claiming that its values were meant to be the values of all humankind. Quite apart from the arrogance, the proposition is absurd, but its absurdity is not readily apparent. The modern age is indubitably good at offering hope; hope does inspire people to live on and to try, and often to do brilliant things.

But, if hope is to be more than a slogan, it must face the hard realities the hopeful cannot abide and the well-off will not. Social theory is not in any way the only endeavor that must face this dilemma. Poetry does, as does science. Religion and culture do and sometimes they do it well enough. In some ways social theory is the weak sister among the imaginative arts. Weak, that is, because it must attack the dreams that, however excellent, can distract attention from the terrors of nights in the cold dirt and weeds under the noisy roadways.

Plus which, social theory, if it takes seriously the realities and the contradictions it is bound to provoke, has one other debilitating responsibility. If it thinks the unthinkable and tells the truth of such things, it makes trouble.

13

Social theory and trouble

How can this be? It is quite apparent to anyone willing to look into the matter that not all social theory is trouble, any more than all of it is poetry. Not only that, but there are endeavors that claim to be social theory that are really plain and, to be frank, disappointing. And there are social theories that are barely readable because their ideas are so finely drawn that it takes months, even years, to get the point clear, much less to discern what trouble is being made, if any.

Still, the incongruity of social theory is that it aims to make trouble even when the trouble it makes is not apparent at first glance. This sometimes (but not always) realized possibility is owing to two historical factors in particular.

Social theory's impure relations with science

First, as social theory has come into its own relatively late in the history of social and culture studies, it has tended to distinguish itself from the more formal sciences one finds in other areas. You would think that social theory belongs properly to sociology, for example. Yet, for a very long while in sociology there was no such thing as social theory. Instead, what theory there was was known by the expression 'sociological theory', by which was meant theory as it could be identified with a formal science of societies. Through the years, sociological theory, so-called, was, as you would expect, the kind of theory that aimed at mathematical expressions of evidence derived from numeric information. Yet, oddly, this attitude never fully prevailed in sociology. Thus, for example, the single most important sociological theorist of modern sociology after the mid-twentieth century was Talcott Parsons (who, I am proud to admit, was one of my teachers). Parsons was famous, and to some notorious, for, yes, attempting to formalize theories of what he called social action; yet all of his formalizations, while abstract, were verbal and not the least mathematical. Thus, among his many very big books was one he edited and introduced with others, *Theories of Society* (1961). His goal in this book was to bring together samples of all the theories and theorists who, in his view, were essential to, in the words of the book's subtitle, 'the foundations of sociological theory'. Yet, what Parsons was doing was actually social theory before the fact.

By the end of the 1960s, the expression 'sociological theory' began to decline somewhat. In its place one increasingly heard of theorists in sociology indentifying their writings as 'social theory'. As late as 1990, James S. Coleman, one of the great and important mathematical sociologists of his time, published *Foundations of Social Theory* (1990), a book that aimed to summarize his life's work in sociological research and of which a quarter of its bulk was devoted to formulae, their solutions meant to prove or illustrate the power of his theories. What he was doing was, in fact, sociological theory. Today, 'sociological theory' is still used, but almost exclusively to signal a theorist's intent to theorize in ways that are either forthrightly or potentially mathematical. Social theory, as the term has come to be used more and more since the last third of the twentieth century rarely attempts to generate mathematical statements except, of course, when the theorist is trying (as Coleman was) to persuade 'real' social theories to take a look at his ideas.

Beyond these events associated with sociological social theory, there was another concurrent and related development that would change everything about what social theory would be. Owing largely to the global events of the 1960s when, to the surprise of the dominant sectors of the modern world, people hitherto ignored began to assert themselves, social theory grew up in many different endeavors. This was, among much else, a time when new social movements replaced older forms of social change and revolution. Then, the settled classes of the modern world encountered civil rights and decoloniza-tion radicals, feminists and anti-war activists, gays and lesbians, former colo-nial subjects and others.

None of these new social movements were as beholden to national ideals or even to the socialist ideals of a universal class of oppressed people. Instead, their political demands were, at first, simply to be heard (this came to be called a poli-tics of cultural recognition). But soon it became evident that they meant to be rec-ognized in order to gain their share of the goods the modern had produced. At first, the comfortable merely hated these radical voices. In time, they were willing to grant them the recognition they demanded – civil rights, fair employment and housing practices, colonial independence. What the comfortable did not want to do was to give them a piece of the economic pie. The history of what followed the early rebellions around the world in the 1960s is long and complex. But, for the time being, we can say that it established, among much else, social theory as a necessary feature of modern (or as some would call to call it postmodern) life.

In that period, from about 1968 down to the present time, the Unthinkable of the modern age began to be thought – at least in the sense that people who, over many centuries, had borne the brunt of modernity's exclusion and of the modern age's refusal to recognize them for who they were, and thus to include them in the progress and benefits many moderns enjoyed, began to speak out and act up. The rebellion of the excluded, if that is the right way to put it, continues even now. There are social theorists in our day who predict that it will continue so long as the excluded of the world are allowed to linger in what Giorgio Agamben has called 'the naked life of humans', excepted from the rights of citizenship and, even, from life itself. But, for the time being, the point to be made is that social theory came to be an activity that would not be contained in the disciplinary requirements of any one of several disciplines. In an important sense, social theory, when at its best, became at long last a poetic of modernity's contradictions – a series of voices giving, if not hope, at least affected rage at the injustices that the modern brought down on them and their people, while promising so much.

As can be readily imagined, such a social theory, even when not poetic, is at least not at home in formal science. Social theory does not, however, abjure facts, or numbers, or formal theories. What it does is work the excesses science cannot fathom, thus to challenge the settled state of social things. Does this mean that social theories of this kind are, as its critics might say, 'ideological', thus 'untrue' or even 'biased'? Yes, of course. How could a mature social theory ask anyone who knows the facts not to be biased against the modern world's false promises, thus siding with the excluded?

THE TROUBLING METHOD OF SOCIAL THEORY

In respect to the second historical fact that explains what social theory has become, it is helpful to state when and where it might have enjoyed its first full and still pertinent expression. Though social theory, since its beginnings in the nineteenth century, has taken on a good many expressions and invented very many new and disturbing methods, it is possible to nominate the social theorist who invented it in a form still workable in our day.

It would not be far wrong to suggest that Karl Marx was the first true modern social theorist and thereby the pioneer of social theory. Marx's many-sided critique of capitalism and all that it entails for the modern world could be said to be the first truly serious social theory, in spite of the fact that he never claimed to be a sociologist, or anything of the like. Indeed, it would be hard to classify what he was. Marx's training was in philosophy. His empirical work was in economic history. His writing, however, was, if not sociology, social theory. What might this mean?

There were three elements to Marx's method that qualify it as social theory – and, I should quickly add, that qualify him as the likely inventor of modern social theory. Those three elements are:

1   Marx's method was to base his theories always on the study of *historical structures*. More than anyone in his day, Marx stood firmly against all philosophical theories of wealth and political economy that gave the first privileges to the moral individual. His focus was the capitalist mode of production, by which he meant the economic structures that, behind the scenes of modern society, imposed the terrible brutalities of class oppression on the inferior, working class.
2   Marx believed in *secrets* – that is, he did not take surface appearances at face value. This was his first and most enduring criticism of early modern theories of the marketplace that believed that market forces would guide economic action and thus lead to economic and social progress. Marx knew better, and he knew better because he painstakingly studied the deep economic history of modern capitalism to the conclusion that modernity's liberal promises of liberty and the good society resulted, in fact, in exploitations of the working class at least as severe as those of the feudal peasant.
3   Marx, a devoted scholar and historical scientist of material structures, never sacrificed his *critical* attitudes and political convictions for the sake of empirical proof. On the contrary, his criticism of modern liberal cultures included the idea that their superficially humanistic ideals of social progress were, below the surface, an appalling sham meant to justify the greed of the bourgeois capitalist.

These three principles – the disciplined *historical study of structures*, the *hermeneutic of hidden factors*, and *the emancipatory power of critical thinking* – lent to social theory a classical model. They demonstrated a way of thinking the Unthinkable without sacrificing evidence, but also without taking the superficial as the real or relinquishing the importance of continuous critical attention to the needs of human beings.

Others who came after did not always follow Marx's lead, but few subsequent social theorists we read today fail to think in something approaching the same way. Each may have emphasized one or several of these principles as they derived them from the classical era – often in response to Marx, but just as often by their own bold challenges to the historical facts before them. Durkheim's theories of culture were, in the end, a hermeneutic of the social force of social structures. Weber's various and many theories of political domination, economic ethics, cultural ideas, among other themes, were likewise a hermeneutic of subjective meanings set against the tremendous force of modern capitalism. Simmel's offbeat essays on the social importance of the stranger in the urban setting reinvented the theory of social forms in ways that, while slight in respect to structures, were deeply attentive to the historical realities of the new urban order. Du Bois's theories of the American Negro and Cooper's of the colored woman's office were, differently, critical reconsiderations of the power of the excluded in challenging the calm of modern liberal values. All, whether directly or indirectly, took their lead from the failures of modern economic and political structures. All were willing to probe behind surface appearances. And all were deeply critical of the prevailing ethos. All, curiously, were, like Marx, poetic, if not poets. And all got themselves into trouble.

If there is one common feature of social theories of the classical period and since, it is a certain spiritual and intellectual courage – a willingness to seek answers where none before had dared look and to ask questions that were (and are) heretical in the eyes of the powerful and influential. Another way to put this is to say that social theory is the art and science of the exile, the stranger, the wanderer, the unsettled, and the displaced. These are the shady characters who know the methods of the excluded and are willing and able to put them to practice. Marx lived in exile. Durkheim left home. Weber quit his university post. Simmel never attained one. Du Bois spent his life engaged in political work. Cooper was a high-school teacher. It is true that, in more recent times, many social theorists have been or are public celebrities. Still, Michel Foucault and Jacques Derrida in France, Jürgen Habermas in Germany, Edward Said and Judith Butler in the United States were or are all among the foremost disturbers of the peace even while having held or holding prominent university positions.

Not all of them used the same language to describe what they were doing. To my tastes, it is Judith Butler, one of today's most influential social theorists, who put it best in the preface to her book, *Gender Trouble* (1990):

Perhaps trouble need not carry such a negative valence. To make trouble was, within the reigning discourse of my childhood, something one should never do precisely because that would get one *in* trouble. The rebellion and its reprimand seemed to be caught up in the same terms, a phenomenon that gave rise to my first critical insight into the ruse of power: The prevailing law threatened one with trouble. Hence, I concluded that trouble is inevitable and the task how best to make, what best way to be in it.

Anyone alive and alert to the world as it is realizes that there is more trouble out there than can be managed. Governments and authorities, so long as they obey the false premises and empty slogans of the modern, will never rid themselves of trouble. In the meantime, social theory – broadly understood as a poetry of facts and a search for real hope – is what is to be done and the trouble to be gotten into if there is to be any real prospect for a knowledge of social things that rings true to those who sleep under bridges to the buzz of finely tuned BMWs racing to nowhere in particular.

REFERENCES

Borges, J., in Alexander Coleman (ed.) (1999 [1964]) *Selected Poems*, New York: Viking.

Coleman, J. (1995) [1990] *Foundations of Social Theory*, Cambridge, MA: Belknap Press.

Cooper, A.J. (1988) [1892] *A Voice from the South*, New York: Oxford University Press.

Darwin, C. (2001) [1859] *On the Origin of Species*, Cambridge, MA: Harvard University Press.

Du Bois, W.E.B. (1989) [1903] *The Souls of Black Folk*, New York: Bantam.

Marx, K. and Engels, F., in Robert C. Tucker (ed.) (1978) [1848] *The Marx–Engels Reader*, 2nd edn, New York: W.W. Norton.

Parsons, T. (1965) [1961] *Theories of Society: Foundations of Modern Sociological Theory*, New York: Free Press.

Simmel, G. (1971) [1908] *On Individuality and Social Forms: Selected Writings*, Donald N. Levine (ed.), Chicago, IL: University of Chicago Press.

Weber, M. (1968) [1905] *Protestant Ethic and the Spirit of Capitalism*, Upper Saddle River, NJ: Prentice-Hall.

2

CLASSICAL SOCIAL THEORY

LARRY RAY

This chapter introduces the ideas of some major classical social theories – especially the quartet of Karl **Marx**, Émile **Durkheim**, Georg **Simmel** and Max Weber – while highlighting some recurring themes and debates that feature in classical sociology. It explains how classical sociology emerged through a debate with the Enlightenment, in which the concept of the 'social' took shape. This was constructed around various themes emphasizing contrasting components of social life – including material, cultural, rational and moral factors. These divergent theorizations set the scene for the play of theoretical oppositions that characterize much subsequent theoretical dispute. For the particular theorists mentioned this is a brief introduction and my intention is to show how what has been passed on to us as the 'classical tradition' contains diverse attempts to address certain core and abiding themes.

What is loosely contained within the 'classical tradition' is an unfinished enterprise of imagining the social in various ways. Contemporary sociology remains, in important respects, indebted to these categories, which overlap, play against each other and combine in the works of individual theorists. However, this is a claim that some dispute. It is sometimes argued that social life changed so irrevocably during the later twentieth century that the concepts and theories of classical sociology are no longer of value for understanding the contemporary world. For example, Ulrich **Beck** writes of an 'epochal break' brought by globalization that renders empty previously central sociological concepts such as those of 'nation' and 'class' – they are he says, 'zombie categories' because 'they are dead but somehow go on living, making us blind to the realities of our lives' (Beck 2000). This catchy phrase 'zombie categories' is often quoted but actually avoids the difficult task of working through what really has been transformed and what purchase existing analysis might still have on social life. The theories and concepts of classical sociology are crucial to this exercise. It is true, of course, that many social developments of the twentieth and twenty-first centuries were unanticipated by classical sociology – for example, the consequences of world wars, the rise and fall of communism and the consequent reconfiguration of the world system, the expansion of the modern state into capillaries of everyday life, the digital technological revolution, new forms of computer mediated networking and lifestyle niches, not to mention globalization and a 24/7 society. Classical analytical frameworks, however, continue to provide ways of understanding contemporary issues.

RECURRENT THEMES AND DEBATES

Sociology emerged with the conditions of **modernity**, that is, the modes of social life and organization that emerged in Europe from about the seventeenth century, subsequently becoming global. The emergence of the modern world entailed dynamic technological and social transformations, leading to a ruthless break with all preceding historical conditions, and a 'never-ending process of internal ruptures and fragmentation within itself' (Harvey 1994: 12). I have argued (Ray 1999) that the circumstances of its emergence have inscribed into sociology a set of antinomies on which sociological theories will tend, implicitly or explicitly, to take a position. By contrast with much earlier philosophy, sociology was historical in the sense that it was concerned less with timeless attributes of human life and more with their historical emergence. The following broad themes can be identified, which appear in different ways in a great deal of social theory.

First, there is the interplay of nature and gender. The growth of capitalism transformed gender relations, something of which classical sociologists were aware, even if their understandings of this were very different from those of contemporary sociologists. It is sometimes suggested that classical sociology ignored gender but this is not so and actually, in some cases, it was an organizing principle in their work. Durkheim (1984), for example, begins with a discussion of 'conjugal solidarity' (the domestic division of labour), which he then takes to be fundamental to social organization and a model for differentiated sociality in general. Theories of gender were often constructed around a dichotomy of nature and society in which the 'natural' was characteristically coded as feminine – thus, for Simmel, the emergence of an 'objective' instrumental culture entailed an irrevocable loss of a 'subjective' feminine one. He does, however, invest his analysis with a romantically loaded and essentialized concept of 'femininity'.

Second, there is a central debate about science and methods. The development of natural science combined with the Enlightenment vision of progress through reason together suggested the possibility of a scientific analysis of society, which occurred in the context of a decline in religious belief and observance and, more generally, the 'crisis of industrial society'. Sociology promised to provide not only a scientific analysis of society that would guide future practice, but also to offer a scientifically based morality and thus resolve problems of social disorganization and conflict. However, this scientistic vision was challenged by a hermeneutic conception, emphasizing essential differences between scientific and cultural knowledge. The debate between naturalism and hermeneutics became a major issue in subsequent sociological theory and this tension is particularly evident in Weber's work.

Third, there is the theme of the duality of social system and social action. We perceive ourselves as agents whose actions have effects. Yet, viewed as a whole, society appears to be a system of interrelated institutions and practices that have unintended consequences. A central rationale for sociology was that the increasing complexity of social organization, combined with markets and bureaucratic organizations, meant that social processes escaped everyday understanding and became susceptible to the specialist understanding of the social sciences. Sociology claimed to be capable of guiding rational (and therefore willed) interventions in the social system. Thus, the duality of action and system became one of the central problems of sociological theory, with some theories opting for action *or* system (e.g. **structuralism**, symbolic interactionism), and others attempting to reconcile the dilemma. All classical sociologists attempted, in some way, to resolve the problem of structure and agency and this debate continues into contemporary sociology – for example, through Giddens's early work on 'structuration' (e.g. Giddens 1984: 25–6).

A fourth sociological debate has centred on the conditions for social solidarity in the midst of often deep and multiple conflicts and social divisions. With the emergence of a market economy it was possible to imagine a self-equilibrating society based on individual rational calculations, although some classical advocates of the market, such as Adam Smith, insisted on the importance of moral sentiments in regulating human conduct. In opposition to *laissez faire* political economists, early theorists such as Saint-Simon, Comte and Durkheim, emphasized the moral, rather than purely instrumental, foundations of social integration. They did not accept the claim of political economists, that 'the pursuit of individual interests produces the greatest good of all'. The uneasy relations between these schools of thought in nineteenth century social theory erupted in the 1880s in the *Methodenstreit* (dispute over method), which resulted in the split between economics and sociology. The ramifications of this dispute continued well into the twentieth century and the sociology of economic life generally situates and embeds market structures within supportive and constraining cultural and institutional systems.

Finally, the development of modern systems of social and economic organization were, from their beginning, accompanied by a Romantic critique of lost communal authentic social relations. This ambivalence within the modern worldview was reproduced within sociology and informed debates about destiny and value of modern industrial society. Many classical sociological theories sought to rediscover community as a counterbalance to mass society. Disenchantment with the consequences of modernity also underlay the growth of hermeneutic methods and wider resistance to **positivism**, which was viewed as an inappropriate application of scientific methods to cultural phenomena. This view was evident in early twentieth century German sociology; for example, the tension in Tönnies between 'community' and 'society'. In Marx, too, we find the paradoxical combination of an enthusiastic endorsement of modernity (e.g. in the *Manifesto of the Communist Party*) with his expectation that post-capitalist society would overcome alienation and re-establish communal regulation and social solidarity. Some contemporary alternative visions, such as deep ecology or eco-feminism, or post-modernist aesthetics, also perhaps draw on

LARRY RAY

anti-modernist cultural traditions. Part of the culture of industrial society is the notion of a rupture with a traditional, communal past, which remains central to sociological theorizing.

DEBATE WITH THE ENLIGHTENMENT

Sociology arrived with the ambitious promise of resolving the crisis of industrial society through the application of scientific inquiry to social organization. Sociology offered a critical diagnosis of the process of modernization of which it was a part. The role of the diffuse intellectual movement loosely understood as the 'Enlightenment' was significant in complex ways. Sociology was not a *direct* legacy of the Enlightenment but it was an elaboration of some of its themes and gave rise to one of the most persistent debates in sociology – whether, and to what extent, it could be 'scientific'. The Enlightenment was to pose a number of issues that provided a context for subsequent social theory, which included:

- Critique of religious thought in the name of scientific validity. Even though many exponents of the new philosophers were deists rather than atheists, they were critical of institutional religion and Diderot, editor of the *l'Encyclopédie*, to which all leading eighteenth century French intellectuals contributed, claimed that humans would progress in peace only if the idea of God was obliterated (Hazard 1965: 407).
- The idea of progress through reason and a linear historical expansion of reason became popular, as philosophy moved away from cyclical theories of the rise and decline of civilizations, which had roots in classical historiography. Condorcet (1743–94) developed an influential progressive history in *Sketch of a Historical Table of the Progress of the Human Mind* (1794).
- Knowledge would enable practical intervention in the world, rather than speculation and contemplation – as Comte subsequently said, 'Knowledge for foresight, foresight for action'.
- For Montesquieu (1689–1755), for example, society was understood as a system of interrelated elements working for mutual benefit and societies were subject to a process of social differentiation into sub-systems in which laws regulate subjects, manners regulate private lives and customs regulate external behaviour. It was thus possible to imagine homologies between social and natural organisms.

However, although these themes of the Enlightenment were important for the subsequent development of sociology, the post-Revolutionary counter-Enlightenment of conservatives such as Louis de Bonald (1754–1840) and Joseph de Maistre (1754–1821) for whom the Enlightenment's critical individualism, combined with the Jacobins' violent assault on the *ancien regime*, had destroyed the bases of social order. Opposed to the notion that society might be founded on reason, de Maistre and de Bonald's social order was based on the slow, invisible work of history. Although informed by a deeply conservative and nostalgic desire to re-create a pre-Revolutionary past, they offered reflections on the nature of social order that were to be echoed in later sociology. For example, de Bonald argued that the practice of ritual sacrifice – whether actual or, as in the Catholic Mass, symbolic – is common to all societies. This could be understood only if one regards the social as a sacred order whose bonds are ritually reaffirmed. This idea was to be particularly important in Durkheim's theory of ritual and, more generally, in his understanding of the non-rational bases of social order.

SAINT-SIMON AND COMTE – ORDER AND PROGRESS

Two figures deserving brief mention are Henri Saint-Simon (1760–1825) and his one-time protégé Auguste Comte (1798–1857). Both were part of the post-Revolutionary generation of French intellectuals who had been educated in the Napoleonic Ecoles Polytechniques, where they had become imbued with a technical and scientific ethos but were, at the same time, disaffected by limited skilled employment opportunities. Many were drawn to socialist and radical movements in Paris – especially those with technocratic schemes for a new society in which technically trained graduates would find their rightful place. For Saint-Simon, the moral crisis threatening Europe could be resolved by immediate construction of a theoretical system unifying all knowledge. Some of his proposals, such as the application of scientific method to the study of society, the organization of a new scientific age in which the state would assume responsibility for social welfare and institutional co-operation in a unified Europe, were later to become widely shared. Anticipating Marx, on whom he exercised some influence, Saint-Simon understood history in terms of class conflict (class defined in terms of functional-occupational groups) between productive and idle classes (Saint-Simon 1975: 158 and 187). Systemizing many of Saint-Simon's ideas and accumulating historical material to support his view, Comte developed a system of 'positive philosophy' which conceived of society as a natural system, subject to objective forces that could be managed by social scientists. 'Society' (which, used in this sense, was still a novel concept) obeyed law-like principles and passed through three states – the Theological, Metaphysical and Positive. In the Theological stage, magical and supernatural worldviews attributed spiritual powers to the immediate physical environment. In the Metaphysical (transitional) state, worldviews were based on natural philosophy and abstract entities of Spirit, Matter, Force and Ultimate Causes. Contemporary European society, however, was entering the Positive Age in which people would renounce the search for metaphysical essences and inhabit a world governed by reason and scientific knowledge. However, both Saint Simon and Comte held that, in a secular age, social solidarity would be maintained through the rituals of a secular religion, which

Comte developed into his Religion of Humanity. Although little read today, Comte was significant in mapping the conceptual terrain for sociology and particularly for posing, if not resolving the question of the foundations of social bonding in complex, post-traditional societies.

KARL MARX – EMANCIPATION AND REVOLUTION

Karl Marx (1818–83) undertook a critical synthesis that brought together in different measures Hegelian philosophy, French socialism and British political economy. Like Saint-Simon, Marx had a vision of the future towards which analysis of the present was orientated. They differed in other respects, though. A great deal of Saint-Simon's work contains plans for future social organization, including draft constitutions, parliaments, professional and scientific associations and a new religion. Marx eschewed this kind of utopian thinking and preferred not to 'write recipes for the soup kitchen of the future' (Månson 2000: 24). Unlike Saint-Simon, moreover, Marx identified a central class conflict *within* capitalism, rather than one between representatives of the decaying and rising social systems.

Marx was centrally concerned with relationships between economy and politics within a progressive historical movement that constituted (class) actors within a context that was structurally determined. Although the 'history of hitherto existing society is the history of class struggle' (Marx and Engels 1967 [1848]) the organizing theme of Marx's theory is that capitalist society has created a social class, the proletariat, whose struggle to abolish its own exploitation will abolish class rule itself and thereby usher in an age in which genuine human history can begin. The logic of this for Marx was that, unlike all previously existing social classes, the proletariat is propertyless (it has only its labour to sell) and therefore no particular interests to defend. The bourgeoisie, when challenging the rule of the aristocratic landed social order, invoked ideas of (especially economic) freedom, civic liberties, democracy and the rule of law and therefore appeared to invoke the universal interests of humanity as a whole but, once bourgeois rule was established, defended the particular interests of capital. The proletariat, however, was structurally determined by its position within the capitalist system of production, yet embodied the truly universal interests of humanity and therefore made possible a leap from necessity (life governed by objective social forces) to freedom – a life based on unconstrained self-conscious organization.

Marx's critique of the capitalist system had many dimensions. That capitalism was a system of exploitation that 'comes dripping from head to foot, from every pore, with blood and dirt' (Marx 1976: chap. 31) could be witnessed in the conditions of poverty, draconian factory discipline and degradation in which much of the new proletariat lived and which have been documented by Engels' *Condition of the Working Class in England* (1844). However, Marx also understood exploitation through a more technical calculation of the rate of extraction of surplus value. At the core of capitalist social relations was the wage as a means of exchange between capital and labour. While this *appeared* to be a fair exchange of labour time (the working day) for money (wages) it was actually exploitative since a portion of the value created by labour was withheld by capital in the form of 'surplus value'. When human labour time is bought as a commodity, it has the peculiar property that its consumption *increases* its value for the owner. In the simple exchange of commodities C–M–C (commodities transformed into money which is transformed back into commodities) money is a medium that enables commodities to be circulated – as, for example, when crops are sold and the money received is spent on clothes and improved fencing for the farm, all of which have use value for their purchaser. However, there is a complex form of circulation M–C–M^1 where money (M) is spent on the purchase of labour power (C) with the intention of generating a greater quantity of money than the buyer had initially (M^1). Marx argued that political economy has no explanation of this increase in value although its origin was really quite simple. If the worker works, for example, a ten-hour day and the first eight of these hours are 'necessary' labour, in that the value created is returned to the worker as wages to cover subsistence needs, the remaining two hours create 'surplus value' that is withheld by capital. It is important to note, though, that surplus value does not equal profit but will 'crystallize' in different measure into rent, interest and profit (Marx 1976: chap. 18). This relationship is concealed partly by the appearance of 'free wage labour' – unlike earlier systems of slavery, serfdom and indentured labour, the wage relation *appears* to be a voluntarily entered and therefore equal contract.

This bears on the much-discussed concept of ideology in Marx. His elaborated theory of ideology is rather sparse ('ruling ideas are ideas of the ruling class') and he suggests that, unlike previous societies such as the ancient world and feudalism, capitalism lacked an ideology represented as a systematic body of beliefs. Rather, the dynamic energies of capitalism drowned 'all bonds of sentiment' in the 'icy waters of egotistical calculation'. Thus, unlike earlier systems of production, capitalism did not have time to create a 'halo' – a body of beliefs and ideas that would provide it with stability. Subsequently, in the face of the survival of capitalism, Marxists have given a great deal of attention to ideology as a means of protecting the system from radical assault, both intellectual and political.

Marx believed that, through the critique of existing political economy, he had discovered the secret self-destructive logic of capitalism – that its core achievement was also its undoing. Competition and technical innovation generate continually more efficient replacement of labour by machinery and therefore the 'organic composition of capital' – the proportion of machinery to living labour – rises. This means that, although the mass of surplus value generated in the system rises, the percentage that is classed as profit (as opposed to fixed overheads and investment) declines, resulting in a long-run crisis of profitability. Further, since machinery replaces living labour, there is a growing 'reserve army of unemployed' who provide cheap labour and depress average proletarian wages. This, in turn, creates relative if not absolute immiseration of the proletariat while

LARRY RAY

undermining markets for mass-produced goods. This is not elaborated in detail in Marx, but the implication of his analysis is that recurrent crises of capitalism would create a revolutionary situation as economic crises combined with growing class consciousness, confidence and organization of the working class, who would mobilize a mass social movement to overthrow capitalism and establish socialism. Despite the failure of this prediction and the disastrous experience of Soviet-type societies, Marxism's ability to combine rigorous theoretical social analysis with political activism, and a belief that history would in the end work out well, perhaps accounts for its abiding appeal to many, especially in a period of global capitalist crisis.

ÉMILE DURKHEIM AND MORAL SOCIALITY

Central to the sociology of Émile Durkheim (1858–1917) were questions about the nature of social solidarity. He elaborated the concept of society as an emergent moral entity in itself, *sui generis*, that was not reducible to any other explanatory level. While Marx and Engels developed a material concept of the social, Durkheim insisted not only on the autonomy of the cultural-symbolic realm, but also on its priority in social development. Durkheim saw economic forms and contracts as embedded in cultural and moral systems – so, for example, contracts depend on trust, which presupposes the existence of society as a moral reality. Further, society is a ritual order, a collective conscience founded on the emotional rhythms of human interaction. In common with positivists, Durkheim regarded sociology as a science, albeit with distinctive methods appropriate to the study of society. In the *Rules of Sociological Method* (1893), Durkheim set out to demonstrate the existence of social realities outside the individual; to separate sociology from philosophy; and to define the subject matter of sociology. The *Rules* began with the famous injunction to 'consider social facts as things' (Durkheim 1964: 2), that is, to regard social norms as objective 'ways of acting, thinking and feeling external to individuals'. This could simply mean that humans acquire social habits that could not have been arrived at spontaneously, but are derived from a pre-existing social world (such as language). But Durkheim gave little attention to peoples' ability to manipulate and distance themselves from social conventions and he tended to write about these with reference to macrosocietal processes. Thus, the persistence (although not origin) of a social form could be explained with reference to the functions it performs for social cohesion and survival (Durkheim 1964: 110). However, a social practice that might be thought of as 'pathological' might not be – for example, contrary to what one might expect, crime is necessary since the collective ritual of punishment serves to reaffirm and strengthen collective sentiments (1964: 81). The three types of social facts identified in the *Rules* – legal codes, social statistics and religious dogmas – correspond to the bases of Durkheim's three major studies: *The Division of Labour* (1895), *Suicide* (1897) and *Elementary Forms of the Religions Life* (1912) respectively.

26

The *Division of Labour* develops an evolutionary theory based on the transition from 'mechanical' (simple) to 'organic' (complex) forms of the division of labour. In the former, beliefs were common to all members (1964: 129); there was a unified collective conscience that was reinforced through public rituals. Legal and moral rules were 'repressive' and punishments were generally severe (Durkheim 1969a: 250). Kinship was the dominant institution in mechanical societies and domestic production formed the basis of social integration. Organic solidarity, on the other hand, is heterogeneous, with a complex and differentiated division of labour, based on specialization, diversification and co-operation. While expanding the scope of individual liberty, the organic division of labour also increases the extent of interdependence among its branches, thus individuals are linked more closely to each other than in mechanical societies. The collective conscience weakens as it fragments into moral codes specific to particular occupations and activities, while religion ceases to be a unifying system of belief. Repressive criminal law diminishes proportionately, as the extent of civil, restitutive law increases. However, this notion of a harmoniously integrated organic division of labour had not been realized in nineteenth century industrial societies, which were characterized by an 'anomic' imbalance between individual expectations and the constraints of social reality. Normative regulation (transmitted via socialization, or 'moral education') acts as a constraint on desires that cannot all be satisfied within a given social environment. This analysis is further developed in *Suicide*, where Durkheim argues that 'suicide varies inversely with the degree of integration of social groups of which the individual forms a part'. He developed a scheme of paired concepts in which egoism and altruism lie at opposite poles of social integration. Egoism, on the one hand, refers to weakening of the ties binding people together – forms of solidarity such as religious ritual, marriage and nationalism bind people to collective integration and their weakening results in higher suicide rates. On the other hand, altruistic suicide is conversely a result of excessive social integration – where custom and habit govern individuals who sacrifice their own life because of commandments from a higher source of authority, such as religious or political allegiances. On a second axis of regulation – weak regulation generates anomic suicide resulting from social dislocations such as rapid industrial and commercial changes. Fatalistic suicide (which he suggested was of largely historical significance) results from an excess of social integration that is so oppressive that the certainty of death is preferable.

This question (fuelled by his involvement in the Dreyfus Affair) led Durkheim to attempt to reconcile individualism and republicanism with the need for sacred legitimation of the social order. An organic, differentiated society is no longer integrated by a common value system but, on the contrary, by respect for human rights, which is the only possible basis of legitimation in a democratic society. However, by contrast with Weber's concept of disenchanted formal rationality, in Durkheim's 'cult of individualism' the rights of the individual acquire sacred significance. Respect for individual rights is the shared moral

LARRY RAY

bond offering institutional regulation of an organic society in which people have divergent interests and beliefs. Indeed, whereas in the *Division of Labour* he regarded individualism with some suspicion, as binding people not to society but to themselves (Durkheim 1984: 140), his later account of the cult of individuality is 'neither anti-social nor egoistic', but involves 'sympathy for all that is human, pity for all sufferings, miseries and greater thirst for justice' (1969b). In this way, Durkheim offers perhaps the first *sociological* theory of human rights which regarded these as deriving not from the individual but from society and therefore as evolving with the moral division of labour.

The significance of religion increased in Durkheim's later work, culminating in *Elementary Forms of the Religious Life* (1912), in which the idea of a collective conscience, as the moral regulator of society, gave way to 'collective representations'. These constitute the symbolic order of society and comprise religious doctrine, legal rules, legends, proverbs, customs and traditions; that is, the symbolic constitution of society. This opened up analysis of society as a symbolic order, which, arguably, led through Marcel Mauss and **Lévi-Strauss** to Roland **Barthes**' semiotics and **Foucault**'s discourse analysis (Alexander 1990: 8). In *Elementary Forms*, Durkheim set out to show that the social is indispensable to understanding the formation of all beliefs, institutions and conceptions since, in religion, we find an 'essential and permanent aspect of humanity'. Thus, to show that religious systems were representations of society would show, too, that categories of scientific knowledge were socially constructed.[1] The idea of a 'class', which is fundamental to all cognitive systems, is an instrument of thought that has been socially constructed in the form of a hierarchy. Thus, systems of knowledge construct relations of subordination and co-ordination, which people would never have thought of organizing in this way had they not already known what a hierarchy was (Durkheim 1976: 148). Similarly, an orientation to space comes initially from the spatial relations with which people are familiar, thus, where the camp has circular form, space is conceived in the form of an immense circle and is subdivided in the same way as the camp (1976: 11–12). The concept of time is derived from the rhythmic activities which punctuate social experience, such as rituals, rites and cycles. The concept of cause as an arrangement of sequences is derived from the logical relations of social organization. The mind then constructs the relationships of cause – effect in the world *a priori* derived from the model offered by society (1976: 363ff).

Elementary Forms aimed to develop a theory of religion based on four hypotheses: religion is socially determined; it is cognitive; ritual expresses and dramatizes social roles; religion is conducive to social solidarity. One of the most famous and controversial claims in *Elementary Forms* is that religion and piety are symbolic representations of the relationship between society and individuals. Society is experienced by individuals as superior and transcendent, a force demanding our acquiescence. It not only creates moral obligations that are external, but it is also continuous while individuals die and are replaced. Thus, as a symbolic representation, the sacred too has features of immortality, transcendence and superior power. People have a dual existence, impersonal and personal, both as a member of society and yet also as a particular person and body existing at a moment in time and space. The essence of religion (as for de Bonald) lies in sacred rituals, which reaffirm social solidarity, and the division between the sacred and profane is an evolutionary universal, found in all societies.

Support for these claims came from the study of 'simple' societies, such as the totemic cultures of Australia and North America, which he believed would possess the 'elementary forms' of all religious practice. Here, the totem is a symbol of collective life, but rather than products of pure imagination, these are derived from external reality, from society, and the object of worship is an anonymous and impersonal force independent of individuals. Totemism is the emblem of the group, which represents the collective to itself through myths and legends. Totemic societies are organized around strictly enforced taboos or interdicts, which are the simplest form of veneration of the sacred. These may be either positive or negative. Positive taboos secure bonds between members of the group, such as the spilling of blood at a sacred rock, which reaffirms the common link between the collective and the object. Negative taboos create prohibitions on forms of contact and conduct, as in the case of prohibited foods or sexual taboos. The incest taboo is both the first interdiction, defining relationships within the group and with others, and also paradigmatic for all other taboos (1969c).

Collective solidarity, moreover, is periodically renewed through rituals that serve in different ways to reaffirm the power of the totem. In these assemblies a 'collective effervescence' reaffirms social integration through four kinds of rites: sacrificial, imitative (taking on qualities of the totem), commemorative (such as ancestor worship), and piacular (expiatory) rites that involve mourning, fasting and weeping, with obligations to slash or tear clothing and flesh, thereby renewing the unity of a group following misfortune. Mourning, however, carries the risk of transforming grief from symbolic into actual violence. Although he was often wrongly regarded as a 'conservative', Durkheim developed radical theoretical reflections on the foundations of the social and the interplay between emotions and collective identities.

GEORG SIMMEL – ELUSIVE SOCIALITY

With Georg Simmel (1856–1917) the emphasis of sociology shifted from an exclusively macroscopic concern towards individuals in interactions. Ambivalence is a keynote of Simmel's sociology. He was reluctant to define terms unambiguously and often develops an argument in one direction, only to appear then to argue the contrary. So, having elaborated his central concept of 'form' as opposed to 'content' in sociology, he said, 'of course, what is form in one respect is content in another' (Simmel 1971: 25). Simmel's critique of sociological reason focused on the activity of subjects who internalized but nonetheless constructed and manipulated social types, which were the categorical basis of social life.

Simmel shared with Durkheim an interest in social differentiation, individualism and competitiveness, although these are taken by each in radically different directions. Simmel opposed functional approaches to the social and emphasized the centrality of conflict and competition in social life. Simmel rejected the idea of 'society' as an organic unity, arguing instead that 'society' was a metaphor for forms of association abstracted from everyday life. Simmel attempted to view society simultaneously from the standpoints of the individual and the social. We reveal parts of ourselves in social interaction, but also hold parts of ourselves back. We present different aspects of the self in different interactions (Simmel 1971: 24). His sociology was not generally written in a way that appealed to data for support but, rather, he invoked a kind of shared intuition, inviting us to recognize the ways of the social in his vignettes and descriptions.

This is not to say that Simmel's sociology was entirely intuitive and unsystematic. Indeed, he was sometimes criticized for writing in an overly formalistic and descriptive way. Simmel's 'formal sociology' was to study the forms of association that made generalized and routinized social interactions possible. Experience is inescapably organized in forms. Try, for example, to imagine colour – one cannot imagine 'pure' colour, but only colours appearing in particular shapes, or forms. There are then two components to experience: a formal, organizing aspect and content, that which is perceived. Another way of understanding this is through Simmel's analogy with geometry. He described sociology as the 'geometry of social life' (Simmel 1971: 28ff) in that, just as geometry was concerned with the abstract relational properties of the material objects, irrespective of their particular content or nature, so sociology would describe the forms through which the content of social life took place.[2] 'Contents' are the materials of sociation – everything that is present in individuals, such as drives, interests, purposes, inclinations and psychic states (Simmel 1971: 24).

To the question, 'How is society possible? Simmel answered that society is an ongoing creation of its subjects and hence, unlike nature, society needs no observer since it is directly realized by its own elements. This occurs through *typification*, the process whereby we construct social categories. In order to interact socially, we must continuously add to and subtract from another's individuality, as Simmel put it. We never encounter anyone as unique (this would be 'formless' experience) but always as 'more and less than they are'. More, because we typify someone as a parent, sister, student, teacher or any such category – attributing characteristics that extend beyond the individual. Less, because we thereby subtract from someone's individuality by relating to them as a bearer of a general category. Society is possible only because of these abstractions that are the basis of formal associations. Forms are relatively stable features of social life – such as superordination and subordination, exchange and competition, inclusion and exclusion – that have regular features irrespective of the particular contexts in which they appear. So conflict and competition, for example, will have a recognizable structure and dynamic whether they appear in the family, in a royal court, or between nations.

Further, there is a balance of individuality and abstraction in different social forms – some are more abstract and impersonal than others. Money exchanges represent a high degree of impersonality and abstraction, whereas love relationships have low typification and higher degrees of individuality. Thus, the affective structure of intimacy is based on what each of the two participants gives or shows only to the one other person and to nobody else. Intimacy then, is based on the exclusive content of a relationship between members, regardless of its specific nature. However, when intimate relations become formalized, as in marriage, their character changes. Marriage is no longer simply an intimate exchange between two people, but is socially regulated and historically transmitted, requiring official recognition by external authorities of law or religion. Nonetheless, modern marriage, Simmel says, seems to have a weaker objective character than unions of the past, allowing a greater degree of individuality, creativity and differentiation (Simmel 1971: 227ff). While relationships of intimacy are becoming less formalized, some public interactions are more relaxed – for example, exchanges between superiors and subordinates become more courteous and apparently egalitarian. Yet sociation is increasingly stylized in that it is pursued playfully as an end in itself. Conversation, for example, becomes an 'art' to be pursued with tact following unspoken rules. Similarly, eroticism as the pursuit of sexual interests is subordinated to coquetry, the play of 'hinted consent and hinted denial', where all participants understand that this is a game not meant to lead to actual seduction (Simmel 1971: 134). Thus, sociability as a play-form becomes an end in itself that mirrors and parodies the serious business of social life.

Yet, the analysis of social forms may reveal a whole world of social relations in apparently unimportant facets of social life. This is illustrated by his concept of the 'senses as forms' (e.g. Simmel 1997: 109–19). A social world may be encapsulated in a glance, revealing mutuality, self-disclosure, concealment and subordination or superordination. The erotic glance contains an 'absorbing moment of playful delight' when two people's eyes meet and both are drawn transiently into an absorbing moment of experience, of 'mutual conspiracy beyond convention'. The glance among lovers constitutes communion and conspiracy beyond social norms. Thus, the eye has a 'uniquely sociological function' of establishing reciprocity and intimacy, a gift to the other, which assumes equality. However, inequality inhibits the glance (it was once considered subversive for a Black in the southern USA to look a White in the eyes) and, where no reciprocity is possible, the eyes are hidden. Thus, we close the eyes of the dead and place a hood over the face of the executed or executioner.

The formation of an objective culture, in which social forms become autonomous and self-sufficient is the outcome of a long developmental process of the human spirit. The instrumentality and calculability of modern life is analysed in Simmel's longest work, *The Philosophy of Money* (1900). Here, he juxtaposes freedom and impersonality with the loss of culture. The development of money, he argues, is an element in a profound cultural trend towards objectification and impersonality. Money is not only evidence of increasing abstraction, but itself becomes more abstract. Once tied to an apparent guarantee of value (gold) it now floats freely and expands into more abstract forms like credit (spending money you have not got, trading on future prices, etc.) imaginary and symbolic worlds that Simmel did not directly anticipate but that his analysis suggested. Money, then, is iconic for the modern age, bringing freedom and depersonalization, proximity and distance. Money and the urban economy reduce spatial distance between people while separating 'nature' from modern life, for which it becomes an object of contemplation. But Simmel saw no possibility of return to pre-capitalist harmony; even if socialism were to replace capitalism it would simply intensify bureaucratic impersonality and the complete calculability of life. This theme of the cultural tragedy of lost wholeness became more explicit in Simmel's last works, such as the 'Crisis of culture' (1916). The tragedy of modern culture arises from the increasing objectivity of life in which world forms (like language, morals and technical and legal systems) lose links with the subject and take on a life of their own. This is a tragedy in the classical sense in that, like the character whose otherwise noble qualities are fatally flawed, the destruction of the unified subject is the necessary result of the very nature of social life. The human being becomes the 'bearer of the compulsion with which this logic rules developments' (Simmel 1997: 72).

Like other 'founding fathers', Simmel was aware that the transformation of gender relationships is one of the core elements of modernization. He went further than most others in regarding the very process of the formation of objective culture as gendered. The separation between subjective and objective culture is also a divide between feminine and masculine culture, in that objective culture was founded on a 'male way of seeing' (Vucht Tijssen 1991). Capitalism intensifies the dominance of male culture, as money creates a division of labour between domestic (female) work and the (paid) work of men, with the consequence that woman's economic value loses substance and she appears to be supported by her husband, a liability which gives rise to dowry (Simmel 1990: 375). Simmel's remedy for the dominance of masculine culture is a reappraisal of the female form of life and the reinforcement of the position of women in society. This could lead towards an independent female culture or to a culture common to men and women that had more female nuances. However, like earlier social theorists, Simmel projected onto women a set of 'natural' attributes. This further illustrates how classical sociology theorized the transformation of gender relations in terms of the nature/society dualism – which was to become a centrally contested division in subsequent sociological theory.

MAX WEBER – THE HUBRIS OF REASON

The debate with the Enlightenment was, in part, about the extent and value of reason in human society and it is with Max Weber (1864–1920) that rationality becomes an unfolding theme in human history. His approach to sociology was framed by the *Methodenstreit*. Weber attempted to define a path for sociology that was both historical and recognized the need for understanding the role of subjective meanings of actors but also met objective standards of evidence. In particular, he developed a method of generalization through the construction of 'ideal types' – intellectual constructs that attempt to abstract from the complexity of actual social life some central defining characteristics that then enable us to compare societies and institutions. One of Weber's most famous ideal-types was his concept of bureaucracy, in which he attempted to identify the core features of modern bureaucracy as opposed to pre-modern 'patrimonial' institutions. Modern bureaucracies he defined in terms of hierarchical authority: a single command centre, impersonality and separation of office from the salaried office-holder, written rules of conduct, specifically defined spheres of expert competence and promotion through a career structure based on merit. Partrimonial bureaucracies he saw as based on personal loyalty and obligations to the ruler, regarding the office as a locus of benefit for personal gain, the exercise of power as discretionary and personalized, rather than rule-following, and judgements made by viewing each case individually (Weber 1978: 235–6).

His concern with bureaucracy as a system of rational action was driven by an overarching project – which is most clearly defined in his posthumously published *Sociology of Religion* – to understand the tendency in modern societies towards *rationalization*. He developed a typology of action – traditional, affective, value-rational and goal-rational. Traditional action is rooted in customary habits of thought and habitual stimuli. Affective action is an emotional response to stimuli. Value-rational (*wertrational*) action involves calculating the most appropriate means to a substantive end (which might itself be non-rational, such as salvation). Goal-rational (*zweckrational*) action calculates both the means and the rationality of the ends – for example, rational accounting in a market economy. In practice, these types of action will appear together (the model is an ideal-type) and Weber was well aware of the complexities of rationality in social life. His famous Protestant Ethic essays, for example, were, in part, an attempt to show how the motivational disposition (the 'spirit of capitalism') necessary for the emergence of a modern capitalist system was the unintended outcome of an attempt by early modern Calvinists to resolve theological problems. For sixteenth and seventeenth century Calvinists (Weber argues), the doctrine of predestination (that those elected to be saved had been determined in advance for eternity) combined with the rejection of a route to salvation through holy sacraments or 'good works' left followers with an 'unprecedented inner loneliness' and uncertainty. In pursuit of 'evidence' of salvation some then followed an ascetic but worldly life of hard work, abstinence and the accumulation of wealth. But since a dissolute life of conspicuous consumption would indicate evidence of damnation rather than salvation, believers began to pursue accumulation as an end itself – thereby the religious (substantive) rational goal of salvation became transposed into the (rational) goal of accumulation and capital growth. Weber's thesis has given rise to more than a century of debate (e.g. Ray 1999: 175–80).

Although Weber did not have a **deterministic** theory of history, he suggested that there was a long-run cultural tendency towards increasing 'rationalization', which was developed 'with full force' in Occidental civilization but is evident

elsewhere. Rationalization involves features such as extending scientific rationality and calculation to 'the conduct of life itself'; secularization or 'disenchantment' (decline of public religious belief which becomes increasingly private);
and especially the growth of bureaucratic systems of action. This is located within
worldviews and is not a unilinear process but is subject to interruption and temporary reversal. Indeed, Weber counterpoised charisma to rationalization and it is
through charisma that personality forces its way into history and is a 'truly revolutionary force' that disrupts bureaucracy and rationalization (Weber 1978:
1117). Charismatic social movements – often headed by leaders claiming divine
inspiration – sweep away conservative bureaucratic procedures but are, in the
end, doomed to routinization. Charisma is subject to routinization in that it must
eventually face the problem of succession, which requires some principle of
selection. At this point, charisma is no longer focused on the qualities of the
leader but rather on the legitimacy of the selection procedures, whether these are
resemblance to the original leader, revelation, election or personal endorsement
of the leader. Since it must always be replaced by some form of procedures,
charisma will tend to develop into either traditional or rational-legal authority
(Weber 1978: 246–8). Similarly, the Charismatic movement of Puritan asceti-
cism became routinized in the capitalist spirit (Mommsen 1987: 35–51). Weber's
view that we are apparently doomed to live in a dull disenchanted world of rationality and bureaucracy (after all, 'the future belongs to bureaucratization') is
open to the suggestion of pessimism, as Coser says, 'He is not a prophet of glad
tidings to come but a harbinger of doom and disaster' (Coser 1977: 233–4).

This view of Weber the pessimist has been influential and has some foundation. He wrote of a bureaucratic nightmare, in which:

> The performance of each individual worker is mathematically measured, each man
> becomes a little cog in the machine and aware of this, his one preoccupation is
> whether he can become a bigger cog ... it is horrible to think that the world could
> one day be filled with these little cogs, little men clinging to little jobs, and striv-
> ing towards bigger ones. ... this passion for bureaucracy is enough to drive one to
> despair.
>
> (Weber 1978: 1402)

This is a view that has less relevance for the contemporary multiplicity of
organizational forms and systems that in some respects progress 'beyond the
"iron cage"' (Reed 2005). But Weber was, arguably, offering a warning regarding a possible future that was not inevitable. He asked whether we can preserve
meaningful existence in a social world dominated by impersonal forces of rationalization. The strengthening of pluralistic democracy and, in particular, the parliamentary committee system that could hold bureaucrats accountable,
represented the possibility of at least mitigating the vista of total control. On the
other hand, Weber's pessimism was highly influential among a generation of
critical social theorists, such as **Adorno** and **Horkheimer**.

CHALLENGES FOR CLASSICAL SOCIOLOGY

Classical sociology was the product of the first Great Transformation of (initially) European societies from largely agrarian to industrial capitalist societies – a period of social change of an extent and intensity probably without precedent in human history. At the moment of its inception, industrial society was already diagnosed as being 'in crisis' – morally, politically, socially and economically. Classical sociology offered systematic critical analysis of its effects, its trajectory and the possibilities for achieving a new equilibrium, which the theorists discussed here envisaged in differing ways. Classical sociology further encapsulated the hopes of the industrial age – the possibilities for a rational, emancipated society of unbounded technological progress and social and individual freedom. It further articulated fears – of atomized individuals in a dull, conformist iron cage of rationality in which a scientific civilization would come to dominate its creators. The twentieth century, then just dawning, was to exceed expectations on both counts but would also post new problems, largely unanticipated by classical theories. Stalinist and Nazi totalitarianism generated, not Weber's dispassionate official, but politicized central bureaucratic control, organizing homicidal mass state terror on a scale previously unimagined. Yet the post-Second World War developed world saw the paradoxical combination of the Damoclean sword of nuclear destruction and the rise of an affluent consumer society in which fundamental contradictions of capitalism appeared, if not resolved, then assuaged within state welfare capitalism. At the same time, the erosion of the imperial, patriarchal and European-centred world of classical sociology gave way to the challenges of anti-colonial movements, second wave feminism and digital technologies that transformed understandings of self and the social. Again, the world after 1989 posed new questions once more – with the collapse of the Soviet 'experiment', the realigned world order and intensifying forces of globalization within a world dominated by issues of global immiseration, renewed capitalist crisis, polarization and environmental catastrophe. The challenge for our understanding of classical social theory is to reveal its relevance to an age in which so much has changed but in which the fundamental dilemmas of social analysis remain.

NOTES

1 Durkheim did, however, try to avoid the possibly relativistic implications of this view by insisting that truth, which requires long and specialist training, embodies the moral authority of the collective (Crook 1991: 47).
2 Simmel did stress that geometry, in contrast to sociology, isolates absolutely pure forms, whereas in sociology abstraction is merely an analytical device. But the analogy is interesting in that it emphasized visual and spatial social relations.

REFERENCES

Alexander, J.C. (ed.) (1990) *Durkheimian Sociology: Cultural Studies*, Cambridge: Cambridge University Press.

Beck, U. (2000) 'The cosmopolitan perspective: the sociology of the second modernity' *Sociology*, 51(1): 79–106.

Coser, L. (1977) *Masters of Sociological Thought*, New York: Harcourt Brace.

Crook, S. (1991) *Modernist Radicalism and Its Aftermath: Foundationalism and Anti-Foundationalism in Radical Social Theory*, London: Routledge.

Durkheim, E. (1964) [1893] *The Division of Labour in Society*, trans. by Wilfred Douglas Halls, London: Macmillan.

—— (1969a) 'Individualism and the intellectuals', *Political Studies*, 17: 14–30.

—— (1969b) 'Deux lois de 'évolution pénale', *Journal Sociologique*, 244–73.

—— (1969c) 'La prohibition de l'inceste et ses origines', *Journal Sociologique*, 37–101.

—— (1976) [1912] *The Elementary Forms of Religious Life*, trans. by J.W. Swain (2nd edition), London: Routledge.

—— (1984) [1893] *The Division of Labour in Society*, trans. by W.D. Halls, New York: Macmillan.

Giddens, A. (1984) *The Constitution of Society: Outline of the Theory of Structuration*, Berkeley, CA: University of California Press.

Harvey, D. (1994) *The Condition of Postmodernity*, Oxford: Blackwell.

Hazard, P. (1965) *European Social Thought in the Eighteenth Century*, Harmondsworth: Penguin.

Månson, P. (2000) 'Karl Marx', in H. Anderson and L.B. Kaspersen (eds), *Classical and Modern Social Theory*, Oxford: Blackwell, pp. 16–33.

Marx, K. (1976) *Capital: A Critique of Political Economy*, vol. 1, Moscow: Progress Publishers.

Marx, K. and Engels, F. (1967) *Manifesto of the Communist Party*, Moscow: Progress Publishers.

Mommsen, W. (1987) 'Personal conduct and societal change', in S. Lash and S. Whimster (eds), *Max Weber, Rationality and Modernity*, London: Allen & Unwin, pp. 35–51.

Ray, L.J. (1999) *Theorizing Classical Sociology*, Milton Keynes: Open University Press.

Reed, M. (2005) 'Beyond the Iron Cage: bureaucracy and democracy in the knowledge economy and society', in P. Du Gay (ed.), *The Values of Bureaucracy*, Oxford: Oxford University Press, pp. 116–40.

Saint-Simon, H. (1975) *Selected Writings on Science, Industry and Social Organization*, ed. and trans. by K. Taylor, London: Croom Helm.

Simmel, G. (1971) *On Individuality and Social Forms*, D. Levine (ed.), Chicago: Chicago University Press.

—— (1990) *The Philosophy of Money*, T. Bottomore and D. Frisby (eds), London: Routledge.

—— (1997) *Simmel on Culture*, D. Frisby and M. Featherstone (eds), London: Sage.

Vucht Tijssen, van L. (1991) 'Women and objective culture: Georg Simmel and Marianne Weber', *Theory Culture and Society*, 8(3): 203–18.

Weber, M. (1978) *Economy and Society*, 2 vols, G. Roth and C. Wittich (eds), London: University of California Press.

—— (1993) *Sociology of Religion*, trans. by Ephraim Fischoff, Boston, MA: Beacon Press.

3

Symbolic Interactionism

Philip Manning and Greg Smith

Herbert Blumer's formulation of symbolic interactionism

Herbert Blumer first used the term 'symbolic interactionism' in print in 1937 and later wrote a very influential book revealingly called *Symbolic Interactionism: Perspective and Method* (1986 [1969]). The title reaffirms that symbolic interactionism is both a perspective, a way of looking at the social world and a method, a way of gathering data about the social world. When Blumer first coined the term, it was in competition with a similar label, 'social behaviorism' that was associated with one of Blumer's mentors, the Chicago philosopher George Herbert Mead. Blumer's neologism soon became widely used and, by the mid-1960s, it had all but replaced Mead's term. However, clearly there is a 20-year period – from the coining of the term to its widespread acceptance – when 'symbolic interactionism' had an uncertain existence and scholarly status.

Herbert Blumer was born in St. Louis, Missouri, in 1900 and died in 1987. Famously, Blumer played professional football for the Chicago Cardinals from 1924 until 1933, when a knee injury ended his career. Thomas Morrione reminds us (2004: 179–83) that, during these years, Blumer rubbed shoulders (literally, presumably) with the football greats of his era: Red Grange, Bronko Nagurski and Jim Thorpe. It is a wonderful story. Blumer the football player would have developed an ability to read the details of opponents' conduct as symbolic indicators of their next moves, a concern central to the sociology he subsequently developed.

In 1937, Blumer introduced the term 'symbolic interactionism' to the academic world in a very low-key way. In response to a request from Emerson Schmidt to write an introductory statement about social psychology for an undergraduate textbook, Blumer presented symbolic interactionism as one promising approach in this relatively new field. With no fanfare and 15 pages into what appeared to be a survey of the literature, Blumer rather casually mentioned that some social psychologists could be described as symbolic interactionists (1986 [1969]: 158). He defended his use of the term by suggesting that symbolic interactionists were a distinctive group of social psychologists who believe that the culture of a specific group consists of 'common symbols' and 'common understanding'. Group members receive extensive training as they are socialized into the group's culture. Later, this produces co-operative behavior and symbolic understanding. Symbolic interactionists should study the symbols and meanings that operate in a specific group and setting, such as a juvenile gang or a hospital.

Blumer initially emphasized Cooley's ideas rather than those of his mentor, George Herbert **Mead**. According to Blumer, Cooley's key contribution is his theory of 'sympathy'. This is the distinctively human ability to 'project oneself into the position of another and to experience his feelings and state of mind' (1986: 167). These feelings are initially those of people sharing our 'primary groups' – family members, friends and people living in our neighborhoods. Building on Cooley's work and running counter to the stimulus–response model favored by behaviorists such as John Watson or, more recently, B.F. Skinner, Blumer suggests that symbolic interactionists are primarily interested in the meanings which group members give to each other's behavior. This does not involve stimulus–response but rather stimulus–interpretation–response, metaphorically akin to a game of tennis, as meanings are batted back and forth and thereby interpreted, reinterpreted and modified (1986: 171–2).

In this seminal statement about symbolic interactionism, Blumer only introduces George Herbert Mead as a theorist of the self toward the end of the paper. Blumer asks us the same question that agitated Mead: how does an individual become an object to himself or herself? Blumer answers this question by drawing upon Mead's account of child development, which emphasizes that all children must pass through both a 'play stage' and a 'game stage', during which they learn to master increasingly complicated role-taking and rule-following behavior.

In 1969, when symbolic interactionism was already 32 years old, Blumer devised a more focused and analytic introduction to symbolic interactionism than the one he had inserted into his 1937 literature review of social psychology. In this later (and much better known) discussion, Blumer suggested that the perspective is based on three straightforward ideas ('premises') and six 'root images'. Each of Blumer's nine claims is remarkably uncontroversial but, taken together, they add up to a highly distinctive approach to the social world.

The first of the three foundational ideas is that 'human beings act toward things on the basis of the meanings that the things have for them' (1986: 2). The second premise is that these meanings are derived from social interaction and group life (1986: 2). The third premise is that 'these meanings are handled in, and modified through, an interpretative process used by the person in dealing with the things he [or she] encounters' (1986: 2).

Blumer then added six root images or basic ideas to these three premises. The first is that social life *'exists in action'* and must be studied as such. The concepts and theories employed by sociologists are only useful to the extent that they clarify the everyday activities in which we are all engaged. Throughout, Blumer is resolute that symbolic interactionists must study the actions occurring in specific, concrete groups. Blumer was therefore careful to anchor symbolic interactionism to empirical concerns and research. The second root image is that of group members interacting with each other. Blumer points out that many sociological and psychological theories see interaction simply as the medium in which social forces or psychological properties are expressed. Instead, attention needs to be given to social interaction in its own right. Human conduct is formed in interaction. Blumer's third root image continues this theme by arguing that the social world is composed of three types of 'object'. It falls to the symbolic interactionist to understand the meanings that are first given to and later modified for each of these three types of object. The three types are the 'physical' (for example, a bicycle) the 'social' (for example, a friend) and the 'abstract' (for example, the judgement that a particular relationship is exploitative). This typology is worthy of careful examination, although Blumer chose not to do so. His central point is that the nature of any object consists of what it means to the person for whom it is an object. The fourth root image is of the person as the possessor of a self or an identity. Most basically this means that humans can be objects of their own reflection, can interact with themselves. Once again, this conception departs from the view, common in the social sciences, that the person is driven by psychological properties or social structural factors. Symbolic interactionism offers a contrary view of the human as an active agent, 'an organism that has to deal with what it notes' (Blumer 1986: 14). Blumer's fifth image presents the person as the interpreter of a 'flow of situations'. Meanings are produced as a continuing and contingent achievement. In this way, the social world is made and remade continuously. Blumer's sixth and last root image emphasizes that our actions are fitted together as joint productions. The resulting joint action, as **Durkheim** recognized, has a life and reality of its own. Many of these joint actions have a stable character because they are repeated in routinized and predictable ways. As a result, they produce well-worn tracks. Blumer gives the example of the church service where both clergy and congregation become very familiar with the conduct and responses that are expected of them.

The strength of Blumer's presentation of symbolic interactionism – as is true for his work in general – is its clarity. The weakness is that, in Blumer's hands, the perspective seems rather bland and perhaps over-committed to the exclusive study of meanings at the expense of other aspects of the social world. It is as if symbolic interactionism were the steamed rice of the sociology world. It is probably good for us but it is hard to get excited about. Out of context and in dry, abstract language, Blumer comes across as being right, but right in an obvious and unremarkable way. Even friendly critics might ask, 'How can so bland a set of ideas produce a distinctive sociological approach?'.

To answer this question, it is helpful to imagine yourself doing a symbolic interactionist project. What will be required? Blumer does not provide a detailed recipe for the conduct of symbolic interactionist research. Rather, he offers some very general guidlelines. He suggests that any research must 'respect the nature of the empirical world' (Blumer 1986: 60) and use methods of investigation that are appropriate to that nature. Blumer favours 'naturalistic inquiry', which seeks close and full familiarity through direct acquaintance with human social life. Blumer identifies two phases in naturalistic inquiry. *Exploration* attempts to build a detailed description of the complexities of the setting under study. Blumer emphasizes that there is nothing 'mere' about the descriptive task. It involves constant probing and attention to sources of information and the images of persons and their activities acquired over the course of investigation. Interviewing may be involved but this will not, in itself, yield straightforward data for, as Anthony Giddens (1984) has argued, group members themselves may only possess 'practical' and not 'discursive' knowledge of the meanings of objects. This means that, although they are skilled everyday agents capable of participating in the life of their group, they may be unable to explain to others what it is that they are doing. *Inspection* is the process of analysis. Once a setting has been depicted, it must be analyzed and particular attention given to 'the empirical content of whatever analytical elements' (Blumer 1986: 43) are identified. The symbolic interactionist must assemble an account of a group's life through the layered meanings applied to objects without initially knowing what these objects are or even how many of these objects exist.

And there are more problems to be solved. Blumer's third premise alerts us to a new area of difficulty: meanings are interpreted and modified during the process of social interaction. This simple statement presents three interwoven challenges to us as symbolic interactionists: we must spend enough time 'in the field' to enable us to grasp the changing meanings given to objects, we must learn the methods of interpretation used by group members and, finally, we must be present during the scenes of social interaction so that we can observe the interpretive process as it plays itself out. By this point it is clear that Blumer is asking a lot of sociologists: his apparently innocuous suggestions translate into a fiendishly difficult form of empirical research. His six root images do nothing to dispel the level of empirical complexity he has in mind; on the contrary, they confirm the problems that will be encountered in realizing Blumer's programmatic statements in empirical research.

Another way of gaining a purchase on Blumer's account of symbolic interactionism is to understand it as more than just an independent theory: it is also a theory that exists in opposition to three alternative approaches in social science. The three approaches that Blumer agitated against are quantification, **structural functionalism** and **psychoanalysis**. Blumer was a symbolic interactionist imperialist; he did not seek reconciliation with these alternative approaches to the study of group life.

Although it is true that Blumer was critical of existing quantitative studies, he rarely singled out specific quantitative projects. In fact, Blumer did not usually identify quantification as a problem; he was, rather, deeply suspicious of the use of variables in sociological research. Perhaps this is only a small semantic difference since, without variables, sociologists have little or nothing to quantify, and so Blumer could fire at a small, vulnerable target as a way of addressing his larger concern.

The second approach opposed by Blumer was the structural functionalism of Talcott Parsons. Strangely, Blumer always criticized Parsons from a distance. In his view, Parsons' work flew high above the ground and hence had no purchase on the intricate processes of meaning creation. Blumer wanted to 'lift the veil' and see social life as it unfolds. He did not want to rely upon ana-lytical schemes that were developed prior to the research and imposed upon the groups being studied. Instead, he wanted sociological theory to emerge from the research itself.

Blumer was similarly dismissive of **Freud** and psychoanalysis. Blumer's Freud was a speculative biological psychologist who stressed impulses and unconscious processes. Blumer apparently had no knowledge of the object-relations school of psychoanalysis that emphasized the central role of transference in the dynamics between patient and analyst. This was Parsons' Freud and one that is – arguably at least – compatible with a symbolic interactionist orientation (see Manning 2005).

This chapter has, so far, pursued a 'narrow' definition of symbolic interaction-ism by concentrating on Blumer's orienting conceptions. However, it is also true that there is a 'broad' definition of symbolic interactionism that is both method-ologically eclectic and only loosely linked to Blumer. Understood broadly, any sociological research that considers the meanings that objects, people and activi-ties have for group members, and the processes whereby these meanings are sus-tained or transformed, is a version of symbolic interactionism. Recently, David Maines (2001) has suggested that the distinction between what we are calling narrow and broad interactionist approaches is the 'fault-line' running through contemporary sociology. This is because the narrow definition of symbolic inter-actionism has become, in his view, a marginalized sociological speciality while at the same time the broad definition has become sociological orthodoxy. The result? No one and everyone is a symbolic interactionist. This, in a nutshell, is the fault-line running through contemporary sociology.

In Gary Fine's view, symbolic interactionism fragmented once Herbert Blumer and his supporters could no longer police the boundaries (Fine 1993: 63). One clear signal of fragmentation was the emergence of a new school of symbolic interac-tionism at the University of Iowa, under the leadership of Manford Kuhn. This post-Second World War development broke the hegemony of the **Chicago School** and reinvigorated the apparently settled debates about the theories, methods and sub-stantive topics appropriate to the field. Kuhn was much more sympathetic to the use of surveys, quantitative data and experimental research than Blumer and, for a brief period, Kuhn's 'Twenty Statements Test' was an influential way of studying self-identity. However, Kuhn's successes were also significant because they reopened discussion about the foundational questions concerning what symbolic interaction-ism really was and what it could be. Once the (bedroom) door was left open by Kuhn, it wasn't long before symbolic interactionists became, in Fine's term, 'intel-lectually promiscuous' (1993: 64). Even though symbolic interactionists have, by and large, retained their ties to Blumer, they have also explored intersecting ideas drawn from **ethnomethodology**, **semiotics**, **feminism**, **post-modernism**, **poststructuralism**, hermeneutics and ordinary language philosophy. On the one hand, this intellectual cross-fertilization has proven to be fruitful and yet, on the other hand, the inevitable fragmentation has also diluted the central ideas of Blumer and his Chicago colleagues. Norman Denzin (1992) has explored the wide range of theoretical and methodological approaches that are now loosely affiliated with symbolic interactionism. Within the confines of this chapter it is plainly impossible to do justice to this range. Instead, we concentrate our attention on interactionism's major founding figure, George Herbert Mead, and its most gifted if wayward practitioner, Erving **Goffman**.

THE ARCHITECT OF SYMBOLIC INTERACTIONISM: GEORGE HERBERT MEAD

Perhaps no one was more bound and determined to preserve the reputation of Mead than Blumer. However, this claim disguises the fact that these two men were very different. Blumer was a pragmatist in the most direct sense of the term: what he couldn't use he threw out or just ignored. He did not seek broad, or even deep, knowledge and was often willing to declare that he either had not read work by major sociologists or had not understood them. Blumer rarely felt the need, for example, to include footnotes or even references in his written work. Instead, Blumer had a keen, almost surgical, sense of what was important and what could be cut out. As a result, his work leaves a smaller but viable set of core sociological concerns in clear view. Although Blumer did not have the stylistic abilities of, for example, Goffman, he did write with a pared down simplicity that was remarkably economic. His writing style was the perfect complement to his theoretical ambitions.

Mead's approach could not have been more different. In an age of specialization, he remained a Renaissance figure, deeply knowledgeable about classical and modern philosophy, theology, social science, history, European and American literature and even biology, physiology and physics. His scholarly goal was to synthesize this diffuse body of knowledge into one theory. This necessarily left him struggling to build bridges between very different bodies of knowledge. Thus, for example, Mead's analysis of the importance of 'taking the role of the other' – an idea that seems to resonate easily with later symbolic interactionist studies – was, for Mead, an extended reflection on the implications of Whitehead's ideas in the philosophy of science and Einstein's contributions to relativity theory in physics for social psychology. Blumer chose to cut through the thicket of issues that interested Mead in order to present a view of his work that had direct relevance to the kind of sociology that he favored.

It is now clear that Mead struggled first to identify and then to write about the central core of ideas that he believed was contained in the different literatures and disciplines that he studied. What were these different disciplines and literatures that both captivated and, in a sense, frustrated Mead? There are four elements that are worth distinguishing. First, Mead was a philosopher with a clear interest in intellectual history. This is demonstrated by his lectures at Chicago, published posthumously as *Movements of Thought in the Nineteenth Century*

(1936). These show Mead drawing on German philosophy, particularly the 'Romantic philosophers' (Fichte, Schelling and Hegel) who were reacting against Kantian thought.

Second, Mead was an admirer of the natural sciences, particularly the broad fields of physics and evolution and the narrow field of physiological psychology. Mead wanted to establish the extent to which social psychology could adopt the methods and assumptions of the natural sciences. Once this was understood, Mead hoped to identify the additional burdens imposed on researchers interested in imprecise objects such as meanings and experiences rather than in inanimate and precise objects such as atoms and molecules. He was also drawn into discussions that combined the romantic idealism of **Hegel** with the evolutionary studies of Darwin, leading him to speculate that social systems may have their own forms of progression and direction (see, particularly, Mead 1962, part IV).

Third, Mead looked to history. As with almost all nineteenth century thinkers, Mead understood the French Revolution as not only the European event that signaled the arrival of **modernity** but also as the test case for the possibility of rapid, fundamental social change. In an even stronger sense, the French Revolution was a test case for the possibility of social engineering. Mead's liberal progressive ambitions were constrained by the realization that, however philosophically and politically desirable were the goals of the Revolution, the storming of the Bastille was followed by the Bloody Terror and, at least in the medium term, a regressive, authoritarian political system (Mead 1936: 51–65).

Fourth, Mead integrated American pragmatism into his own view of social psychology. In particular, Mead was impressed by his Michigan and Chicago colleague, John Dewey and by the Harvard philosopher, William James. Their ideas and, in some cases, their concepts, were springboards for his own distinctive theory. Although Dewey was undoubtedly a tremendous influence on Mead, it is important to remember that they were only departmental colleagues in the early stages of Mead's career. Following a disagreement with the President of the University of Chicago, Dewey resigned his position in 1904. Mead, however, stayed on at the University of Chicago for another 27 years, until he died in 1931.

However, Mead does owe a key debt to Dewey, derived from Dewey's early observations about the 'reflex arc'. This informed both Mead and Dewey's functionalist psychology and, in what amounts to the same thing, their version of behaviorism. In his 1896 paper, 'The Reflex Arc in Psychology', Dewey undermined the causal sequence of stimulus and response. Instead of understanding a response as caused by a stimulus, Dewey proposed that both a response and a stimulus are interwoven 'distinctions of function'; they are 'phases' during which functional roles are exchanged and 'what is at one moment a guided response may at the next moment become a guiding influence' (Cook 1993: 49). The stimulus cannot, according to Dewey, simply produce a response because each stimulus must first be interpreted in some way (Thayer 1968: 188). The implication of Dewey's argument for Mead's social psychology was that the social world must be analyzed as an interdependent set of parts that, by definition, mutually influence each other. Rather than cause and effect, there is unity and process, and these two ideas became critical for later symbolic interactionists.

In a direct way, Mead translated Dewey's abstract ideas about unity and process into a procedure for understanding the idea of the 'self'. In a formulation that seems to us to be reminiscent of Freud but was, for Mead, one that indicated his debt to William James, Mead suggested that the self is a reflexive entity that possesses both an 'I' and a 'me'. The 'I' and the 'me' are not connected by stimulus and response; rather, each informs the other, giving the person a sense of unity. Mead understood the 'me' to be the 'attitude of the generalized other'. He meant by this that we all possess a 'me', insofar as we have internalized a set of community standards. However, we do not internalize the 'me' passively. Instead, as reflexive beings who can be objects to ourselves, we think about the community standards that have become incorporated into our identities. This process leads Cook to call the 'I' an 'agent of reconstruction' (1993: 51).

Mead's behaviorism was a response to the behaviorism of John Watson. Mead understood and supported a broad version of behaviorism that he defined as: 'an approach to the study of experience of the individual from the point of view of his conduct, particularly, but not exclusively, the conduct as it is observable by others' (1962: 2). The hedge 'but not exclusively' is, in fact, very consequential, since it made the domain of 'social' behaviorism much wider than Watsonian behaviorism. By contrast, like Cooley, Mead wanted a broader approach that could include the field of introspection, even though this was not directly observable. With the inclusion of a few words, then, Mead had opened sociology's door to the investigation of internal states and internal worlds. Mead began to describe his psychology as behavioristic rather than functionalist in order to emphasize the social component of behavior that is captured by the 'I' and the 'me' (see Cook 1993: 70).

The focus of sociological interest in Mead has been on the second section of his masterpiece, *Mind, Self and Society* (1962 [1934]) that contains a sustained investigation of the dynamic interplay between the self and the social group. As suggested earlier, Mead's intention is to show that a person's sense of self is significantly (but not completely) formed through the internalization of the norms and values of the different groups to which he or she belongs. These group standards are internalized rather than simply learned, indicating that they are fused into the person's sense of self. Whereas a knowledgeable outsider might simply understand that group members will probably feel, for example, anger in response to a certain event, insiders both understand that this is the likely response and actually feel anger themselves: their blood boils too. Thus, the Meadian self has discursive, emotional and even visceral reactions that are simultaneously the 'property' of the person and the group.

A person's self is not and cannot be present at birth. Rather, Mead suggests, it emerges during 'social experience and activity' (1962: 135). These experiences and activities take place in groups and the socialization and later internalization of group standards is a prerequisite for group membership. Mead outlined a developmental schema that children pass through as they master socialization and internalizations skills. This involves a critical passage from a 'play stage' to a 'game stage'. During the former, children take on the roles of 'significant others' that have a concrete existence for them, such as their own parents, or perhaps the roles of specific comic book figures, such as Spiderman or Catwoman. Later, they enter a game stage where they understand the different roles played by members of the group. This allows children to play the roles of 'generalized others' that exist only in the abstract, such as police officers or bank robbers. During the game stage, children's activities become structured by rules and bounded in space and time, thereby preparing them for the practical constraints of adult life (1962: 150–64).

Since we qualify for membership of multiple groups, it follows that we also have multiple personalities, a state of affairs that Mead considers to be 'normal' (1962: 142–3). As part of the creation of multiple personalities, we internalize the requirements of membership for each group. In Mead's vocabulary, we adopt the 'morale' of each group and this gives us a sense of belonging (1962: 160). It is much more powerful than the morale we have when we belong to a large, undifferentiated group, such as a town, to which we may feel only a slight attachment. . . .

In order to conceptualize the process of forming a normal multiple personality, Mead introduced a famous distinction between the 'I' and the 'me'. The 'me' characterizes the attitudes of the group and, as such, contains community standards: 'The "me" represents a definite organization of the community there in our own attitudes. . .' (1962: 178). Since we simultaneously belong to multiple groups, we must also have more than one 'me'. The 'me' 'is the organized set of attitudes of others which one . . . assumes' (1962: 175). By assuming these attitudes, the person internalizes them. The 'me' is therefore the attitude of the generalized other that the child learned to adopt repeatedly during the game stage.

A person with an overdeveloped 'me' is a hyper-conformist whose 'ideas are exactly the same as those of his neighbors' with only limited and 'unconscious' adjustments (1962: 200). To counteract the mechanical behavior that results from this, Mead argued that we also have an 'I' that is each person's (that is, each organism's) response to attitudes of the generalized other contained in each me (1962: 175). The self is formed out of the 'conversation' between the 'I' and the 'me' (1962: 179). This conceptualization of **identity** is complicated by the fact that each person has multiple personalities and is therefore composed of more than one 'I' and 'me'. As a result, we are all therefore composed through multiple internal conversations.

Although not of immediate interest to Mead himself, it is not difficult to see that sociologists could understand Mead's delineation of the 'me' as something that could be empirically investigated. Mead inadvertently positioned himself as the inventor of a set of ideas crying out for a qualitative method of inquiry to ascertain the content of the 'me' that is formed in and by specific social groups. Since the 'me' is the property of both the person and the group, it can be studied, in the manner of Durkheim, without recourse to the psychological investigation of the individual. This is because the 'me' imposes an external constraint on the individual that exists *sui generis*. The 'me' can therefore be understood as a Durkheimian 'social fact'.

The 'I' in Mead's theory is harder to pin down and, as Lewis (1979) has shown, Mead used the term in different ways. However, at a minimum, the 'I' is the response made by the person to the dictates of the generalized other. It is a repository of impulses that are regulated, in fact censored, by the 'me'. Lewis (1979) has argued that commentators on Mead have often falsely reduced the concept of the 'I' to either a 'remedial' or a 'residual' status. He suggests that both approaches fail because they separate Mead's conceptualization of the 'I' from his overarching account of social behaviorism. Understood as a remedy, Mead's 'I' is interpreted as a way of avoiding a **deterministic** conception of self. Understood as a residue, it is a way of accounting for the unpredictability of human conduct. In effect, these two interpretations are two sides of the same coin. These problems occurred in part because Mead's used the term 'I' 'equivocally' (1979: 266).

Although Mead's version of behaviorism was certainly a social psychology, it was also a political theory. Indeed, this observation can and should be put more forcefully: Mead's social psychology proposed a political solution to existing economic and social problems in the America of the early twentieth century. In this regard, Mead was comparable to other pragmatists of his day. Mead wanted to find a post-Christian way of establishing a democratic and inclusive society that was capable of providing general prosperity. Despite (or perhaps because of) his thoroughly Protestant upbringing, Mead did not believe that the then thriving social Gospel movement was a viable means of realizing the American dream for the large immigrant and recently relocated populations that overwhelmed Chicago and other Northern cities following the Civil War. If Mead could not sustain his own Christian faith, how could he propose this as a general solution to the anomic and exploitative conditions that were documented so well by Chicago sociologists and the muckraking exposé novels of Theodore Dreiser and Upton Sinclair? Mead's lost religion must also be understood against the backdrop of the Baptist origins of the University of Chicago and its chief patron, John D. Rockefeller, as well as the heartfelt ambitions for the social Gospel movement nurtured by prominent Chicago sociologists, notably Albion Small and Charles Henderson. Once we seek to read Mead's work as part social psychology, part political theory, then the different aspects of his life form a coherent whole. Mead's civic work, carried out through the City Club, Hull House and the University of Chicago itself, was a practical attempt to realize the theoretical ambitions laid out in his writings.

ERVING GOFFMAN

Erving Goffman (1922–82) perhaps did more than any other single figure to popularize the perspective of symbolic interactionism. He cut an intellectually distinctive figure within and beyond sociology. In a series of books and papers published from the early 1950s to the early 1980s, he focused on the organization of observable, everyday behavior in a range of work, domestic, institutional and informal settings in contemporary society. Using a variety of qualitative methods, Goffman developed concepts and classifications to describe and analyze the different elements of social interaction. These concepts were heuristic, simplifying tools for sociological analysis that did not capture the complexity of lived experience. Rather, they were designed to identify features of the social organization of interaction. Although these concepts simplified lived experience, their 'experience near' standing is testified by the shock of recognition readers often encounter when reading Goffman's writings as they realize that they too have done or felt something exactly as Goffman describes it. In addition to the study of everyday social interaction, Goffman retained a strong interest in the sociology of mental illness. This began in the 1950s, when he conducted ethnographic research at a large hospital, Saint Elizabeths (the apostrophe is usually omitted) in Washington DC. He considered the study of everyday interaction and the study of mental illness as two sides of the same coin. Like Freud, Goffman suggested that much could be learned about ordinary events by studying extraordinary behavior.

Within the interactionist tradition, and specifically that part of it associated with the Second Chicago School (Fine 1995), Goffman is often regarded as 'the special one'. Yet he remained ambivalent about characterizing his work as symbolic interactionist. Speaking in 1980 (Verhoeven 1993), he acknowledged that he had as much right to be described as an interactionist as anyone. However, he remained diffident about the label throughout his career. This was part of his more general resistance to the intellectual shorthands that he considered such oversimplifications encouraged. Goffman agreed that he found Blumer's social psychology 'congenial', but complained that his writings lacked the content that could help to guide substantive sociological enquiry. Interactionist premises broadly consistent with those articulated by Blumer often seem to be presumed as a basis for investigation by Goffman, but he looked elsewhere – to the likes of Émile Durkheim, A.R. Radcliffe-Brown, Kenneth Burke and W. Lloyd Warner – for the resources and inspiration to develop his own interactional analyses.

Erving Goffman was born in 1922 in Mannville, Alberta, Canada, the second of two children of Ukrainian Jewish émigrés. Starting as a science student in Manitoba, Goffman graduated from the University of Toronto in 1945, where he studied anthropology and sociology. Goffman began graduate study in sociology at the University of Chicago, which at that time was a hive of activity, with its student numbers swelled to near breaking point by the G.I. Bill. In 1949, Goffman successfully completed all the requirements for his Master's degree and for his doctoral dissertation, Goffman chose to study rural life in the Shetlands Islands. This setting was a world apart from the hustle, heterogeneity and sprawl of Chicago life. In December 1949, Goffman arrived on Unst, a small, crofting community at the northern end of the Shetland Isles. Variously describing himself as an anthropologist and as a student of agricultural techniques, Goffman actually studied social interaction among the islanders, concentrating on the encounters occurring in the island's only hotel. After initially suspecting that he was a spy, the islanders warmed to Goffman, who stayed there until May 1951.

In 1953, Goffman was awarded his doctorate from the University of Chicago and, in 1954, left Chicago to begin ethnographic work at Saint Elizabeths in Washington, D.C. The ensuing book – *Asylums* (1961) – would become one of the most influential sociological works of the twentieth century.

In 1958, Goffman began work at the University of California at Berkeley, at the invitation of Herbert Blumer, who himself had moved to California from Chicago six years earlier. Goffman's academic career progressed very rapidly and he became a Full Professor in 1962. In the decade from 1959–69 Goffman published seven significant books – a remarkable achievement. Goffman's social interest in blackjack also became a scholarly one: he returned to school to earn certification to become a blackjack dealer, a position he occupied periodically at the Station Plaza Casino in Las Vegas, where he was later promoted to 'pit boss'. This experience was intended as research for an anticipated ethnographic project of the social world of the gambler. However, nothing was ever published, although his paper 'Where the action is' gives tantalizing clues to what the full-length study might have looked like.

In 1968, Goffman resigned from Berkeley in order to accept a Benjamin Franklin Chair in Anthropology and Sociology at the University of Pennsylvania. He continued to be a very productive scholar, publishing *Relations in Public* (1971), his hoped-for magnum opus, *Frame Analysis* (1974), *Gender Advertisements* (1979) and *Forms of Talk* (1981) and was at the height of his powers when he died in 1982.

Goffman's overarching theme is the investigation of face-to-face interaction, primarily among the unacquainted. At the beginning and end of his career (but curiously, not in the middle) he referred to this as the study of the interaction order. The primary focus of this investigation was the identification and classification of the different elements of face-to-face interaction. The subsidiary tasks involved the use of theatrical and game metaphors to explore the tactical dimension of the interaction order, a ritual model that highlighted the part played by tact and respect and an analysis of the role of reflexivity in social life, particularly as revealed through the notion of 'framing' and its analytic refinements. In addition, Goffman made significant contributions in works of broad popular appeal to the sociologies of mental illness, stigma and gender.

The interaction order is a conceptual map to each and every occasion of face-to-face interaction. This map is therefore intended to cover behavior in, among other places, restaurants, elevators, stadiums and dinner parties. Literally speaking, all face-to-face interaction requires the 'co-presence' of participants; that is, people must sense that others are close enough to them to be able to register whatever it is that they are doing. In *Behavior in Public Places* (1963a: 13–22) Goffman distinguished three types of co-presence: the 'gathering', the 'situation' and the 'social occasion'. For Goffman, a gathering is simply a coming together of two or more people, a situation occurs whenever there is 'mutual monitoring' and a social occasion is the wider social entity that brings together a particular group of people to a specific time and place. Thus, a social occasion such as a birthday party becomes the background against which gatherings and situations can occur. For each of these types of co-presence there are distinctive patterns of 'communication traffic order' regulated by a distinct moral code that Goffman calls the 'situational proprieties' (1963a: 24). These patterns are 'focused' when there is a single focus of attention and 'unfocused' when there is not.

Focused interaction occurs when people 'extend one another a special communication license and sustain a special type of mutual activity' (1963a: 83). This involves 'face-work' of various kinds among friends, acquaintances and, under special circumstances, the unacquainted. The initiation and continuation of unwanted focused interaction was, for Goffman, an interesting topic in its own right.

Unfocused interaction predominates in urban settings where people are unacquainted with each other. Even if efforts are made to slow down the flow of information, people 'read' each other through 'body idiom' and perceived 'involvement'. Through our body idiom people glean information about us by judging us against conventional standards. Our body idiom therefore consists of impressions that either we willingly 'give' or inadvertently 'give off' (Goffman 1963a: 13–14). Involvement refers to the attention we give – or fail to give – to the social situations in which we find ourselves. It is an internal state that others perceive through observable, behavioral markers. Frequently, people simultaneously manage both a 'main' and a 'side' involvement, as when a student listens to a lecture and doodles on a notepad at the same time. The group and the present situation determine what constitutes a 'dominant' involvement. By contrast, a 'subordinate' involvement is whatever the group tolerates, once appropriate respect is shown for the dominant focus of group attention.

Ritual regard for the unacquainted is preserved in unfocused interaction through 'civil inattention'. This involves initial eye contact among the unacquainted and then a studious looking away. The practice is likened to passing cars dipping their lights. Thus, the function of civil inattention appears to be to display mutual regard and the absence of threat. Civil inattention is the cardinal rule regulating behavior between the unacquainted in public places. Goffman's point is that we do not simply ignore unacquainted others. Rather, we comport ourselves in such a manner as to indicate absence of threat.

Goffman extended the analysis of the interaction to the presentation of relationships in public settings. Understood in these terms, we are 'sign vehicles': our body idiom conveys information about ourselves and our social relationships. This will often be sensitive material that has to be handled delicately by others, with appropriate ritual care. In *Relations in Public* (1971) Goffman used an ethological perspective to analyze how people negotiate their way around often packed urban spaces, mark their territories while so doing, signal their relationships to others by various 'tie-signs' and manage their appearances so as to appear normal or unre-markable. By these elaborate means we all contribute to what Herbert Spencer called 'government of ceremonial observance'. To fail to do so sounds alarm bells for others because it threatens the predictability and routinization of everyday encounters. Thus, Goffman was able to show the interwoven complexity, neces-sity and fragility of ordinary conduct.

Goffman began fieldwork in 1955 at Saint Elizabeths Hospital, a large facility housing about 7,000 patients. It is important to remember that this research was conducted at a time when psychiatry was heavily influenced by psychoanalysis, just before the rise of psychopharmacology. Psychoanalysis and psychiatry were therefore interwoven fields at the height of their pres-tige. Sociology was then a small but emerging discipline thought to have connections to the study of interpersonal difficulties. Goffman was, then, unwittingly ideally placed to study the final moments of the psychiatric hospital as it was then understood. Goffman's perspective was somewhat different: as a product of the Chicago School of Sociology, he understood himself to have a special obligation to side with the 'underdog' and to criti-cize institutionalized authority.

Goffman spent about a year and a half at Saint Elizabeths, collecting the ethnographic data that informed *Asylums* (1961). As with his dissertation, this book is highly unusual: it provides very little detailed information about the hos-pital; rather it conveys a 'tone of life' (Fine and Martin 1990: 93). Goffman investigated the characteristics of 'total institutions', of which he took Saint Elizabeths as an exemplar. All total institutions sequester inmates, set schedules and monitor behavior. Inmates are subjected to 'batch living' and its attendant indignities. Goffman drew on both his own data and research from other total institutions, such as monasteries, prisons and boarding schools to produce a gen-eral theory of the characteristics of the total institution.

Goffman provided a subtle and moving account of the process whereby a person can become a candidate for institutionalization. Pre-patients pass through a 'betrayal funnel', as the people they trust most – family and friends – conspire against them, reporting their questionable actions to physicians and other members of the 'circuit of agents' who often play a decisive role in the decision-making process.

Once institutionalized, inmates experience 'civil death' as they lose many of the freedoms that they had taken for granted. There is a further 'mortification of self' as patients are standardized: they are given regulation clothes and subjected to a myriad of indignities. Unco-operative patients are punished by being placed in an unpleasant ward, ostensibly for their own good. Patients may advance through the ward system only through good behavior, taken by the psychiatrists as indicative of improving mental health.

Asylums remains a controversial book. It is a provocative new approach to ethnography, in which the traditional case study is transformed into comparative analysis, producing an ethnography, not of a place, but of a concept; in this case, that of the total institution (Manning 1992). Goffman's findings are also controversial because they suggest that psychiatrists may have weak clinical knowledge. The central issue for Goffman is that, although everyone commits 'situational improprieties', only some of these cases of inappropriate behavior are considered by psychiatrists (and others) to be 'symptomatic' of mental illness. Psychiatrists need, but lack, a 'technical mapping' that could distinguish symptomatic from non-symptomatic situational improprieties. Thus, the occasionally transparent, often latent, message of *Asylums* is that psychiatrists lack a scientific understanding of mental illness and rely instead on lay interpretations. As a result, Goffman thought that psychiatrists routinely misunderstood the behavior of their patients. This aspect of Goffman's work placed a special burden on his analysis to demonstrate how sociological knowledge can undermine psychiatric knowledge. Probably he failed to do this; however, his analysis of Saint Elizabeths did contribute positively to the reevaluation of psychiatry and the treatment of the mentally ill (see Manning 1999).

In the early 1960s, Goffman also analyzed the interpersonal management of stigma. *Stigma* (1963b) emerged out of lectures he gave at the University of California at Berkeley but the idea had its origins during Goffman's fieldwork at St Elizabeths. The predicament typically faced by the ex-patient is generalized to cover a very wide range of situations. Goffman defined a stigma as a 'deeply discrediting' attribute in the context of a set of relationships (1963b: 3). He distinguished three types: abominations of the body, blemishes of character and tribal stigmata (1963b: 4). The focus of his analysis was primarily the stigmatized person's techniques of 'information control' by which discrediting, undisclosed information could be managed. Goffman recognized that the management of potentially damaging information was critical for three aspects of our identity: the 'personal', the 'social' and the 'ego'. Our personal identity is what makes each of us unique; it consists of 'identity pegs' (such as fingerprints) and life histories (1963b: 57). Our social identity is what others understand about us by virtue of the groups to which we belong. Our ego identity refers to what we think about ourselves. Goffman introduced the term 'identity politics' to characterize the often troubled interactions between the stigmatized, the groups who represent them, 'normals' and the 'own' (who understand the world of the stigmatized without being stigmatized themselves). In the latter part of *Stigma*, Goffman suggested that we are all stigmatized in some situations and at some points in our lives. At best, we are 'discreditable' if we are not already 'discredited'. Thus, there is a continuum rather than a binary opposition between normals and the stigmatized. The stigmatized are not a type of person or outcast class but rather a perspective – creatures of the interaction roles they play not the attributes they possess. Stigma, Goffman shows, is more a matter of difference than deviance in any consequential sense of the term.

Goffman's social constructionism again comes to the fore in his gender studies, apparently prompted by the feminist interests of his students, an interest that tapped into Goffman's own longer-standing recognition of the distinctive interactional predicaments routinely faced by women. Goffman (1977, 1979) advances a conception of gender difference that anticipates Judith Butler's (1990) celebrated performative theory of gender by more than a decade. He suggests that, rather than taking gender as a kind of cultural overlay of biologically grounded essential differences between men and women, we can instead see gender as constructed through the culturally-provided arrays of conduct deemed specific to men and women respectively. Goffman's most convincing demonstration is given in *Gender Advertisements* (1979), where some 500 advertising images are analyzed as illustrations of such gender codes as the 'feminine touch', the 'ritualization of subordination' and 'licensed withdrawal'. These gendered ways of touching objects, assuming subordinate postures and symbolically opting out of confronting the full implications of what is transpiring in a situation, make up for Goffman 'the shadow and the substance' of gender difference. There is no need to account for the markers of femininity and masculinity in terms of differences in the natures of men and women grounded in biology. These markers are socially constructed and culturally learned. What we take to be mere markers of some more fundamental biological differences are the very sources of our gendered identities.

Goffman's analyses are distinguished by their inventive use of a range of metaphorical resources, most particularly the metaphors of theatre, game and strategy, ritual and frame. In *The Presentation of Self in Everyday Life* (1959) Goffman outlined a conceptual framework in which any occasion of face-to-face interaction can be interpreted as a theatrical performance. Expanding the ideas of Kenneth Burke's 'dramatistic' approach, Goffman developed his own 'dramaturgical' investigations based on six themes: the performance, the team, the region, discrepant roles, communication out of character and impression management. Dramaturgy offers re-descriptions of familiar events in which there is a heightened sense of suspicion. Nothing in Goffman's dramaturgical world is quite what it seems.

Since nearly all of us are skilled in the arts of impression management, we monitor aspects of the people's conduct and the impressions that they unconsciously give off. Goffman's actors seek to deceive others while seeing through the deceptive practices of others. Even when among team members in backstage areas, our performances are not necessarily more authentic, although there we often 'knowingly contradict' (1959: 114) our front-stage behavior. Goffman's dramaturgical world is thus one of misdirection in which general suspicion is necessary. In fact, Goffman (1969) later developed an interest in espionage practices precisely because he recognized these as extensions of everyday behavior. This way of thinking was perhaps part of a broader cultural shift in the United States: the safe assumptions of mainstream Americans in the 1950s were being challenged by the radicalized generation of the 1960s. To some degree, Goffman gave expression to this emerging sentiment.

Goffman (1969) speculated that his adaptation of game theory was a possible successor to Blumer's symbolic interactionism. Rather than focusing on the production of meanings, the definition of the situation and relevant symbols, as Blumer advocated, Goffman proposed the study of 'strategic interaction', using the vocabulary outlined above. For unclear reasons, neither Goffman nor anyone else developed this proposal, and the relationship between symbolic interactionism and strategic interaction has been largely ignored.

The ritual metaphor is Goffman's third major metaphorical resource. Goffman draws on Durkheim's thinking about religious ritual from *Elementary Forms of the Religious Life* (1912) and adapts it for the secular contexts of the interaction order. In any encounter, tactical considerations must be set alongside tactful ones. Ritual is the notion that articulates the various forms of care, courtesy and respect for the other person as well as oneself. Of course, Goffman is worldly enough to recognize that many encounters do not involve warm expressions of regard for the other, but rather the opposite – insult and contempt. Ritual considerations might best be thought of as occupying a continuum. Goffman's early work identifies the major forms of ritual conduct (deference and demeanour) and ritual process ('face-work'). Through the 'line' the person takes in any encounter, that is the view of themselves, others and the situation expressed through verbal and non-verbal acts, a person claims a certain 'face'. This face is a 'positive social value', sustained by what transpires in an encounter. The ritual metaphor in Goffman's interactional analyses offers a counterbalance to the egoistic elements prominent in his deployment of dramaturgical and strategic metaphors.

Goffman expected *Frame Analysis* (1974) to be his crowning achievement: the 586-page book took a decade to prepare and marked a subtle departure from his earlier work. In this project, Goffman emphasized reflexive aspects of social life – that is, the ways in which what we think about what we do affects the performance of the activity itself. This was showcased in the book's preface, in which Goffman interrogated the idea of writing a preface itself. Goffman defined a frame as a way of organizing experiences: we use frames to identify what is taking place. For example, a story may be a joke, a warning, a lesson, an invitation and so on. Frame analysis is therefore the study of the 'organization of experience'. The most fundamental frameworks are 'primary frameworks', which reveal what is 'really' happening either in the natural or social world. The meaning of a primary framework can be challenged in various ways. It can also be 'keyed': this occurs when its meaning is transformed into something patterned on but independent of the initial frame. For example, a keying may convince us that what appears to be a fight is in fact just play. However, caution is needed because every keying can itself be re-keyed. In addition to keys, there are 'fabrications'. These are frames that are designed to mislead others. Fabrications are 'benign' when they are for the benefit of the audience or 'exploitative' when they are for the benefit of the fabricator. In an attempt to prevent the keying, re-keying and fabrications of frames, we often attempt to 'anchor' them so that audiences can accept them as real.

Goffman extended this analysis into an investigation of various kinds of talk. These essays were published together as *Forms of Talk* (1981). The central theme of the five essays was the 'footing' of talk. This referred to the participant's projected self during a conversation. Thus, we can change footing by realigning ourselves. This is simply another way of discussing a change in the relevant frame for events. Goffman gave the example of the then President Nixon commenting on the dress style of the reporter, Helen Thomas. Goffman argued that this interlude was intended by President Nixon to be a brief time-out from the formal duties of the day, a moment in which he could reveal himself as an ordinary, if sharp-witted man who could thrive without the protection of presidential authority. Goffman suggested that in this President Nixon failed, as his performance was too wooden and his jokes were laughed at only out of respect for his office. This small example, taken from one of his final projects, epitomizes his overall concern: the development of general classifications to be used to understand concrete examples of the interaction order.

REFERENCES AND RECOMMENDED FURTHER READING

Blumer, Herbert (1986) [1969] *Symbolic Interactionism*, Berkeley, CA: University of California Press.
Cooley, Charles (1964) [1902] *Human Nature and Social Order*, New York: Schocken Books.
Cook, G. (1993) *George Herbert Mead*, Champaign, IL: University of Illinois Press.
Fine, Gary (ed.) (1995) *A Second Chicago School?*, Chicago: University of Chicago Press.
Fine, Gary and Martin, D. (1990) 'A partisan view: sarcasm, satire and irony as voices in Erving Goffman's asylums', *Journal of Contemporary Ethnography*, 19(1): 89–115.
Giddens, Anthony (1984) *The Constitution of Society*, Cambridge: Polity.
Goffman, Erving (1959) *The Presentation of Self in Everyday Life*, New York: Doubleday, Anchor.
—— (1961) *Asylums*, Harmondsworth: Penguin.
—— (1963a) *Behavior in Public Places: Notes on the Social Organization of Gatherings*, New York: Free Press.
—— (1963b) *Stigma: Notes on the Management of Spoiled Identity*, Englewood Cliffs, NJ: Prentice-Hall.
—— (1967) *Interaction Ritual: Essays on Face-to-Face Behavior*, New York: Anchor.
—— (1969) *Strategic Interaction*, Philadelphia, PA: University of Pennsylvania Press.
—— (1971) *Relations in Public: Microstudies of the Public Order*, New York: Basic Books.
—— (1974) *Frame Analysis: An Essay on the Organization of Experience*, New York: Harper & Row.
—— (1977) 'The arrangement between the sexes', *Theory and Society*, 4(3): 301–31.
—— (1981) *Forms of Talk*, Oxford: Blackwell.
—— (1983) 'The Interaction Order', *American Sociological Review*, 48: 1–17.
Lewis, J.D. (1979) 'A social behaviorist interpretation of the Meadian "I"', *American Journal of Sociology*, 85: 261–87.
Maines, D. (2001) *The Faultline of Consciousness: A View of Interactionism in Sociology*, Chicago, IL: Aldine.

Manning, P. (1992) *Erving Goffman and Modern Sociology*, Stanford, CA: Stanford University Press.

—— (1999) 'Ethnographic coats and tents', in *Goffman and Social Organization: Studies in a Sociological Legacy*, Greg Smith (ed.), London: Routledge.

—— (2000) 'Credibility, agency and the Interaction Order', *Symbolic Interaction*, 23(3): 283–97.

—— (2005) *Freud and American Sociology*, Cambridge: Polity.

Mead, G.H. (1936) *Movements of Thought in the Nineteenth Century*, C.W. Morris (ed.), Chicago, IL: Chicago University Press.

Morrione, T. (ed.) (2004) *George Herbert Mead and Human Conduct*, Walnut Creek, CA: AltaMira Press.

Smith, Greg (ed.) (1999) *Goffman and Social Organization: Studies in a Sociological Legacy*, London: Routledge.

Thayer, H.S. (1968) *Meaning and Action: A Critical History of Pragmatism*, New York: Bobbs-Merrill.

Verhoeven, Jeff (1993) 'An interview with Erving Goffman, 1980', *Research on Language and Social Interaction*, 26(3): 317–48.

Winkin, Yves (1988) *Erving Goffman: Les Moments et Leurs Hommes*, Paris: Minuit.

4

SOCIAL THEORY AND PSYCHOANALYSIS

ANTHONY ELLIOTT

No modern thinker has affected our views on **identity** and sexuality as forcefully as Sigmund **Freud**. And, arguably, psychoanalysis has exerted (and continues to exert) a massive influence over modern social thought. Yet what is the relevance of Freud and **psychoanalysis** to today's world? What does psychoanalysis have to offer our understanding of contemporary social life? It was Nietzsche who spoke of the importance of time to our own self-understanding of mortality. Deeply influenced by Nietzsche, Freud saw time as deeply interwoven with pain, depression and mourning – that is, our ability to confront the most distressing and painful aspects of life is what makes us truly human. The capacity of people to bear guilt and tolerate periods of depression, in a psychoanalytic frame, is essential to personal growth and change. But self-understanding requires attention to our inner world, and this, of course, takes time – a scarce 'commodity' in our speed-driven information age. The psychoanalytic notion of repressed desire, in particular, has provided for a new cultural emphasis on identity, sexuality, the body, feeling and emotion. From the affirmative politics of countercultural movements during the 1960s to various feminist currents in the 1980s and 1990s, psychoanalysis has been drawn on extensively to reshape the concerns of contemporary social and political thought. But the broader point is that psychoanalytic ideas have deeply infiltrated the culture of contemporary societies. From Woody Allen's *Annie Hall* to Marie Cardinal's *The Words to Say It*, from Paul Riceour's *Freud and Philosophy* to Jacques Derrida's *The Post Card*, psychoanalytic ideas pervade our intellectual life and culture. Freudian psychoanalysis is both a doctrine and dogma of our age; it influences our everyday understanding of ourselves, other people, and the world in which we live.

In this chapter, after sketching some of the core concepts of psychoanalytic theory, I consider the relevance and power of psychoanalysis in terms of social-theoretical debates in the social sciences. Throughout, the chapter attempts to defend the view that psychoanalytic theory has much to offer social theorists in the analysis of subjectivity, ideology, sexual politics, and in coming to terms with crises in contemporary culture.

THE LEGACY OF FREUD

It is now more than a century since psychoanalysis emerged under the direction of a single man, Sigmund Freud. Freud, working from his private neurological practice, founded psychoanalysis in late nineteenth-century Vienna as both a therapy and a theory of the human mind. Therapeutically, psychoanalysis is perhaps best known as the 'talking cure' – a slogan used to describe the magical power of language to relieve mental suffering. The nub of the talking cure is known as 'free association.' The patient says to the analyst everything that comes to mind, no matter how trivial or unpleasant. This gives the analyst access to the patient's imagined desires and narrative histories, which may then be interpreted and reconstructed within a clinical session. The aim of psychoanalysis as a clinical practice is to uncover the hidden passions and disruptive emotional conflicts that fuel neurosis and other forms of mental suffering, in order to relieve the patient of his or her distressing symptoms.

Theoretically, psychoanalysis is rooted in a set of dynamic models concerning psychic functioning. The unconscious, repression, drives, representation, trauma, narcissism, denial, displacement: these are the core dimensions of the Freudian account of selfhood. For Freud, the subject does not exist independently of sexuality, libidinal enjoyment, fantasy, or the social and patriarchal codes of cultural life. In fact, the human subject of Enlightenment reason – an identity seemingly self-identical to itself – is deconstructed by psychoanalysis as a kind of fantasy, and one which is itself secretly libidinal. Knowledge, for Freud as for Schopenhauer and Nietzsche, is internal to the world of desire. In the light of Freudian psychoanalysis, a whole series of contemporary ideological oppositions – the intellect and emotion, commerce and pleasure, masculinity and femininity, rationality and irrationality – are potentially open to displacement.

One of Freud's most substantial findings is that there are psychical phenomena which are not available to consciousness, but which nevertheless exert a determining influence on everyday life. In his celebrated meta-psychological essay 'The Unconscious' written in 1914, Freud argued that the individual's self-understanding is not immediately available to itself, that consciousness is not the expression of some core of continuous selfhood. On the contrary, the human subject is, for Freud, a *split* subject, torn between consciousness of self and repressed desire. For Freud, examination of the language of his patients revealed a profound turbulence of passion behind all draftings of self-identity, a radical *otherness* at the heart of subjective life. In discussing human subjectivity, Freud divides the psyche into the unconscious, preconscious and conscious. The preconscious can be thought of as a vast storehouse of memories, most of which may be recalled at will. By contrast, unconscious memories and desires are cut off, or buried, from consciousness. According to Freud, the unconscious is not 'another' consciousness but a separate psychic system with its own distinct processes and mechanisms. The unconscious, Freud comments, is indifferent to reality; it knows no causality or contradiction or logic or negation; it is entirely given over to the search for pleasure and libidinal enjoyment. Moreover, the unconscious cannot be known directly and is, rather, detected only through its effects, through the distortions it inflicts on consciousness.

Rejecting the idea that consciousness can provide a foundation for subjectivity and knowledge, Freud traces the psychic effects of our early dependence on others – usually our parents – in terms of our biologically fixed needs. The infant, Freud says, is incapable of surviving without the provision of care, warmth and nourishment from others. However – and this is fundamental in Freud – human needs always outstrip the biological, linked as needs are to the attaining of pleasure. Freud's exemplary case is the small child sucking milk from her or his mother's breast. After the infant's biological need for nourishment is satisfied, there is the emergence of a certain pleasure in sucking itself, which for Freud is a kind of prototype for the complexity of our erotic lives. From this angle, sexuality is not some preordained, unitary biological force that springs into existence fully formed at birth. Sexuality is created, not pre-packaged. For Freud, sexuality is 'polymorphously perverse.'

In Freud's view, we become the identities we are because we have inside us buried identifications with people we have previously loved (and also hated), most usually our parents. And yet, the foundational loss to which we must respond, and which in effect sets in motion the unfolding of our unconscious sexual fantasies, remains that of the maternal body. The break-up or restructuring of our primary emotional tie to the maternal body is, in fact, so significant that it becomes the founding moment, not only of individuation and differentiation, but also sexual and gender difference. Loss and gender affinity are directly linked in Freud's theory to the Oedipus complex, the psyche's entry into received social meanings. For Freud, the Oedipus complex is the nodal point of sexual development, the symbolic internalization of a lost, tabooed object of desire. In the act of internalizing the loss of the pre-Oedipal mother, the infant's relationship with the father (or, more accurately, symbolic representations of paternal power) becomes crucial for the consolidation of both selfhood and gender identity. Trust in the inter-subjective nature of social life begins here: the father, holding a structural position which is outside and other to this imaginary sphere, functions to *break* the child/mother dyad, thus referring the child to the wider culture and social network. The paternal prohibition on desire for the mother, which is experienced as castration, at once instantiates repressed desire and refers the infant beyond itself, to an external world of social meanings. And yet, the work of culture, according to Freud, is always outstripped by unconscious desire, the return of the repressed. Identity, sexuality, gender, and signification: these are all radically divided between an ongoing development of conscious self-awareness and the unconscious, or repressed desire.

THE FRANKFURT SCHOOL: DOMINATION AFTER FREUD

Freud's relevance to social theory remains perhaps nowhere better dramatized than in the various writings of the first generation of **critical theorists** associated with the Frankfurt Institute of Social Research. The **Frankfurt School**, as it came to be called, was formed in the decade prior to the Nazi reign of terror in Germany and, not surprisingly, many of its leading theorists conducted numerous studies seeking to grasp the wave of political irrationalism and totalitarianism sweeping Western Europe. In a daring theoretical move, the School brought Freudian categories to bear upon the sociological analysis of everyday life, in order to fathom the myriad ways that political power imprints itself upon the internal world of human subjects and, more specifically, to critically examine the obscene, meaningless kind of evil that Hitler had unleashed. Of the School's attempts to fathom the psychopathologies of fascism, the writings of **Adorno**, **Marcuse** and **Fromm** stand out in particular; each of these authors, in quite different ways, drew upon Freudian categories to figure out the core dynamics and pathologies of post-liberal rationality, culture and politics, and also to trace the sociological deadlocks of **modernity** itself. The result was a dramatic underscoring of both the political dimensions of psychoanalysis and also the psychodynamic elements of public political life.

The philosophical backdrop to the Frankfurt School's engagement with Freud and psychoanalysis was spelt out in particular detail by Adorno, who sketched along with co-author Max **Horkheimer** – in *Dialectic of Enlightenment* – a bleak portrait of the personal and political pathologies of instrumental rationality. Humanization of drives and passions, resulting in the transformation from blind instinct to consciousness of self, was, for Adorno, necessary to release the subject from its enslavement to Nature. But, in a tragic irony, the unconscious forces facilitating the achievement of autonomy undergo a mind-shattering repression that leaves the subject marked by inner division, isolation and compulsion. The Janus-face of this forging of the self is clearly discerned in Adorno's historicization of Freud's Oedipus complex. According to Adorno, the bourgeois liberal subject repressed unconscious desire in and through Oedipal prohibitions and, as a consequence, achieved a level of self-control in order to reproduce capitalist social relations. But not so in the administered world of modernity. In post-liberal societies, changes in family life mean that the father no longer functions as an agency of social repression. Instead, individuals are increasingly brought under the sway of the logic of techno-rationality itself, as registered in and through the rise of 'culture industries.' The concept of 'repressive desublimation' is crucial here. The shift from simple to advanced modernity comes about through the destruction of the psychological dimensions of human experience: the socialization of the unconscious in the administered world directly loops the id and the superego at the expense of the mediating agency of the ego itself.

What has been of lasting value is the Frankfurt School's use of Freud in its demonstration of why human subjects, apparently without resistance, submit to the dominant ideologies of late capitalism. The general explanatory model developed by the Frankfurt School to study the socio-psychological dimension of the relation between the individual and culture has received considerable attention in social theory. The following discussion concentrates principally on the social-theoretical reconstructions of psychoanalysis offered by Fromm and Marcuse.

ERICH FROMM

Fromm, who had been practicing as an analyst since 1926 and was a member of the Frankfurt Psychoanalytic Institute, sought in his early studies to integrate Freud's theory of the unconscious with **Marx**ist sociology. Influenced by Wilhelm Reich's book *Character Analysis*, which connects society to the repressed unconscious, Fromm became preoccupied with the cultural consequences of sexual repression, as well as the mediating influence of the family between the economy and the individual. According to Fromm, Freudian psychoanalysis must supplement Marxism in order to grasp how social structures influence, indeed shape, the inner dimensions of human subjectivity. Fromm's concern with the effects of repression, however, differed substantially from the analysis worked out by Reich. In Fromm's view, Reich had been unable to develop an adequate theory of social reproduction because he had reduced Freud's theory of sexuality to a monadic focus on genital sexuality. Yet Freudian psychoanalysis, Fromm maintained, was fundamentally a 'social psychology.' For Fromm, the individual must be understood in his or her relation to others.

The bourgeois nuclear family, Fromm says, is pivotal to understanding the links between individual repression, cultural reproduction and ideological domination. An agency of social reproduction, the family is described as 'the essential medium through which the economic situation exerts its ... influence on the individual's psyche.' Fromm contends that the family implants regression at the heart of subjectivity, sustains economic conditions as ideology, and infuses perceptions of the self as submissive, self-effacing, and powerless. The central message of Fromm's early work is that the destructive effects of late capitalism are not only centered in economic mechanisms and institutions, but involve the anchoring of domination within the inner life and psychodynamic struggles of each individual.

As the 1930s progressed, Fromm became increasingly skeptical of orthodox Freudianism. He strongly criticized Freud's notion of the death drive for its biological reductionism, and argued that it only served to legitimate, at a theoretical level, the destructive and aggressive tendencies of capitalism. Significantly, Fromm also became influenced by neo-Freudian analysts – such as Harry Stack Sullivan and Karen Homey – who stressed larger social and cultural factors in the constitution of selfhood. This emphasis on cultural contributions to identity-formation was underscored by Fromm in his major books, *Escape from Freedom* and *The Sane Society*, both of which argued the idea of an essential 'nature of man,' a nature repressed and distorted by capitalist patterns of domination.

Although Fromm's early studies on the integration of individuals into capitalism was broadly accepted by other members of the Frankfurt School, his subsequent, more sociological, diagnosis of an essential human nature twisted out of shape by capitalism was strongly rejected. Marcuse, for example, charged Fromm (and other neo-Freudian revisionists) with undoing the critical force of Freud's most important ideas, such as the unconscious, repression and infantile sexuality. According to Marcuse, Fromm's revisionism underwrites the smooth functioning of the ego only by displacing the dislocating nature of the unconscious. Marcuse sums up the central point in the following way:

> Whereas Freud, focusing on the vicissitudes of the primary drives, discovered society in the most concealed layer of the genus and individual man, the revisionists, aiming at the reified, ready-made form rather than at the origin of the societal institutions and relations, fail to comprehend what these institutions and relations have done to the personality that they are supposed to fulfill.
>
> (Marcuse, 1974: 240–1)

Fromm's attempt to add sociological factors to psychoanalysis, says Marcuse, results in a false political optimism as well as a liquidation of what is truly revolutionary in Freud: the discovery of the repressed unconscious.

HERBERT MARCUSE

Marcuse, like Fromm, views psychological and political repression as being deeply interwoven. For Marcuse, Freudian psychoanalysis is relevant for tracing the exercise of domination upon the inner world of the subject, for understanding how capitalism and mass culture shape personal desires, and for analyzing the possibilities of human emancipation. Unlike Fromm, however, Marcuse rejects the view that sociological and historical factors must be added to Freudian theory. Instead, Marcuse seeks to unfold the liberative potential in Freud's work from the inside out, in order to reveal its radical political edge.

Marcuse's reconceptualization of psychoanalysis seeks to develop the 'political and sociological substance' of Freud's work. His analysis proceeds from an acceptance of some of the core claims of psychoanalysis. These include the theory of the unconscious, the conflict between the pleasure and reality principles, the life and death drives, and the view that civilization entails sexual repression. Marcuse contends, however, that Freud was wrong about the permanent cultural necessity of psychological repression. Marcuse agrees that all social reproduction demands a certain level of repression. Yet what Freud did not see, Marcuse argues, is that capitalism creates a crippling (though impermanent) burden of repression. From this angle, individuals are, in fact, adapting to the destructive forces of capitalist domination, forces that masquerade as the 'reality principle.'

These provocative ideas are developed by Marcuse in his classic *Eros and Civilization* and *Five Lectures*. The key to Marcuse's interpretation of Freud is the division of repression into 'basic' and 'surplus.' Basic repression refers to that minimum level of libidinal renunciation deemed necessary for facing social life. What this means, in short, is that a certain amount of repression underlies the constitution of the 'socialized subject,' a subject capable of sustaining the business

ANTHONY ELLIOTT

of social and sexual reproduction. By contrast, surplus repression refers to the intensification of restraint created in and through asymmetrical relations of power. Marcuse points to patriarchy (especially in terms of family relationships) and to the workplace as socio-symbolic fields containing a surplus of repression. This repressive surplus, says Marcuse, operates through the 'performance principle,' a culturally specific form of reality structured by the economic order of capitalism. For Marcuse, the destructive psychological effects of this principle are highly consequential. 'Performance' recasts individuals as mere 'things' or 'objects,' replaces eroticism with genital sexuality and fashions a disciplining of the human body (what Marcuse terms 'repressive desublimation') in order to prevent repressed desire from interfering with capitalist exchange values.

Marcuse presses this reinterpretation of Freud into a critical theory of the psychic costs of modernity. In Marcuse's view, the massive social and industrial transformations which have occurred in the twentieth century – changes in systems of economy and technology as well as cultural production – have produced a radical escalation in psychological repression. The more technocapitalism has advanced, he argues, the more repression has become surplus. The immense productive capacities released by technology, modernism and monopoly capitalism have been turned back upon the individual subject with a vengeance. As a consequence, the personal sphere is subject to decomposition and fragmentation. According to Marcuse, the psychoanalytic division of the individual into id, ego, and superego is no longer relevant. A weakening in patriarchal authority within the bourgeois nuclear family, accompanied by the impact of the mass media and commodified culture, has led to an authority-bound, manipulated sense of identity.

Notwithstanding this bleak picture of the contemporary epoch, Marcuse was optimistic about social change. In one sense, he used Freudian psychoanalysis against itself, to trace the emancipatory potentials of modernity. He argued that the performance principle, ironically, generates the economic and social conditions necessary for a radical transformation of society. That is, the material affluence generated by capitalism opens the way for undoing surplus repression. Emancipation, for Marcuse, is linked to a reconciliation between culture, nature, and unconscious pleasure, what he termed 'libidinal rationality.' The preconditions for the realization of libidinal rationality include the overcoming of the split between pleasure and reality, life and death, and a recovery of repressed needs and aspirations. Through changes in fantasy structures and the social context, Marcuse says, society can become re-eroticized.

Marcuse's analysis of contemporary ideological pressures toward 'surplus repression' contains many insights, but it is also clear that there are important limitations to his approach. For one thing, he fails to point, in anything but the most general way, to how ideology transforms repression from 'basic' into 'surplus,' and so it is far from easy to grasp the complex ways in which culture implants political domination upon the emotional economy of subjects. Similarly, the argument that reason or rationality can be located in repressed drives (the notion of 'libidinal rationality') is underdeveloped. Marcuse's work fails to analyze in any substantive way intersubjective social relationships. Instead, his vision of political autonomy is one in which repressed drives become liberated, and thus transfigurative of social relations. From this angle, some critics have suggested that Marcuse's conception of the relation between repressed desire and social transformation is individualistic and asocial in character.

RETURNING TO FREUD: JACQUES LACAN

Many psychoanalytic theorists have identified loss as central to self-constitution. From the fall from pre-Oedipal Eden, in which the small infant becomes separated from the maternal body, through the alarming and painful terrors of the Oedipal constellation, and on to subsequent adult disappointments, rejections and negations: loss infiltrates all emotional transactions between self and others, and so, in a sense, is at the root from which desire flows uncontrollably. Yet, while the intricate connections between loss and selfhood have been underwritten throughout the history of psychoanalysis, perhaps the most remarkable contribution remains that elaborated by the French psychoanalyst Jacques **Lacan**. The world of illusion which we fashion to avoid the traumatic and impenetrable mysteries of loss are, for Lacan, the very stuff out of which we are made. According to Lacan, the individual subject is constituted in and through loss, as an excess of lack. In a radical revision of Freud, largely through a widening of the horizons of psychoanalysis to embrace **structuralist** linguistics and **post-structuralist** theories of discourse, Lacan makes lack the cause which ensures that, as human subjects, we are continually falling short, failing, fading, and lapsing.

The world of sense-perception, for Lacan as for Freud, is born from immersion in a sublimely opaque realm of images, of very early experience of imaginings and imagos, of primitive fantasies of the body of another. Lacan calls this realm, caught between wonderful delight and terrifying anguish, the Imaginary. The Imaginary for Lacan is a prelinguistic, pre-Oedipal register, solely visual in operation and in which desire slides around and recircles an endless array of part-objects – breasts, lips, gaze, skin. According to Lacan, this imaginary drafting of the world of illusion, of wholeness, is broken apart once the infant comes to identify with, and introject, things or objects beyond itself, thus shifting beyond the lures of the Imaginary. This primordial moment of separation is devastating, a loss so painful that it results in a *primary repression* of the pre-Oedipal connection to the maternal sphere, a repression which, in one stroke, founds the repressed unconscious. Once severed from primary identification with the pre-Oedipal mother, the infant is projected into the realm of language, the differences internal to signification that Lacan calls the Other, or the Symbolic order. The Symbolic in Lacan's theory is a plane of received social meanings, logic, differentiation. Symbolization and language permit the subject to represent desire, both to itself and to others. Yet the representation of desire, says Lacan, is always stained by a scar of imaginary, maternal identification.

Lacan theorizes the imaginary tribulations of self-constitution largely through a novel consideration of Freud's theory of narcissism. In 'The Mirror Stage as Formative of the Function of the I,' (1977) Lacan contends that the infant apprehends a sense of bodily unity through the recognition of its image in a mirror. The 'mirror' provides the infant with a consoling image of itself as unified and self-sufficient. This reflecting mirror image is not at all, however, what it seems. Lacan says that what the mirror produces is a 'mirage of coherence,' an alienating *misrecognition*. In short, the mirror *lies*. Mirroring leads the infant to imagine itself as stable and unified, when in fact psychical space is fragmented, and the infant's physical movements unco-ordinated. The reflecting mirror leads the infant into an unfettered realm of narcissism, underpinned by hate and aggression, given the unbridgeable gap between ideal and actuality.

The imaginary can thus be described as a kind of archaic realm of distorted mirror images, a spatial world of indistinction between self and other, from which primary narcissism and aggressivity are drawn as key building blocks in the formation of identity. But, if the Imaginary order is already an alienation of desire, then the same is certainly true of the Symbolic order of language. The Symbolic, says Lacan, smashes the mirror unity of the Imaginary. For Lacan, as for Freud, this happens with the entry of the father into the psychic world of the child. In disturbing the mother–child link, the Oedipal father breaks up the self–other unity of the Imaginary order. For Lacan, language is the fundamental medium which structures the Oedipal process. The child enters the symbolic via language, which ushers in temporal, spatial and logical differences, which are foundational to self and other, subject and object. Language, for Lacan, is an intersubjective order of symbolization which carries the force of cultural sanctions, of what he terms 'the Law of the Father' – for it is in and through language that the subject attempts a reconstruction of lost, imagined unities.

Rewriting the unconscious and Oedipus in terms of the symbolic dimensions of language, Lacan's theoretical point of reference is the structural linguistics of Ferdinand de **Saussure**. It is not possible here to provide an adequate exegesis of Lacan's appropriation and reconstruction of Saussure's ideas; in what follows I shall only emphasize certain aspects of Lacan's use of Saussure's structural linguistics, particularly those aspects most relevant to the concerns of social theory. In Saussurian linguistics, language is explicated as a system of internal differences. In this view, signs are made up of a signifier (a sound or image) and a signified (the concept or meaning evoked). The meaning of a word arises through its differences from other words: a pencil, for example, is not a pen; a book is not a pamphlet, not a magazine, not a newspaper. Words, as such, do not 'mean' their objects. Language creates meaning only through an internal play of differences. While Lacan accepts the key elements of Saussure's structural linguistics, he radicalizes the relation between the signifier and the signified. Lacan will have nothing of the Saussurian search for the signified, or concept, however 'arbitrary' the relation between signifiers that generates meaning may be. Instead, Lacan inverts Saussure's interpretation of the sign, asserting that the signifier has primacy over the signified in the production of meaning. In Lacan's psychoanalytic reading, the two orders of discourse are always separated by censorship, marked by a bar of repression. The signified, says Lacan, cannot be elucidated once and for all since it is always 'sinking' or 'fading' into the unconscious; the signified is, in effect, always just another signifier. And, for Lacan, the signifier is itself coterminous with the unconscious.

Language, as a system of differences, constitutes the subject's repressed desire through and through. The subject, once severed from the narcissistic fullness of the Imaginary, is inserted into linguistic and symbolic structures that both generate the unconscious and allow for its contents to traverse the intersubjective field of culture. Access to ourselves and others, however, is complicated by the fact that desire is itself an 'effect of the signifier,' an outcrop of the spacings or differences of linguistic structures. From this angle, the unconscious is less a realm on the 'inside' of the individual, or 'underneath' language, than an intersubjective space *between* subjects – located in those gaps which separate word from word, meaning from meaning. 'The exteriority of the symbolic in relation to man,' says Lacan, 'is the very notion of the unconscious.' Or, in Lacan's infamous slogan: 'the unconscious is structured like a language.'

CRITICISMS OF LACAN'S FREUD

Lacan's re-reading of Freud has powerfully influenced contemporary social theory. His emphasis on the centrality of symbolic structures in the constitution of the subject, as well as the disruption caused to these structures through the fracturing effects of the unconscious, has been of core importance to recent debates concerning **identity**. His stress on the complicated interweaving of language and desire has been original and provocative. Significantly, his work has served as a useful corrective to social-theoretical accounts that portray the self as the site of rational psychological functioning. Moreover, his linguistic reconceptualization of the unconscious powerfully deconstructs theories of representation which presume that mind and world automatically fit together.

There are many limitations, however, with the Lacanian account of subjectivity and social relations. The most important of these, as concerns identity, is Lacan's claim that individuality involves an inescapable sentence of alienation. While it is undeniable that Freud viewed miscognition as internally tied to ego-formation, Lacan's version of this process involves a number of substantive problems. Consider the following: what is it that allows the individual to (mis)recognize itself from its mirror image? How, exactly, does it cash in on this conferring of selfhood? The problem with the argument that the mirror distorts is that it fails to specify the psychic capacities which make any such misrecognition possible. That is, Lacan's account fails to detail how the mirror is constituted as *real*. Related to this is the criticism that Lacan's linguistic reconceptualization of psychoanalysis actually suppresses the radical implications of Freud's discovery of the unconscious by structuralizing it, reducing it to a chance play of signifiers.

In this respect, Lacan's claim that the unconscious is naturally tied to language has come under fire. Here the criticism is that the unconscious is the precondition of language and not the reverse.

Equally serious are the criticisms that have been made of Lacan's account of culture. Lacan's linkage of the 'subject of the unconscious' with the idea of the 'arbitrary nature of the sign' raises the thorny problem of the replication of ideological power. In this connection, Lacan fails to explain how some ideological and political meanings predominate over others in the shaping of the personal sphere. Instead, cultural domination is equated with language as such. It is the subjection of the individual to the symbolic, to the force of the Law, which accounts for the fall of the subject. However, as Dews (1987) argues, Lacan's equation of language with domination seriously downplays the importance of power, ideology, and social institutions in the reproduction of cultural life.

LACANIAN AND POST-LACANIAN SOCIAL THEORY

In his famous essay, 'Ideology and Ideological State Apparatuses,' the French Marxist philosopher Louis **Althusser** sought to integrate structural Marxism and Lacanian psychoanalysis in order to understand the workings of ideology in modern societies. Althusser (1971) traces ideology as a discourse which leads the individuals to support the reproduction of ruling class power. Althusser argued that society and political life are experienced less in the public world of institutions than in the fantasy realm of the imaginary. 'All ideology' writes Althusser, 'represents in its necessarily imaginary distortion is not the existing relations of production ... but above all the (imaginary) relationship of individuals to the relations of production and the relations that derive from them.' From this angle, ideology provides an imaginary centering to everyday life; ideology confers identity on the self and Others, and makes the individual feel valued within the social, cultural network.

What are the psychic mechanisms which underpin ideology? Echoing Lacan, Althusser argues that ideology functions in and through *mirroring*. Like the Lacanian child in front of its mirror-image, the ideological mirror implants received social meanings at the heart of the subject's world. Yet, as in the mirror stage, the constitution of social forms necessarily involves a misrecognition, since ideology idealizes and distorts the intersubjective world of society, culture, and politics. Through a 'subjection' to ideological discourses of class, race, gender, nationalism, and the like, the individual comes to *misrecognize* itself as an autonomous, self-legislating subject. Imaginary misrecognition occurs through a process that Althusser terms 'interpellation'. It is in and through ideology that society 'interpellates' the individual as a 'subject,' at once conferring identity and subjecting the individual to that social position. This interweaving of signification and imaginary misrecognition, Althusser contends, is rooted in 'Ideological state apparatuses,' which include schools, trade unions, the mass media and the like, and whose function is to ensure the subjection of individuals to different social positions in modern class-based societies. That human subjects should come to overlook the nature of their real decentered subjectivity, says Althusser, is precisely the function of ideology – thus serving to reinforce the dominant power interests of late capitalism.

The theory of ideology developed by Althusser, with its implicit use of Lacanian psychoanalysis, marks one of the major sources of stimulus in twentieth-century social thought. It sets out an array of ideas about the relations between the personal and social domains, the imaginary and institutional life. Althusser's argument that ideology is an indispensable imaginary medium for social reproduction is provocative and important, and it did much to discredit traditional Marxist theories of ideology as mere false consciousness. Like the unconscious for Freud, ideology for Althusser is eternal. However, it is now widely agreed that there are many problems with Althusser's account of ideology. Most importantly, Althusser's argument about the mirroring distortion of ideology runs into the same kind of theoretical dead end as does Lacan's account of the imaginary. That is, in order for an individual subject to (mis)recognize itself in and through ideological discourse, then surely she or he must already possess certain affective capacities for subjective response.

Whatever these shortcomings, the Althusserian/Lacanian model remains a powerful source of influence in contemporary social theory. Indeed, Althusser's Lacan has recently been examined with new interest as concerns the study of subjectivity, society and culture. Fredric **Jameson** (1984) argues for a return to the Lacanian underpinnings of Althusser's social theory in order to fashion what he calls a 'cognitive mapping' of postmodern symbolic forms. So too, Slavoj Žižek recasts the Althusserian model of 'interpellation' in order to trace the fantasy identifications created in and through cultural forms such as media and film.

FEMINISM AND PSYCHOANALYSIS

In recent years, some of the most important conceptual advances in psychoanalytic social theory have come from **feminist** debates on sexual subjectivity and gender hierarchy. Broadly speaking, the major division in psychoanalytic feminism is between Anglo-American object relations theory on the one hand, and French Lacanian and post-Lacanian theory on the other. Through the object-relations perspective, feminist theorists analyze sexuality and gender against the backdrop of interpersonal relationships – with particular emphasis on the pre-Oedipal child–mother bond. Post-structuralist feminists indebted to Lacanian psychoanalysis, by contrast, deconstruct gender terms with reference to the structuring power of the order of the Symbolic, of language as such. What follows concentrates for the most part on developments in feminist theories of sexual difference that draw from, rework or transfigure Lacanian theory. The central concerns that are touched on include an exploration of the political ramifications of psychoanalysis, the psychic forces which affect women's desexualization and lack of **agency** in modern culture, the relationship between maternal

67

ANTHONY ELLIOTT

and paternal power in infant development, and the connections between sexuality, the body, and its pleasures. For, in addressing these issues, feminist psychoanalytic theorists have sought to enlarge their understandings of polarized sexual identities in modern societies and to rethink the possibilities for restructuring existing forms of gender power.

Lacanian psychoanalysis is probably the most influential current in feminist social theory today. In Lacan's deployment of Saussurian linguistics, as noted above, meaning arises from difference. In the order of language, a signifier attains reference to a signified through the exclusion of other signifiers. In patriarchal culture, that which is excluded is the *feminine*: woman is denied a voice of her own. Lacan thus claims, in what is regarded by many as a clear indication of his antifeminism, that 'The Woman does not exist.' Linking the unconscious with the essentially patriarchal organization of language and culture, Lacan defines the feminine in the negative. Woman as the Other, as something which is outside the symbolic order: this is what gives the masculine unconscious its self-presence as power and authority.

For Lacan, as for Freud, the phallus is the marker of sexual difference *par excellence.* The father and his phallus smash the incestuous unity of the mother–infant bond, and thereby refer the infant to the wider cultural, social network. In contrast to Freud, however, Lacan claims to conceptually disconnect the phallus from any linkage with the penis. The phallus, says Lacan, is illusory, fictitious, imaginary. It exists less in the sense of biology than in a kind of fantasy realm which merges desire with power, omnipotence, and wholeness. In Lacanian theory, the power that the phallus promises is directly tied to maternal, imaginary space. According to Lacan, the infant wishes to be loved exclusively by the mother. The infant painfully learns, however, that the mother's desire is invested elsewhere: in the phallus. Significantly, this discovery occurs at the same time that the infant is discovering itself in language, as a *separate subject.* In this connection, it is important to note that Lacan says that *both* sexes enter the symbolic order of language as castrated. The infant's separation from maternal space is experienced as a devastating loss. The pain of this loss *is* castration, from which sexual subjectivity becomes deeply interwoven with absence and lack.

Lacan was not much interested in the social application of his theories, but this has not prevented feminists from making critical appropriations of Lacanian psychoanalysis for rethinking the social theory of gender. Interest in Lacan's ideas for feminism was initiated in the English-speaking world by Juliet Mitchell who, in her magisterial *Psychoanalysis and Feminism* (1974), used Freud and Lacan to explore the contemporary gender system. In Mitchell's Lacanian-based feminism, an analysis of sexual politics is developed which stresses that the symbolic order of language creates sexual division. Gendered subjectivity, for Mitchell, is necessarily tied to a fundamental loss: that of maternal, imaginary space. In this connection, the phallus, as 'transcendental signifier,' functions as an imaginary lining or construction which marks the lack of the human subject at the level of sexual division. Yet the crucial point, according to Mitchell, is that these imaginary scenarios position

68

males and females within unequal gender relations. Man is constituted as a self-determining, autonomous agent, and woman as the lacking Other, as sexual object. Using Lacanian theory against itself, however, Mitchell also explores potentialities for gender transformation. Though the phallus may stand for entry to the symbolic order, Mitchell claims, it is an imaginary object that either sex can secure once and for all.

Though generating much interest at the time, most commentators would now agree that Mitchell's analysis of gender contains serious theoretical and political difficulties. It seems to assume, for example, that the social reproduction of sexuality and gender is a relatively stable affair, without allowing room for the contradictions and ambiguities of split subjectivity and the unconscious. This involves important political implications. For, if women are symbolically fixed in relation to masculinity as the lacking Other, via a repression of desire, then it remains far from clear why women would ever feel compelled to question or challenge the contemporary gender system. This point can be made in another way. The Lacanian specification of the feminine as that which is always defined negatively – lack, the Other, the dark continent – carries a number of theoretical and political ambiguities. On the one hand, Lacan's doctrines have been a valuable theoretical resource for feminists analyzing how women are rendered the excluded Other in patriarchal discourse and culture. On the other hand, the recurring problem for feminism, when set within Lacanian parameters, is that all dimensions of human sexuality become inscribed within the signifier and therefore trapped by the Law. Lacan's reduction of the feminine to mere oppositeness implies that woman can be defined only as *mirror* to the masculine subject, and thus can never escape the domination of a rigidly genderized discourse.

In opposition to Lacan, however, a number of French feminists have recently sought to articulate an alternative vision of female sexual subjectivity in French psychoanalysis. This approach to revaluing the feminine is generally referred to as post-Lacanian feminism, though it is worth briefly expanding on this label. This branch of feminist psychoanalysis is generally considered 'Lacanian' because theorists associated with it adopt a broadly structuralist interpretation of gender categories, situating woman as the excluded Other of masculinist discourse and culture. Yet this approach is also 'anti-Lacanian' since such theorists tend to oppose the view that woman can only be defined as the mirror opposite of the masculine subject, and thus never escape the domination of a rigidly genderized discourse. Broadly speaking, post-Lacanian feminists evoke a positive image of femininity, an image that underscores the multiple and plural dimensions of women's sexuality. Hélène Cixous, for example, speaks of the rhythms, flows and sensations of the feminine libidinal economy, contrasting this with the exaggerated masculinist stress on genital sexuality. Woman, says Cixous, has the 'capacity to depropriate unselfishly, body without end, without appendage, without principal "parts" . . . Her libido is cosmic, just as her unconscious is worldwide.' Similarly, Luce Irigaray locates the feminine in the multiplicity of bodily sensations arising from the lips, vagina, clitoris, breasts. In contrast to the imperial phallic compulsiveness of male sexuality, women's capacity and need for sexual expression resides in the multiplicity and flux of feminine desire itself. As Irigaray says of woman: 'Her sexuality, always at least double, is in fact *plural*.' Women, argues Irigaray, need to establish a different relationship to feminine sexuality, establishing a range of displacements to patriarchy through writing as a cultural practice. Speaking the feminine, for Irigaray, can potentially transform the oppressive sexed identities of patriarchy. In her more recent work, particularly *An Ethics of Sexual Difference* (1993) and *To Be Two* (2000), Irigaray situates the renegotiation of identities in the frame of ethics, specifically the dilemma of recognizing the otherness of the other sex. An ethics of sexual difference, she argues, would respect the Other in her or his own right, with regard to considerations of finitude, mortality, creation and the divine.

Finally, we can find another meeting point of feminist and psychoanalytic theories in the work of **Kristeva**, who elaborates the idea of a specifically feminine mode of being which dislocates patriarchal language and culture. In *Revolution in Poetic Language*, Kristeva contrasts the Lacanian symbolic, the Law which the father embodies, with the multiple libidinal forces of the 'semiotic.' The semiotic is a realm of prelinguistic experience – including feelings, drives, and rhythms experienced by the infant in its pre-Oedipal relation to the mother. According to Kristeva, our semiotic longing for the pre-Oedipal mother, though repressed with entry to the symbolic, remains present in the unconscious and cannot be shut off from society and culture. The semiotic, Kristeva says, is present in the rhythms, slips, and silences in speech; and it is subversive of the Law of the Father since it is rooted in a pre-patriarchal connection with the feminine. Yet Kristeva denies that the feminine semiotic has any intrinsic link with gender, because it stems from the pre-Oedipal phase and is thus *prior* to sexual difference. Thus, if the semiotic is 'feminine,' it is a femininity that is always potentially available to women and men in their efforts to transform gender power. Kristeva looks to the semiotic as a means of subverting the male-dominated symbolic order. She finds a clear expression of the semiotic in the writings of avant-garde authors, such as Mallarmé, Lautréamont, and Artaud, writing which she feels defies patriarchal language. Kristeva also locates semiotic subversion in pregnancy. The psychic experience of giving birth, Kristeva says, reproduces 'the radical ordeal of the splitting of the subject: redoubling of the body, separation and coexistence of the self and of an other, of nature and consciousness, of physiology and speech.'

In her more recent work, especially *Black Sun* and *New Maladies of the Soul*, Kristeva situates the emotional turmoil produced by contemporary culture with reference to depression, mourning and melancholia. In depression, argues Kristeva, there is an emotional disinvestment from the Symbolic, from language as such. The depressed person, overwhelmed by sadness, suffers from a paralysis of symbolic activity. In effect, language fails to substitute for what has been lost at the level of the psyche. The loss of loved ones, the loss of ideals, the loss of pasts: as the depressed person loses all interest in the surrounding world, in language itself, psychic energy shifts to a more primitive mode of functioning, to a maternal, drive-orientated form of experience. In short, depression produces a trauma of symbolic identification, a trauma which unleashes the power of semiotic energy. In the force field of the semiotic – rhythms, semantic shifts, changes in intimation – Kristeva finds a means to connect the unspoken experience of the depressed person to established meaning, thereby facilitating an emotional reorganization of the self.

The foregoing feminist theories represent one of the most important areas of contemporary psychoanalytic criticism. They help to explain, more clearly than conventional Lacanian accounts, the ways in which dominant sexual ideologies penetrate everyday life, and also explore the radicalizing possibilities of a feminine transformation of gender. But assumptions are made in these theories which need to be questioned. For one thing, the male-dominated Law is opposed in these accounts either by the woman's body or the subversive relationship of women to language. However, some feminists have argued that this merely reinstates a 'female essence' prior to the construction of sexual subjectivity, and is therefore in danger of reinforcing traditional gender divisions through an unintended biologism. Related to this is the concern that these theories erase the mediating factors which link fantasy and social reality, either by displacing the psychoanalytic account of the construction of sexual difference (as in the case of Irigaray and Cixous), or by essentialism (as with Kristeva's merging of the semiotic and motherhood).

REFERENCES AND RECOMMENDED FURTHER READING

Adorno, T. and M. Horkheimer (2002) [1944] *Dialectic of Enlightenment: Philosophical Fragments*, Stanford, CA: Stanford University Press.
Althusser, L. (1971) 'Ideology and ideological state apparatuses', in *Lenin and Philosophy and Other Essays*, London: New Left Books, pp. 121–73.
Dews, P. (1987) *Logics of Disintegration*, London: Verso.
Elliott, A. (1999) *Social Theory and Psychoanalysis in Transition: Self and Society from Freud to Kristeva*, 2nd Edition, London: Free Association Books.
—— (2002) *Psychoanalytic Theory: An Introduction*, 2nd Edition, Durham, NC: Duke University Press.
—— (2004) *Social Theory Since Freud*, Routledge, London.
Freud, S. (1961) [1900] 'The Interpretation of Dreams', in J. Strachey (ed.) *The Standard Edition of the Complete Psychological Works of Sigmund Freud*, Vol. IV, London: Hogarth Press, pp. 1–610.
—— (1961) [1930] 'Civilization and Its Discontents', in J. Strachey (ed.) *The Standard Edition of the Complete Psychological Works of Sigmund Freud*, Vol. XXI, London: Hogarth Press, pp. 57–145.
Fromm, E. (1941) *Escape from Freedom*, New York: Farrar & Rinehart.
Irigaray, L. (1985) *This Sex Which Is Not One*, Ithaca, NY: Cornell University Press.
—— (1993) *An Ethics of Sexual Difference*, Ithaca, NY: Cornell University Press.
—— (2000) *To Be Two*, London: Athlone.

Kristeva, J. (1984) [1974] *Revolution in Poetic Language*, New York: Columbia University Press.

—— (1986) 'Stabat Mater', in T. Moi (ed.) *The Kristeva Reader*, Oxford: Blackwell, pp. 160–87.

—— (1987) *Tales of Love*, New York: Columbia University Press.

—— (1989) *Black Sun: Depression and Melancholia*, New York: Columbia University Press.

—— (1991) *Strangers to Ourselves*, New York: Columbia University Press.

Lacan, J. (1977) [1949] 'The Mirror Stage as formative of the function of the I', in J.-A. Miller (ed.) *Ecrits: A Selection*, London: Tavistock Press, pp. 1–7.

—— (1977) [1953] 'The field and function of speech and language in psychoanalysis', in J.-A. Miller (ed.) *Ecrits: A Selection*, London: Tavistock Press, pp. 30–113.

—— (1977) [1957] 'The agency of the letter in the unconscious or reason since Freud', in J.-A. Miller (ed.) *Ecrits: A Selection*, London: Tavistock Press, pp. 146–78.

—— (1979) *The Four Fundamental Concepts of Psychoanalysis*, Harmondsworth: Penguin.

—— (1988) *The Seminar of Jacques Lacan, Vol. 1: Freud's Paper on Technique 1953–54*, Cambridge: Cambridge University Press.

—— (1992) *The Ethics of Psychoanalysis 1959–60: The Seminar of Jacques Lacan*, London: Routledge.

—— (1998a) *The Seminar of Jacques Lacan, Vol. 2: The Ego in Freud's Theory and in the Technique of Psychoanalysis 1954–5*, Cambridge: Cambridge University Press.

—— (1998b) *The Seminar, Book XX: Encore, On Feminine Sexuality*, London: Tavistock Press.

Marcuse, H. (1956) *Eros and Civilization*, New York: Vintage Books.

—— (1964) *One-Dimensional Man*, Boston, MA: Beacon Press.

—— (1970) *Five Lectures: Psychoanalysis, Politics and Utopia*, trans. by Jeremy J. Shapiro and Shierry M. Weber, Boston, MA: Beacon Press.

—— (1974) [1955] *Eros and Civilization*, Boston, MA: Beacon Press.

Mitchell, J. (1974) *Psychoanalysis and Feminism*, London: Penguin Books.

—— (1984) *Women: The Longest Revolution*, New York: Pantheon Books.

5

STRUCTURALIST AND POST-STRUCTURALIST SOCIAL THEORY

DANIEL CHAFFEE

Social theory has been heavily influenced by **structuralism** and **post-structuralism**. While many sciences use structures to think about the world, structuralism and post-structuralism view structure as both a thing and as a method. They hold that cultural symbols, customs, language and writing are far more dense than meets the eye. Some critics have argued that the theorists of structuralism and post-structuralism, such figures as Roland **Barthes**, Michael **Foucault**, Jacques **Derrida**, and Claude **Lévi-Strauss**, amongst others, are too loosely connected to constitute a distinct school of thought. There are, however, certain elements of structuralism that do link them. In particular, a focus on how language is central to social life is key to both structuralist and post-structualist social theory. While often unacknowledged, Karl Marx is the first structural thinker, and his economic theory of exchange is essential to structural thought. I briefly review **Marx** and **Saussure**, before examining the work of Lévi-Strauss and Derrida. I conclude by outlining some criticisms of structuralism and post-structuralism.

STRUCTURES AND STRUCTURALISM

All fields of empirical study can be said to begin with a structural assumption. Namely, that the objects under examination, and their relationships, have a prior order that can be discerned. This holds true for structures in the natural and the social world. Organisms, buildings and languages are all structural systems which have objects that are related to the whole. According to the Oxford English Dictionary, structure is 'The mutual relation of the constituent parts or elements of a whole as determining its peculiar nature or character; make, frame.' However, for structuralism, structure is not something that simply exists; structures do not exist until they are defined. This holds true for physical structures as well as social structures. The particular relationship that holds elements in mutual relation is an obscure one. While it might seem that something like a university building just exists, the structure that is a building relies on a definition of building. Structures, social and physical, rely on a structural assumption of the relationship of the parts of elements.

In the social sciences, two kinds of structural assumptions are used (Boudon 1971). Structure means not only the totality but also the method used to observe the structures. Some, like the psychologist Piaget, use structure to mean a set of interrelated objects that form a whole with distinct properties. This is the assumption that holds that structure is a starting point for analysis. However, in social theory, the study of structures has focused more on the method of discerning structures. Most structuralisms, from Marx to contemporary versions of social thought, have focused on meaning as being generated or understood through study and method. An examination of the elements in question, focusing on the invisible aspects of structure, yields information about the structuring force. The measurement, and definition, of something is indeed what yields the coherence of its elements.

Karl Marx is the first social theorist to offer a rigorous structural theory. As I will consider later in the chapter, many of the criticisms aimed at Marx are true of later structuralist theories. Marx's declaration of a structural scandal at work in the modern world is summed up in the first line of the communist manifesto that he wrote with Engels, 'The history of all hitherto existing society is the history of class struggles' (Marx and Engels 2005 [1848]: 1). They identified the fact that capitalism was a new form of economic system that was every bit as exploitative as slavery or feudalism. Capitalism, as a system, alienates the worker by separating him from the means of production, and thus preventing him from controlling his own life. In *Capital I*, Marx outlines the structural force of capitalism that systematically exploits the worker. Specifically, it is the factory system, owned by the capitalist class, moved by the structural logic of capital, that extracts value from workers by extending the working day and by cutting wages.

Marx's theory of structures is built around the concept of mutual relations, in particular his theory of exchange values is the process by which capitalism generates capital. The structural whole of the economy is the market, which is the collection of the elements that are traded, namely commodities. Commodities are any things, material or immaterial, which have exchange value on the market. The value that a commodity trades at is not necessarily its use value. One can get a drink of water from a public water fountain, or pay $2 for a bottle of water that may or may not have come from a tap somewhere else. Water, which is free, has a relatively high use value. In comparison, single malt scotch whisky has little or no use value for human life and costs at least $40 a bottle. This strange fact of economic exchange entails a sociology of economic exchange. For any commodity to be exchanged for a value, it must be different in kind but equivalent in value. The modern measure of equivalence between different commodities is the money system, which is itself a structured social convention, and that convention must be well-understood by the parties to an exchange. The implication is that, for the commodity to have exchange value, it must, in principle, bear a relation to all other commodities in the economy.

In Marx's view, the general theory of exchange values was the key to capitalism's particularly deceptive but vicious exploitation (or, in the term of his youth, estrangement). One of the reasons that exchanged commodities must be qualitatively different but quantitatively equivalent is that the qualitative difference is the only way to account for profit, which he defined as 'surplus value.' If all exchanges, even between different commodities, are between precisely equal values, then there is no way to explain surplus-value. The most vicious instance of surplus-value is the labor power of the worker who is forced to sell his labor for wages that the capitalist covers in a few hours and the rest of the working day becomes surplus value for the capitalist whom Marx called 'Mr. Moneybags,' who 'must be so lucky as to find . . . a commodity whose use-value possesses the peculiar property of being a source of value, whose actual consumption . . . is a creation of value' (Marx 1978 [1867]). Obviously, in most (if not all), forms of mass production, wages will be as low as possible while the working day must be as long as possible – otherwise, under capitalism, there can be no surplus value, hence no profit. Thus, the structural inequality of capitalism is based on the general theory of exchange value, and workers are open to exploitation by the larger society.

Ferdinand de Saussure (1858–1913), a Swiss linguist, is most often credited with being the founder of structuralism. He outlined his theory of structural linguistics in a series of lectures, published posthumously as *Course in General Linguistics* (1916). These lectures challenged the then dominant view of language, which posited an inherent and natural connection between words and things in the world that they reference. For Saussure, the bond between the thing (signified) and the word (signifier) is constructed through social convention. Hence, his structuralist assertion, 'If we could collect the totality of word patterns stored in all those individuals, we should have the social bond which constitutes their language' (Saussure 1974: 13). Language is a social institution, a collection of individual elements, and must be viewed through a general theory of social and economic values, which he called a **semiology** (the science of signs).

Semiology was Saussure's guiding idea and, much like the work of Marx, focused on the question of exchange. Saussure writes,

> Even outside language all values are apparently governed by the same paradoxical principle. They are always composed:
>
> 1. of a dissimilar thing that can be exchanged for the thing of which the value is to be determined; and
> 2. of similar things that can be compared with the thing of which the value is to be determined.
>
> (Saussure 1974 [1916]: 116–17)

Or, more generally, 'Sciences are concerned with *a system for equating things of different orders* – labor and wages in one and a signified and a signifier in the other' (1974 [1916]: 116). As in Marx, the key to the exchange of values in human communities is different qualities assessed by a system of equivalencies. Saussure makes a distinction in the sign between the signifier (sounds, written text and images) and the signified (the image that the signifer refers to), which together make up the sign. Signs have value, or meaning, through their place in language.

Saussure makes a distinction between *la parole* (speech/speaking) and *la langue* (language as a system). Speaking is the work of individuals in producing spoken statements, or signs that are observable (literally, audible). Language, for Saussure, is a kind of 'collective intelligence' that extends beyond individual speakers ordering speech into meaningful statements. In this sense, language exhibits the most difficult feature of structures – their invisibility. Nobody has ever laid eyes on the English language, yet we are able to draw on its rules of grammar and syntax to engage in meaningful communication. When these rules of language are used in everyday speaking, the rules are observed in their use. While the language is invisible, the individual speaker has to be competent in it to produce meaningful speech.

The social system of language, argues Saussure, is thus radically arbitrary. This is not a form of nihilism, but rather the view that value and meaning are determined through social convention. The connections between signs and their meanings are established through difference. The primary mode of difference for Saussure is binary oppositions: woman is constituted as a sign, as distinct from man, hot from cold, day from night and so forth. This entails the social proposition that words (or, more generally, signs), thereby, cannot be based in nature. If the English 'tree' is innately correct, then there would be no French *'arbre.'* Both are different signs for the same meaning. Likewise, within a language, the exchange of meanings in speech depends on the ability of speakers to recognize similarities and differences. 'Tree' has meaning for competent speakers because it is different from other words. In effect, words operate in spoken languages just as do commodities in economies. Members of the language community, like buyers and sellers in economies, share community-wide conventions that are used to determine values – money (usually) in the case of economies, signs in the case of languages. The value or meaning of a particular sign is determined socially.

French Structuralism

It could be said that the high-water mark of structuralism was, roughly speaking, the two decades from 1945 to 1965 in France. Although structuralism is best known as a French phenomenon, there were British and American versions of structural thinking that were influential around this time. Following on the linguistic insights of Saussure, and with an eye towards Marx, several social theorists in France developed structuralisms. Claude Lévi-Strauss (1908–) is the undisputed father of structuralism and one of the only thinkers of the movement to accept the label of 'structuralist.' He was exposed to structuralism during his time in New York with the Russian linguist Roman Jakobson, who is said to have coined the term. Structuralism was, at least in part, a reaction to the dominant post-war trends of existentialism and **phenomenology** that focused heavily on the subject. When Lévi-Strauss was developing his structuralism, the cultural and human sciences were caught in a debate between naturalism and humanism. Structuralism moves the focus away from the subject and onto the cultural process of signification. The key here is representation. What role does culture play in how signs are deployed? Many thinkers, most notably existentialists, were locked into asserting that human individuals were autonomous from culture. For Lévi-Strauss, structuralism provided a direction for social science to investigate, in particular the cultural process of representation. He was very much interested in creating a formal science of structures. He writes,

> By pursing conditions where systems of truth become mutually convertible and can therefore be simultaneously admissible for several subjects, the ensemble of these conditions acquires the character of an object endowed by a reality proper to itself and independent of the subject.
>
> (Lévi-Strauss 1970: 44)

In constructing his structural anthropology, Lévi-Strauss employed Saussure's structural linguistics as well as the work of Émile Durkheim (1965 [1912]) and French anthropologist Marcel Mauss (1990 [1924]). Lévi-Strauss's early work on kinship is a characteristic example of his structuralist anthropology. Drawing on Durkheim's *Elementary forms of Religious Life*, and Marcel Mauss's essay 'The Gift,' Lévi-Strauss focused on the symbolic units of culture. Ethnography is, at least in part, about uncovering the work of cultural symbols. Lévi-Strauss argued that structuralism was better suited to the work of ethnography because the cultural objects under investigation have an indefinite number of features that are arbitrarily highlighted and enforced. By paying attention to the structuring patterns, the structural anthropologist can not only pick up on the obvious symbols, but also make note of symbols and practices that may be important.

However, Lévi-Strauss argues, in contrast to classical anthropology, that the task is not to find the best symbol for the job, but rather to use analysis to reduce down to the smallest units of culture. In *Elementary Structures of Kinship* (1969 [1949]) Lévi-Strauss argues, again in contrast to classical anthropology, that the nuclear family is not the basic unit, but rather that kinship is a system of generalized exchange; that marriage rules, social class, and kinship are all representations of an unconscious exchange system based on the law of exogamy. In particular, kinship is based on the exchange of women. He writes, 'The prohibition of incest is less a rule prohibiting marriage with the mother, sister or daughter, than a rule obliging the mother, sister or daughter to be given to others. It is the supreme rule of the gift' (1969 [1949]: 481). Thus, the exchange of women forms the basis of society, governed by the rule of reciprocity.

For Lévi-Strauss, the task of structural anthropology is to search for the structure that makes sense of seemingly unrelated events. He writes,

Behind what seemed to be the superficial contingency and incoherent diversity of the laws governing marriage, I discerned a small number of simple principles, thanks to which a very complex set of mass of customs and practices, at first sight absurd (and generally held to be so), could be reduced to a meaningful system.

(Lévi-Strauss 1975 [1964]: 10)

In his later work, Lévi-Strauss focused on myths as a means of opening up cross-cultural comparison. Given that, for each cultural object, there are an infinite number of relationships, Lévi-Strauss suggested that the myth is a way of realizing aspects of elements that may not be directly present. For example, from Sophocles to Shakespeare to Freud there are numerous versions of the Oedipus myth. By comparing the versions over time he isolated, among others, two recurrent mythemic elements: Oedipus kills his father and Oedipus marries his mother. He then interprets the elements as, in effect, signifiers of a universal human conflict between hate and love toward parents or, more formally, between under-attachment to one parent and over-attachment to the other. At one point, he proposed that his structuralism was meant to be a science of the human mind (by which he meant *esprit*, human spirit or even culture). He argued that myths and structural elements resided in the unconscious of each individual.

Like Lévi-Strauss, Roland Barthes (1915–80) developed a mode of investigation of the ways in which culture functions through the meaning of signs. Barthes, as an eclectic thinker, showed the ways in which signs that are thought to be neutral are, in fact, imbued with power. His structuralist book *Mythologies* investigates many different aspects of French culture from advertising to the Tour de France. His aim, however, was to decode the process by which myths turn something cultural into Nature. He analyses the cover of the magazine *Paris-Match*, which portrays a young black man in the French national colors. In this, the historical operations of an imperial France are portrayed as natural. Thus, his structural method uncovers the political interests that are hidden by the function of the myth.

Jacques Lacan (1901–81) applied a structural linguistics to his influential reinterpretations of Freud's theory of the Unconscious. Drawing on Saussure's structural linguistics, Lacan gave us the infamous slogan, 'the unconscious is structured like a language' ('The Agency of the Letter in the Unconscious, or Reason Since Freud' 1977 [1957]). Though his work is notorious for being cryptic and opaque, one aspect of his revision of Freud was to critique the idea of consciousness. His influential seminar 'The Mirror Stage' (1949) outlines the supposed moment when an infant sees herself and believes the specular image to represent a unity or self. However, the image cast back from the mirror is an Imaginary self. Somewhat later, Louis **Althusser** (1918–90) used Lacan's seminar on the mirror stage to refine Marxism's theory of culture by drawing the parallel between the mirror stage and culture as an imaginary (in which a culture is presented as if it were a totality bigger and more true than truth itself. The link to Marx is in the retention of Marx's claim that culture is an inversion of reality. Likewise, Lacan stresses that mental consciousness is an illusion of the psyche. For Lacan, the Unconscious is an inherently disorganizing force, and is therefore essential to the understanding of the totality of consciousness.

POST-STRUCTURALISM

Post-structuralism is, at once, a critique and a continuation of the structuralist method. Anthony **Giddens** writes,

> The relational character of wholes, the arbitrary nature of the sign, and the notion of difference are concepts which run though structuralist and post-structuralist per-spectives as a whole. At the same time they are the source of some of the main fea-tures which tend to separate the structuralist authors from their post-structuralist successors.
>
> (Giddens 1987: 81)

Post-structuralism is a radicalization of structuralism, one that picks up with par-ticular force on the political question of how cultural practices become 'natural,' and it has therefore become an important conceptual resource for queer theory and post-colonial theory, amongst other theories.

Jacques Derrida's (1930–2004) post-structuralism is, itself, one of the most famous critiques of structuralism. He acknowledges that post-structuralism relies on a prior structuralism. He delivered his critique of structuralism, a paper entitled 'Structure, sign and play in the discourse of the human sciences' in 1966 at the American Johns Hopkins University. His paper primarily critiques Lévi-Strauss, but also structuralism in general. He begins by referring to an 'event' in the 'history of the concept of structure' that provoked a rupture in Western his-tory (Derrida 1978: 278). Derrida's underlying argument is a critique of the very idea of structure by associating it with all prior structuring elements that under-mine the free play of signs in human thought and discourse.

> It could be shown that all the names related to fundamentals, to principles, or to the center have always designated an invariable presence – *eidos, arch , telos ener-gia, ousia* (essence, substance, subject), *al thia*, transcendentality, consciousness, God, man, and so forth.
>
> (Derrida 1978: 279–80)

This is a list of the centers of other belief systems, but what of structuralism's center? The structure is both that which organizes and the organizing belief. He writes, 'the center is, paradoxically, within the structure and outside it' (Derrida 1978: 279). The irony is that the structure is both that which structures and that which escapes structure.

In 1967, Derrida published three books that formed the core of his philosophical argument: *Of Grammatology* (1976), *Speech and Phenomena* (1967) and *Writing and Difference* (1978). His now infamous method of deconstruction is a way of rereading texts to uncover the silences in the history of philosophical and social thought and, as he acknowledges, to create silences of its own. Deconstruction seeks to engage the internal logic of texts. Derrida applied deconstruction most famously to Western philosophy. Philosophy, and Western culture more generally, have privileged speech over writing. Speech is seen as a form of direct communication between self-present subjects, while writing is eschewed as indirect. He develops this point through a critique of Saussure's structural linguistics. Derrida argues that Saussure's distinction between signifier and signified is a metaphysical one, which implies that the signifier is more intelligible than the signified. Speech is privileged over the external reality. The problem is that speech, or voice, in the modern West is assumed to be the representative of an inner self (or, one might say, the soul of meaning). This idea that meanings can be present in human interaction is the principle of the Center he attacks. Thus, Derrida argues that writing is a form of communication in which the meaning is always deferred and mediated. Derrida's idea is that, though there is much to be gained from Saussure's semiology, its theory of the spoken sign as the presence of a meaning participates in the modern centering of social thought, thus limiting the free play of signification. Meaning is something that can only be investigated at a remove.

Derrida also engages Saussure on the question of meaning being generated through difference. Derrida's concept of difference is one of his most famous and highlights his argument that writing is central to meaning. *Différance*, which Derrida famously said is neither word nor concept, it is both. Différance is a deliberate misspelling of the French verb *différer* that means both 'to differ' and 'to defer.' Spelled differently, it sounds the same; it has to be seen written for the play to be understood. The dual meanings of the verb are both the point. Meaning is created through an endless chain of difference, and thus meaning is always deferred. When you read a sentence, or make an interpretation of a myth, the meaning has been delayed and will always be delayed because there is always another interpretation. There is no ultimate end to the endless play of signifiers. Derrida highlights the fact that structure involves constant shifting. He writes,

> Différance is thus a structure and a movement which can only be grasped in relation to the opposition of present/absent. Différance is the systematic play of differences, or traces of differences, of the *spacing* whereby elements are connected to one-another.
>
> (Derrida 1972, cited in Giddens 1979: 31)

The play of difference makes a bold statement for the possibility of identity. Much like Lacan's revision of Freud's Ego, Derrida's theory of *différance* implies that self-presence is an impossibility. He writes of *différance*,

It confirms that the subject, and first of all the conscious and speaking subject, depends upon the system of differences and the movement of *différance*, that the subject is not present, nor above all present to itself before *différance*, that the subject is constituted only in being divided from itself, in becoming space, in temporizing, in deferral.

(Derrida 1981: 29)

Social differences are delayed and ignored through the endless chain of signification that spaces and temporalizes. To reread, the process of signification has turned into a powerful political statement and Derrida's deconstruction has been influential in queer theory and post-colonialism. For Edward Said (1978), the West has presented itself as the center of culture, but relies on an Other, 'the Orient,' not an actual place on the globe, but a construction of Other by a culture with pretensions of centrality.

Michel Foucault (1926–84), a celebrated French social theorist who greatly contributed to the post-structuralist movement, came to public notice at much the same time as Derrida in a series of books on subjects such as the history of madness, the clinic, and the prison. Foucault, like Barthes, became known for critiquing beliefs, thoughts and social actions that are held to be 'normal.' While Derrida was very much focused on the philosophical critique of structure, Foucault focused on historical analysis, calling his method 'geneology' or 'archaeology.' In tracing the history of language, Foucault explicitly draws out the connections between language and power. Arguably, his most notorious book of the 1960s was *The Order of Things: An Archaeology of the Human Sciences* (1966), which was, by his own tacit admission, a strong structuralist history of the birth of modern social thought. His archaeology of social knowledge (covering the birth of modern methods for treating both the mentally and physically ill, and the rehabilitative prison) aimed to demonstrate that modern thought came into being by, in Althusser's word, an epistemological break – that is, a sudden structural shift occurring late in the eighteenth century when modern society was coming into its own.

Though Derrida and Foucault worked in quite different fields and lived very different lives, the similarities between them are hard to miss. Where Derrida attacked the idea of the center, Foucault attacked the ideal of the original Subject. Where Derrida juxtaposed differences and deferrals of meaning to the voice as the presence of meanings, Foucault offered (in *Archaeology of Knowledge* in 1969) the concept of discursive formations which served, among other effects, to identify the power of silences and prohibitions in the history of social discourses as key to understanding how power in the modern world works through the silencing of oppositions.

From this rather formalized theory of the late 1960s, Foucault turned to his influential theory of power as knowledge in *History of Sexuality I* (1981 [1976]), in which he devastated the modern Enlightenment idea that knowledge offered emancipation from the limiting effects of power. On the contrary, Foucault said that, in the modern world, knowledge is the social component of power. This represents is another turning point in his own structural theories and in the history of structuralism. As Marx and others after him understood, power as a top-down effect – the dominant class exploiting the poor – Foucault said that power is just as much bottom-up. Power is structured by knowledge (or, one might say, by culture), which effectively forms the modern individual – the human subject is thereby subjugated. Thus, Foucault's interest in the human sciences, including now the practical sciences of sexualities, is the completion of Marx's failed structuralism. A strong materialist theory can never explain the modern method of taming the subjects of the industrial era because, however degraded the worker is, he participates in his own degradation. Foucault left no doubt that top-down domination is at work, but it works not through overt force so much as, one might say, persuasion – the gentle force of practical knowledge taught to schoolchildren, patients, penitents, and university students through the social formation of the modern world.

Post-structuralism has become an important influence in some **feminist** theory and queer theory. Notably Judith **Butler** (1956–) has developed an important critique of sex and gender as natural categories. She argues that feminism, having developed gender as separate from biological sex, cannot move forward in a constructive way because gender has again been created as a new 'natural' category. In contrast, she asserts that gender and sex are a performance. Through enacting certain modes of dress, action, and other social scripts, gender is created through repetitive performance (Butler 1990). Her radical argument about performativity breaks with traditional structural binaries and focuses on the endless play of difference that is involved in living gender. Eve Kosofsky Sedgwick (1950–2009) is one of the most central figures of gay theory. Her argument, outlined in the influential book *Epistemology of the Closet* (1992) picks up on Foucault's argument about the proliferation of the discourse of sexuality in Western culture. She argues that sexuality has become the most influential discourse and, in particular, the binary of homo/heterosexuality has become central not only to sexuality, but to Western culture as a whole. The catch is that the hetero/homo binary is unclear and that the politics of difference should be mapped out to clarify the power dynamics.

CRITICISMS OF STRUCTURALISM AND POST-STRUCTURALISM

One of the most common criticisms of stucturalisms is that they are inherently **deterministic** and unable sufficiently to account for the human individual, the acting subject. In Marx's structural account, the worker is a kind of cultural dope, participating in his own exploitation. This criticism, when aimed at Marx, while fair, ignores the fact that he meant his structuralism to be a historically based account of the actual conditions of working men and women in a social structure, the very essence of which was the alienation of human individuals. To be a worker under capitalism is to be alienated. Marx's structuralism serves as a near-perfect illustration of the properties of all structuralisms by illustrating how structures are the salient and organizing features of fields that cannot be directly observed but must be reconstructed historically and analytically. Most famously for Marx, the key structure is the mode of production. Vitally, in contrast to the market-place, the key attribute of the mode of production is its concealment, as the shop floor is a private space, not open to ready inspection.

One of the abiding questions posed to all structuralisms concerns the question of social change and how it happens. Marx gave an answer, namely that the workers of the world should unite and throw off the bonds of capitalism. This was supposed to happen through revolution; however, history has revealed that communist revolutions are never easy and the subsequent systems to be far from the future that Marx envisioned. Part of the difficulty of change is that structuralisms tend to focus on structures as fixed. Saussure argued that structures should be studied synchronically, that is language at only one point in history, not over time. Those that followed Saussure, however they tried to shake this, seemed stuck with structure as a fixed, but necessary, abstraction. Lévi-Strauss's myth seems to hover outside time. This is ironic in that he strove in his work to connect cultures across geographies and times through the study of systems of myths: particular social systems frozen in time. This runs against Marx's fierce argument that, to come to terms with a social reality, one must think of it historically.

Derrida and Foucault sidestepped Saussure's focus on the synchronic by looking at the historical dimensions of language. In text and discourse, not only is the structure important, but also the spacing of the elements in the structure. Thus, to say that temporality is the only issue, does not come to terms with their arguments. This way in which structuralisms reveal that which has been repressed is particularly troubling. While Foucault and Derrida develop historically sensitive structural arguments that unpack the hierarchies of power imbued in the way we communicate, a process that involves more than a question of temporality, these arguments also focus on the normative powers of structures to control the language we use. However, as they are both aware, the human subject is still at the mercy of language and there is no new system but, rather, a new controlling ideology. The awareness of power and how it functions does not alter the fact that we still must use language to function socially. Further, as many critics point out, Derrida and Foucault make similar bold pronouncements about the world: there is nothing outside of text or discourse.

In a world so dominated by language, where there is nothing outside of language, how is it that social change occurs? Saussure separated language, as form, from speech, and those that followed his approach continued to focus on the signifier as the primary point of study. Though post-structuralism radicalized the function of the signifier, it is still unclear how it is that the individual element, the signifier can come to change the structural system. Linguistic change, for Saussure, happens blindly. The system simply alters. For Lévi-Strauss, change is something that was located in the unconscious or, for post-structuralists, the human individual is always displaced from self-knowledge. Simon Clarke is highly skeptical of Lévi-Strauss on this point, that 'the creative power of the subject has to be taken away as soon as it is acknowledged and given to a mechanism inscribed in the biological constitution of the mind' (Clarke 1981: 171 cited in Giddens 1987: 79).

Anthony Giddens argues that the major deficiency of structuralism and post-structuralism is that they fail to generate a sufficient account of reference. That is, they never explicate the connection between signifer and signified, a problem with Saussure's structural linguistics that is only increased in post-structuralist radicalisms. Giddens asserts that they do not have an account of the social power structures that shape the ways in which we are able to use language. Context, argues Giddens, should be central to any account of language. Further, he claims, structuralism and post-structuralism do not have a generative account of social structures. For Giddens, linguistic competence means more than just mastering grammar and syntax: there is something more to social competence. He writes,

> Knowing a language certainly means knowing syntactical rules but, equally important, to know a language is to acquire a range of methodological devices, involved both with the production of utterances themselves and with the constitution and reconstitution of social life in the daily context of social activity.
>
> (Giddens 1987: 80)

This is an expression of his theory of structuration, which critiques structuralism by focusing on how it is that the use of language by agents is integral to the formation and constitution not only of language, but of social life in general.

CONCLUSION

Giddens highlights the fact that structures are both constraining and enabling. Structures are not something that merely entrap individuals, but when we invoke structures, such as language, they allow us to communicate effectively: they enable communication. It is hard to think of a social science without making reference to social structures of some kind. Societies, nations, cultures, like the natural world, are all structured things – in both a constraining and an enabling way. Thus, perhaps the best lesson to take from structuralism and post-structuralism is the dynamic play of structures. As Derrida realized, post-structuralism is a powerful cultural critique, a way of investigating the hidden workings of power at play in the very way we communicate and create social meaning. But, at the same time, he told a cautionary tale concerning the moment of structural rupture, a paradoxical point of redoubling. Social and cultural structures create subjects through determining meaning, a process that is completely social.

REFERENCES AND RECOMMENDED FURTHER READING

Althusser, Louis (1972) [1969] 'Ideology and ideological state apparatuses: notes toward an investigation', in *Lenin and Philosophy and Other Essays*, trans. by Ben Brewster, London: Monthly Review Press.
Barthes, Roland (1968) [1953] *Elements of Semiology*, New York: Hill & Wang.
—— (1972) [1957] *Mythologies*, New York: Hill & Wang.

Boudon, R. (1971) *Uses of Structuralism*, trans. by Michalina Vaughan, London: Heinemann.

Butler, Judith (1990) *Gender Trouble: Feminism and the Subversion of Identity*, London: Routledge.

—— (2004) *Undoing Gender*, London: Routledge.

Clarke, Simon (1981) *The Foundations of Structuralism*, Brighton, Sussex: Harvester.

Derrida, Jacques (1973 [1967]) *Speech and Phenomena and Other Essays on Husserl's Theory of Signs*, trans. by David B. Allison, Evanston, IL: Northwestern University Press.

—— (1976 [1967]) *Of Grammatology*, trans. by Gayatri Chakravorty Spivak, Baltimore, MD: Johns Hopkins University Press.

—— (1978) 'Structure, sign and play in the discourse of human sciences', in *Writing and Difference*, trans. by Alan Bass, London: Routledge and Kegan Paul.

—— (1978) *Writing and Difference*, trans. by Alan Bass, London: Routledge.

—— (1981 [1972]) *Positions*, trans. by Alan Bass, Chicago: University of Chicago Press.

Durkheim, Émile (1965) [1912] *Elementary Forms of Religious Life*, New York: Free Press.

Foucault, Michael (1966) *The Order of Things: An Archaeology of the Human Sciences*, London: Tavistock.

—— (1972) [1969] *The Archaeology of Knowledge*, trans. from the French by A.M. Sheridan Smith, London: Tavistock.

—— (1981) [1976] *The History of Sexuality*, Vol. 1, trans. from the French by Robert Hurley, Harmondsworth: Penguin.

Giddens, Anthony (1987) *Social Theory and Modern Sociology*, Cambridge: Polity Press.

Lacan, J. (1977) *Ecrits: A Selection*, New York: W.W. Norton.

Lévi-Strauss, C. (1969) [1949] *The Elementary Structures of Kinship*, revised edition, trans. from the French by James Harle Bell, John Richard von Sturmer and Rodney Needham (ed.), London: Eyre & Spottiswoode.

—— (1963) [1958] *Structural anthropology*, trans. by Claire Jacobson and Brooke Grundfest Schoepf, London: Penguin Press.

—— (1970) 'Overture to *Le Cru et le cuit*', in Jacques Ehrmann (ed.), *Structuralism*, New York: Anchor.

—— (1975) [1964] *The Raw and the Cooked*, New York: Harper & Row.

Marx, Karl (1978) [1844] 'Estranged labour', in *The Marx–Engels Reader*, Robert Tucker (ed.), New York: W.W. Norton.

—— (1978) [1867] '*Capital*, Vol. I', in *The Marx–Engels Reader*, Robert Tucker (ed.), New York: W.W. Norton.

Marx, Karl and Engels, Friedrich (2005) [1848] *Manifesto of the Communist Party*, New York: Cosimo.

Mauss, Marcel (1990) [1924] *The Gift: Forms and Functions of Exchange in Archaic Societies*, London: Routledge.

Runciman, W.G. (1970) 'What is structuralism?', in *Sociology in Its Place and Other Essays*, Cambridge: Cambridge University Press, pp. 45–58.

Saussure, Ferdinand de (1974) [1916] *Course in General Linguistics*, ed. Charles Bally and Albert Sechehaye in collaboration with Albert Riedlinger; trans. from the French by Wade Baskin, London: Fontana.

Sedgwick, Eve Kosofsky (1992) *Epistemology of the Closet*, Berkeley, CA: University of California Press.

Sturrock, John (1979) *Structuralism and Since*, Oxford: Oxford University Press.

6

THEORIES OF STRUCTURATION

ANTHONY ELLIOTT

The question of the relation between the individual and society, or individual subject and social structure, has been a core preoccupation of social theory. Broadly speaking, this question has been dealt with in most versions of social theory by either emphasizing the creative powers of the individual self, or by stressing the determining role of social structures in our lives. That is to say, a dualism is evident in the very way in which the large bulk of social theorists have addressed the question of the relation between self and society. Conceptual approaches that pay particular attention to theorizing human **agency** and social actors have contributed a great deal to understanding how individual action and daily interaction are structured by broader social, political and cultural sources. Social theories influenced by symbolic interactionism, hermeneutics and **psychoanalysis**, for example, all allegedly fall into such 'subjectivist' categories. Yet, while underscoring the importance of individual agency and personal life to social critique, such frameworks encounter serious problems in providing conceptions of institutional transformation or social structure. By contrast, conceptual approaches that stress the determining influence of social structures in our lives powerfully highlight the force of institutions in the production and reproduction of society. In such 'objectivistic' approaches within social theory, from **functionalism** to systems-theory, there is a methodological break with the immediate experience of individual agents and a focus instead on the changing structural conditions of modern industrial societies. But, again, there are serious limitations here. One key limitation of 'objectivist' social theories is that, by according priority to structure over action, a **deterministic** flavor is accorded to the social world and the practical activities of the individuals who make up that world. Many social scientists argue that such determinism is especially evident in certain versions of classical social thought; for example, in the writings of **Durkheim** and **Marx** – in which society often appears as a force external to the agent, exercising constraint over individual action.

In more recent versions of social theory, there have been new attempts to move beyond either 'action approaches' or 'structural analysis'. Considering anew the issue of how the actions of individual agents are related to the structural features of the society from which they spring, social theorists have sought to consider in more detailed ways how action and structure actually presuppose one another. As we will see throughout this chapter, this means that social scientists must seek to provide an account of the conditions and consequences of action as directly embroiled with structure. In this chapter,

I will concentrate on two major attempts in contemporary social theory to account for how reproduced practices have their own distinct structural properties. This approach in social theory is sometimes labeled structuration, and in what follows I shall review the seminal contributions of Anthony **Giddens** and Pierre **Bourdieu**.

STRUCTURATION THEORY: ANTHONY GIDDENS

Anthony Giddens first came to international prominence in social theory with the publication of his first book, *Capitalism and Modern Social Theory*, which appeared in 1971. The book remains, to this day, one of the most referenced sociological textbooks on Marx, **Weber** and Durkheim. In examining the origins of classical sociology in *Capitalism and Modern Social Theory*, Giddens set out the rudiments of a project concerned to reinterpret the theoretical foundations of the social sciences – a project he steadfastly developed from his Durkheimian-titled *New Rules of Sociological Method* (1976) to *Politics, Sociology and Social Theory* (1995). In doing so, Giddens sought to develop some interesting sounding – indeed, quite novel – answers to questions that have long plagued social theorists seeking to grasp the complex, contradictory interactions of individual agency on the one hand, and social structure on the other. An indication of the novelty of Giddens's approach to the self/society problem can be easily gleaned by looking at his magisterial book, *The Constitution of Society* (1984). Regarded as one of the most important books since the grand sociological theorizing of Talcott Parsons, *The Constitution of Society* presented a whole new vocabulary for grasping the age of modernization: 'structuration', 'reflexivity', 'time–space distantiation', 'double hermeneutic', and 'ontological security' – to name just a few terms introduced by Giddens. Subsequent to *The Constitution of Society*, Giddens produced an astonishing range of books. His analysis of warfare, its new technologies and globalization, as developed in *The Nation-State and Violence* (1985), has been highly influential in political science and international relations. *The Consequences of Modernity* (1990) was Giddens's response to **postmodernism**, in which he argued that the West and the developed industrial societies were entering conditions of 'reflexive modernization'. And in *Modernity and Self-Identity* (1991) and *The Transformation of Intimacy* (1992), he addressed issues of the self, **identity**, intimacy and sexuality in the context of social transformations sweeping the globe.

My aim in the first section of this chapter is to provide a brief overview of Giddens's writings in social theory. Given the broad sweep of his interests, as well as his exceptional productivity, I have decided to concentrate on two specific aspects of Giddens's work, namely (a) structuration theory, and (b) **modernity** and modernization, as filtered through the lens of Giddens's theory of structuration. After examining Giddens's more substantive contributions to social theory, I shall turn to consider some of the issues raised by his critics.

GIDDENS'S THEORY OF STRUCTURATION

In a series of books, principally *New Rules of Sociological Method* (1976), *Central Problems in Social Theory* (1979), and *The Constitution of Society* (1984), Giddens sets out a highly original conceptualization of the relation between action and structure, agent and system, individual and society. Broadly speaking, Giddens argues that it is not possible to resolve the question of how the action of individual agents is related to the structural features of society by merely supplementing or augmenting one emphasis through reference to the other. In an attempt to move beyond such dualism, Giddens borrowed the term 'structuration' from French. The starting point of his analysis is not society as fixed and given, but rather the active flow of social life. In contrast to approaches that downgrade agency, Giddens argues that people are knowledgeable about the social structures they produce and reproduce through their conduct. Society, he argues, can be understood as a complex of recurrent practices which form institutions. For Giddens, the central task of social theory is to grasp how action is structured in everyday contexts of social practices, while simultaneously recognizing that the structural elements of action are reproduced by the performance of action. Giddens thus proposes that the dualism of agency and structure should instead be understood as complementary terms of a duality, the 'duality of structure'. 'By the duality of structure', writes Giddens, 'I mean that social structures are both constituted by human agency, and yet at the same time are the very medium of this constitution'.

Perhaps the most useful way to gain a purchase on the radical aspects of Giddens's social theory is by contrasting his conception of structure with the mainstream sociological literature. Sociologists have tended to conceptualize structure in terms of institutional constraint, often in a quasi-hydraulical or mechanical fashion, such that structure is likened to the biological workings of the body or the girders of a building. Giddens strongly rejects functionalist, biological and empiricist analyses of structure. Following the 'linguistic turn' in twentieth century social theory, Giddens critically draws upon **structuralist** and **post-structuralist** theory, specifically the relationship posited between language and speech in linguistics. He does this, not because society is structured like a language (as structuralists have argued), but because he believes that language can be taken as exemplifying core aspects of social life. Language, according to Giddens, has a virtual existence; it 'exists' outside of time and space, and is only present in its instantiations as speech or writing. By contrast, speech presupposes a subject and exists in time/space intersections. In Giddens's reading of structural linguistics, the subject draws from the rules of language in order to produce a phrase or sentence and, in so doing, contributes to the reproduction of that language as a whole. Giddens draws extensively from such a conception of the structures of language in order to account for structures of action. His theorem is that agents draw from structures in order to perform and carry out social interactions and, in so doing, contribute to the reproduction of institutions and structures. This analysis leads to a very specific conception of structure and social systems. 'Structure', writes Giddens (1984: 26), 'has no existence independent of the knowledge that agents have about what they do in their day-to-day activity'.

Giddens's theoretical approach emphasizes that structures should be conceptualized as 'rules and resources': the application of rules which comprise structure may be regarded as generating differential access to social, economic, cultural and political resources. In *The Constitution of Society* (1984) Giddens argues that the sense of 'rule' most relevant to understanding social life is that which pertains to mathematical formulae – for instance, if the sequence is 2, 4, 6, 8, the formula is $x = x_1 + 2$. Understanding a formula, says Giddens, enables an agent to carry on in social life in a routine manner and to apply the rule in a range of different contexts. The same is true of bureaucratic rules, traffic rules, rules of football, rules of grammar, rules of social etiquette: to know a rule does not necessarily mean that one is able explicitly to formulate the principle, but it does mean that one can use the rule 'to go on' in social life. 'The rules and resources of social action', writes Giddens, 'are at the same time the means of systems reproduction' (1984: 19). Systems reproduction, as Giddens conceives it, is complex and contradictory, involving structures, systems and institutions. Social systems, for Giddens, are not equivalent to structures. Social systems are regularized patterns of interaction; such systems are, in turn, structured by rules and resources. Institutions are understood by Giddens as involving different modalities in and through which structuration occurs. Political institutions, for example, involve the generation of commands over people in relation to issues of authorization, signification and legitimation; economic institutions, by contrast, involve the allocation of resources through processes of signification and legitimation.

To understand this recursive quality of social life, it is necessary also to consider Giddens's discussion of human agency and individual subjectivity. Action, according to Giddens, must be analytically distinguished from the 'acts' of an individual. Whereas acts are discrete segments of individual doing, action refers to the continuous flow of people's social practices. On a general plane, Giddens advances a 'stratification model' of the human subject comprising three levels of knowledge or motivation: *discursive consciousness*, *practical consciousness* and the *unconscious*. He explains this stratification model of agency in *The Constitution of Society* as follows:

> Human agents or actors – I use these terms interchangeably – have, as an inherent aspect of what they do, the capacity to understand what they do while they do it. The reflexive capacities of the human actor are characteristically involved in a continuous manner with the flow of day-to-day conduct in the contexts of social activity. But reflexivity operates only partly on a discursive level. What agents know about what they do, and why they do it – their knowledgeability *as* agents – is largely carried in practical consciousness. Practical consciousness consists of all the things which actors know tacitly about how to 'go on' in the

contexts of social life without being able to give them direct discursive expression. The significance of practical consciousness is a leading theme of the book, and it has to be distinguished from both consciousness (discursive consciousness) and the unconscious.

(1984: xxii–xxiii)

Discursive consciousness thus refers to what agents are able to say, both to themselves and to others, about their own action; as Giddens repeatedly emphasizes, agents are knowledgeable about what they are doing and this awareness often has a highly discursive component. *Practical consciousness* also refers to what actors know about their own actions, beliefs and motivations, but it is practical in the sense that it cannot be expressed discursively; what cannot be put into words, Giddens says, following Wittgenstein, is what has to be done. Human beings know about their activities and the world in a sense that cannot be readily articulated; such practical stocks of knowledge are central, according to Giddens, to the project of social scientific research. Finally, the *unconscious*, says Giddens, is also a crucial feature of human motivation and is differentiated from discursive and practical consciousness by the barrier of repression.

While Giddens accords the unconscious a residual role in the reproduction of social life (as something that 'erupts' at moments of stress or crisis), he nonetheless makes considerable use of psychoanalytical theory in order to theorize the routine patterning of social relations. Drawing from **Freud**, **Lacan** and Erikson, Giddens argues that the emotional presence and absence of the primary caretaker (most usually, the mother) provides the foundation for a sense of what he terms 'ontological security', as well as trust in the taken-for-granted, routine nature of social life. Indeed, the routine is accorded a central place in Giddens's social theory for (a) grasping the production and maintenance of ontological security, and (b) comprehending the modes of socialization by which actors learn the implicit rules of how to go on in social life. To do this, Giddens draws from a vast array of sociological micro-theorists, including **Goffman** and Garfinkel. His debt to **ethnomethodology** and **phenomenology** is reflected in much of the language of structuration theory, as is evident from his references to 'skilled performances', 'copresence', 'seriality', 'contextuality', 'knowledgeability' and 'mutual knowledge'.

In the last few paragraphs I have noted how Giddens approaches issues of human action, agency and subjectivity. It is important to link these more subjective aspects of his social theory back to issues of social practices and structures in order to grasp his emphasis on duality in structuration theory. Agents, according to Giddens, draw on the rules and resources of structures and, in so doing, contribute to the systemic reproduction of institutions, systems and structures. In studying social life, says Giddens, it is important to recognize the role of 'methodological bracketing'. Giddens argues that the social sciences simultaneously pursue *institutional analysis*, in which the structural features of society are analyzed, and the *analysis of strategic conduct*, in which the manner which actors carry on social interaction is studied. These different levels of analysis are central to social scientific research, and both are crucial to structuration theory. Connected to this, Giddens argues that the subjects of study of the social sciences are concept-using agents, individuals whose concepts enter into the manner in which their actions are constituted. He calls this intersection of the social world, as constituted by lay-actors on the one hand, and the metalanguages created by social scientists on the other, the 'double hermeneutic'.

MODERNITY REAPPRAISED: GIDDENS'S THEORY OF STRUCTURATION IN ACTION

The theory of structuration, as developed by Giddens, has been viewed by some social scientists as a largely dry, abstract affair. For some, the very term 'structuration' was, in fact, off-putting. Indeed, Giddens's seemingly endless deployment of neologisms – or some supposed – seemed to be more about grand systems-building than confronting the fast-changing nature of society in conditions of advanced modernization. Perhaps in response to some such criticisms of the theory of structuration, and certainly in response to the massive social changes unleashed throughout the late 1980s and 1990s as a result of advanced modernity, Giddens turned to address a range of topics – including modernity, globalization, identity, sexuality and intimacy – in his late writings. In all of these writings, the theory of structuration – whilst rarely discussed in any detail – is drawn upon by Giddens to rethink the state of the world today. Giddens's late writings can thus be viewed, from one angle at least, as the application of structuration theory to some of the big social issues of our times.

In *The Consequences of Modernity* (1990) and *Modernity and Self-Identity* (1991), Giddens develops a comprehensive analysis of the complex relation between self and society in the late modern age. Rejecting Marx's equation of modernity with capitalism, and wary of Weber's portrait of the iron cage of bureaucracy, Giddens instead presents an image of modernity as a juggernaut. As with structuration theory, Giddens's approach to modernity involves considerable terminological innovation: 'embedding and disembedding mechanisms', 'symbolic tokens', 'expert systems', 'the dialectic of trust and risk' and, crucially, 'reflexivity'. Reflexivity, according to Giddens, should be conceived as a continuous flow of individual and collective 'self-monitoring'. 'The reflexivity of modern social life', writes Giddens, 'consists in the fact that social practices are constantly examined and reformed in the light of incoming information about those very practices, thus constitutively altering their character' (1990: 38). Elsewhere Giddens (1991: 28) writes:

> To live in the 'world' produced by high modernity has the feeling of riding a juggernaut. It is not just that more or less continuous and profound processes of change occur; rather, change does not consistently conform either to human expectation or to human control.

The experiential character of contemporary daily life is well grasped by two of Giddens's key concepts: *trust and risk* as interwoven with *abstract systems*. For Giddens, the relation between individual subjectivity and social contexts of action is a highly mobile one; and it is something that we make sense of and utilize through 'abstract systems'. Abstract systems are institutional domains of technical and social knowledge: they include systems of expertise of all kinds, from local forms of knowledge to science, technology and mass communications. Giddens is underscoring much more than simply the impact of expertise on people's lives, far-reaching though that is. Rather, Giddens extends the notion of expertise to cover 'trust relations' – the personal and collective investment of active trust in social life. The psychological investment of trust contributes to the power of specialized, expert knowledge – indeed, it lies at the bedrock of our Age of Experts – and also plays a key role in the forging of a sense of security in day-to-day social life.

Trust and security are thus both a condition and an outcome of social reflexivity. Giddens sees the reflexive appropriation of expert knowledge as fundamental in a globalizing, culturally cosmopolitan society. While a key aim may be the regularization of stability and order in our identities and in society, reflexive modernity is radically experimental and is constantly producing new types of incalculable risk and insecurity. This means that, whether we like it or not, we must recognize the ambivalence of a social universe of expanded reflexivity: there are no clear paths of individual or social development in the late modern age. On the contrary, human attempts at control of the social world are undertaken against a reflexive backdrop of a variety of other ways of doing things. Giddens offers the following overview in relation to global warming as an example:

> Many experts consider that global warming is occurring and they may be right. The hypothesis is disputed by some, however, and it has even been suggested that the real trend, if there is one at all, is in the opposite direction, towards the cooling of the global climate. Probably the most that can be said with some surety is that we cannot be certain that global warming is *not* occurring. Yet such a conditional conclusion will yield not a precise calculation of risks but rather an array of 'scenarios' – whose plausibility will be influenced, among other things, by how many people become convinced of the thesis of global warming and take action on that basis. In the social world, where institutional reflexivity has become a central constituent, the complexity of 'scenarios' is even more marked.
>
> (in Beck *et al.* 1994: 59)

The complexity of 'scenarios' is thus central to our engagement with the wider social world. Reflexivity, according to Giddens, influences the way in which these scenarios are constructed, perceived, coped with and reacted to.

In *The Transformation of Intimacy* (1992), Giddens connects the notion of reflexivity to sexuality, gender and intimate relationships. With modernization and the decline of tradition, says Giddens, the sexual life of the human subject becomes a 'project' that has to be managed and defined against the backdrop of new opportunities and risks – including, for example, artificial insemination, experiments in ectogenesis (the creation of human life without pregnancy), AIDS, sexual harassment, and the like. Linking gender to new technologies, Giddens argues that we live in an era of 'plastic sexuality'. 'Plastic sexuality' (1992: 2), writes Giddens, 'is decentred sexuality, freed from the needs of reproduction . . . and from the rule of the phallus, from the overweening importance of male sexual experience'. Sexuality thus becomes open-ended; elaborated, not through pre-given roles, but through reflexively forged relationships. The self today, as the rise of therapy testifies, is faced with profound dilemmas in respect of sexuality. 'Who am I?', 'What do I desire?', 'What satisfactions do I want from sexual relations?' – these are core issues for the self, according to Giddens. This does not mean that sexual experience occurs without institutional constraint, however. Giddens contends that the development of modern institutions produces a 'sequestration of experience' – sexual, existential and moral – which squeeze to the sidelines core problems relating to sexuality, intimacy, mortality and death (see Elliott 1992).

Giddens, in other words, adopts an idealist language of autonomy, stressing as he does the creativity of action and the modernist drive to absolute self-realization, while remaining suspicious of intellectual traditions that prioritize subjects over objects, or actors over structures. This comes out very clearly in his work on the changing connections between marriage, the family and self-identity. According to Giddens, individuals today actively engage with novel opportunities and dangers that arise as a consequence of dramatic transformations affecting self-identity, sexuality and intimacy. For Giddens, divorce is undeniably a personal crisis, involving significant pain, loss and grief. Yet many people, he argues, take positive steps to work through the emotional dilemmas generated by marriage breakdown. In addition to dealing with financial issues and matters affecting how children should be brought up, separation and divorce also call into play a reflexive emotional engagement with the self. Charting territory from the past (where things went wrong, missed opportunities, etc.) and for the future (alternative possibilities, chances for self-actualization, etc.) necessarily involves experimenting with a new sense of self. This can lead to emotional growth, new understandings of self and strengthened intimacies. Against the conservative critique of marriage breakdown, Giddens sees the self opening out to constructive renewal. Remarriage and the changing nature of family life are crucial in this respect. As he develops this point:

> Many people, adults and children, now live in stepfamilies – not usually, as in previous eras, as a consequence of the death of a spouse, but because of the re-forming of marriage ties after divorce. A child in a stepfamily may have two mothers and fathers, two sets of brothers and sisters, together with other complex kin connections resulting from the multiple marriages of parents. Even the terminology is

ANTHONY ELLIOTT

difficult: should a stepmother be called 'mother' by the child, or called by her name? Negotiating such problems might be arduous and psychologically costly for all parties; yet opportunities for novel kinds of fulfilling social relations plainly also exist. One thing we can be sure of is that the changes involved here are not just external to the individual. These new forms of extended family ties have to be established by the very persons who find themselves most directly caught up in them.

(1991: 13)

Marital separation, as portrayed by Giddens, implicates the self in an open project: tracing over the past, imagining the future, dealing with complex family problems and experimenting with a new sense of identity. Further experimentation with marriage and intimate relationships will necessarily involve anxieties, risks and opportunities. But, as Giddens emphasizes, the relation between self and society is a highly fluid one, involving negotiation, change and development.

The manner in which current social practices shape future life outcomes is nowhere more in evidence than in the conjunction of divorce statistics, the reckoning of probability ratios for success or failure in intimate relationships and the decision to get married. As Giddens rightly points out, statistics about marriage and divorce do not exist in a social vacuum; everyone, he says, is in some sense aware of how present gender uncertainties affect long-term relationships. When people marry or remarry today, according to Giddens, they do so against a societal backdrop of high divorce statistics, knowledge of which alters a person's understanding and conception of what marriage actually is. It is precisely this reflexive monitoring of relationships that, in turn, transforms expectations about, and aspirations for, marriage and intimacy. The relationship between self, society and reflexivity is thus a highly dynamic one, involving the continual overturning of traditional ways of doing things.

CRITICISMS OF GIDDENS'S THEORY OF STRUCTURATION

Having briefly discussed Giddens's theory of structuration, I want now to consider some of the major criticisms of his social theory.

In several celebrated critiques, Margaret Archer (1982, 1990) argues not only that it is undesirable to amalgamate agency with structure, but that it is necessary to treat structure and agency as analytically distinct in order to deal with core methodological and substantive problems in the social sciences. At the core of Archer's critique of Giddens is an anxiety about his claim that structures have no existence independent of the knowledge that human subjects have about what they do in their daily lives. She argues that Giddens's structuration theory fails to accord sufficient ontological status to the pre-existence of social forms, specifically the impact of social distributions of populations on human action. Archer juxtaposes to Giddens a morphogenetic theory which focuses on the dialectical interplay between agency and the emergent properties of social systems. Similarly, Nicos Mouzelis (1995) argues that, while the notion of structuration is appropriate to routine social practices where agents carry out their actions without undue levels of reflection, there are other forms of social life which require that structure and agency be kept apart. Theoretical reflection upon the social world, for example, involves dualism in Mouzelis's eyes, since there is a shift from the individual to the collective level and this necessarily depends on a distancing of our immediate, everyday lives from broader social structures.

In an especially sharp critique of Giddens's structuration theory, John B. Thompson (1989) questions the analytical value of (a) the notion of rules and resources for grasping social structure, and (b) conceiving of structural constraint as modeled on certain linguistic and grammatical forms. According to Thompson, Giddens's account of rules and resources is vague and misleading. Linguistic and grammatical rules, says Thompson, are important forms of constraint upon human action; however, they are not the only forms of constraint in social life and, indeed, when considering social constraint, the core issue is to understand how an agent's range of alternatives is limited. Thompson acknowledges that Giddens goes some distance towards accounting for this by distinguishing between structure, system and institutions. But, again, he questions Giddens's account of the transformational properties of structures and suggests that there is confusion here between structural and institutional constraint. A worker at the Ford Motor Company, notes Thompson, can be said to contribute to the reproduction of the institution, and thus also be said to contribute to the reproduction of capitalism as a structure, to the extent that the worker pursues their everyday employment activities. However, it is also possible that the worker might undertake activities that threaten or transform the institution, but without similarly transforming their structural conditions. 'Every act of production and reproduction', writes Thompson (1989: 70), 'may also be a potential act of transformation, as Giddens rightly insists; but the extent to which an action transforms an institution does not coincide with the extent to which social structure is thereby transformed'.

Other critics have likewise targeted Giddens's conceptualization of subjectivity, agency and the agent. Bryan S. Turner, for example, finds Giddens's theory of the human agent lacking a sufficient account of embodiment (Turner 1992). Alan Sica has suggested that, notwithstanding his commitment to macro social theory, Giddens's borrowings from Garfinkel, Goffman, Erikson and others indicates an awareness that a theory of the subject and its complex darkness has been central to the project of contemporary social theory. Sica writes:

> Giddens reinvolves himself with the subjective' because he knows that a general theory of action will surely fail that does not come to terms with it. But he fondly thinks, it seems, that by inventing a new vocabulary, by bringing in the ubiquitous

'duality of structure' or 'reflexive rationalization of conduct', he can make good his escape from both the calcified Marxism without a subject (Althusser) or sloppy-hearted Parsonism, which is all norms, values and wishes.

(1989: 48)

Sica's argument here rests on a particular sociological reading of the relations between the reflexive monitoring of action, the routinization of day-to-day social processes and the material condition in which all activities are located and undertaken. There is a sense, for Sica, in which Giddens tries to outflank both Althusserian Marxism and Parsonian sociology, only to find that the crippling dualism of subjectivity and objectivity reappears in his beloved sociological upgrading of the routine (whatever is done habitually). On this view, Giddens's ethnomethodological imperialism not only produces a risky suppression of the material conditions structuring routinized activities, but also cancels those unconscious or symbolic dimensions of human experience untrammeled by routine or convention.

There is something intriguingly divided about Giddens's self-actualizing 'subject of routinization', who is at once structured and structuring, commanding and contextual, a post-Freudian master coolly keeping the unconscious contained within the realm of the habitual, while all the time remaining unquestionably in ethnomethodological control. Yet these polarities have less to do with Giddens's fundamental concept of routinization as such; rather, sociological problems arise – for reasons I shall explore subsequently – as a consequence of the manner in which Giddens attempts to force an ontological division between discursive and practical consciousness on the one side, and the unconscious dimensions of subjectivity or agency on the other. But, for the moment, let us stay with Sica's complaint that Giddens's vision of a routinized subject is disturbingly ungrounded in socio-structural or moral-normative concerns. There can be little doubt that Giddens makes the concept of routinization central to the constitution and reproduction of history and consciousness. 'Routine', writes Giddens (1984: 60) 'is integral both to the continuity of the personality of the agent, as he or she moves along the paths of daily activities, and to the institutions of society, which *are* such only through their continued reproduction'. This is not an expression of sociological determinism (in the sense that all action is pre-programmed) nor political conservatism: there is no logical reason why the reflexively constituted process of social reproduction demands an acceptance of *particular* habitual practices. Rather, Giddens's grounding of ontological security in routinization suggests that both existing and alternative (or oppositional) forms of life demand some sort of motivational commitment to the integration of habitual practices across space and time.

Where Giddens's sociology of routinization is problematic is not in its privileging of the capabilities of actors to 'go on' in the contexts of social life without necessarily being able to give them direct discursive expression, but in its

assumption that practical consciousness brackets, limits and contains unconscious representation and repressed desire. For Giddens, the repetition of activities which are undertaken in like manner day after day provides the grounding
for what he terms 'ontological security', protecting against the unwanted erup-
tion of anxiety. Predictable routines keep the unconscious at bay. And yet anyone with a psychoanalytic ear reading of Giddens's sociology of routinization is
likely to feel unsympathetic to such a characterization of the nature of the unconscious. Concentrating mainly on the notion of repression leaves Giddens to give
sociological expression to the widespread cultural fantasy that the fracturing
effects of the unconscious must be limited, held in check. But, even in the terms
of his own stratification model, one has only to raise a few psychoanalytically-
inspired questions to see the problems here. What kind of good is it to practical
consciousness to bracket anxiety at the level of the unconscious? Does such
'bracketing' lead to autonomy of action – that is, does it guarantee it, as it were?
What of Freud's speaking up for unconscious passion, for the strangeness and
otherness of emotional life, a life not dominated by system or custom? Such concerns are not easily addressed from the standpoint of Giddens's structuration
theory, a point underscored by both psychoanalytic-inspired critics and **feminists**. (For further discussion see Anthony Elliott, *Critical Visions*, Rowman and
Littlefield, 2003, chapter 2.)

PIERRE BOURDIEU: *HABITUS* AND PRACTICAL SOCIAL LIFE

The French sociologist Bourdieu also developed, over several decades, a highly
influential account of the complex interrelations between self and society, the individual agent and social structure. Like Giddens, Bourdieu is interested in the habits
of whole societies. In developing this research interest, Bourdieu coined the term
habitus, by which he meant the institutionalized process by which well-practiced
habits bridge individuals and the wider social things of which they are part. Also,
like Giddens, Bourdieu argues that social actors exhibit intricate and complex
understandings of the social conditions which influence, and are in turn influenced
by, their personal decisions and private lives. Bourdieu's formulation is that actors
possess a 'sense of the game', which is the basis from which people deploy a kind
of semi-automatic grasp of what is appropriate to differing social situations.

In *Outline of a Theory of Practice* (1977) Bourdieu detailed the concept of
habitus – that is, how individual dispositions interlock with the specific cultural
characteristics of society. 'The structures constitutive of a particular type of
environment', writes Bourdieu, 'produce the *habitus*, systems of durable dispositions, structured structures predisposed to function as structuring structures'.
Note that social structures for Bourdieu do not actually *determine* individual
action. On the contrary, *habitus* is a flexible, open-ended structuring system, one
which enables social actors to have numerous creative strategies at their disposal
and thus to cope with unforeseen social structures.

Bourdieu developed his concept of *habitus* from his anthropological studies of the Kabyle tribespeople and, in particular, from close sociological analysis of gift exchanges in Kabyle society. Bourdieu considers that structuralism is correct in its initial diagnosis that society possesses a reality that precedes the individual. This is the point, for example, that language pre-exists us as speaking agents, and will subsequently continue as a social institution long after we have left the planet. If this is so, Bourdieu supposes, then structuralism is right to claim that language has the power to regulate, even shape, our individual speech-acts – whether we realize it or not. But, where structuralism is palpably insufficient, according to Bourdieu, lies in its reduction of social action to a mechanical system of rules which imposes itself on individuals. Studying the intricacies of gift exchange in Kabyle society, Bourdieu finds that men's sense of honor is facilitated less by an application of pre-established rules than by carrying out a whole range of practices – such as 'playing with the tempo' of response and acknowledgment of a gift. An actor's response to the receipt of a gift is not therefore socially determined by the application of mechanical rules, and nor is it a matter of mere private judgement. Rather, it involves the creative artistry of the recipient, experimenting within a fluid structuring structure, one marked by group norms of acceptable practice, obligation, reciprocity and honor.

Habitus, in the sense of deeply ingrained dispositions, is a structuring feature of social practices, but it is more than just that. If our practical, or habitual, behaviors have a degree of consistency to them, this is because our bodies are literally moulded into certain forms that interlock with existing social arrangements. One way of thinking about how *habitus* reaches all the way down into bodily needs and dispositions is to consider the process that sociologists call 'socialization'. The notion of socialization refers, broadly speaking, to the training or regulation of children within the structure of bigger social things. The learning of good manners at home or respect for figures of authority at school are examples of the socialization process. Bourdieu's account of how *habitus* penetrates the body – what he calls the 'corporeal hexis' – is similar to the idea of socialization, but is much broader in scope. Socialization conveys too strongly the sense of active or conscious learning, and this is not how Bourdieu thinks we come to act in the world. Instead, he is interested in getting at the subtle ways in which messages are relayed to people over time, such that cultural norms become routine patterns of behavior and, thus, withdrawn from consciousness. The parent who routinely tells their son or daughter to 'sit up straight' at dinner, or who instructs their child to 'always say thank you' when offered food at the home of a fellow class-mate, is thus going about the business of reproducing the *habitus* of modern society. This is the sense, too, in which *habitus* bites deeply into the very bodies of individuals – structuring the ways in which people come to talk, walk, act and eat. *Habitus*, thus, is deeply interwoven with the stylization of bodies.

What has been discussed so far about social practices and bodies is central to the analysis of human action, and yet it hardly needs saying that – for regular social life to get up and running – such practices must be anchored in wider institutional contexts. Bourdieu seeks to do this by introducing the notion of 'field', by which he means the structured space of positions in which an individual in located. For Bourdieu, there are various kinds of fields – educational, economic and cultural – which contain different kinds of social properties and characteristics. A field, says Bourdieu, pre-exists the individual. It ascribes an objective place to individuals within the broader scheme of social things, and thereby serves as a relation of force between individuals and groups engaged in struggles within certain fields. It is in and through our social interactions in fields – whether these be educational, financial, sporting or scientific – that actors struggle to assert themselves as distinct or noteworthy in the eyes of others and the wider society. Bourdieu calls such struggle the search for 'cultural capital'. Through this notion of capital, which is principally cultural in its form and impact, Bourdieu directs our attention to the means whereby social inequalities are generated through classifications of power, displays of taste and acts of individual consumption. In *Distinction: A Social Critique of the Judgment of Taste* (1984), Bourdieu developed a brilliant analysis of the habits and tastes of French society – which he divided into the working class, the lower middle class and the upper middle class. His argument, broadly speaking, was that, whilst economics is the baseline of social order, the struggle for social distinction is played out with other forms of capital too – notably, cultural capital and symbolic capital. Culture, then, is the sense of fine living, manners, refinement or an elegant ease of social interaction that lies at the centre of how individuals demonstrate social sophistication. Such social sophistication requires certain economic capital – for example, expensive private schools. But social struggles for distinction have a cultural dimension too: cultivation of the self is also a matter of learning, aesthetics, the arts.

CRITICISM OF BOURDIEU

Bourdieu's work has been subjected to criticisms from various quarters. Critics have questioned, for example, the adequacy of the concept of *habitus* to address the complexity of social experience. The criticism here is that *habitus* overemphasizes the *containment* of cultural dispositions within social structures – thereby downgrading the capacity of individuals to negotiate or transform existing social systems through their creative actions. There may be some truth to this charge, but the criticism needs more precision. Bourdieu's *habitus* emerged as a theoretical innovation in the aftermath of structuralism and post-structuralism; it fitted well enough with a political and intellectual climate in which dissent was still possible, but now conceptualized in a fashion that fully broke with individualistic ways of understanding the world. Society, for Bourdieu, was less the outcome of individual acts and choices than a structuring, structured field of dispositions in which individuals mobilize themselves and act to exclude others on the base of relevant cultural capital. The *habitus*, in other words, refers to an objectivity ('society') that inscribes itself within identity. There is something about social production which is both enabling and coercive. What is most dynamic about *habitus* for Bourdieu is its status as the condition of sociality: the *habitus* prescribes the kinds of agency demanded by culture. Yet, whilst this viewpoint was in some general sense radical, it seemed on the whole to have little of interest to say about specific issues of identity (the concrete negotiations of the self in relation to social relations), even if Bourdieu had provided a whole range of sociological enquiries, from education to aesthetics. Part of the difficulty in this respect is that Bourdieu might be said not to have broken with structuralism thoroughly enough, in the sense that structures in his work continue to confer on us our agency – to such a degree that we misrecognize our fate as our choice. In doing so, Bourdieu's *habitus* neglects the creativity of action which individuals bring to all encounters with social and cultural processes – a matter of profound significance to the question of social change.

The debate over Bourdieu's contributions to social theory has also addressed many other issues. One central criticism concerns certain *assumptions about society* that Bourdieu appears to make in his various sociological analyses. Some critics contend, for example, that he takes the economy for granted, leaving unanalyzed the role of economic forces in social life. Whilst Bourdieu was widely seen as sympathetic to the political left, the politics of his social theory were somewhat oblique; he certainly distanced himself from Marx and Marxism. Against this backdrop, some have argued that he elevated cultural capital over economic capital, thus tending to skirt issues of economic oppression. A more interesting line of criticism, in my view, is that his account of symbolic violence assumes a certain kind of consensus with respect to the norms and values that are central in society. This is less a matter of assuming that people openly agree with one another about societal values than a presupposition that those who exercise cultural and symbolic capital are perceived by others as 'legitimate' bearers of social authority. That is to say, Bourdieu can be criticized for conceptualizing social practice in terms of how social stability is sustained. Such an approach allows him to develop powerful insights into how symbolic domination is wielded in contemporary societies, and yet these insights, arguably, come at the sociological cost of understanding how social structures – or ways of acting with cultural capital – can be changed. In short, *habitus* might not be so overwhelmingly rigid.

Conclusion

Theories of structuration, as represented in the writings of Giddens and Bourdieu, have influenced social theorists seeking to find conceptual pathways beyond the dualism of 'subjectivism' and 'objectivism'. The notion that action is structured in everyday contexts, in and through which the structural features of society are reproduced, has been a major advancement of recent social thought. Giddens's concept of 'reflexivity' and Bourdieu's notion of 'habitus' represent, in quite different ways, original formulations of how to rethink the self/society dualism in social theory. The systematic study of processes of structuration has been developed in many various ways in recent social theory, and the contributions of – amongst others – John B. Thompson, David Held, Loic Waquant, Charles Lemert, Lois McNay, Jeffrey Prager and Patricia Clough all offer important new frameworks based to some substantial degree on structuration theories. Understanding the complex ways in which action and structure intersect in a world increasingly interconnected, mobile and fluid remains a core challenge of social theory in the twenty-first century.

REFERENCES AND RECOMMENDED FURTHER READING

Archer, M. (1982) 'Morphogenesis vs. structuration', *British Journal of Sociology*, 33: 455–83.
—— (1990) 'Human agency and social structure', in J. Clark, C. Modgil and S. Modgil (eds), *Anthony Giddens: Consensus and Controversy*, New York: Falmer.
Beck, U., Giddens, A. and Lash, S. (1994) *Reflexive Modernisation: Politics, Tradition and Aesthetics in the Modern Social Order*, Stanford, CA: Stanford University Press.
Bourdieu, P. (1977) [1972] *Outline of a Theory of Practice*, Cambridge: Cambridge University Press.
—— (1984) *Distinction: A Social Critique of the Judgment of Taste*, London: Routledge and Kegan Paul.
—— (1988) [1984] *Homo Academicus*, Cambridge: Polity Press.
—— (1991) *Language and Symbolic Power*, Cambridge: Polity Press.
—— (1993) *The Field of Cultural Production*, Cambridge: Polity Press.
—— (1995) *The Rules of Art: Genesis and Structure of the Literary Field*, Stanford, CA: Stanford University Press.
—— (1996a) *On Television and Journalism*, London: Pluto Press.
—— (1996b) *The State Nobility: Elite Schools in the Field of Power*, Cambridge: Polity Press.
—— (2000) *Weight of the World: Social Suffering in Contemporary Society*, Stanford, CA: Stanford University Press.
Elliott, A. (1992) *Social Theory and Psychoanalysis in Transition: Self and Society from Freud to Kristeva*, Oxford: Blackwell.
—— (2003) *Critical Visions: New Directions in Social Theory*, Lanham, MD: Rowman & Littlefield.
—— (2009) *Contemporary Social Theory: An Introduction*, London: Routledge.
Giddens, A. (1971) *Capitalism and Modern Social Theory: An Analysis of the Writings of Marx, Durkheim and Max Weber*, Cambridge: Cambridge University Press.
—— (1976) *New Rules of Sociological Method*, Cambridge: Cambridge University Press.
—— (1979) *Central Problems in Social Theory: Action, Structure, and Contradiction in Social Analysis*, London: Macmillan.
—— (1984) *The Constitution of Society: Outline of the Theory of Structuration*, Cambridge: Polity Press.
—— (1987) [1985] *The Nation-State and Violence*, Berkeley, CA: University of California Press.
—— (1990) *The Consequences of Modernity*, Stanford, CA: Stanford University Press.
—— (1991) *Modernity and Self-identity: Self and Society in the Late Modern Age*, Stanford, CA: Stanford University Press.
—— (1992) *The Transformation of Intimacy: Sexuality, Love, and Eroticism in Modern Societies*, Stanford, CA: Stanford University Press.
—— (1995) *Politics, Sociology and Social Theory*, Cambridge: Polity Press.
Mouzelis, N. (1995) *Sociological Theory: What Went Wrong?*, London: Routledge.
Thompson, J. B. (1989) 'The theory of structuration', in D. Held and J. B. Thompson (eds), *Social Theory of Modern Societies: Giddens and his Critics*, Cambridge: Cambridge University Press.
Turner, B.S. (1992) *Regulating Bodies*, London: Routledge.

7

SOCIAL THEORY OF THE BODY

MARY HOLMES

The contemporary world is apparently obsessed by bodily appearance. Social theory of the body can help to explain this, through thinking about how bodies are shaped by social contexts. There is a long history of thought relating to embodiment, but body theory as a specific field within the social sciences did not develop until the 1980s. There are three reasons why it emerged (Blaikie *et al.* 2003). First, there was the intellectual desire to improve on the mind versus body dualism that Western thought inherited from René Descartes (1596–1650). He was a French philosopher whose radical view of human being was based on his argument – 'I think therefore I am'. This favouring of 'pure' reasoning minds over messy bodies was used by dominant social groups such as male upper-class elites to justify holding political power. Their supposedly superior intellect was deemed to fit them for ruling the allegedly weak-minded 'lower classes' and women, who were thought slaves to their flesh (Bordo 1987; Pateman 1988; 1989). Social theorists have long challenged such prejudices with arguments that lack of education, not naturally inferior brains, prevented women and other excluded groups from greater engagement in intellectual debates (e.g. Wollstonecraft (1985) [1792]). Nevertheless, people still struggle to think of minds as part of bodies rather than 'higher' and separate from them. This dualism is not the only way to think about bodies. Non-Western traditions in China, Japan and India are examples of alternative assessments which understand body and mind as more connected (Blaikie *et al.* 2003; Kasulis *et al.* 1993). And, indeed, Western views have altered, due to political changes which are the second reason behind the emergence of body theory. From the 1960s, social movements such as feminism, black power, gay liberation and the disability movement challenged dominant ideas about what was a 'normal' body. Third, social theory on the body became an essential tool in trying to make sense of a society and culture placing increasing importance on bodily appearance (Blaikie *et al.* 2003).

In social theory, embodiment is understood not as a 'natural' fact but as a product of social forces. This social constructionism intellectually battles biological essentialism, which assumes that there is some essence, some bodily property (e.g. a certain gene), that determines our actions. Good social theory acknowledges the biological, but an important part of constructionism has been to criticize scientific and medical ideas about bodies. This chapter begins with these criticisms, examining how labelling certain bodies as 'normal' has marginalized other types of bodies (for example, 'homosexual' or 'disabled'). It is not just science and medicine that define and shape bodies, but other social institutions such as family and the education system. These institutions influence bodily practices and circulate **discourse**s (ways of thinking and talking) about bodies. The second section discusses debates about how practices and discourses repress, regulate or are experienced by actual bodies. Ideas about bodies and bodies themselves are diverse and changing. The final section addresses a key social change, looking at the increasing importance of bodily appearance in everyday life. This chapter will argue that such importance can best be understood, but also questioned, by seeing bodies as belonging to thinking, doing and feeling people who exist and interact in a changing social world.

THE MEDICALIZATION OF BODIES: FOUCAULT AND THE SOCIOLOGY OF MEDICINE

Science and medicine have not always been the ultimate authorities on the body. One of the 'founding fathers' of sociology, Max **Weber**, argued that its dominance came about with **modernity**, a new phase in human history comprising an eighteenth-century shift in knowledge known as the Enlightenment, followed by the **Industrial Revolution**. Weber thought one of modernity's main characteristics was disenchantment. Rationality replaced religion and superstition as the basis of knowledge, and science became the new holder of 'The Truth' (Weber 1968 [1921], 1981 [1927]). Scientists were especially interested in the workings of the human body, but knew relatively little about it. Dissection of human cadavers was very rare prior to the sixteenth century because the powerful Church saw it as desecration. Anatomical dissections did become more common throughout Europe from the eighteenth century, but were still frowned upon, so it was largely the bodies of executed criminals which were used. When supplies ran short, 'body snatchers' robbed graves and sold the corpses to medical schools. In 1827, the money a body fetched was good enough to tempt the infamous pair Burke and Hare to murder 17 people and sell their bodies to the Edinburgh medical college (Macdonald 2005). Dissection eventually became a routine part of the medical training carried out in teaching hospitals (or clinics) as medicine became increasingly powerful.

The medicalization of the body refers to the process by which medical knowledge about bodies became dominant. The fragmenting and objectifying medical gaze became all-powerful, as charted by the hugely influential French historian of ideas, Michel **Foucault** (1973 [1963]). Bodily processes, previously part of everyday life, have been taken out of their ordinary sphere and fallen under the control of medical experts (Illich 1976). In wealthier nations, those born in the early twentieth century were highly likely to be born at home. By late in the century, home births were almost non-existent and childbirth was surrounded by doctors and technology (Howson 2004: 132–8; Oakley

1980). Similarly, death is now seldom managed by the family at home, despite most people wishing to die there. Around 80 per cent of people die in hospital (Flory *et al.* 2004, Office of National Statistics 2008: 299, Wilson *et al.* 2001). Indeed, dying is sequestered away like a dirty secret to which no one will admit (see Ariès 1983, Elias 1985, Lawton 1998). Medicalization also extends to arenas such as mental illness (Foucault 1967 [1961]) and sexuality (Foucault 1990 [1976]); a process Foucault understands by retheorizing power. He argues that, within modernity people no longer do what they are told because of fear of physical punishment. Instead, power becomes diffused, an abstract system heavily reliant on surveillance. Knowledge is both obtained from and used in watching and controlling people. Scientists attempt to classify everything into categories and types, and this brings new forms of control. Foucault (1990 [1976]) illustrates how this happened with the development of a science of sex. Victorian sexologists, like Richard Freiherr von Krafft-Ebing (1951 [1886]) and Havelock Ellis (1898–1928), put together detailed studies of sexual behaviour, nearly all focused on identifying 'abnormal' expressions of sexuality. Classifying sexual diversity into 'normal' versus 'abnormal' changed conceptions of sexuality. It was no longer seen as a form of behaviour, but as a fundamental aspect of a person. Having sex with persons of the same sex now defined someone as a homosexual, rather than being something they sometimes did. This labelling was used, often contrary to the wishes of the sexologists, to control homosexuality by criminalizing it and/or treating it as a disease. This implied that homosexuals needed to be cured. Even as late as the 1970s, 'treatments' such as aversion therapy were given, which involved showing the patient same-sex erotic pictures and then giving them vomit-inducing drugs, or painful electric shocks. But this relied on externally imposed physical punishment and was extremely ineffective in altering the sexual orientation of 'patients' (King *et al.* 2004).

Medical knowledge is most powerful in defining and (re)making bodies when people internalize ideas about what is 'normal' and 'healthy' and try to discipline their own bodies to conform (Foucault 1973 [1963]). There is some debate about whether the model for the 'normal' body was male, and whether this has made women particularly subject to medicalization (see Howson 2004: 48 –51, 128–30). However, anyone who does not fit the 'normal' category – be they underweight or overweight, disabled or chronically ill – is likely to be passed from one set of 'experts' to another and to become subject to a great deal of surveillance and control by the medical profession. Sociologist Ivan Illich (1976) even argues that the medical profession causes much ill-health, from infections passed on in hospitals, to drug side-effects, to the general 'un-health' it causes by taking away from people the ability to deal with their own well-being.

Whether people passively submit to processes of medicalization is much contested. Disability campaigners, for example, blame the social environment for being disabling, rather than accepting biomedical models of disability as dysfunction. For instance, stairs disable people in wheelchairs, not paralysis (see Oliver 1996). Despite its dominance, scientific medicine is not the only factor shaping bodies.

SOCIAL BODIES

Bodies are shaped through social structures (the way society is organized) and through social processes. Socialization is a key process, which teaches children how to be acceptable members of their society; for example, parents potty-train children and teach them to eat with a knife and fork. Also, social structures in the form of social institutions such as family, education, work and the mass media all produce bodies in ways particular to time and place. Karl **Marx**'s best friend, Friedrich Engels (1845), provides an example when describing the impact of the new nineteenth century factories that came about with industrialization. The poor worked at physically demanding jobs until their bodies were literally worn out; that is, if they did not die first from a work-related accident or illness brought on by long hours and terrible working and living conditions. The rapid urbanization accompanying industrialization turned the mass of the population into city dwellers. Georg **Simmel** (1950 [1908]), an early German sociologist, proposed that people could not deal with all the sensations and people around them in a complex city, so they developed a new blasé attitude, learning to ignore the mass of humanity.

'Humanity' had a changing social meaning and, in particular, became increasingly gendered. Thomas Laqueur (1990) shows that, prior to the eighteenth century, there was a one-sex model which understood women's bodies as a less-developed version of the male body, with their genitals remaining folded up inside them. Only later did a two-sex model develop in which male and female bodies were seen as distinctly different. Femininity and masculinity no longer meant types of behaviour that either men or women could exhibit. Femininity became linked to female bodies and masculinity to male bodies. The labelling of newborns as either male or female is crucial in producing individual bodies that conform to current social expectations about femininity and masculinity. Social meanings transform biology (e.g. Kessler and McKenna 1985), but social theorists of the body differ in terms of how they understand the social shaping of bodies.

Society represses bodies

People do not do whatever they like most of the time. Few have sex with everyone they find attractive. Most neighbours manage to avoid killing each other, even if they find each other unbearable. Women tend not to pee in the street, even if desperate to urinate. Folk try to refrain from picking their nose in public. All this involves an element of control, which, according to Sigmund Freud (1961 [1930]), involves repression of our natural drives. The drives push us to satisfy bodily needs and desires, like the desire for sex. Repressing drives is what he thinks makes a civilized society possible; it enables an orderly and advanced world. However, bodily needs simmer under the surface and always threaten to return. Thus, embodied individuals are in tension with the demands of an ordered society, which says 'no' to their free expression.

The civilizing process is one in which bodies and emotions have become increasingly subject to social controls since the medieval period. Norbert Elias (2000/1939), a German Jewish sociologist who fled to Britain in 1935, developed Freud's ideas. He identified the social aspects of this 'civilizing process' in Europe as socialization, rationalization and individualization. Children are socialized to control their bodily functions and greater bodily and emotional restraint are increasingly expected from everyone. Rationalization sees social rules proliferate so that bodies are subject to growing regulation. Finally, there is a change of consciousness resulting in individualization. Communal sharing is gradually replaced by individuated practices. People stop drinking from the same cup and eating from a common dish. Bed-sharing becomes something done only with a sexual partner. These changes occur because of shifts of power in which the aristocracy lose their dominance and become partly dependent on the upcoming new middle classes, based especially on trade. A process of pacification also takes place. The violence of medieval society is succeeded by a state monopoly on legitimate violence and aggression is regulated in the form of sport or military discipline. Control is exercised through social means rather than by external force. New instruments like the fork, the handkerchief and the toilet are developed to assist in the exercise of self-restraint and concealment of bodily functions. These began as luxury items, distinguishing the upper classes. High status was associated with repressing 'natural' functions and conforming to social rules requiring bodily and emotional restraint.

Rules about bodily restraint have been highly gendered. Pioneering French feminist philosopher Simone de **Beauvoir** (1989 [1949]) struggles with what she sees as women's socially induced inability to transcend their bodies and find a higher form of existence. Her most famous book, *The Second Sex*, explains women's embodiment not as a natural fact but as something that is socially created. This is summarized in her statement that 'one is not born, but rather becomes, a woman' (de Beauvoir 1989 [1949]: 267). Women learn to act in 'feminine' ways. Such constructionism continued to be the centrepiece of most feminist theories of the body in the 1960s and 1970s. Constructionism usually emphasizes external social constraints. A focus on increasing inner self-restraint can ignore some of the ways in which bodily expression has become freer. For example, it is no longer shocking to have sex outside of marriage (Wouters 2004). 'Civilized' society does not simply say 'no' to bodily expression, it regulates it.

Society regulates bodies

Understanding bodies as socially regulated draws on Foucault's contention that power produces disciplined bodies. He explicitly rejects the idea of increasing repression of the body as society becomes 'more civilized' (Foucault 1990

[1976]). He thinks that history is not a story of society or power, increasingly saying 'no' to the body. For example, conventional histories tended to present the Victorians as the pinnacle of sexual repression – afraid to have the legs of their pianos on view in case they might remind men of women's ankles. On the contrary, Foucault points out that the Victorians couldn't stop talking about sex and that it was precisely Victorians such as Freud and Ellis and Kraft-Ebing who prompted prolific 'scientific' discourse about sex at the same time that newspapers were constantly peddling stories about 'morality' and 'fallen women' (prostitutes). The increasing prominence of science and medicine is crucial in regulating and governing bodies, their principles of power/knowledge contagious. Surveillance is used in an array of social institutions and discourses, from schools to prisons to psychiatry, to try to compel people to discipline themselves to conform to social norms (Foucault 1979 [1975], 1967 [1961]).

The importance of power relations in producing certain kinds of bodies has long been attested to by **feminist** thinkers, especially those associated with second wave feminism as a social movement. These 1970s feminists analysed the oppression of women as it related to their bodies. Oppression may seem a strong word but, over 40 years ago, women had limited power within a male-dominated society. There are different approaches within feminist theorizing (see Holmes 2007), but almost all see women's and men's bodies as social products. The radical suggestion of some feminists was that women's lower social position produced bodily weakness, rather than being derived from it. Kate Millet's (1972 [1970]) work is the classic example of this argument, positing that relationships between women and men were power relationships in which men tried to maintain their dominance and oppress women, partly by claiming that men were strong and women weak. She argued that brute strength was no longer essential within modern technological society and that these biological differences in strength were not 'natural' but 'culturally encouraged, through breeding, diet, and exercise' (Millet 1972: 27). For Millet, it is social inequalities in a male-dominated society which shape bodies and reinforce women's dependency. Thus, a key demand of the feminist movement was that women gain greater control of their bodies, especially their reproductivity. One response was women's health groups, in which women shared their knowledge of their bodies with each other in order to help them challenge medical models (Howson 2004: 130–2).

Some feminists have adapted Foucault's ideas on regulation to better illustrate the gendered nature of most disciplinary processes, from medicine to media to beauty (e.g. Black 2004, Bordo 1993, Howson 2001). Analyses of medical interventions, cosmetic surgery, beauty and body work all further understanding of the large role of social forces and social rules in making bodies masculine and feminine. While extremely valuable, such work can sometimes struggle to represent embodied complexity because of its constant drift toward the social level for explanations.

Feminist philosophers, Moira Gatens and Elizabeth Grosz, attempted to create a corporeal feminism, which looked to the bodily level for explaining actions.

They did not want to return to essentialism and ignore social construction, instead mounting an ambitious effort to rethink ideas about space, time and power and to reconsider how women are represented and how bodies are understood (Howson 2005: 118). However, corporeal feminism failed to develop adequate tools to analyse social inequalities between bodies of differing 'race', 'class' or ability. The possibilities are interesting but the influence of corporeal feminism was also limited by its overly philosophical approach, divorced from women's everyday embodied experiences (Beasley 2005: 70; Howson 2005: 121).

Symbolic interactionism provided more analysis of bodies as fundamentally constructed by the everyday social meanings given to them. This tradition emanated from early twentieth century social psychologist G.H. **Mead**'s (1962) interest in how our selves and social worlds are formed via the meanings we give to the actions of others. The best known exponent of symbolic interactionism was American sociologist Erving **Goffman**. He developed the dramaturgical approach to analysing social interaction, initially outlined in *The Presentation of Self in Everyday Life* (Goffman 1987 [1959]). This approach uses the metaphor of people as actors performing roles to analyse how people try to present the best version of themselves to different 'audiences' within their everyday lives. Someone may perform the role of the model employee to the boss and then go home and be a genial slob in front of the family. Goffman recognizes that the body is the vital instrument by which we impress, disappoint, disgust or delight others. How people stand, how they talk and how they dress are used to try to create a certain impression.

Bodies can upset efforts to give a good impression, for example if they have stigma: characteristics that are socially problematic. Goffman (1968) argues that these characteristics are not intrinsically bad but result in the bearer being thought of as not 'normal', and perhaps inferior, according to the social expectations of the time (Howson 2004: 23–4). Bodily stigma might include facial scarring or the lack of a limb. Stigma relating to character might include having a criminal record or being a prostitute. There are also tribal stigma which come from being a member of a marginalized social group such as an ethnic or religious minority. Currently, Muslim women and men in Western societies are likely to be stigmatized if indentifiable by their dress. Many Westerners will not treat them 'normally' in interactions and the usual rules of interaction break down. People can become embarrassed and start to question how to interact with the stigmatized person, or try to avoid having to interact. Tribal stigma affects whole categories of people with bodies not considered 'normal'.

As a tribal stigma, gender signifies women's bodies as deviant in ways requiring special rules of interaction. Regarding all women as stigmatized may seem surprising, but there are many ways in which women still do not enjoy full equality (see Holmes 2007). Goffman (1979) argues, in his book analysing advertisements, that interaction rules make interactions between women and men a constant display of dominant beliefs in men's power over women. He is critical, for example, of how men are almost always portrayed looking down at women, sometimes placing a territory-claiming hand on their shoulder. Overall, he argues that advertisements picture women in ways that make them look inferior to, and possessed by, masterful and authoritative men. This is one illustration of how embodied interactions reinforce gender norms. Gender is made by acting and responding to others' actions according to rules about how to be 'feminine' and 'masculine'. The question is why people follow the rules and thus maintain social order?

The maintenance of social order is a central problem in social theory, but debates have paid insufficient attention to bodies. Bryan Turner's (1984) pioneering text, *The Body in Society* seeks to remedy this and was key in establishing the body as a field and setting an agenda. Turner is influenced by theorists such as Marx, Weber, Parsons and Foucault, but produces original thinking on the need to make the body central to social theory. For Turner, order is a problem of 'the government of the body' (Turner 1984: 2). Society has to attend to that problem by dealing with reproducing its population, and regulating, disciplining and representing bodies. These efforts have consequences for different social groups. For example, Turner uses Foucault's work to discuss how governments have attempted to regulate women's sexuality. Hysteria emerged in the early twentieth as a nervous condition that women were thought to risk if they did not have children. Turner (1984: 102–3) argues that, if women were showing the kinds of 'irrational' behaviour labelled as symptoms of hysteria, it was not because of a 'wandering womb', but because they were having to deal with being told to marry and reproduce while simultaneously being told to delay marriage to help slow the rapid population growth which was causing concern. They were subject to bodily management.

Men's bodies are also subject to social management, but attention to this point came later and required feminist prompting. Men achieved power by presenting themselves as disembodied rational beings (Bordo 1987, Lloyd 1984, Pateman 1988, 1989) but, by the late 1980s, the political challenge of feminism and other social changes had brought about a shift. Media representations of male bodies as muscularly macho became common in the 1980s, just as masculine identity was undergoing significant changes in which bodily strength was becoming less important and consumption more so (e.g. Mort 1988). The decline of manufacturing in many Western nations and the rise of service industries saw many men lose their traditional role as breadwinner, and/or shift away from work involving physical labour. Traditionally, the more privileged type of male body is what David Morgan (1993) refers to as the 'classical' type. This is associated with upper-class bodies that are very controlled and usually well-dressed. These are contrasted with 'grotesque' male bodies, associated with the working class. Although attributed with a raw, and supposedly violent, 'natural' power, they are usually negatively described as lacking restraint. Australian sociologist R.W. Connell (1995) varies slightly in identifying 'muscular' as the privileged kind of masculine body, but also emphasizes the importance of bodily control in displaying oneself as masculine. Connell's extremely significant work on masculinities developed a notion of hegemonic masculinity to describe dominant meanings about masculinity. The hegemonically masculine is a shifting ideal that is engaged with and approached, but never really attained, by individuals. It is defined as not homosexual and not feminine. A hegemonically masculine form of embodiment is one that is authoritative and claims space. Although most men may not conform to the hegemonically masculine, they and their bodies are judged in these terms and they will shape their identity and body in relation to it.

There are questions about the extent to which social norms determine the shaping or disciplining of women's and men's bodies. There is some doubt about whether people are the docile bodies that Foucault and followers imply. We often see messy and undisciplined bodies around us (Blaikie *et al.* 2003, Crossley 2004). Structures and social meaning do not entirely govern bodies. Individuals have some **agency**, some ability to shape their body and how bodies are experienced may be complex.

Bodies are experienced by individuals within a social world

Phenomenology is the study of experiences, and can inform analysis of bodies as the centre of our being and the means by which we perceive and think about the world. In the 1940s, Frenchman Maurice **Merleau-Ponty** (2001 [1962]) began publishing his philosophic conceptualization of the 'body-subject' to counter Cartesian dualism. For him, we are bodies who see, feel and think about the world according to our embodied position within it. Phenomenological social theory examines 'the social processes people depend on to categorize sense data as phenomena and examines the extent to which these phenomena are shared' (Howson 2004: 35). For Merleau-Ponty, inter-corporeality, or the way we act towards others and our social situation, is important in understanding embodiment as fundamentally social. Iris Young (1990) is particularly noted for using such a phenomenological approach to explain how most women come to experience their body as having limited capacities, which, for instance, may make them 'throw like a girl'.

Embodied experience includes much routine action which constitutes a person's *habitus*. Another Frenchman – Pierre **Bourdieu**, takes the term *habitus* from Marcel Mauss (1973: 70) who uses it to describe learned techniques of using the body, like learning culturally different ways to walk. For Bourdieu (e.g. 1987), *habitus* refers to durable principles which reproduce the practices of a social class. In other words, it is the ways of being and doing learned and practised by members of a class (Howson and Inglis 2001: 310). Bodily practices are instilled by social structures such as class, but embodied agents reproduce social conditions through the practice of bodily dispositions and tastes typical of their class. Dispositions include things like accents, ways of moving and ways of eating that are not 'natural' but learned and they depend on inheriting capital. In Marxist thinking, capital referred to monetary wealth, but Bourdieu called that economic capital and also analysed cultural capital (knowledge of the 'right' kinds of things) and social capital (having useful social contacts). Those with high cultural and social capital are able to distinguish themselves from others because of the higher social value given to the kinds of dispositions and tastes embedded as part of their class upbringing. Class is reproduced by people distinguishing themselves via their tastes and dispositions. 'Good' taste is what the more powerful middle and upper classes say it is, defined in contrast to 'bad' taste, usually associated with the working classes. For example, a taste for 'good' coffee can be used to reinforce class boundaries. In the fairly recent arrival of a café society to British shores, the middle classes initially defined having a coffee as a tasteful trend. However, as the trend for café visits spread to the working classes, who pursued it by frequenting chains such as Starbucks, portions of the middle classes defined those chains as being in 'bad taste' and retreated to independently run cafés or smaller European-styled chains. Tastes in dress and bodily comportment are subject to similar judgements about what is 'good' taste. The middle and upper classes have considerably more power to enforce their taste by excluding or deriding working class people who do not meet those standards when they apply for jobs or have a night out on the town (see Skeggs 1997, 2005). However, the body itself is a form of capital. This physical capital can be used to acquire other forms of capital. Boxers can fight for money (Wacquant 1995) and working class women can try to use their feminine appearance to get 'better' men and 'better' jobs (Skeggs 1997). This may recognize agency to some degree, but inserting phenomenology into social theory has not been entirely successful in escaping **structuralist** emphasis on social forces like class. The actual everyday experiences of embodied people tend to disappear (Howson and Inglis 2001).

The abstractions and neatening tendencies of social theory can over-generalize diverse and subjective bodily experiences. For this reason, some of the best work on bodies has an empirical element, or at least deals with embodiment in more specific contexts. The breadth of this work, some already mentioned, is impressive. It ranges from discussion of sexual bodies (e.g. Weeks 1985), to bodies in pain (e.g. Bendelow and Williams 1995, Scarry 1985), ageing bodies (e.g. Hepworth 1995), sporting bodies (e.g. Probyn 2000), self-starving bodies (e.g. Bordo 1993) and technological bodies (e.g. Haraway 1985). Yet there are generalizations to be made about the current social conditions in which a diversity of bodily experiences arise.

BODIES IN CONTEMPORARY SOCIETY

As noted at the beginning of this chapter, a key reason for increased theoretical interest in the body is social changes which have made individuals extremely body-conscious. This body-consciousness is argued to have come from social shifts towards individualism and consumerism within a globalized social environment. These 'isms describe a society in which individuals are expected to be responsible for themselves and in which the purchase of things is deemed crucial to a good life. Within this individualistic consumer society, bodily needs are mostly met by purchasing goods and services, but bodies themselves must also be marketable. Having the right 'look' is essential for getting the 'right' job and the 'right' lifestyle. Bodily appearance is assumed to indicate the kind of person you are and therefore bodies must be carefully maintained by buying gym membership or beauty treatments or cosmetic surgery (Featherstone 1991, Lemert and Elliott 2006). In contemporary society, the body is treated as an ongoing project (see Shilling 1993), but one that is still highly gendered (e.g. Black 2004, Davis 2002). As the influence of tradition (how things were always done) on practices is lost, individuals are forced to become reflexive. They must think about and act on the range of information and choices available to them. Habit cannot control actions as much as previously and people must create their own biographies, an activity highly focused on shaping the kind of body which displays the individual as healthy, sexy and in control (Beck *et al.* 1994). Yet mass wastage of human life is arguably the other side of these processes. In order for the privileged to consume in safety, workers in marginalized countries are exploited, the environment is degraded, borders are strictly guarded against refugees and wars are fought over resources like oil (Bauman 2000, 2003). Bodies are controlled, but also try to exercise control.

Body maintenance and body modification (such as tattooing or cosmetic surgery) are practised by increasing numbers of people (Lemert and Elliott 2006), but not everyone conforms to current body ideals. On the one hand, technology is making us into cyborgs – human/machine composites with pacemakers, fake breasts or performance-enhancing running shoes (Haraway 1985). On the other hand, experiences of pain and dysfunction (Bendelow and Williams 1995, Braidotti 2001, Scarry 1985) and trends like the rise in obesity remind us of the often undisciplined nature of bodies. Such trends also raise questions about the extent to which body-consciousness is as obsessive a concern as has been implied (Crossley 2004). Much thinking has attended to problematic aspects of embodiment rather than to how people may feel in, about and through their bodies in mundane circumstances (Leder 1990).

More work on emotions is needed to do justice to the current complex intersections between bodily experience and social constraints. A major step in going beyond mind–body dualism and its privileging of cognitive reasoning is to consider how embodiment is felt, not just via sight, sound, smell and touch, but via emotions. Our embodied sense of self is highly emotional (Burkitt 1997, Lupton 1998), but most social theory of the body struggles to analyse the complex experiences of pleasure, boredom and pain people go through in their everyday lives. How we feel in and about our bodies and the bodies of others is crucial in understanding the contemporary social world.

Conclusion

Western thinking has been heavily influenced by the Cartesian dualistic model of mind as a separate controller of the body. This became a key pillar of scientific and medical understandings of the body, dominant from the eighteenth century.

Everyday knowledge about and experience of bodies are now typically secondary to expert opinion. Many bodily processes are subjected to intense medical observation and technological procedures. A whole range of human experiences become medicalized, from birth and death to mental illness and sexuality. Many positive health outcomes may have resulted, but individuals are made responsible for their bodies according to expert classifications of 'normal'. Given that what is 'normal' has typically been defined in relation to the white, male, straight, able body, others have been disempowered by medicalization. Nevertheless, there are ways in which medicalization has been resisted and medicine itself has not been untouched by efforts to give more attention to social factors in shaping bodies.

Social theory has been foremost in thinking through how the social world affects our bodies. Three main threads in this thinking have been identified: a notion of bodies as repressed within 'civilized' societies, a conception of bodies as regulated by social structures and ideas and an approach which attends to the experiencing of bodies. Each has their strengths and weaknesses. The first gives a powerful explanation of how biology is important, but its demands are dealt with more strictly as society changes. Questions remain about whether society does 'say no' to bodies, or increasingly classifies them. The second thread has been enormously fruitful in making sense of that classification and its implications for the control of populations and of various marginal groups within those populations. Yet, it has tended to render bodies as overly passive objects of regulation. The third, broadly phenomenological, approach has been important in trying to appreciate the active embodiment of individuals, albeit seeing body-subjects as absolutely social. The richness of bodily experience is still often lost in these explanations.

Recent social theory of the body both makes use of and tries to develop existing approaches in order to better understand our everyday embodied lives. The messy and unregulated aspects of bodies have been attended to particularly in work on ageing, pain, death and dying. It may be a body-obsessed social world, but not everyone is willing or able to conform to social ideals. There are horrendous inequalities worldwide between the fleshily comfortable and those starved and scratching out life. Bodily experiences combine thought, action and feeling in ways related to, but not entirely determined by different physical and social environments. What all social theorists continue to offer is a way to understand different embodied lives, not as 'natural' outcomes related to biological 'facts', but as products of a social world which human beings have created. The advantages of recognizing the social shaping of bodies is that change can be both understood and enabled.

REFERENCES

Ariès, P. (1983) *The Hour of Our Death*, trans. by H. Weaver, Harmondsworth: Penguin.
Bauman, Z. (2000) *Liquid Modernity*, Cambridge: Polity.
—— (2003) *Wasted Lives: Modernity and Its Outcasts*, Cambridge: Polity.

Beasley, C. (2005) *Gender and Sexuality: Critical Theories, Critical Thinkers*, London: Sage.

Black, P. (2004) *The Beauty Industry: Gender, Culture, Pleasure*, London: Routledge.

Blaikie, A., Hepworth, M., Holmes, M., Howson, A. and Inglis, D. (2003) 'The sociology of the body: genesis, development and futures', in A. Blaikie, M. Hepworth, M. Holmes, A. Howson, D. Inglis and S. Sartain (eds), *The Body: Critical Concepts in Sociology*, London: Routledge.

Beauvoir, S. de (1989) [1949] *The Second Sex*, New York: Vintage.

Beck, U., Giddens, A. and Lash, S. (1994) *Reflexive Modernisation: Politics, Tradition and Aesthetics in the Modern Social Order*, Cambridge: Polity.

Bendelow G. and Williams S. (1995) 'Pain and mind–body dualism: a sociological approach', *Body and Society*, 1(2), 83–103.

Bordo, S. (1987) 'The Cartesian masculinization of thought', in S. Harding and J. O'Barr (eds), *Sex and Scientific Inquiry*, Chicago: University of Chicago Press.

—— (1993) *Unbearable Weight: Feminism, Western Culture and the Body*, Berkeley, CA: University of California Press.

Bourdieu, P. (1987) *Distinction: A Social Critique of the Judgement of Taste*, Cambridge, MA: Harvard University Press.

—— (1990) [1987] *In Other Words: Essays Toward a Reflective Sociology*, Stanford, CA: Stanford University Press.

Braidotti, R. (2001) *Metamorphoses: Towards a Materialist Theory of Becoming*, Cambridge: Polity.

Burkitt, I. (1997) 'Social relationships and emotions', *Sociology*, 31(1): 37–55.

Connell, R.W. (1995) *Masculinities*, Sydney: Allen & Unwin.

Crossley N. (2004) 'Fat is a sociological issue: obesity rates in late modern "body-conscious" societies', *Social Theory & Health*, 2(3): 222–53.

Davis, K. (2002) '"A dubious equality": men, women and cosmetic surgery', *Body and Society*, 8(1): 49–65.

Elias, N. (1985) *The Loneliness of the Dying*, Oxford: Basil Blackwell.

—— (2000) [1939] *The Civilizing Process: Sociogenetic and Psychogenetic Investigations*, Oxford: Blackwell.

Ellis, H. (1898–1928) *Studies in the Psychology of Sex*, 7 Vols, Philadelphia, PA: F.A. Davis.

Engels, F. (1958) [1845] *The Condition of the Working Class in England*, Stanford, CA: Stanford University Press.

Featherstone, M. (1991) 'The body in consumer culture', in M. Featherstone, M. Hepworth and B. Turner (eds), *The Body: Social Process and Cultural Theory*, London: Sage.

Featherstone, M., Hepworth, H. and Turner, B. (eds) (1991) *The Body: Social Process and Cultural Theory*, London: Sage.

Flory, J., Young-Xu, Y., Gurol, I., Levinsky, N., Ash, A. and Emanuel, E. (2004) 'Place of death: US trends since 1980', *Health Affairs*, 23(3): 194–200.

Foucault, M. (1967) [1961] *Madness and Civilization: A History of Insanity in the Age of Reason*, trans. by R. Howard, London: Tavistock.

—— (1973) [1963] *The Birth of the Clinic: An Archeology of Medical Perception*, trans. by A.M. Sheridan, London: Tavistock.

—— (1979) [1975] *Discipline and Punish: The Birth of the Prison*, trans. by A.S. Smith, Harmondsworth: Penguin.

—— (1990) [1976] *The History of Sexuality: Vol. 1. An Introduction*, trans. by R. Hurley, London: Penguin.

Freud, S. (1961) [1930] *Civilization and Its Discontents*, trans. by J. Strachey, New York: W.W. Norton.

Goffman, E. (1968) [1963] *Stigma: Notes on the Management of Spoiled Identity*, Harmondsworth: Penguin.

—— (1979) *Gender Advertisements*, Basingstoke: Macmillan.

—— (1987) [1959] *The Presentation of Self in Everyday Life*, Harmondsworth: Penguin.

Haraway D.J. (1985) 'A manifesto for cyborgs: science, technology and socialist feminism', *Socialist Review*, 80: 65–108.

Hepworth, M. (1995) 'Positive ageing: what is the message?', in R. Bunton, S. Nettleton and R. Burrows (eds), *The Sociology of Health Promotion: Critical Analyses of Consumption, Lifestyle and Risk*, London: Routledge, pp. 176–90.

Holmes, M. (2007) *What is Gender? Sociological Approaches*, London: Sage.

Howson, A. (2001) '"Watching you – watching me": visualising techniques and the cervix', *Women's Studies International Forum*, 24(1): 97–109.

—— (2004) *The Body in Society: An Introduction*, Cambridge: Polity.

—— (2005) *Embodying Gender*, London: Sage.

Howson, A. and Inglis, D. (2001) 'The body in sociology: tensions inside and outside sociological thought', *Sociological Review*, 49: 297–317.

Illich, I. (1976) *Medical Nemesis: The Expropriation of Health*, Harmondsworth: Penguin.

Kasulis T.P., Ames, R.T. and Dissanayake, W. (eds) (1993) *Self as Body in Asian Theory and Practice*, New York: State University of New York Press.

Kessler, S.J. and McKenna, W. (1985) [1978] *Gender: An Ethnomethodological Approach*, Chicago: University of Chicago Press.

King, M., Smith, G. and Bartlett, A. (2004) 'Treatments of homosexuality since the 1950s – an oral history: the experience of professionals', *British Medical Journal*, 328, 429, doi: 10.1136/bmj.37984.496725.EE, accessed at BMJ.com on 13 July 2009.

Kraft-Ebing, R. (1951) [1886] *Psychopathia Sexualis English*, London: Staples Press.

Laqueur, T. (1990) *Making Sex: Body and Gender from the Greeks to Freud*, Cambridge, MA: Harvard University Press.

Lawton J. (1998) 'Contemporary hospice care: the sequestration of the unbounded body and "dirty dying"', *Sociology of Health and Illness*, 20(2): 121–43.

Leder, D. (1990) *The Absent Body*, Chicago: University of Chicago Press.

Lemert, C. and Elliott, A. (2006) *The New Individualism: The Emotional Costs of Globalization*, London: Routledge.

Lloyd, G. (1984) *The Man of Reason: 'Male' and 'Female' in Western Philosophy*, Minneapolis: University of Minnesota Press.

Lupton, D. (1998) *The Emotional Self: A Sociocultural Exploration*, London: Sage.

MacDonald, H.P. (2005) *Human Remains: Episodes in Human Dissection*, Carlton, VIC: Melbourne University Press.

Mauss, M. (1973) 'Techniques of the body', *Economy and Society*, 2(1): 70–88.

Mead, G.H. (1962) *Mind, Self, and Society: From the Standpoint of a Social Behaviourist*, Chicago: University of Chicago Press.

Merleau-Ponty, M. (2001) [1962] *Phenomenology of Perception*, trans. by C. Smith, London: Sage.

Millet, K. (1972) [1970] *Sexual Politics*, London: Abacus.

Morgan, D. (1993) 'You too can have a body like mine: reflections on the male body and masculinities', in S. Scott and D. Morgan (eds), *Body Matters: Essays on the Sociology of the Body*, London: Falmer.

Mort, F. (1988) '"Boys" own? Masculinity, style and popular culture', in R. Rutherford and J. Chapman (eds), *Male Order: Unwrapping Masculinity*, London: Lawrence & Wishart.

Oakley, A. (1980) *Women Confined: Towards a Sociology of Childbirth*, Oxford: Martin Robertson.

Office for National Statistics (2008) *Mortality Statistics: Deaths Registered in 2006 (DR-06)*, Newport: ONS. Available at http://www.statistics.gov.uk/statbase/Product.asp?vlnk=15096 (accessed 13 July 2009).

Oliver, M. (1996) *Understanding Disability*, London: Macmillan.

Pateman, C. (1988) *The Sexual Contract*, Stanford, CA: Stanford University Press.

—— (1989) *The Disorder of Women: Democracy, Feminism and Political Theory*, Cambridge: Polity Press.

Probyn, E. (2000) 'Sporting bodies: dynamics of shame and pride', *Body and Society*, 6(1): 13–28.

Scarry, E. (1985) *The Body in Pain: The Making and the Unmaking of the World*, Oxford: Oxford University Press.

Shilling, C. (1993) *The Body and Social Theory*, London: Sage.

Simmel, G. (1950) [1908] 'The metropolis and mental life', in K. Wolff (ed. and trans.), *The Sociology of Georg Simmel*, New York: Free Press, pp. 409–24.

Skeggs, B. (1997) *Formations of Class and Gender: Becoming Respectable*, London: Sage.

—— (2005) 'The making of class and gender through visualizing moral subject formation', *Sociology*, 39(5): 965–82.

Turner, B. (1984) *The Body in Society*, Oxford: Basil Blackwell.

Wacquant, L. (1995) 'Pugs at work: bodily capital and bodily labour among professional boxers', *Body and Society*, 1: 65–93.

Weber, M. (1968) [1921] *Economy and Society*, 3 vols, Totowa, NJ: Bedminster Press.

—— (1981) [1927] *General Economic History*, New Brunswick, NJ: Transaction.

Weeks, J. (1985) *Sexuality and Its Discontents*, London: Routledge.

Wilson, D.M., Northcott, H.C., Truman, C.D., Smith, S.L., Anderson, M.C., Fainsinger, R.L. and Stingl, M.J. (2001) 'Location of death in Canada', *Evaluation and the Health Professions*, 24(4): 385–403.

Wollstonecraft, M. (1985) [1792] *Vindication of the Rights of Woman*, Harmondsworth: Penguin.

Wouters, C. (2004) 'Changing regimes of manners and emotions: from disciplining to informalizing', in S. Loyal and S. Quilley (eds), *The Sociology of Norbert Elias*, Cambridge: Cambridge University Press, pp. 193–211.

Young, I.M. (1990) 'Throwing like a girl: a phenomenology of feminine body comportment, motility, and spatiality', in *Throwing Like a Girl and Other Essays in Feminist Philosophy and Social Theory*, Bloomington: Indiana University Press.

8

POSTMODERN SOCIAL THEORY

SAM HAN

Within the nebulous field of contemporary academic discourse, the once hotly-contested debates on 'the postmodern' have all but faded completely. For many, this is a good thing. As those who agree with this sentiment would have it, the debates surrounding 'the postmodern', '**postmodernism**' and 'postmodernity', though they provided some temporary excitement within intellectual circles, ended up confusing a lot more people than helping them to understand anything. For them, this is due to, among other things, the 'obtuse' writing-style of many authors and scholars with postmodern sympathies. And, indeed, for the adherents of the postmodern backlash, the eventual fizzling out of the postmodern wave was well overdue. Likewise, those who were not necessarily stalwart defenders of the postmodern, but had believed there to be something substantive in its philosophy, have equally shied away from the concept. It is very difficult to find, among theorists today, those who would welcome the label of 'postmodernist'.

Nevertheless, the fact that 'postmodernism' no longer pops up as a keyword within journal articles does not mean that its conceptual and political challenges to various disciplines have been wiped clean away. In fact, it can be argued that they have spread unnoticed throughout so many disciplinary traditions that they have now become normalized. For example, the skepticism towards a Universal Truth, an idea associated with postmodernism mostly due to philosopher Jean-François **Lyotard**'s *The Postmodern Condition* (1984), is readily discussed in a positive light among intellectuals who would not, for the life of them, consider themselves to be postmodern. Hence, this 'decline' may be the worst nightmare of the anti-postmoderns; for, despite their disdain, postmodernism has leaked through the crevices of the disciplines and, undoubtedly, also social theory.

In this chapter, I will use 'the postmodern' to encompass 'postmodernism' as well as 'postmodernity'. By using the generalized category, my aim is to draw attention to the variety of ways in which 'postmodern' is tagged onto numerous phenomena and, ultimately, to clarify a clearly baffling topic for many. To do so, it will be important to take seriously one of the ideas most readily attributed to postmodern thought – the attention to language and **discourse**. This is especially daunting today as the word 'postmodern' creeps up every now and then outside of scholarly literature, usually misused horribly by the author. In mainstream public discourse in the United States, the label 'postmodern' continues to be the favorite adjective to tack onto anything considered intellectually 'fuzzy'. Recently, it has even been deployed in the press coverage of the US presidential elections to describe Barack Obama. Jonah Goldberg in an op-ed for the national daily *USA Today* wrote:

> The Obama campaign has a postmodern feel to it because more than anything else, it seems to be about itself. Its relationship to reality is almost theoretical. Sure, the campaign has policy proposals, but they are props to advance the narrative of a grand movement existing in order to be a movement galvanized around the singular ideal of movement-ness. Obama's followers are . . . hooked on a feeling. 'We are the ones we have been waiting for!' Well, of course you are.
>
> (Goldberg 2008)

We can see from Goldberg's rather caustic characterization of the postmodern that it remains an empty signifier for self-referentiality ('a grand movement centered around movement') and overt theoretical interest ('reality is almost theoretical'). The intended image of the postmodern is clear for writers like Goldberg and others. It is a catch-all for those who are considered not only 'out-there' but unserious. And, by attaching this term to then candidate Obama, the conservative Goldberg was certainly trying to paint him in a negative light. It is this kind of silly mistake which we want to avoid.

So where did 'postmodern' come from and what does it have to do with social theory? Many scholars suggest that the term 'postmodern' began in the arts (painting specifically), then moved to the realm of architecture and finally blossomed in full force in high literary theory, through which it finally found its way into the mainstream public discourse in the 1980s. As a result, some of the best works dealing with the postmodern have been written by literary theorists and art historians. Perhaps the most significant and best known among them is Fredric **Jameson**, a literary theorist by training, who has written on numerous topics including **Marxism**, **structuralism** and science fiction. He argues that postmodernism is the cultural reflection of a certain mode of capitalism, which he describes, following Ernest Mandel, as 'late-capitalism'. In his widely-read essay, 'Postmodernism, or the cultural logic of late capitalism,' Jameson outlines a historical **aesthetic** analysis (using a method he calls 'periodization') of the postmodern, rooted in his very unorthodox Marxism.

> The case for its [postmodernism's] existence depends on the hypothesis of some radical break or *coupure*, generally traced back to the end of the 1950s or the early 1960s.
>
> As the word itself suggests, this break is most often related to notions of the waning or extinction of the hundred-year-old modern movement (or to its ideological or aesthetic repudiation). Thus, abstract expressionism in painting, existentialism in philosophy, the final forms of representation in the novel, the films of the great

auteurs, or the modernist school of poetry (as institutionalized and canonized in the works of Wallace Stevens): all these are now seen as the final, extraordinary flowering of a high modernist impulse which is spent and exhausted with them.

(Jameson 1984: 53)

However, postmodernism's impact on social theory, it is believed, was considerably later, and, for the most part, minimal, although it is interesting that Lyotard cites *sociology* as the originator of the term in his famous study (1984: xxiii). Even if he were inaccurate, the question – what is postmodern social theory? – is still a significant one, especially since many studies of the postmodern have only minimally considered the impact of the postmodern on social theory.

One of the recurring themes in the debates on the postmodern, and consequently in this chapter, is that of crisis. 'Postmodern', for many, indicated not only a transformation but a crisis in the values, culture and aesthetics of the modern. This crisis was sometimes articulated as 'the end' of modern life. The Italian philosopher and theologian, Gianni Vattimo, for instance, authored a book called *The End of Modernity* (1991). To approach the question of 'crisis' and 'end' and to figure out what exactly the 'postmodern' means in postmodern social theory, it will be helpful to view just the phrase 'postmodern social theory'. It can be taken to have two meanings. The first is to believe that postmodern social theory is, in effect, postmodern*ist* social theory. That is to say, within this interpretation, postmodern is a modifier that entails a certain theoretical or philosophical disposition, what I will call throughout this chapter the 'positional' approach. The second view would be to see the 'postmodern' in 'postmodern social theory' as a conditional modifier, one which stems from a socio-historical epoch known as 'postmodernity'. This approach is what I will call the 'historicist' approach, and it is favored by mostly post-Marxist theorists, such as Jameson, but also by geographer David Harvey, whose book *The Conditions of Postmodernity* (1994) takes into consideration changes in the global financial system to produce the social condition of 'postmodernity'. In turn, it is the aim of this chapter to investigate what I earlier referred to as the permeation of 'the postmodern' in social theory, by looking closely at various thinkers, including Jameson but also Jean-François Lyotard, Jürgen **Habermas**, Richard Rorty and Jean **Baudrillard**, who have weighed on the postmodern and exemplify these two approaches.

There is absolutely no guarantee that the reader will come out with the feeling of understanding postmodern social theory *in toto* because, in a sense, 'the postmodern' is, among other things, about smashing totalities. However, what this chapter does attempt to do is to provide the reader with some basic co-ordinates to navigate the murky waters by reading a debate on, not simply accounts of, the postmodern. What reading the debate closely will, hopefully, achieve is not only an explication of the concepts surrounding the postmodern but also what is *at stake*.

THE CRISIS OF CAPITALISM: FREDRIC JAMESON

Jameson utilizes the figure of 'the end' and 'crisis' in his analysis of contemporary culture and capitalism. Beginning with his explosive article on postmodernism that appeared in the *New Left Review* in 1984, and his subsequent book based on the article, he has emerged as perhaps the most learned voice in the 'historicist' approach to the study of the postmodern. There are many reasons for this, but most significant is his allegiance to a certain brand of unorthodox Marxism and his knack for cultural analysis.

Postmodernism, according to Jameson, is the end to the divide between aesthetic production and commodity production which, in turn, is a signal for a new brand of capitalism.

> The frantic economic urgency of producing fresh waves of ever more novel-seeming goods (from clothing to airplanes), at ever greater rates of turnover, now assigns an increasingly essential structural function and position to aesthetic innovation and experimentation.
>
> (Jameson 1984: 56)

Capitalism, long believed by Marxists and neoclassical economists alike to be a fundamentally economic phenomenon requires, for Jameson, not only a cultural aspect but essentially works *through* culture. Yet, as he readily acknowledges, the fact that capitalism requires an ideological component ('superstructure') has long been a vital component of Marxist theory. However, Jameson's argument cannot simply be labeled a rearticulation of Marx's or even **Gramsci**'s conceptions of 'ideology' because Jameson believes there to be a fundamental transformation in the workings of capitalism, effecting a new society as a whole. Hence, he acknowledges some intellectual affinity with the writings of Daniel Bell, the sociologist responsible for the term 'post-industrial society'.

> [I]ndeed, theories of the postmodern – whether celebratory or couched in the language of moral revulsion and denunciation – bear a strong family resemblance to all those more ambitious sociological generalizations which, at much the same time, bring us the news of the arrival and inauguration of a whole new type of society, most famously baptized 'post-industrial society' (Daniel Bell), but often also designated consumer society, media society, information society, electronic society or 'high tech', and the like. Such theories have the obvious ideological mission of demonstrating, to their own relief, that the new social formation in question no longer obeys the laws of classical capitalism, namely the primacy of industrial production and the omnipresence of class struggle. The Marxist tradition has therefore resisted them with vehemence, with the signal exception of the economist Ernest Mandel, whose book *Late*

Capitalism sets out not merely to anatomize the historic originality of this new society (which he sees as a third stage or moment in the evolution of capital), but also to demonstrate that it is, if anything, a *purer* stage of capitalism than any of the moments that preceded it.

(Jameson 1984: 55)

Jameson therefore utilizes postmodernism as an intervention within Marxist theory, to haul it into crisis. It has too long either simply ignored aesthetics or seen it as secondary in importance. This intra-Marxist mission of Jameson's is reflected also in the Marxist theorists from whom he draws – Theodor **Adorno** and Herbert **Marcuse**. Culture, or more specifically *aesthetics*, is not a mirror of capitalism, but an essential component. It is this analytical centrality of aesthetics in the analysis of capitalism that differentiates Jameson's 'postmodern' from other approaches that will be considered below.

One aspect of postmodernism is the blurring of the boundaries between high and 'mass' culture. Mass culture is, of course, one of the major concepts utilized not only by Adorno and **Horkheimer** in the famous chapter on 'the culture industry' in The *Dialectic of the Enlightenment* (2002), but also in Marcuse's *One Dimensional Man* (1964). This 'effacement of boundaries' can be seen, argues Jameson, in the rising interest in:

the whole landscape of advertising and motels, of the Las Vegas strip, of the late show and Grade-B Hollywood film, of so-called paraliterature with its airport paperback categories of the gothic and the romance, the popular biography, the murder mystery and the science fiction or fantasy novel. They no longer 'quote' such 'texts' as a Joyce might have done, or a Mahler; they incorporate them, to the point where the line between high art and commercial forms seems increasingly difficult to draw.

(Jameson 1998: 112)

Here, Jameson identifies a crisis in not only capitalism, but in the space of art and literature, which in the classical-modernist mode was 'oppositional'.

It emerged with the business society of the gilded age as scandalous and offensive to the middle-class public – ugly, dissonant, bohemian, sexually shocking. It was something to make fun of (when the police were not called in to seize the books or close the exhibitions): an offense to good taste and to common sense, or, as Freud and Marcuse would have put it, a provocative challenge to the reigning reality – and performance-principles of the early 20th-century middle class society.

(Jameson 1998: 124)

Whereas the high modernism of Joyce or Mahler preserved a somewhat autonomous and critical space, removed from the mundane, humdrum of mass or popular culture, figures like Andy Warhol in the visual arts and Robert Venture in architecture not only incorporated it in their work but championed it. Jameson's critique of postmodernism is political – in short, whereas high-modernist culture used to be resistant, it is now wholly subsumed and normalized by bourgeois, capitalist society.

> Not only are Joyce and Picasso no longer weird and repulsive, they have become classics and now look rather realistic to us. Meanwhile, there is very little in either the form or the content of contemporary art that the contemporary society finds intolerable and scandalous. The most offensive forms of this art – punk rock, say, or what is called sexually explicit material – are all taken in stride by society, and they are commercially successful, unlike the productions of the older high modernism ... [C]ommodity production and in particular our clothing, furniture, buildings and other artifacts are now intimately tied in with styling changes which derive from artistic experimentation; our advertising, for example, is fed by postmodernism in all the arts and inconceivable without it.
>
> (Jameson 1998: 124)

Thus, Jameson suggests that not only have changes in middle-class tastes rendered art and literature devoid of political opposition (an argument which Slovenian philosopher Slavoj Žižek has rightly identified as an updated form of Marx's 'commodification') but that postmodernism *needs* commercial art for its existence. Commodity production and artistic production are no longer distinguishable in this sense. It is this sort of 'aesthetic populism' of postmodernism that Jameson believes to be representative of a larger dynamic in the evolution of capitalism. Ultimately, the postmodern in postmodern social theory, according to Jameson, is a 'periodizing concept, whose function is to correlate the emergence of new formal features in culture with the emergence of a new type of social life and a new economic order' (Jameson 1998: 113).

THE CRISIS OF KNOWLEDGE: JEAN-FRANÇOIS LYOTARD

One of the most well-known postmodern pronouncements is Lyotard's oft-quoted definition of the postmodern 'as incredulity toward metanarratives' (Jameson 1998: xxiv). Many sympathetic and unsympathetic interpreters of Lyotard have attributed to him what has widely been cited as the **epistemological** grounding of postmodern theory. Yet, as is the case with many things associated with the postmodern, this interpretation has been riddled with misreading. One of the points of confusion has come from Lyotard's work, especially *The Postmodern Condition*, being read as the explication of an intellectual stance, that is, as a postmodern*ist* stance. Though, indeed, Lyotard's own words do have something to do with that, it is not necessarily a fair reading of him since it is not his purpose to argue for a sharp break between the modern and postmodern because, in part, he suggests that the break was already taking place when he was writing in the 1970s.

In giving his report on knowledge, Lyotard outlines which modern tenets he believes to be in critical condition.

I will use the term *modern* to designate any science that legitimates itself with reference to a metadiscourse of this kind making an explicit appeal to some grand narrative, such as the dialectics of Spirit, the hermeneutics of meaning, the emancipation of the rational or working subject, or the creation of wealth. For example, the rule of consensus between the sender and addressee of a statement with truth-value is deemed acceptable if it is cast in terms of a possible unanimity between rational minds: this is the Enlightenment narrative, in which the hero of knowledge works toward a good ethico-political end – universal peace. As can be seen from this example, if a metanarrative implying a philosophy of history is used to legitimate knowledge, questions are raised concerning the validity of the institutions governing the social bond: these must be legitimated as well. Thus justice is consigned to the grand narrative in the same way as truth.

(Jameson 1998: xxiii)

In this paragraph, which precedes the famous declaration of incredulity, Lyotard compiles a list of what he believes to be modern tenets. It is not full of esoteric, strictly philosophical concerns but, rather, the intellectual grounds of modern culture. Indeed, one of the main objects of critique is the process of the legitimation of knowledge itself, which Fredric Jameson notes in his foreword to the English translation is a direct critique of German social theorist Jürgen Habermas. Lyotard asks how the truth-value of any statement is evaluated, believing there to be a metaphysical undergirding – the real significance of the term 'metanarrative' – at work. This he calls the 'rule of consensus,' which relies on the meeting of rational minds. This 'rule of consensus' is nothing other than the law of equivalence that constitutes the conditions of possibility for modern grand narratives, such as 'truth' and 'justice,' to list just two that Lyotard mentions. And, importantly for our purposes, Lyotard brings his critique of legitimate knowledge to the level of the social bond, specifically institutions, which he identifies as the legislators of legitimacy in the realm of knowledge. This 'regime' of legitimate knowledge, Lyotard puts under the heading of 'narrative'.

The crisis of the modern is the crisis of narrative. So what is happening to narrative? 'The narrative function,' he writes, 'is losing its functors, its great hero, its great dangers, its great voyages, its great goal. It is being dispersed in clouds of narrative language elements – narrative, but also denotative, prescriptive, descriptive, and so on'. And the social bond?

> Thus the society of the future falls less within the province of a Newtonian anthropology (such as structuralism or systems theory) than a pragmatics of language particles. There are many different language games – a heterogeneity of elements. They only give rise to institutions in patches – local determinism.
>
> (Jameson 1998: xxiv)

While the epistemological critiques of Lyotard have been well commented upon, Lyotard's explicit references and commentary on the 'social bond' have not yet been analyzed to the same extent. This section will connect Lyotard's epistemology to his social theory.

One recurring theme within the scholarly treatment of the postmodern has been the turn to language (sometimes called 'the linguistic turn'), regarding which many analysts have rightly pointed to the work of Ludwig Wittgenstein, the Austrian philosopher, who was one of the first analytic philosophers to look at ordinary language or language in-use. On this point, Lyotard falls in line. Undoubtedly, his references to 'language games' and 'language particles' are direct borrowings from Wittgenstein and it is true that he is one of Lyotard's lasting influences. However, Lyotard does not simply reiterate Wittgenstein's philosophy of ordinary language but extracts from him a critique of consensus in increasingly 'computerized' societies, which is parallel to the kind of methodological move Wittgenstein made in analytic philosophy, which was to look at aspects of everyday life, not solely metaphysics.

According to Lyotard, the status of knowledge has been shifting since the immediate post-Second World War years, during which Western societies experienced a shift from industrial to post-industrial societies. Additionally, this socioeconomic shift also marked a parallel shift, which he describes as the transition to the postmodern age; thus, for Lyotard, industrial to post-industrial in the socioeconomic roughly correlates to the modern and post-modern in the cultural realm. One of the clearest of indications of the shift to post-industrial society is the increased penetration of media technologies throughout various sectors of society. 'The nature of knowledge cannot survive unchanged within this context of general transformation,' Lyotard argues. The epistemological result of the 'computerization of societies' is the dominance of scientific knowledge, which for Lyotard has an instrumental quality. In other words, scientific knowledge exists in information commodities, thereby undermining any sense of knowledge as an end in itself. One of the main products of the Enlightenment was the pursuit of knowledge for the sake of knowledge, which Immanuel Kant captured in his famous dictum: 'Dare to know'. To be sure, Kant had no small part in the hegemony of 'scientific objectivity', but the kind of power which scientific knowledge has maintained since the nineteenth century has been supported by technology. In other words, the progressive accumulative aspect of science (that it continually builds, gets better and more accurate) has been mostly unchallenged, thus eliding the question of legitimation. In point of fact, Lyotard is suggesting that scientific knowledge is a discourse, involved in language games, not simply truth-incarnate.

The question of the legitimacy of science has been indissociably linked to that of the legitimation of the legislator since the time of Plato. From this point of view, the right to decide what is true is not independent of the right to decide what is just, even if the statements consigned to these two authorities differ in nature. The point is that there is a strict interlinkage between the kind of language called 'science' and the kind called 'ethics and politics': they both stem from the same perspective, the same 'choice' if you will – the choice called 'the Occident' . . . revealing that knowledge and power are simply two sides of the same question (Jameson 1998: 8).

Lyotard's 'outing' of scientific legitimacy as a largely Eurocentric enterprise brings together the two seemingly separate issues – knowledge and government, which resonates with Michel Foucault's concept of power/knowledge. Ultimately, the point he is trying to make is that truth, which under the modern regime of knowledge, is agreed upon and thus universal, can only be uttered through what Wittgenstein calls a 'language game'. More simply, that all statements or 'utterances' are

> defined in terms of rules specifying their properties and the uses to which they can be put – in exactly the same way as the game of chess is defined by a set of rules determining the properties of each of the pieces, in other words, the proper way to move them.
>
> (Jameson 1998: 10)

By suggesting that science participates in a language game, Lyotard challenges the accepted wisdom of science and, in turn, knowledge, as merely a 'mirror of nature,' a phrase Richard Rorty uses in his well-known book *Philosophy and the Mirror of Nature*.

> Understood in this way, knowledge is what makes someone capable of forming 'good' denotative utterances, but also 'good' prescriptive and 'good' evaluative utterances. . . . It is not a competence relative to a particular class of statements (for example, cognitive ones) to the exclusion of all others.
>
> (Jameson 1998: 18)

But, in addition to scientific knowledge, Lyotard also notes that there is still a complementary knowledge that exists alongside it – narrative knowledge. Narrative knowledge takes shape in customs, as customs are another type of knowledge – *savoir-faire* (know-how). Traditional or customary knowledge, what Émile Durkheim and Marcel Mauss may have once called culture or 'collective reality,' frequently comes in the form of narration. In traditional-narrative

SAM HAN

knowledge, authority comes from the narrator having heard the story themselves. It is assumed that the narratee will, in turn, be able to occupy the position of the narrator after he or she listens to the story. On the other hand, the 'pragmatics' of scientific knowledge differ drastically from those of customary knowledge based on narration. Scientific knowledge is based on the principles of referentiality and validity, which underlie what used to be called 'verification' in the nineteenth century and what is today called 'falsification'. Referentiality and validity ensure that the rules of engagement are followed, acting as the condition for entrance into the language game. Unlike customary knowledge, authority is not so easily transferred but is handed down through education training. But, in the increasingly computerized field of knowledge, science, also trapped by the logic of technology, is forced to lean on narration for legitimation. The dynamics of this appeal to narrative by science are based on the construction of a metasubject – humanity. In turn, this becomes the seedbed for the notion of progress, in which 'the people' become the subject of this progress. Hence, in the narrative of scientific progress, 'the name of the hero is the people, the sign of legitimacy is the people's consensus, and their mode of creating norms is deliberation' (Jameson 1998: 30) and the end is the emancipation of humanity.

In Lyotard's estimation, the compensatory appeal to narrative has been ultimately failing for science, and other grand narratives, since the Second World War due to the technologies that have become so prevalent. As Bernard Stiegler (1998) and others have argued, these technologies, especially digital technologies, are based on discontinuity; this makes it nearly impossible to achieve the mode of unification necessitated by any grand narrative. The emergence of new languages, such as machine languages, game theory, musical notation and non-destructive logic, bears no small burden of responsibility for this. What we have in the postmodern age is a plethora of 'little narratives' which no longer uphold the abstract subject of 'the people', as their hero nor do they hold the promise of emancipation. On the contrary, little narratives do not rely on consensus and unity.

Lyotard's views are in clear contrast to those of Jürgen Habermas, whose work privileges precisely the themes that Lyotard argues as modern, and thus on the decline–consensus and unity. This disagreement, however, is not simply a skirmish between two philosophers at the level of ideas. Their differences have consequences for social theory. One aspect of these differences is precisely on this point regarding unity. Lyotard argues that Habermas, who had been quite critical of another German social theorist Niklas Luhmann, has more in common with systems theory, of which Luhmann was a main proponent, than he would like to admit. Habermas's line of criticism leveled at Luhmann was that systems theory offered no place for emancipation – in short, that it lacked any kind of politics. But Lyotard levels a similar critique at Habermas's insistence on consensus to solve the crisis of legitimation.

It is easy to see what function this recourse plays in Habermas's argument against Luhmann. *Diskurs* is his ultimate weapon against the theory of the stable system. The cause is good, but the argument is not. Consensus has become an outmoded and suspect value. But justice as a value is neither outmoded nor suspect. We must thus arrive at an idea and practice of justice that is not linked to that of consensus (Jameson 1998: 66).

Diskurs, Habermas's word for the search for a universal consensus, troubles Lyotard on two grounds. First, universal consensus would mean that all the speakers must come to an agreement on the rules of engagement. According to Lyotard's reading of Wittgenstein, language games are heteromorphous. In other words, the rules are constantly changing. Second, Habermas assumes that the goal of language is consensus. Lyotard argues that consensus cannot be the end of the language but merely a state of language. Habermas's *Diskurs*, for Lyotard, functions to discourage dissent. If there were going to be consensus, it cannot reach for universality but rather locality.

THE CRISIS OF MODERN CULTURE: JÜRGEN HABERMAS

It would be unfair simply to read Habermas through Lyotard. Habermas has been one of the most ardent and reasoned critics of the postmodern. As a sociologist and philosopher in the tradition of the **Frankfurt School**, Habermas has maintained a certain hope in the project of Enlightenment. This has already been evidenced in the section on Lyotard, as Lyotard has accused him of inheriting the Enlightenment in an uncritical fashion. But this is not a point which Habermas would contest. His reading of modernity as 'an incomplete project' is one of his most well-known formulations on the subject (Habermas 1998: 3).

In his attempt to recover some aspects of the modern, Habermas delves more deeply than Lyotard into what 'modern' really means.

> With varying content the term 'modern' again and again expresses the consciousness of an epoch that relates itself to the past of antiquity, in order to view itself as the result of a transition from the old to the new.
>
> (Habermas 1998: 3)

There are different aspects to modernity – aesthetic, cultural and societal. The modern, as he says, was not a fixed ideal.

> The most recent modernism simply makes an abstract opposition between tradition and the present; and we are, in a way, still the contemporaries of that kind of aesthetic modernity which first appeared in the midst of the nineteenth century.
>
> (Habermas 1998: 4)

But this is not necessarily the case for all 'modernisms,' Habermas says. Each modernism has its own relation to the past and present. Aesthetic modernity, found in the work of Baudelaire as well as the Dadaists and surrealists, focused on a changed consciousness of time. The value was placed on 'the transitory, the elusive and ephemeral, [and] the very celebration of dynamism' (Habermas 1998: 5), which he interprets as the longing for an immaculate present. This rejection of the historical embodied by so many of the artists associated with aesthetic modernism is thus found in the theory of the modern put forth.

> Modernity revolts against the normalizing functions of tradition; modernity lives on the experience of rebelling against all that is normative. This revolt is one way to neutralize the standards of both morality and utility.
>
> (Habermas 1998: 5)

The waning of this aesthetic tradition is clear; but does this signal the end of modernity itself? There are certainly many that believe so. One whom Habermas mentions is American sociologist Daniel Bell, a neoconservative, who has suggested that the crisis of Western societies is one of cultural modernism. That is to say that the regulative and normative functions of culture have been infected with the surrealist rebellion of aesthetic modernism. 'Because of the forces of modernism, the principle of unlimited self-realization, the demand for authentic self-experience and the subjectivism of hyperstimulated sensitivity have come to be dominant' (Habermas 1998: 6), unleashing hedonism throughout society. The only way in which norms can be re-established, according to those like Bell, would be through a religious revival that restores faith in tradition, offering clearly defined individual identities.

While he does not agree with the politics of Bell, Habermas does see wisdom in Bell's thesis that there is a divergence between society and culture. As Habermas points out, this divergence has been a gradual process, beginning in the nineteenth century, which Max Weber had already noted. But, for Habermas, neoconservative thinkers like Bell too easily confuse cultural modernity and societal modernization.

The neoconservative doctrine blurs the relationship between the welcomed process of societal modernization on the one hand, and the lamented cultural development on the other. The neoconservative does not uncover the economic and social causes for the altered attitudes towards work, consumption, achievement and leisure. Consequently, he attributes all of the following – hedonism, the lack of social identification, the lack of obedience, narcissism, the withdrawal from status and achievement competition – to the domain of 'culture'. In fact, however, culture is intervening in the creation of all these problems in only a very indirect and mediated fashion (Habermas 1998: 7).

This distinction between Habermas's own position and the neoconservative position is mainly a methodological one, with a slight twist. It is merely a matter of where Habermas locates the root of the 'crisis' of modern values and modern life. Whereas, for Bell, it was the injection of aesthetic modernism into mainstream cultural life, for Habermas, it is the pressures of capitalism – the logic of economic growth and rationality – 'colonizing' the life-world, into every form of human existence. This, in Habermas's view, is an effect of societal modernization, not cultural modernism. Hence, we see in his critique of Daniel Bell not so much a political departure as an argumentative quibble. This is not to suggest that Habermas is in any way a neoconservative. Many who are Habermas scholars have already, and correctly in my estimation, labeled Habermas a liberal, though this fact is surely debatable.

But, in point of fact, Habermas too sees a crisis occurring in modern life, one in which he acknowledges the role of the intellectual heritage of the Enlightenment. Although he has been one of the Enlightenment's most noted defenders in recent times, he does so critically, in much the same way as his forebears of the critical theory tradition – Theodor Adorno and Max Horkheimer in their 1944 masterpiece *The Dialectic of the Enlightenment*. One of the ways in which Habermas upholds the Enlightenment tradition is through a rereading of the Weberian notion of rationalization.

The project of modernity, formulated in the eighteenth century by the philosophers of the Enlightenment, consisted in their efforts to develop objective science, universal morality and law and autonomous art according to their inner logic. At the same time, this project intended to release the cognitive potentials of each of these domains from their esoteric forms. The Enlightenment philosophers wanted to utilize this accumulation of specialized culture for the enrichment of everyday life – that is to say, for the rational organization of everyday social life (Habermas 1998: 9).

Habermas's definition of the project of modernity is characterized by an optimistic view of the rationalization of everyday life. Where it went wrong, Habermas says, is the point at which the rationalization process transforms into specialization, thereby separating itself from 'the hermeneutics of everyday communication' (Habermas 1998: 9).

The political question is, do we ultimately jettison the project of modernity or are there bits and pieces worth saving? This might be the critical point of difference between Lyotard and Habermas. Clearly, Habermas believes that the project of modernity, though it should be rationally criticized, should not be discarded altogether. Habermas leaves us an interesting an alternative:

> In sum, the project of modernity has not yet been fulfilled. . . . The project aims at a differentiated relinking of modern culture with an everyday praxis that still depends on vital heritages, but would be impoverished through mere traditionalism. This new connection, however, can only be established under the condition that societal modernization will also be steered in a different direction. The life-world has to become able to develop institutions out of itself which set limits to the internal dynamics and imperatives of an almost autonomous economic system and its administrative complements.

> (Habermas 1998: 13)

THE CRISIS OF THE UNIVERSAL: RICHARD RORTY AND
JEAN BAUDRILLARD

Thus far we have looked at various perspectives on the postmodern, some of which are clearly sympathetic (Lyotard) and some which are not (Habermas), while others defy such binaries (Jameson). But, no matter where the authors' sympathies lie, there is surely an identifiable recurrence of the thematic of crisis in the writings dealing with the postmodern. By looking at two additional figures, Richard Rorty and Jean Baudrillard, we continue with the theme of 'crisis' to track a crisis of the largest proportions – a crisis in the universal and of reality. The universal is one of the most fundamental precepts of modern life, in particular modern science. As Alfred North Whitehead argues in *Science and the Modern World* (1925), abstraction, which is the foundation for mathematics, necessitates a notion of the universal. 'Reality' is, indeed, the ultimate universal, since it is constantly used as a transcendent, overarching reference for all. That is to say, it is assumed that we all live in the *same* reality.

Richard Rorty lays out what he believes to be up for grabs in the debate between Habermas and Lyotard in a classic essay 'Habermas and Lyotard on Postmodernity' (1985). Though, at first glance, the disagreement is about metanarratives, according to Rorty, it is, more specifically, about the status of the universal. Even Habermas's largely sympathetic critics, he notes, accuse him of overreaching in his attempt to construct a universal in support of liberal politics. Hence, the French writers that Habermas criticizes are most skeptical of his idea of 'true consensus', which relies precisely on a universal agreement of the rules of conduct as well as what constitutes subjectivity. This is also an area of contention for Lyotard since the subject-formation entailed in Habermas's schema would undoubtedly be equated to the adoption of bourgeois values, within which Habermas believes emancipatory elements of the Enlightenment to remain.

For Rorty, the attempt to reclaim bourgeois ideals is Habermas's weakest defense of modernity. Bourgeois ideals, according to Habermas, are repositories for Reason that have not been corrupted by the technological knowledge of the system. Although interpreting Lyotard's misgivings about Habermas, Rorty asks a question that does not arise for Lyotard. Rorty sharply inquires: why not just be frankly ethnocentric? That is to say, what constitute bourgeois ideals are, in effect, the political norms of Western democracies. And, if it is the case that Habermas wishes to hold onto bourgeois ideals, then why not simply make the implicit ethnocentrism explicit?

Modern science will appear to be something which a certain group of human beings invented, in the same sense in which these same people can be said to have invented Protestantism, parliamentary government and Romantic poetry. What Habermas calls the 'self-reflection of the sciences' will thus consist not in the attempt to 'ground' scientists' practices (for example, free exchange of information, normal problem-solving and revolutionary paradigm-creation) in something larger or broader, but rather of attempts to show how these practices link up with, or contrast with, other practices of the same group or of other groups (Rorty 1985: 166).

Continuing his evaluation of Lyotard's critique of Habermas's philosophy of science, Rorty highlights the significance of Lyotard's insistence that the 'aims and procedures of scientists and those of politicians' are fundamentally the same (Rorty 1985: 166). Habermas very much maintains some positive 'inner dynamic' to scientific knowledge which he believes aids humanity's trajectory towards emancipation. Today, we do not have scientific knowledge proper, Habermas would say, but rather technoscience, in which scientific knowledge is co-opted by the enslaving logic of technology, trapping human beings in an 'iron cage' that even Max Weber would have had trouble envisaging. Quite simply, Lyotard does not afford science this special privilege, whereas Habermas does. For Rorty, Habermas does so in the service of liberal politics. Without the conception of Progress through Reason, founded on the principle of 'universal consensus,' Habermas sees no grounds for his politics of emancipation. But, as a fellow liberal, Rorty ultimately believes Habermas's unbridled faith in Reason and universality to be misplaced.

So, if science or Reason cannot be seen as grounds for a universal, what about 'reality'? One of the most vehement critics of 'reality' is Jean Baudrillard, the French philosopher and social theorist, who famously declared the First Gulf War not to have taken place. (In fact, he did believe that it took place, but more through informational waves of radar and television than in physical reality.) While never declaring himself postmodern, Baudrillard was perhaps the chief figure whom critics of the postmodern would use as a straw man. There are several reasons for this, one of them being his rather unorthodox writing style, which in his later years began to resemble less and less North American conventions of 'scholarly' writing. Additionally, Baudrillard purposely utilizes hyperbole in order to make his point. Hence, many of his writings have been misused and poorly interpreted.

One of the ideas most closely associated with Baudrillard is that of the 'hyperreal'. It is perhaps one of his most famous ideas (though not necessarily most important in the grand scheme of philosophical writings) due to the purported claim by the Wachowski brothers, the writer-directors of *The Matrix* films that they were inspired by Baudrillard. In fact, Neo, the lead character portrayed by Keanu Reeves is, at one point, reading a copy of *Simulacra and Simulation* in the film. The hyperreal, Baudrillard explains, is an effect of the crisis in the exchange-relation between meaning and substance. Or, to put it in the terms of Whitehead, it is a fundamental change in the process of abstraction.

Abstraction today is no longer that of the map, the double, the mirror or the concept. Simulation is no longer that of a territory, a referential being or a substance. It is the generation by models of a real without origin or reality: a hyperreal. The territory no

longer precedes the map, nor survives it. Henceforth, it is the map that precedes the
territory – *precession of simulacra* – it is the map that engenders the territory . . . It
is the real, and not the map, whose vestiges subsist here and there . . . The desert of
the real itself.

(Baudrillard 1988: 166)

As it is usually understood, abstraction is a process by which there must be a
referent, an object, a thing. A map, in this instance, is an abstraction of the territory. But, according to Baudrillard, the map *precedes* the territory. That is to
say, there is no longer any privilege given to the origin because, as Baudrillard
alludes to in referring to 'generation by models,' of the computerized society in
which we all live. 'The real,' he writes, 'is produced from miniaturized units,
from matrices, memory banks, and command models – and with these it can be
reproduced an indefinite number of times' (Baudrillard 1988: 167). And, indeed,
a most notoriously famous illustration Baudrillard gives is that of Disneyland as
'the perfect mode of all the entangled orders of simulation'(Baudrillard 1988:
171). According to Baudrillard, one can find the 'objective profile of the United
States' throughout Disneyland:

All its values are exalted here, in miniature and comic-strip form. Embalmed and
pacified . . . Disneyland is presented as imaginary in order to make us believe that
the rest is real, when in fact all of Los Angeles and the America surrounding it are
no longer real, but of the order of the hyperreal and of simulation. It is no longer
a question of a false representation of reality (ideology), but of concealing the fact
that the real is no longer real, and thus of saving the reality principle.

(Baudrillard 1988: 171)

Here, in Baudrillard, we see an analysis of postmodernism which differs
slightly from Jameson. Whereas Jameson sees the cultural dominant of late-
capitalism in postmodernism, meaning that a certain type of aesthetic regime
dominates alongside a new form of capitalism, Baudrillard argues in a more
technologically materialist vein that reality itself, not simply capitalism, is
altered at its foundation. And yet there is some connection, which makes them
both historicist postmodern social theorists. Baudrillard, like Jameson, argues
that something has indeed changed; that is to say, there is a clear 'break' from
one mode of social life to another. In Baudrillard's words:

Something has changed, and the Faustian, Promethean (perhaps Oedipal) period of
production and consumption gives way to the 'proteinic' era of networks, to the
narcissistic and protean era of connections, contact, contiguity, feedback and generalized interface that goes with the universe of communication.

(Baudrillard 1998: 127)

Moreover, what distinguishes Baudrillard's work, along with Lyotard's, on the postmodern from that of others is his keen eye for the shifting landscape of media technologies. Though Jameson does, indeed, come close when mentioning aesthetics, there is no reckoning with the fundamental impact of new media technologies on modern life, which mostly saw technologies in an instrumental (in effect, anthropocentric) mode. It seems that, today, in the era of technomedia, in which the boundary between the virtual and the real are quickly vanishing (see Han 2007), Baudrillard and Lyotard seem not to be as delusional as they once did.

And finally, to conclude on the question of what is at stake in the debates on the postmodern, we should return to the theme of crisis. Despite the clear and abounding differences among Jameson, Lyotard, Habermas, Rorty and Baudrillard, there seems to be no disagreement on the existence of some fundamental transformation in the social order. Hence, one point is clear. Although sociologists such as Bell and Alain Touraine had pointed out an earlier major shift, suggesting that so-called liberal democracies in the West had moved into a stage of 'post-industrial society', it took the debates on the postmodern to bring the shift to the forefront. The crises of capitalism (Jameson), knowledge (Lyotard), modern culture (Habermas) and the universal (Rorty and Baudrillard), challenged social theory to rethink not only the tenets of modernity but also the implicit values of modern social theory since the 'founders' (Marx, Weber and Durkheim), namely, stability and order – two interlocking ideas that modern social theory took as given and good, which Jameson would potentially label as the 'political unconscious' of modern social theory.

If something has indeed ended or changed fundamentally, a premise with which even Habermas and Jameson seem to agree, then it is the task of social theory to take stock and reckon with it, just as the classical social theorists did when modernity was in its nascent stages. Though he so expertly defends the project of the Enlightenment and modernity, Habermas nevertheless acknowledges the *incomplete* nature of modernity, striking a rather unusual resonance with Bruno Latour, a sociologist who has frequently been lumped in with 'postmodernism' and author of a book entitled *We Have Never Been Modern*. If there is a 'lesson' to be learned from the debates on the postmodern, it must be the critical evaluation of what modernity attempted to portray as natural. It is this call to be radical, in the real sense of the term – to get to the root and, in turn, not to fear crisis but to think alongside it, which, I think, makes the postmodern a truly important moment in the history of social theory. Judging from the intellectual stagnation in the field of contemporary social theory, at least in the United States, it seems that it is one that more students of social theory must revisit.

REFERENCES

Baudrillard, Jean (1988) *Jean Baudrillard: Selected Writings*, Mark Poster (ed.), Stanford, CA: Stanford University Press.
—— (1998) 'Ecstasy of communication', in Hal Foster (ed.), *The Anti-Aesthetic: Essays on Postmodern Culture*, New York: The New Press.

Bell, Daniel (1973) *The Coming of Post-Industrial Society*, New York: Basic Books.

Foster, Hal (ed.) (1998) *The Anti-Aesthetic: Essays on Postmodern Culture*, New York: The New Press.

Goldberg, Jonah (2008) 'Obama, the postmodernist', *USA Today*, 5 August.

Habermas, Jürgen (1998) 'Modernity – an incomplete project', in Hal Foster (ed.), *The Anti-Aesthetic: Essays on Postmodern Culture*, New York: The New Press.

Han, Sam (2007) *Navigating Technomedia: Caught in the Web*, Lanham, MD: Rowman & Littlefield.

Jameson, Fredric (1984) 'Postmodernism, or the cultural logic of late capitalism', *New Left Review*, I/146, July–August.

Latour, Bruno (2008) *We Have Never been Modern*, Cambridge, MA: Harvard University Press.

Lyotard, Jean-François (1984) *The Postmodern Condition: A Report on Knowledge*, trans. by Geoffrey Bennington and Brian Massumi, Minneapolis: University of Minnesota Press.

Rorty, Richard (1979) *Philosophy and the Mirror of Nature*, Princeton, NJ: Princeton University Press.

—— (1985) 'Habermas and Lyotard on Postmodernity', in Richard J. Bernstein (ed.), *Habermas and Modernity*, Cambridge, MA: MIT Press.

Stiegler, B. (1998) [1994] *Technics and Time, 1: The Fault of Epimetheus*, trans. by George Collins and Richard Beardsworth, Stanford, CA: Stanford University Press.

Vattimo, Gianni (1991) *The End of Modernity: Nihilism and Hermeneutics in Postmodern Culture*, Baltimore, MD: Johns Hopkins University Press.

Whitehead, Alfred North (1925) *Science in the Modern World*, New York: Free Press.

9
IDENTITY AND SOCIAL THEORY

ANN BRANAMAN

Self, **identity**, and subjectivity are central topics in contemporary social theory.[1] In some respects, the relationship between self and society has been a core concern in social theory since the classical period of sociology: in Europe, the discipline's founders – **Marx, Durkheim, Weber**, and **Simmel** – analyzed the impact of the structures of modern societies on the subjective experience of individuals and, across the Atlantic, George Herbert **Mead** developed the idea of the 'social self' (1934). But, despite initial interest, the topic largely disappeared from sociology by the middle of the twentieth century. For most sociologists of that era, the self was uninteresting. It was non-existent to those influenced by behaviorism and schooled in its empirical rigors; it was the province of psychological reductionism to those entranced by disciplinary boundaries; it was the passively determined product of social institutions to both **functionalists** and, insofar as they were known to mainstream sociologists, dominant schools of Marxist thought. In the final decades of the twentieth century, though, issues of self, identity, agency, and subjective experience emerged as central topics of analysis and debate among social theorists (Elliott 2001). In a collection published in 1996, Stuart Hall referred to a 'veritable discourse explosion' around matters of identity (Hall and Du Gay 1996: 1), while a few years later Zygmunt **Bauman** (2001) commented that the explosion had triggered an avalanche.

This chapter will focus on two broad and overlapping areas of development within social theory: (a) analyses of and disagreements over the relationship between social change, self and identity, and (b) theoretical work on identity that developed from the confluence of **post-structuralist** critique and identity politics. Exploration of these two areas will frame many of the most important debates within contemporary social theory, and particularly critical social theory; additionally, it will allow the exploration of a broad range of influential social theorists and theoretical perspectives. Under the rubric of the first theme, this chapter will discuss one significant pathway to the current theoretical prominence of concepts of self, identity and subjectivity: classical social theorists' analyses of the relationship between modernity and subjective experience; early theorists such as **Marcuse** and **Fromm**, who integrated Marxian and Freudian theory to analyze the damaging and repressing psychological effects of twentieth century capitalist modernity; Foucault's influential work on the regulation of self, identity, and subjective experience as **modernity**'s primary strategy of social control; and theories of the impact of recent social change – variously designated as **postmodernity**, late modernity, advanced capitalism, detraditionalization and individualization, liquid modernity, neoliberalism, and/or globalization – on subjectivity, self and identity. Under the rubric of the second theme, the chapter will focus on a second significant pathway to the current theoretical prominence of the concept of identity: the 'new social movements' of race, class, gender and sexuality; their connection to **psychoanalytically**-oriented **feminist** and postcolonial theories of the subjective effects of identity-based structures of power and domination; poststructuralist critiques of and contributions to concepts of identity in this new body of critical social theory; emerging tensions between critical social theory of identity and some fundamental insights of post-structuralism; and an array of critical responses to those tensions.

Through these two themes, the chapter will explore some of the terrain that has been covered by the avalanche that Bauman described. Much of it, though, must await the excavation of others.

THE SELF AND SOCIAL CHANGE

Classical social theory

Self, identity, and subjectivity were central concerns of the classical sociologists Marx, Durkheim, Weber, and Simmel as they observed the social changes sweeping through European societies in the nineteenth century. Convinced that the emergent self in Western modernity was shaped by industrial capitalism (Burkitt 2008), they studied the subjective experience of individuals as a means of understanding macro-level social change. Additionally, though, they asked – with varying degrees of explicitness – whether these social changes advanced or hindered the development of the autonomous and rational self celebrated by Enlightenment thinkers.

Karl Marx (1978) analyzed how the organization of labor under capitalism alienated humans from themselves and others. He argued that lack of control over the means of production deprived people of the highest human fulfillment: the exercise of consciousness and will in one's labor and life in cooperation with others. In Marx's view, only a communal and democratic organization of society could realize the highest potential of the human species.

Self-identity and subjectivity were equally central for Émile Durkheim (1951, 1964, 1973). He argued that the complex division of labor in industrial capitalism broke down social solidarity and built up individuality: his concepts of 'anomie' and 'egoism' pointed to the deleterious social and personal consequences of the untrammeled self. While recognizing the excesses of modern individualism, Durkheim nevertheless defended the Enlightenment value of 'moral individualism,' arguing that shared commitment to human **rights** and dignity was the only possible basis of social solidarity in a society too complex to agree on anything more specific. To make individualism compatible with the necessary level of social solidarity, Durkheim envisioned it as tempered by adequate levels of social integration and social regulation: norms to guide and give meaning to people's lives; meaningful connections to other people.

Weber (1946, 1958) analyzed the effect of modernity on subjectivity largely through his analysis of the dehumanizing effects of bureaucracy and formal rationality. Although he acknowledged the negative implications of modern social structures for the self, he was far more interested in the impact of a distinctly modern cultural formation: a Western culture shaped by secularized Protestantism and its prescription of a rationalized life bound by relentless instrumentality. For Weber, the alienation produced by this 'iron cage' could only be overcome by asserting choice in and accepting responsibility for the shaping of one's own life. As Burkitt puts it in his discussion of Weber, '[s]elf-hood is therefore an idea to be attained, rather than a fact of modern life in Western bureaucratic capitalism' (Burkitt 2008).

Simmel (1971, 1978) analyzed some of the same cultural trends that intrigued Weber, asking how the conditions of modern, urban, and capitalist societies shaped the mental lives of individuals. Strangers exchanging money for goods and services were caught up in a profound cultural transformation: abstraction, depersonalization, instrumentality, calculation, and fungibility combined to create a new form of life in which all things could be bought and sold, reduced to a common denominator, and drained of distinctiveness. Under these circumstances, a new subjectivity emerged: the blasé cynicism that characterized the mental life of the metropolis. However, as Ritzer (2000) reminds us, Simmel also conceded the liberating possibilities of the money economy and the urban way of life. Both permitted people to escape the constraints of their social groups, limit their obligations to others, develop increasingly individuated selves, and pursue – insofar as they could acquire the material resources to do so – new ways of life and forms of pleasure.

Even though each of the classical sociologists analyzed the effects of modernity on subjectivity and self, they viewed these effects as entirely secondary and determined by social structures. Subjectivity and self were less intrinsically interesting than they were useful as a baseline measure of the adequacy of nascent modern institutions. By the mid-twentieth century, however, subjectivity and identity themselves became the primary focus of social theorists struggling to understand the direction of social change.

Marxist theory tempered by Freudian insight: the Frankfurt School

Marx predicted that heightened suffering and emergent class consciousness among the proletariat would produce a mass movement for economic change but, only a few decades into the twentieth century, Marxist theorists were forced to struggle with the failure of this prediction. One influential response to this theoretical challenge came from the so-called **Frankfurt School**. Its members adapted **Freudian** theory to offer a critical analysis of the repressive psychological effects of capitalist modernity, using psychodynamic theory to explain how human subjectivity had been suborned by capitalism in ways that reduced opposition to the status quo. Shifting away from the analysis of political economy and towards an analysis of culture and subjectivity, they argued that the social revolution envisioned by Marx required a radical liberation of human subjectivity as a precondition to any social movement for economic and political change (Kellner 1989a).

Because modern capitalism was able to dominate the modern self, that self was unable to experience the intrapsychic distress predicted by Marx; without intrapsychic distress, there was no impetus to invent a new world. **Horkheimer** referred to the 'end of the individual' (Horkheimer 1947), Marcuse to the 'one-dimensional man' (Marcuse 1964), Adorno to 'pseudo-individuality' (Adorno and Bernstein 2001), and Fromm to 'alienated consumption' (Fromm 1955) . Each critiqued the false reconciliation between capitalist society and the self, that was based on a new and prepossessing basis for identity: mass-produced consumer goods and commoditized leisure. For example, according to Adorno, the emergent culture industry helped to replace critical human consciousness with blind conformity to the status quo; it made prevailing social conditions seem like the 'good life' and offered a wide array of 'substitute gratifications' that lessened human suffering but ultimately cheated people of the best forms of gratification by causing them to lose sight of any alternative to the status quo. Similarly, Marcuse argued that the new social order of consumerism had swept away the intrapsychic conflict that Freud had observed and mistakenly believed to be eternal, resulting in what Marcuse called the 'one-dimensional man'. He argued that, without perceptible conflict between social and individual needs, humans lost the 'depth dimension' in their psyches and, with it, the motivation for social revolution. While none of the Frankfurt School theorists saw an easy route to reclaiming human subjectivity from its thrall to capitalism, Marcuse was cautiously optimistic that some segments of the population were not fully psychically integrated into the existing society, thereby still experiencing enough internal distress to prod them to question superficial happiness and seek genuine forms of fulfillment. In tiny pockets of human misery, he found hope for a better future.

Foucault and post-structuralism

Whereas the Frankfurt School theorists believed that intrapsychic conflict could awaken desire for 'true' happiness and freedom, the critique of core Enlightenment beliefs by Foucault and other post-structuralist theorists initiated a very different way of thinking about the self and its relationship to domination and liberation. Foucault and the Frankfurt School theorists had similarly critical orientations towards the institutions of modernity and the subtlety with which they drew upon self and subjectivity to produce mass conformity and social domination. They differed profoundly in their relationship to Enlightenment notions of reason, the rational subject, and freedom or liberation. Central to the philosophical orientation of most Frankfurt School theorists was a belief in Enlightenment values of reason and freedom, and a conviction that the human capacity to make sound judgements rationally (such as between 'true' and 'false' needs) was under siege. Underlying their critique was an abiding belief in core Enlightenment values and a hope – meager, but still alive – in the possibility of the yet-to-be-fulfilled Enlightenment project. Post-structuralist thinkers, including Foucault, challenged basic Enlightenment notions by making the following arguments: (a) reason is not absolute but is a product of discourse; (b) the 'rational subject' is a fiction *constituted* by discourse; and (c) liberation or freedom as abstract and totalizing values are meaningless. Most importantly for thinking about matters of self and identity, Foucault viewed the 'deep psychic interior' that Marcuse and others wished to liberate as not only constructed by discourse but itself a core instrument of modern social control.

In Foucault's studies of psychiatry, penology and other 'disciplinary technologies,' he argued that these institutions created deep selves as a means of control. The triumph of the process was a self devoted to its own observation and regulation in the interests of social standards of reason and righteousness (1965, 1977). For Foucault, self-scrutiny produced self-regulation, even when it appeared freely chosen and ostensibly rebelled against repression. Famously, in *The History of Sexuality*, Volume 1 (1978), he argued that the fiction of repressed impulses intensified self-monitoring and self-judgement and, ultimately, social control: the modern myth of the elusive 'true self' only deepened scrutiny of self and rendered the scrutinizer more susceptible to the pressures of prevailing normative standards. In the Foucauldian modern self, there is little possibility of meaningful challenge to a social order that has created this form of selfhood. The logic of the interrogation of the self – from 'who am I?' to 'am I looking deeply enough?' to 'how am I supposed to be?' – is, for Foucault, the logic of a modern social control apparatus that has deputized every citizen: the modern self is only a pretext for implementing a new form of control. Building on Foucault's insight, a considerable body of scholarly work over the past few decades has analyzed various processes by which selves are monitored and controlled in the contemporary period (for example, Bartky 1990, Rose 1990, Foucault, Burchell *et al.* 1991, Du Gay 1996, Rose 1996, Dean 1999, Hazleden 2003, Füredi 2004, Cremin 2005, Skeggs 2005).

Contemporary theories of self and identity

Foucault focused on the self that emerged from the complex set of social changes that produced *modernity*: the emergent modern self was the historically-specific product of institutions and discourses aimed primarily at producing a highly disciplined, self-monitoring subjectivity. But, according to some social theorists, the social changes of the twentieth century have produced a new kind of self that has supplanted this disciplined subjectivity. Theories of postmodern selves (for example, Kellner 1989a, Baudrillard 1990a, Baudrillard

1990b, Jameson 1991, Baudrillard 1994, Turkle 1995, Sennett 1998, Bauman 2001) portray selves as far less orderly, fragmented, 'deep' and stable than those analyzed by Foucault as characteristic of the modern era. According to Elliott (2001), postmodern theories of the self have three core aspects: (1) an emphasis on fragmentation of the self; (2) 'a narcissistic preoccupation with appearance, image and style'; and (3) an elevation of value of dream, hallucination and madness 'at the expense of common stocks of knowledge or rationality' (Elliott 2001: 136). These postmodern theories differ in whether they see the self as narcotized and largely obliterated or fraught with anxiety about its fragility and transience.

Many analysts of this emergent form of self stress the ways in which this new cultural order enervates people and renders their selves thin, vague, and insubstantial (Baudrillard 1990a, 1990b, Jameson 1991, Baudrillard 1994, Baudrillard 2007). For example, French sociologist Jean **Baudrillard** argues that selves are diminished by the elaborate 'hyperreal' social environment created by the late twentieth-century's explosion of media: intoxicating, prepossessing and rapidly-shifting images become more powerful realities than the immediate physical and social environment. Seduced and bedazzled by these images and their simulated worlds, people lack motivation and means to sustain either the disciplined self described by Foucault or the thoughtful self proposed by the Enlightenment ideal. In the postmodern era, as the rapid transmission of sounds and images intensifies, the self becomes a shallow spectator. People consume the endless sounds and images of mass culture with a blasé attitude (*pace* Simmel) only slightly tempered by pleasurable moments that fail to add up to any lasting pleasure. Adorno's worst fears for the impact of 'the culture industry' on the self have been exceeded: not only is there no impetus for social change, but there is no longer much impetus even for the construction of individual identity.

In contrast to theories like Baudrillard's, that stress how postmodernity enervates or obliterates the self, other theorists of postmodern (or late modern) individualization – Anthony **Giddens**, Ulrich **Beck** and Elizabeth Beck-Gernsheim, and Zygmunt Bauman – observe a postmodern self that retains sufficient integrity and energy to be tormented, anxious and confused – and, for at least a few observers, to sometimes thrive in this hyper-changing world.

Giddens (1991, 1992, 2000) argues that the late modern era requires that the self become a 'reflexive project' that is provisional, improvisational, and unmoored from tradition. When de-traditionalization extended from the public sphere to the private sphere of self, intimacy, and everyday life, the last bit of solid social ground fell away: people were forced to live reflectively – strategically, thoughtfully, anxiously – in all spheres of life. The self must now be under constant revision as new lifestyle choices emerge and former ones become less viable. The threat of failure and meaninglessness looms behind this reflexive project: people lack guidance and validation for the lives they lead and the selves they fashion (Giddens 1991: 32). Anxiety and uncertainty can overwhelm reflexivity and revision and, Giddens argues, 'the dark side of decision making is the rise of addictions and compulsions. Addiction comes into play when choice, which should be driven by autonomy, is subverted by anxiety' (Giddens 2000: 64–5). Although his work concedes the pitfalls of self-reflexivity, Giddens offers a largely optimistic portrayal of the increased possibilities for freedom and choice provided through the project of identity in the late modern age: the reflexive self has a level of autonomy and rationality that fulfills some of the Enlightenment's promises, bringing the rewards of self-mastery and self-authorship to its creator.

Although their analysis of the implications of de-traditionalization for self and identity is similar to Giddens', Beck and Beck-Gernsheim depart from him in their emphasis on its darker consequences. They focus on the precarious identities constructed in the context of an institutionalized individualization imposed by the disintegration of social categories and forms of social integration such as class, social status, gender, family, and neighborhood.

> Individualization is a compulsion, albeit a paradoxical one, to create, to stage-manage, not only one's own biography but the bonds and networks surrounding it, and to do this amid changing preferences and at successive stages of life, while constantly adapting to the conditions of the labour market, the education system, the welfare state, etc.
>
> (Beck and Beck-Gernsheim 2002: 4)

Individualization has several pernicious consequences. The task of 'stage managing' a biography is an anxious one. 'The normal biography thus becomes the "elective biography", the "reflexive biography", the "do-it-yourself biography"' (Beck and Beck-Gernsheim 2002: 3). While offering the possibility of mastery, the do-it-yourself biography can easily fail as a project – especially for those with limited resources to successfully navigate the treacherous waters of rapid social change. Additionally, this do-it-yourself biography must be constructed under relentlessly stressful daily circumstances. Ubiquitous social change makes everyday life uncertain. The security of daily routine vanishes, replaced by 'a cloud of possibilities to be thought about and negotiated' (2002: 6). 'Think, calculate, plan, adjust, negotiate, define, revoke (with everything constantly starting again from the beginning): these are the imperatives of the "precarious freedoms" that are taking hold of life as modernity advances' (2002: 6). In this world of uncertainty and anxiety, psychotherapies proliferate as individuals seek authorities to answer the question 'Who am I and what do I want?' (2002: 7). 'God, nature and the social system are being progressively replaced . . . by the individual –confused, astray, helpless, and at a loss' (2002: 8).

Bauman similarly emphasizes the precariousness of identity in the late modern age: postmodernity or 'liquid modernity' has more uncertainty, contingency, and ambivalence than the earlier modern period. Early modernity gave individuals the task of constructing identities through personal achievement, but they remained embedded in relatively well-defined social positions.

ANN BRANAMAN

The 'self-identification' task put before men and women once the stiff frame of estates had been broken in the early modern era boiled down to the challenge of living 'true to kind' ('keeping up with the Joneses'): of actively conforming to the established social types and models of conduct, of imitating, following the pattern, 'acculturating', not falling out of step, not deviating from the norm.

(Bauman 2001: 145)

In the individualization of the contemporary era, though, 'not just the individual *placements* in society, but the *places* to which individuals may gain access and in which they may wish to settle are melting fast and can hardly serve as targets for "life projects"' (2001: 146). The conditions of life in advanced modern societies, in Bauman's view, conspire 'against distant goals, life-long projects, lasting commitments, eternal alliances, immutable identities' (Bauman 1996: 51).

Bauman attributes much of the precariousness of identity to the precariousness of lives under global capitalism. Mirroring late-twentieth century markets, postmodern social circumstances pressure individuals to maintain loose attachments to everything from institutions to identities. As the environment changes, the self must change. But the constant renovation of identity requires resources and, frequently, assistance from a range of experts. It provokes anxiety, even for those with the resources to manage it well, as they are haunted by 'fears of being caught napping, of failing to catch up with fast-moving events, of being left behind . . . of missing the moment that calls for a change of tack before crossing the point of no return' (Bauman 2005: 2). For the less affluent majority, the race is lost before it begins: they lack the resources to construct and manage a self appropriate to their rapidly-changing environments. They dwell painfully and anxiously in the gap between 'individuality as fate and individuality as a practical capacity for self-assertion' (Bauman 2001: 47). Although the various fundamentalisms promise shelter from the struggle, it may be impossible to escape: even neo-traditionalists remain perpetually anxious about whether they have found an identity that is a haven from a mercilessly volatile environment.

The socially stratified nature of the individualization of the late modern age is a prominent theme in the debates about the heightened reflexivity of the contemporary period and criticisms of those who celebrate it (see Adams 2007 for a recent review). As Adams argues:

The key proposition to be considered is whether or not the recent social changes . . . really do allow more people, more of the time, the power to transform their selves, via heightened reflexive self-awareness and what the specific social distribution and availability of this 'power' is, if it does exist.

(Adams 2007: 50)

Few deny heightened reflexivity in the lives of *some*, but the critics argue for a more differentiated analysis that examines how class, gender, and other bases of social differentiation shape individuals' experience (cf., Lash 1994, Charlesworth 2000, McNay 2000, Adkins 2002, Devine 2005, Hey 2005, Skeggs 2005). An emerging consensus among social theorists is that the reflexive project of the post/late modern period is decisively shaped by systems of inequality.

IDENTITY, POWER, AND IDENTITY POLITICS

New perspectives on inequality emerged from the 'new social movements' of the 1960s. Departing from the Old Left's exclusive focus on social class, these movements focused on gender, race, sexuality and other previously-ignored systems of domination and subordination. Parting company with meliorist strategies for producing 'equal opportunity' largely through legal change, these movements pointed to systems of repression that functioned as much at the level of the intra-psychic as the legal: political change without intra-psychic change would be ineffectual. 'The personal is political,' as the feminist slogan put it.

Psychoanalytic-feminist and postcolonial theories

Following the logic of this slogan, feminist theorists in the 1970s and 1980s confronted issues about self and identity that had been explored earlier by post-colonial theorists of the 1950s and 1960s. Postcolonial theorists asked why the colonized clung to the worldview established by the colonizer; feminist theorists asked how and why women remained attached to a feminine identity shaped by patriarchy. Independent of one another, both sets of theorists explored the utility of psychoanalytic theory to answer these questions.

Psychoanalytically oriented postcolonial theory (Fanon 1965, Memmi 1965, Fanon 1967 [1952], Césaire 1972 [1950]) identified three crucial intrapsychic dynamics of colonialism: the colonizers' projection of disavowed qualities onto the colonized native populations, the conflicted but psychically damaging internalization of these projections by the colonized, and the pathological and dehumanizing effects of colonialism on the colonizer. As Fanon put it, 'The Negro enslaved by his inferiority, the white man enslaved by his superiority alike behave in accordance with a neurotic orientation' (Fanon 1967: 60).

The Anglophone psychoanalytic feminist theorists made a similar case (Mitchell 1974, Dinnerstein 1976, Chodorow 1978, Benjamin 1988). They argued that gender identities under patriarchy were distorted, pathological, and fraught with contradiction. Masculinity was fraught with anxiety and defined precariously in opposition to and superiority over femininity; women's sense of self tended to shore up this unstable masculinity, as their anxieties about independent agency motivated them to support men in their superior stance.

Psychoanalytic feminist and postcolonial theory developed a complex relationship with post-structuralism, one that continues to frame contemporary issues in critical social theory. Feminist and postcolonial theory enthusiastically joined the post-structuralists' project of deconstructing the Enlightenment's valorization of autonomy and rationality: if these ideals were born out of the neuroses of domination (i.e., patriarchy and colonialism), then they could no longer hold their position in the humanist pantheon. But the psychoanalytically-oriented critical theories parted company with post-structuralism over questions of identity, self and subjectivity: the former continued in the Enlightenment tradition of seeking a society in which the self was undamaged, free, 'natural'; the latter insisted that all selves were products of discourse and power, and that no self held a privileged or 'natural' position. This same ambivalence colored the relationship between post-structuralism, French psychoanalytic feminist theory, and the next wave of postcolonial theory (for example, Said 1978, Nandy 1983, Bhabha 2004). They had a shared interest in exposing the irrational forces lurking behind the purportedly rational, deconstructing binary oppositions embedded in Western discourse: male/female, masculine/feminine, active/passive, independent/dependent, reason/emotion, culture/nature, rational/irrational. French feminist theorists, especially **Kristeva** (1982, 1984, Kristeva and Moi 1986), insisted that something existed beyond and outside discourse – forces and drives that inhabited the imaginary and disrupted the ordinary, serving as both a check on and a challenge to discourse. Postcolonial theory insisted that colonial discourse was riven through with repressed anxieties about how to sustain a representation of the colonized that was palpably untrue. Unlike post-structuralists, feminist and postcolonial theorists were intent on a social theory that never lost sight of its political mission – and never lost sight of what was hidden from sight by dominant structures of power and discourse.

Post-structuralism, identity, and social critique: theoretical controversies

In one important respect, the post-structuralist critique of the Enlightenment subject was compatible with the social constructionist perspective shared by most feminist social theorists: both agreed that humans do not possess core selves capable of autonomous rationality. Most feminists in the 1970s eschewed biological essentialism: they emphasized the distinction between sex as a biological fact and gender as a social (and socially constructed) fact. This emphasis fostered a pervasive interest in the analysis of social processes that constructed difference and inequality between men and women. Theorists had widely different ideas about when and how gendered identity was constructed – in early childhood, through language and discourse, via situational performances – but there was no debate about the fact of construction.

Postmodern feminist theorists, though, soon identified a form of essentialism in the constructionist arguments of 'second wave' feminist social theory (cf., Hill Collins 1990, Nicholson 1990, Butler and Scott 1992, Findlen 1995, Walker 1995) They charged that, just as the Enlightenment *philosophes* confused a particular kind of person – European, educated, male, rational, autonomous – with a universal human nature, so too did feminist analysts often confuse a particular *kind* of woman with the category of 'woman.' Early social constructionist theories – including, for example, Chodorow's *The Reproduction of Mothering* – were criticized for their focus on white, middle-class, Western, heterosexual people living in the male breadwinner–female homemaker suburban families. Influenced by theories of poststructuralism and the political insights of the new social movements based on race and sexuality, critics charged that this kind of analysis neglected the experiences of the many women and men whose race, nationality, class, sexuality, culture or other important differences caused gender to shape their lives very differently.

By undermining Eurocentric and masculinist ideas of human nature, poststructuralist deconstruction contributed to 'third wave' feminist theorists' deconstruction of the supposedly universal 'woman' that they found implicit in many 'second wave' feminist theories. Intersectionality theory emerged from this deconstruction, proposing that the 'intersection of vectors of oppression and privilege create variations in both the forms and the intensity of people's experience of oppression' (Goodman and Ritzer 2008: 479). Throughout the 1980s and 1990s, feminist social theory focused on the systematic analysis of how the intersection of race, class, gender, sexuality, nationality, religion or disability resulted in a diverse range of experience and interests among women, such that it was impossible to speak of the interests of 'women' in the abstract (Hooks 1981, Moraga and Anzaldúa 1981, Lorde 1984, Anzaldúa 1987, Spivak, Landry *et al.* 1996, Heywood and Drake 1997, Hill Collins 1998, Hooks 2000, Freedman 2002, McCall 2005). Intersectionality theory was closely allied with the emergence of postmodern feminism, particularly as postmodern feminism questioned the unity of the identity 'woman' (Haraway 1991, 2004, Butler 2006 [1990]). Thus, from one perspective, post-structuralism made a significant contribution to the development of feminist social theory: the decentering of the purportedly universal; the reorientation of the field's focus; a corrective complexity in ideas about the categories of 'man' and 'woman.'

In another respect, though, post-structuralist ideas presented an almost insurmountable challenge to the political projects of feminist and other critically oriented social theorists. The post-structuralist view of identity as a fiction – and the idea that *all* identities were products of power and discourse, none more real than any other – was problematic for critical theories seeking to distinguish between pathological and healthy identities. Post-structuralism's key challenge was this: if all identities are products of discourse and power relations and all standards for evaluating identities are equally products of discourse and power relations, how is it possible to defend the position that some identities are pathological or neurotic while others are healthier and saner? Although many feminist theorists (for example, Diamond and Quinby 1988, Bartky 1990, Sawicki 1991, Bordo 1993, McNay 1993, Ramazanoglu 1993, McLaren 2002) built upon Foucault's argument that modern subjectivity was a product of discourse and power relations, most balked at the post-structuralist insistence that all subjectivities had the same

ANN BRANAMAN

ontological status and that varying subjectivities did not also vary in their relationships to system of oppression. Psychoanalytic feminist and postcolonial theories argued that the creation of new forms of identity and subjectivity were essential to dismantling patriarchal and colonial hierarchies. And even critical social theorists who did not take a psychoanalytic approach nonetheless shared the view that identities were central to the maintenance or subversion of systems of domination and subordination: although critique of particular identities had to proceed through careful analysis, it could not be abandoned (Habermas 1981, Best and Kellner 1991, Benhabib 1992, 1995, Nicholson and Seidman 1995, Fraser 1997, Hartsock 1998, Moya and Hames-Garcia 2000, Fraser and Honneth 2003, Appiah 2005, Alcoff 2006). Thus, even as contemporary critical social theorists acknowledged the importance of the post-structuralist challenge to Enlightenment notions of reason, freedom, and autonomous and rational subjectivity, they continued to insist that the critical role of social theory could not be abandoned. They maintained the conviction that some social arrangements and some identities were more morally justifiable than others, and most continued to argue that the moral soundness of social arrangements is reflected – albeit imperfectly – in the miseries and fragilities of the selves constructed within them (cf., Habermas 1981, Rorty 1989)

Rethinking identity for a critical social theory

In general, then, critical social theorists have chosen to see the deconstructionist critique as requiring them to be cautious in their work on identity issues rather than to abandon it. As Stuart Hall argues, certain key questions – most importantly, questions of agency and politics – cannot be fruitfully engaged without some concept of identity (Hall and Du Gay 1996: 2) Within the context of critical social theory, some version of Hall's position is widely shared; analysts concede the usefulness of the concept of identity to understand the nexus of agency, politics and social change. **Agency** refers to the ability of an individual to take an action or have a thought that is not determined by his or her social context or biography, and critical social theorists ask: when and how does agency appear? Under what circumstances is it progressive in its impact? Some identities are considered to have a greater likelihood of fostering agency than others: identities that are difficult to inhabit, in tension with one's subjectivity, a source of resentment or other distress. Politics is the struggle over social arrangements and priorities and, at least for **critical theorists**, the key question about politics is: under what circumstances and through what means are humans capable of purposeful social change that fundamentally shifts the status quo? For many analysts, the answer to this question is: when individuals are mobilized around an identity that is invested with passion and promise. While Hall and others recognize that the concept of identity may require reformulation – perhaps through the activation of a related concept, such as identification – they remain convinced that understanding the phenomenon dubbed 'identity' is key to answering these questions. If identity reflects dominant discourse and power relations, then not all identities will be equally easy to embrace. To many critical theorists, an uneasy identity remains – as it was for the early theorists of the Frankfurt School – fruitful ground for resistance to domination and the quest for social change. If the uneasily assumed identity is a discursive construction, the restlessness of its bearer might serve as a motivation to talk back: to, quite literally, break the system of discursive constraints.

So, despite the post-structuralist challenge, social theorists generally agree that self and identity are central to the 'anti-authority' struggles that have deepened in recent decades. As Foucault put it:

> the anti-authority struggles – opposition to the power of men over women, of parents over children, of psychiatry over the mentally ill, of administration over the ways people live – of recent years are struggles which question the status of the individual.
>
> (Foucault 1982: 212–13)

An array of strategies have been explored for resistance to the illegitimate exercise of authority, and social theorists have contributed analyses of the legitimacy of various forms of authority (for example, Lukes 1974, Miller 1986, Wartenberg 1992) and various modes of resistance. The most familiar forms of resistance are, of course, the most publicly accessible ones: cultural rejoinders to devaluation, ranging from the positive affirmation of the devalued identity to reasoned responses to the substance of devaluation; legal and political struggles against the institutions that embody illegitimate authority; some form of withdrawal from the devaluing authority, intended to nurture resilience and build supportive community. For the purposes of critical social theory, though, there are two particularly interesting but relatively obscure strategies of resistance, both of which both have roots in Foucault's discussions of the subject and the self: the strategy of identity subversion and the strategy of critical identity.

According to the strategy of identity subversion, the most effective way to engage in anti-authority struggles is to refuse the form of subjectivity offered by the authority. For Foucault, subjectivity is a technique of power which:

> applies itself to immediate everyday life, categorizes the individual, marks him by his own individuality, attaches him to his own identity, imposes a law of truth on him which he must recognize and which others have to recognize in him.
>
> (Foucault 1982: 212)

In short, subjectivity binds the individual to an identity which is constituted in discourse and power relations (Foucault 1982). Foucault put this strategy cryptically: 'Maybe the target nowadays is not to discover what we are, but to refuse what we are' (1982: 216).

The strategy of identity subversion is most apparent in 'queer theory': a body of scholarly work that emerged in the 1990s in response to gay, lesbian, and feminist studies. Queer theory builds on Foucault's critical insights concerning the dominant view – shared by both the heterosexual mainstream and the gay and lesbian mainstream – of homosexuality as an identity. Foucault acknowledged the strategic usefulness of homosexuality as an *identity* in fostering a politically-mobilized and socially-supportive community of gays and lesbians. As social theorist Jeffrey Weeks has pointed out, the argument of a distinctive and biologically-given homosexual identity was a strategically useful fiction. But Foucault never ceased to be troubled by the movement's reliance on the idea of sexuality as an 'identity.' In Foucault's view, the gay and lesbian movement in the USA effectively adopted the views of the late nineteenth century medical experts who defined the homosexual as a distinct kind of person, with the only difference being that they celebrated rather than pathologized gay and lesbian identities (Seidman 1994)

Queer theory, deeply influenced by Foucault and post-structuralism, challenges the idea of 'the homosexual' (or 'the gay man' or 'the lesbian') as part of a strategy to dethrone a categorical system that began with 'the heterosexual' and consequently will always offer the homosexual a lesser place. Rather than challenging homophobia and anti-gay discrimination by positively affirming gay or lesbian identity, 'queer politics' aim to break up the sexual identity system that produces oppression and exclusion. Eve Sedgwick argues that the modern homo – heterosexual dichotomy not only produces social hierarchy but does so on the basis of sexual identities that limit our view of the diversity of sexualities. She says:

> It is a rather amazing fact that, of the very many dimensions along which the genital activity of one person can be differentiated from that of another (dimensions that include preference for certain acts, certain zones or sensations, certain physical types, a certain frequency, certain symbolic investments, certain relations of age or power, a certain species, a certain number of participants, etc. etc. etc.), precisely one, the gender of object choice, emerged from the turn of the century, and has remained as *the* dimension denoted by the now ubiquitous category of 'sexual orientation'.

> (Sedgwick 1990: 8)

Identity subversion raises the question of the degree to which a social order can do away with firm social categories without producing untenable psychic distress – a question that is explored extensively in social theory about the postmodern condition (Flax 1990, Glass 1993).

If the strategy of identity subversion seeks to wreck the identity categories, the strategy of critical identity seeks to make identities deeper, more sophisticated, and more deliberate. Thus developed, identity can be a stronger basis for movements of social transformation. Interestingly, this approach is foreshadowed in some of Foucault's last musings about the self. In one of his last interviews, in a seeming divergence from his earlier position, Foucault explained that he saw a useful point of resistance to domination in the relationship of 'self to self' (Foucault 1988: 10). He explained that the problem was not to dissolve relations of power:

> in the utopia of a perfectly transparent communication, but to give one's self the rules of law, the techniques of management, and also the ethics, the ethos, the practice of self, which would allow these games of power to be played with a minimum of domination.
>
> (Foucault 1988: 18)

In contrast to Foucault's earlier preferred strategy of identity subversion, this strategy suggests that what one does is as important as what one resists – which, ironically, might be read as a return to a humanist critical foundation. Certainly, it was a late-in-life call to a form of introspection that an earlier Foucault would have dismissed.

Proponents of the critical-self strategy presuppose the dangers of an uncritical embrace of any particular form of subjectivity, but nonetheless attempt to conceptualize identity in a way that permits the possibility of critical agency despite embeddedness in relations of power. In the 1980s and 1990s, many feminist and other critical theorists dedicated themselves to developing such alternative conceptions (for example, Dallmayr 1981, Kristeva and Moi 1986, Hassan 1987, Moi 1987, Agger 1992, Bourdieu and Wacquant 1992). Rosenau (1992) provided an overview of some of the notable efforts by the late 1990s to revive the subject by 'affirmative postmodernists' who opposed the 'total destruction of the voluntary, meaningful, and communal subject identity' (Rosenau 1992: 57). Alain Touraine (1988), for example, envisioned a subject who eschewed the modern subject's striving for conquest, but defensively struggled for autonomy in a world where autonomous self-definition had become very difficult, seeking to 'construct a new identity by appealing to life, personal freedom, and creativity' (Rosenau 1992: 58). Although consensus has not developed around any of these normative proposals for a revised concept of the subject, the proliferation of scholarly work in this period dedicated to developing post-Enlightenment concepts of subjectivity illustrates the profoundly unsettling impact of post-structuralist ideas for critical social theorists interested in progressive politics – and the earnestness with which theorists approached the task of rehabilitating one of their central goals.

Two other responses to post-structuralist critiques of identity – standpoint theories and the 'realist' theory of identity – are less normative and more focused on analysis of the experience of those who inhabit marginalized and subordinated positions in society. Standpoint theories (Harding 1986, Hill Collins 1990, Smith 1990, Hartsock 1998) are tempered by the insights of post-structuralism but energized by the insights that can be gleaned from the systematic study of subordinated identities. They argue that people understand the world only from a particular standpoint and that all standpoints are inevitably partial. But they depart from the post-structuralist position by building on Marx's insight that human consciousness is shaped by the material conditions of life and rejecting the argument that discourse is more important than those material positions. While post-structuralists argue that identities, knowledge, and standards for critique are determined by discourse, standpoint theories counter by arguing that the embodied experiences of everyday life can provide a perspective that may contradict dominant discourses: however, because discourse is a powerful counterforce to what is gleaned from material conditions, the materially-based perspective will have difficulty finding language for its insights – and, at this juncture, the work of the analyst begins. Patricia Hill Collins, for example, combs through the lyrics of African-American women's blues songs as part of her inductive reconstruction of an African-American women's standpoint. Because the materially-generated perspective of devalued and marginalized people is rarely reflected in dominant discourse, their standpoint – derived through analysis of their words and practices – can provide a powerful corrective to dominant discourse. When the crystallized and distilled knowledge of the standpoint is returned to the community from which it was gleaned, it can serve as a basis for further insight and a resource for political action.

With some similarities to the starting point of standpoint theory, the 'realist theory of identity' has been developed primarily by scholars in the humanities (for example, Alcoff *et al.* 2006). This perspective affirms some of the key points of anti-essentialist critiques of identity but disagrees fundamentally with the notion that identities are merely fictions or discursive effects that serve only to maintain social hierarchies. In their introduction to a collection of essays by like-minded scholars, Alcoff and Mohanty (2006) define the realist theory of identity as follows:

> We contend that identities can be no less real for being socially and historically situated, and for being relational, dynamic, and, at times, ideological entrapments. . . . Identities are markers for history, social location, and positionality. . . . The theoretical issue concerning identities is not whether they are constructed (they always are, since they are social kinds) but what difference different kinds of construction make. . . . Social identities can be mired in distorted ideologies, by they can also be the lenses through which we learn to view our world accurately. Our identities are not just imposed on us by society. Often we create positive and meaningful identities that enable us to better understand and negotiate the social world. . . . Like identities, identity politics in itself is neither positive nor negative. At its minimum, it is a claim that identities are politically relevant, an irrefutable fact. Identities are the locus and nodal point by which political structures are played out, mobilized, reinforced, and sometimes challenged. . . . Obviously, identities can be recognized in pernicious ways . . . , for the purposes of discrimination.

But it is a false dilemma to suppose that we should *either* accept pernicious uses of identity *or* pretend they do not exist.

(Alcoff and Mohanty 2006: 6)

NOTE

1 These terms have a family of meanings within social theory. Identity most frequently refers to a person's location in a social category, often imposed on an individual but sometimes elective: priest, Jew, woman, Indianapolis Colts fan. Subjectivity most frequently refers to a high personal point of view: the world that is directly or immediately experienced, not inexplicable to others but not directly knowable by them. The self has a highly variable history of uses, but tends to refer to what individuals mean when they say 'I': that sense of who I am, distinct from others, as I exist in the world. But, although these terms are often used distinctly, they are sometimes used interchangeably. Arguably, when I have a large number of social categories that appropriately describe me, my identity is not some simple sum of them: instead, it is what I present, construct or affirm – something more complex than an accounting of categories and closer to what is often meant by 'self'. Arguably, my subjectivity is both shaped by and foundational to my self: by some lights, my subjective experiences (including my reflections on those experiences and those narratives that I construct to order and interpret them) are my self. Different theorists, then, use these terms in somewhat different ways – as will become clear in the contexts in which they are explored in this chapter.

REFERENCES

Adams, M. (2007) *Self and Social Change*, Los Angeles, CA: Sage.

Adkins, L. (2002) *Revisions: Gender and Sexuality in Late Modernity*, Milton Keynes: Open University Press.

Adorno, T.W. and Bernstein, J.M. (2001) *The Culture Industry: Selected Essays on Mass Culture*, London: Routledge.

Agger, B. (1992) *The Discourse of Domination: From the Frankfurt School to Postmodernism*, Evanston, IL: Northwestern University Press.

Alcoff, L. (2006) *Visible Identities: Race, Gender, and the Self*, New York: Oxford University Press.

Alcoff, L., Hames-García, M., Mohanty, P. and Moya, P. (eds) (2006) [2000] *Identity Politics Reconsidered*, New York: Palgrave Macmillan.

Anzaldúa, G. (1987) *Borderlands: The New Mestiza = La Frontera*, San Francisco, CA: Spinsters/Aunt Lute.

Appiah, K.A. (2005) *The Ethics of Identity*, Princeton, NJ: Princeton University Press.

Bartky, S.L. (1990) *Femininity and Domination: Studies in the Phenomenology of Oppression*, New York: Routledge.

Baudrillard, J. (1990) *Fatal Strategies*, London: Pluto.

—— (1990) *Seduction*, New York: St Martin's Press.

—— (1994) *Simulacra and Simulation*, Ann Arbor, MI: University of Michigan Press.

—— (2007) *In the Shadow of the Silent Majorities, or, The End of the Social*, Los Angeles and Cambridge, MA: Semiotext(e), distributed by MIT Press.

Bauman, Z. (2001) *The Individualized Society*, Cambridge: Polity Press.

—— (2005) *Liquid Life*, Cambridge: Polity Press.

ANN BRANAMAN

Beck, U. and Beck-Gernsheim, E. (2002) *Individualization: Institutionalized Individualism and Its Social and Political Consequences*, London: Sage.
Benhabib, S. (1992) *Situating The Self: Gender, Community, and Postmodernism in Contemporary Ethics*, New York: Routledge.
—— (1995) *Feminist Contentions: A Philosophical Exchange*, New York: Routledge.
Benjamin, J. (1988) *The Bonds of Love: Psychoanalysis, Feminism, and the Problem of Domination*, New York: Pantheon Books.
Best, S. and Kellner, D. (1991) *Postmodern Theory: Critical Interrogations*, Basingstoke: Macmillan.
Bhabha, H.K. (2004) *The Location of Culture*, London: Routledge.
Bordo, S. (1993) *Unbearable Weight: Feminism, Western Culture, and the Body*, Berkeley, CA: University of California Press.
Bourdieu, P. and Wacquant, L.J.D. (1992) *An Invitation to Reflexive Sociology*, Chicago: University of Chicago Press.
Burkitt, I. (2008) *Social Selves: Theories of Self and Society*, Thousand Oaks, CA: Sage.
Butler, J. (2006) *Gender Trouble: Feminism and the Subversion of Identity*, New York: Routledge.
Butler, J. and Scott, J.W. (1992) *Feminists Theorize the Political*, New York: Routledge.
Césaire, A. (1972) *Discourse on Colonialism*, New York: MR.
Charlesworth, S.J. (2000). *A Phenomenology of Working Class Experience*, Cambridge: Cambridge University Press.
Chodorow, N. (1978) *The Reproduction of Mothering: Psychoanalysis and the Sociology of Gender*, Berkeley, CA: University of California Press.
Cremin, C. S. (2005) 'Profiling the personal: configuration of teenage biographies to employment norms', *Sociology*, 39(2): 315–32.
Dallmayr, F.R. (1981) *Twilight of Subjectivity: Contributions to a Post-Individualist Theory of Politics*, Amherst, MA: University of Massachusetts Press.
Dean, M. (1999) *Governmentality: Power and Rule in Modern Society*, London: Sage.
Devine, F. (2005) *Rethinking Class: Culture, Identities and Lifestyles*, New York: Palgrave Macmillan.
Diamond, I. and Quinby, L. (1988) *Feminism & Foucault: Reflections on Resistance*, Boston, MA: Northeastern University Press.
Dinnerstein, D. (1976) *The Mermaid and the Minotaur: Sexual Arrangements and Human Malaise*, New York: Harper & Row.
Du Gay, P. (1996) *Consumption and Identity at Work*, London: Sage.
Durkheim, E. (1951) *Suicide, a Study in Sociology*, Glencoe, IL: Free Press.
—— (1964) *The Division of Labor in Society*, New York: Free Press of Glencoe.
—— (1973) *On Morality and Society: Selected Writings*, Chicago: University of Chicago Press.
Elliott, A. (2001) *Concepts of the Self*, Cambridge: Polity
Fanon, F. (1965) *The Wretched of the Earth*, New York: Grove Press.
—— (1967) *Black Skin, White Masks*, New York: Grove Press.
Findlen, B. (1995) *Listen Up: Voices from the Next Feminist Generation*, Seattle, WA: Seal Press.
Flax, J. (1990) *Thinking Fragments: Psychoanalysis, Feminism, and Postmodernism in the Contemporary West*, Berkeley, CA: University of California Press.
Foucault, M. (1965) *Madness and Civilization: A History of Insanity in the Age of Reason*, New York: Pantheon Books.
—— (1977) *Discipline and Punish: The Birth of the Prison*, New York: Pantheon Books.

152

—— (1978) *The History of Sexuality*, New York: Pantheon Books.

—— (1982) 'The subject and power', in *Michel Foucault: Beyond Structuralism and Hermeneutics*, (ed.) H.L. Dreyfus and P. Rabinow, Brighton, Sussex: Harvester.

—— (1988) 'The ethic of care for the self as a practice of freedom', in *The Final Foucault*, (ed.) J.W. Bernauer and D.M. Rasmussen, Cambridge, MA: MIT Press.

Foucault, M., G. Burchell, *et al.* (1991) *The Foucault Effect: Studies in Governmentality: With Two Lectures by and an Interview with Michel Foucault*, Chicago: University of Chicago Press.

Fraser, N. (1997) *Justice Interruptus: Critical Reflections on the 'Postsocialist' Condition*, New York: Routledge.

Fraser, N. and Honneth, A. (2003) *Redistribution or Recognition?: A Political–Philosophical Exchange*, London: Verso.

Freedman, E.B. (2002) *No Turning Back: The History of Feminism and the Future of Women*, New York: Ballantine Books.

Fromm, E. (1955) *The Sane Society*, New York: Rinehart.

Füredi, F. (2004) *Therapy Culture: Cultivating Vulnerability in an Uncertain Age*, London: Routledge.

Giddens, A. (1991) *Modernity and Self-identity: Self and Society in the Late Modern Age*, Stanford, CA: Stanford University Press.

—— (1992) *The Transformation of Intimacy: Sexuality, Love, and Eroticism in Modern Societies*, Stanford, CA: Stanford University Press.

—— (2000) *Runaway World: How Globalization is Reshaping our Lives*, New York: Routledge.

Glass, J. M. (1993) *Shattered Selves: Multiple Personality in a Postmodern World*, Ithaca, NY: Cornell University Press.

Goodman, D. and Ritzer, G. (2008) *Sociological Theory*, Columbus, OH: McGraw-Hill.

Habermas, J. (1981) 'Psychic thermidor and the rebirth of rebellious subjectivity', *Praxis International*, 1(1): 79–86.

Hall, S. and Du Gay, P. (1996) *Questions of Cultural Identity*, London: Sage.

Haraway, D.J. (1991) *Simians, Cyborgs, and Women: The Reinvention of Nature*, New York: Routledge.

—— (2004) *The Haraway Reader*, New York: Routledge.

Harding, S.G. (1986) *The Science Question in Feminism*, Ithaca, NY: Cornell University Press.

Hartsock, N.C.M. (1998) *The Feminist Standpoint Revisited and Other Essays*, Boulder, CO: Westview Press.

Hassan, I.H. (1987) *The Postmodern Turn: Essays in Postmodern Theory and Culture*, Columbus, OH: Ohio State University Press.

Hazleden, R. (2003) 'Love yourself: the relationship of the self with itself in popular self-help texts', *Journal of Sociology*, 39(4): 413–28.

Hey, V. (2005) 'The contrasting social logics of sociality and survival: cultures of classed be/longing in late modernity', *Sociology*, 39(5): 855–72.

Heywood, L. and Drake, J. (1997) *Third Wave Agenda: Being Feminist, Doing Feminism*, Minneapolis, NM: University of Minnesota Press.

Hill Collins, P. (1990) *Black Feminist Thought: Knowledge, Consciousness, and the Politics of Empowerment*, Boston, MA: Unwin Hyman.

—— (1998) *Fighting Words: Black Women and the Search for Justice*, Minneapolis, MN: University of Minnesota Press.

hooks, B. (1981) *Ain't I a Woman: Black Women and Feminism*, Boston, MA: South End Press.

—— (2000) *Feminist Theory: From Margin to Center*, Cambridge, MA: South End Press.

Horkheimer, M. (1947) *Eclipse of Reason*, New York: Oxford University Press.

Jameson, F. (1991) *Postmodernism, or, The Cultural Logic of Late Capitalism*, Durham, NC: Duke University Press.

Kellner, D. (1989a) *Critical Theory, Marxism, and Modernity*, Baltimore, MD: Johns Hopkins University Press.

—— (1989b) *Jean Baudrillard: From Marxism to Postmodernism and Beyond*, Stanford, CA: Stanford University Press.

Kristeva, J. (1982) *Powers of Horror: An Essay on Abjection*, New York: Columbia University Press.

—— (1984) *Revolution in Poetic Language*, New York: Columbia University Press.

Kristeva, J. and Moi, T. (1986) *The Kristeva Reader*, New York: Columbia University Press.

Lash, S. (1994) 'Reflexivity and its doubles: structure, aesthetics, community', *Reflexive Modernization*, U. Beck, A. Giddens and S. Lash, Cambridge: Polity Press.

Lorde, A. (1984) *Sister Outsider: Essays and Speeches*, Trumansburg, NY: Crossing Press.

Lukes, S. (1974) *Power: A Radical View*, London: Macmillan.

McCall, L. (2005) 'The complexity of intersectionality', *Signs: Journal of Women in Culture & Society*, 30(3): 1771–800.

McLaren, M.A. (2002) *Feminism, Foucault, and Embodied Subjectivity*, Albany, NY: State University of New York Press.

McNay, L. (1993) *Foucault and Feminism: Power, Gender, and the Self*, Boston, MA: Northeastern University Press.

—— (2000) *Gender and Agency: Reconfiguring the Subject in Feminist and Social Theory*, Cambridge: Polity Press and Blackwell.

Marcuse, H. (1964) *One-Dimensional Man: Studies in the Ideology of Advanced Industrial Society*, Boston, MA: Beacon Press.

Marx, K. (1978) 'Economic and philosophic manuscripts of 1844', *The Mark–Engels Reader*, (ed.) R.C. Tucker, New York: W.W. Norton.

Mead, G.H. and Morris, C.W. (1934) *Mind, Self and Society from the Standpoint of a Social Behaviorist*, Chicago, IL: The University of Chicago Press.

Memmi, A. (1965) *The Colonizer and the Colonized*, New York: Orion Press.

Miller, J.B. (1986) *Toward a New Psychology of Women*, Boston, MA: Beacon Press.

Mitchell, J. (1974) *Psychoanalysis and Feminism*, London: Allen Lane.

Moi, T. (1987) *French Feminist Thought: A Reader*, Oxford: Blackwell.

Moraga, C. and Anzaldúa, G. (1981) *This Bridge Called My Back: Writings by Radical Women of Color*, Watertown, MA: Persephone Press.

Moya, P.M.L. and Hames-Garcia, M.R. (2000) *Reclaiming Identity: Realist Theory and the Predicament of Postmodernism*, Berkeley, CA: University of California Press.

Nandy, A. (1983) *The Intimate Enemy: Loss and Recovery of Self Under Colonialism*, Delhi: Oxford.

Nicholson, L.J. (1990) *Feminism/Postmodernism*, New York: Routledge.

Nicholson, L.J. and Seidman, S. (1995) *Social Postmodernism: Beyond Identity Politics*, Cambridge: Cambridge University Press.

Ramazanoglu, C. (1993) *Up Against Foucault: Explorations of Some Tensions Between Foucault and Feminism*, London: Routledge.

Ritzer, G. (2000) *Classical Sociological Theory*, Boston, MA: McGraw Hill.

Rorty, R. (1989) *Contingency, Irony, and Solidarity*, Cambridge: Cambridge University Press.

Rose, N.S. (1990) *Governing the Soul: The Shaping of the Private Self*, London: Routledge.

—— (1996) *Inventing Our Selves: Psychology, Power, and Personhood*, Cambridge: Cambridge University Press.

Rosenau, P. (1992) *Post-Modernism and the Social Sciences: Insights, Inroads and Intrusions*, Princeton, NJ: Princeton University Press.

Said, E.W. (1978) *Orientalism*, New York: Pantheon Books.

Sawicki, J. (1991) *Disciplining Foucault: Feminism, Power, and the Body*, New York: Routledge.

Sedgwick, E.K. (1990) *Epistemology of the Closet*, Berkeley, CA: University of California Press.

Seidman, S. (1994) *Contested Knowledge: Social Theory in the Postmodern Era*, Malden, MA: Blackwell.

Sennett, R. (1998) *The Corrosion of Character: The Personal Consequences of Work in the New Capitalism*, New York: W.W. Norton.

Simmel, G. (1971) *On Individuality and Social Forms: Selected Writings*, Chicago, IL: University of Chicago Press.

—— (1978) *The Philosophy of Money*, London: Routledge & Kegan Paul.

Skeggs, B. (2005) 'The making of class and gender through visualizing moral subject formation', *Sociology*, 39(5): 965–82.

Smith, D.E. (1990) *The Conceptual Practices of Power: A Feminist Sociology of Knowledge*, Boston, MA: Northeastern University Press.

Spivak, G.C., Landry, D., *et al.* (1996) *The Spivak Reader: Selected Works of Gayatri Chakravorty Spivak*, New York: Routledge.

Touraine, A. (1988) *Return of the Actor: A Social Theory in Postindustrial Society*, Minnesota, MN: University of Minnesota.

Turkle, S. (1995) *Life on the Screen: Identity in the Age of the Internet*, New York: Simon & Schuster.

Walker, R. (1995) *To Be Real: Telling The Truth and Changing the Face of Feminism*, New York: Anchor Books.

Wartenberg, T.E. (1992) *Rethinking Power*, Albany, NY: State University of New York Press.

Weber, M. (1958) *The Protestant Ethic and the Spirit of Capitalism*, New York: Scribner.

Weber, M., Gerth, H.H., *et al.* (1946) *From Max Weber: Essays in Sociology*, New York: Oxford University Press.

10

NEW MEDIA, POPULAR CULTURE AND SOCIAL THEORY

NICK STEVENSON

The analysis of new media has become a central preoccupation within social theory. This has a number of reasons, not least because of the centrality of the metaphor of the network in seeking to characterize the modern post-industrial or knowledge society. If, as John Urry (2000: 33–7) has argued, networks are less vertical structures than they are different points of interconnection between people, objects and institutions, then such features would seem to have profound implications for how we understand society. Technological networks are best represented as flows across borders. In these terms, globalization is more about different levels of interconnection than a dominant world region seeking to impose its way of life upon others. The development of mobile phones, the Internet, multi-channel television and other features would seemingly weaken the power of vertical institutions to organize our **identities**. In a world of relatively fluid global networks, this potentially unfixes the task of making human identity from particular locations and places. Manuel Castells (2006: 14–17) argues that the network has helped to institute a new global social structure which he calls informationalism. Informationalism is a new form of capitalism where the main source of productivity is the application of knowledge. If industrialism was geared towards economic growth, informationalism, it can be argued, relies on both technological development and the development of knowledge. Castells argues that, since the 1980s, capitalism has restructured itself via the **Information Revolution** to allow for the emergence of a genuinely interdependent economy. In this respect, the Internet is to the knowledge economy what the factory system was to the Industrial Revolution. If, since the 1980s, states all over the world have deregulated their economies and increasingly privatized the public realm, they have done so to aid the introduction of a technological economy that is capable of interconnecting different world regions simultaneously. The virtual economy has promoted intensified global levels of interconnection while, at the same time, enhancing patterns of global exclusion. The new knowledge economy is not based on the idea of a mass society or concerns about information shortage but, rather, operates in a new paradigm where media messages and products become increasingly customized for the intended consumers. The development of new markets in television, proliferation of interactive websites and other features does not, of course, imply a loss of control by media corporations. However, the rise of digital interactive media has helped to promote more horizontal forms of communication linking the global to the local. The rapid development of blog sites, MySpace and, of course, mobile phones has had a dramatic effect on the construction of popular culture and experience (Castells 2007).

The arrival of a mass computing culture has had a profound impact on our daily lives. Here, I think that Castells has identified a key source of contradiction for both our society and for any thinking about new media. The first source of contradiction is that the networked and computer-connected cultures of modern society create networks and connections in a way that mainly 'reinforces existing social patterns' (Castells 1996: 363). In this respect, the development of new media enhances the cosmopolitan orientations and sense of solidarity amongst elites, whereas more excluded sections of the population continue to uphold identities that are mainly local. Yet, once large sections of the population gain access to the Internet, it does seem to provide them with new opportunities for human interaction and human sociability. The networked society potentially links citizens and consumers into increasingly pluralized worlds of information through a diversity of websites and interactive media. As Alberto Melucci (1996: 43) has argued, when some of the 'anchors' to our collective identities are broken down we become aware of the multiple possibilities of living in an information-driven society. For many people today we are increasingly linked to others through the fast links provided by computer terminals.

In this respect, Castells (1996: 371–3) argues that the unification of mass television is replaced by the increasing differentiation of the audience by a number of sociological co-ordinates (in particular class and age), making important distinctions between those who are 'interacted' upon and those doing the 'interacting'. This becomes a key divide in the network age. Without technological development, global capitalism would have been a much more limited phenomenon of our times. New media, then, promotes interconnection, disconnection and exclusion as well as commodification, all at the same time. What is required therefore are social and cultural theories which are able to do justice to the profound ambivalences of the new media age and that resist being overly partial in their analysis. If the new media age points towards a second Industrial Revolution, we will need to be careful that the way in which we analyse this transformation marks points of continuity as well as radical breaks from previous waves of media analysis. We also need to resist the idea that the new cultures of the media age are simply imposed from above by the operations of large conglomerate and media industries, no matter how powerful these might seem. While there remains a considerable amount of disagreement among media scholars concerning the extent to which new media have a democratic potential absent within old media (namely, television, radio and the press) such features should not be dismissed too quickly. Instead, like the radical historian E.P. Thompson's (1968) work on the Industrial Revolution, I shall seek to argue that the new media cultures are actively made from above and below.

TECHNOLOGY AND CULTURAL FORM

Whatever the insights of the network age, this is not the first time that social and cultural theory has tried to develop a complex analysis of the arrival of 'new' media. At this point, I wish to return to some of the critical questions that came along with the arrival of a mass television age in the 1960s. In particular, I continue to be struck by the contribution of Raymond Williams (1974) in developing a similarly complex analysis from which we still have much to learn. Williams explicitly sought to move the argument beyond that promoted by two competing and highly influential trends within social theory in respect of television.

First, the work of **Adorno** and **Horkheimer** (1973 [1944]) had developed a theory of the culture industry outlining the progressive commodification and industrial organization of culture. The dominant culture of capitalist-controlled media and communication industries sought to repress all forms of heterogeneity from the cultural sphere. The culture industry promoted a media culture of mass distraction and could seemingly only be criticized by utopian moments of transcendence found in some artistic forms. If Williams does not seek to deny the extent to which new technological forms are moulded by the dominant capitalist society, he resists the pessimistic conclusions of the culture industry approach. For Williams, technologies need to be understood more concretely in their social and historical context, while seeking to understand how their meanings and uses are transformed over time. Popular culture was not simply controlled by capitalism, but had an important role to play in helping to forge more civic and democratically inspired identities. These features are not really evident in the idea of the culture industry, given the emphasis that is placed on how technologies have allowed elites in totalitarian Europe and capitalist America to control subject populations. Missing from this context is the role that cultural technologies might play in helping to promote more democratically inspired identities and movements for change.

Second, the writing of Marshall McLuhan (1994) had gained a considerable amount of popular prominence in the 1960s. McLuhan's (1994) arguments were a direct challenge to the media's more politically radical critics, arguing that it was the historical transformation of technological media that was most significant in assessing the media's importance. In this, McLuhan had traced through the three main stages of media development as oral, print-based and electronic media. Anticipating much of the later writing on globalization, McLuhan (1994: 34–5) argues that an electronic culture swept aside the hierarchical and uniform forms of cultural production associated with print. As we have seen with the arrival of the Internet, electronic cultures have no connecting center and produce relatively hybridized and de-centralized cultural flows. Ultimately, electronic communications returned society to a condition like that of a village, thereby destroying the individualizing effect of book culture. For Williams (1974), McLuhan's work is interesting as it takes seriously the structuring role of technology, but he also writes about it outside of the structuring power of the dominant institutions that help to shape our culture. McLuhan's writing, then, is no less **deterministic** than the culture industry thesis, given its lack of historical specificity and concrete analysis. For Williams, both of these approaches were examples of technological determinism, whereby a given technology or associated set of technologies is analysed outside of its complex forms of intersection with questions of history, **structure** and meaning.

Alternatively, Williams argues that the 'effect' of the arrival of new technologies is not the direct institution of a completely new society. Like Castells, Williams offers a vision of media and technology that becomes adapted to and partially helps to transform the dominant capitalist society. In making this argument, Williams notes that television was developed without any clear idea as to how it might eventually become used, but then takes on a particular technological form in the context of what he calls 'mobile privitization' (Williams 1974: 26). Over the historical course of capitalist development, people increasing live in relative isolation from the rest of the community in transportable family units. The requirement of capitalism for both new markets of consumption and a relatively mobile labour force helps to determine the specific cultural shape of television and how it fits into domestic settings. The history of television is also shaped by a mix of public and private institutions that helps to structure the nature of its programming and much of its output. In particular, Williams is concerned with whether ideas of public service might become increasingly eroded by more Americanized capitalist-driven models of television. For Williams, the United States, as the dominant world power, had particular interests in seeking not only to shape the commercial character of television, but also a particular consumerist lifestyle that promoted a 'good life' based on the practices of consumption rather than the democratic civic norms of citizenship. Yet, if Williams was critical of technological determinism, he also suggested that 'we must be careful not to substitute it for the notion of a determined technology' (Williams 1974: 130). If technology developed under certain economic, political and cultural conditions, Williams was keen to remind us that these determinations were multiple rather than singular.

In Williams's analysis, technological development is a complex business, involving not only the intentions of elites, but also alternative uses that might be developed by the wider population and social movements. The historical, political and technological development of television could all have happened differently. Here, Williams (1974: 131) offers an example from the history of popular education where, after the Industrial Revolution, the ruling class wanted the working population to read rather than write. If they were to operate complex machinery and, of course, improve themselves morally by reading works of scripture, then basic levels of literacy were a pre-requisite to becoming a citizen. However, in the 1830s, during the rise of Chartism, if ordinary people were able to read the Bible, they could also choose to read radical publications and more fully engage with radical popular movements. Here there is, perhaps, a lesson for those who have been (like Adorno and McLuhan) either too pessimistic or optimistic with respect to the democratizing potential of more interactive technologies. As Douglas Kellner (2005) has argued, there is a marked tendency in much of the literature on new media and technology to treat it as leading to either liberation or oppression. The consequences of viewing media in these terms have long and complex histories that we need to learn to navigate carefully. By viewing new technologies through binary discourses, I would claim that we miss points of genuine ambivalence and, of course, the ways in which a number of complex elements can become mixed in with one another. The great strength of Williams's more complex analysis of technological culture and change is that his writing seeks to position 'new' media cultures in a way that resists the polarized thinking evident in earlier strands of social theory.

The development of the knowledge economy requires masses of people to become computer literate. This has had a profound effect on education, increasing the numbers of people coming into higher education while developing a concern about transferable skills and measurable outcomes. As Hardt and Negri (2000: 289) argue, the information-based society develops 'a new mode of becoming human'. The world of just-in-time production, computer screens and fast communication fosters a world where 'we increasingly think like computers' (Hardt and Negri 2000: 291). If the capitalist economy requires increasing numbers of people to develop computing skills and receive a university education then, in the context of an information-based economy, such a situation would seem offer opportunities as well as dangers. Bill Readings (1996) has argued that the development of the information economy has seen the increasing corporatization of universities as they compete in a global education market for expanding numbers of students. If the mission of the universities of the past was to preserve the national culture, then today they draw upon a number of bureaucratic performance indicators to prove 'excellence'. Inevitably, the economic need for universities to produce new generations of computer-literate students has led to justified concerns about the loss of the idea of a meaningful education (Evans 2004). There are justified fears about institutions of higher learning becoming an employment training ground, thereby marginalizing the universities' civic and, indeed, critical role.

While concerns about 'training' large numbers students for employment markets are well taken, they can, of course, become overstated. In his early writing, Williams was deeply critical of the ways in which radicals and conservatives dismissed the culture of the common people as that of 'the masses'. Metaphors of the 'mob' and the 'brute' rolled too easily off the tongue (Williams 1958: 303). Notably, a similar tone is sometimes discernable within some of the critical commentary on the changing patterns in higher education and popular culture more generally. This argument that new generations of young people are gaining access to the world-wide web while also receiving a university education has at least a potentially progressive viability for the development of democratic and civic cultures. Yet, what was important for Williams was the need to develop more democratic, critical and responsive relations within education and popular media more generally. Democratic cultures more ordinarily needed to help foster commonly available cultures of criticism, reciprocity and dialogue (Williams 1958: 305). The development of arguably more interactive and technologically horizontal modes of communication would then need to be assessed in terms of these values.

THE RETURN OF THE SPECTACLE

Recently, in order to help understand the ways in which capitalism has transformed popular culture and the mediated public realm, there has been a re-emergence of interest in the idea of the society of the spectacle. Douglas Kellner (2003) argues that media spectacles have become a key organizing principle of the dominant capitalist society. Following the earlier work of Debord (1994), Kellner argues that the society of the spectacle reproduces itself through the promotion of reified images of sensation and scandal. Similarly, Mary Kaldor (2003: 123) has argued that there has emerged a new kind of warfare that should be called 'spectacle war'. Spectacle wars uses advanced weapon and missile technology in order to both maximize impact and minimize the casualties of the spatially separated nation. Spectacle wars have a tendency to be extremely destructive in terms of the loss of life, have a huge media impact and downplay humanitarian considerations. The spectacle then provides the link between new forms of warfare and the arrival of the consumer society.

   In Debord's original formation, just as workers are separated from the products of their labour through capitalist social relations, so images take on an autonomous appearance that has little connection with everyday life. The masses consume dramatic images of human misery and suffering, which increasingly take on the appearance of unreality. In this respect, the spectacle is not the effect of technology but is the product of a centralized capitalist society that institutes an 'essentially one-way flow of information' (Debord 1994: 19). Capitalist domination is built on alienation, as people learn to recognize their needs and desires through the images and commodities offered by the dominant system. Needs and desires, then, are not arrived at autonomously, but through a society of affluence where people are driven to consume images and commodities, built on 'the ceaseless manufacture of pseudo-needs' (Debord 1994: 33). The society of the spectacle has its roots in the economy and represents the further penetration of capitalism into the psyche of modern citizens. Notably, however, some forms of **critical theory** and **Marxism** have been complicit with the dominance of the spectacle through the imposition of similarly authoritarian modes of struggle and rule. For Debord, if the alienation effect of the spectacle is to be defeated, then the subjugated would need to revolt against their imposed passivity and 'purely contemplative role' (Debord 1994: 87). Alienation can only be countered by entering into social and political struggle that has rejected alienated forms of life. This demands a 'theory of praxis entering into two-way communication with practical struggles' (Debord 1994: 89).

The other way in which the spectacle dominates the lives of modern citizens is through the elimination of historical knowledge. If the rise of capitalism eclipsed the dominance of cyclical time of the medieval world, then it did so by instituting irreversible time. For Debord this involves ideas of progress that came along with capitalist modernity and calculable time necessary for the disciplining of labour and the production of commodities, but also spectacular time. Spectacular time prevents the development of historical knowledge since it organizes information through the media as dramatic events that are quickly displaced and forgotten. Similarly, Fredric **Jameson** (1991) has argued that commodity capitalism has instituted a society of the timeless present. Notably, such features could only be resisted once 'dialogue has taken up arms to impose its own conditions upon the world' (Debord 1994: 154).

Debord was, perhaps, among the first to grasp the emerging connections between capitalism, technology and media that have became increasingly concentrated upon the spectacular. The reconfiguration of capitalism in the age of information has massively expanded the reach of transnational corporations into the fabric of everyday life. The development of superinformation highways through the digital convergence of the computer, telephone and the television set provide new, profitable markets for the future (McChesney 2000, Schiller 2000). Furthermore, despite the interactive nature of new media through the production of high-definition television, digital images and computer games have arguably led to the enhancement of spectacular capitalism.

For Kellner, updating Debord's original reflections, in the society of the spectacle fashion, fashion models, celebrities and icons become increasingly important. Culture is increasingly dominated by the power of certain images and brands. Society's central feature is the dominance of a new form of technocapitalism, whereby capital accumulation, the knowledge revolution and new technology have combined to produce a new kind of society. The culture of the spectacle instigates a new form of domination of mass distraction, profit and the continuing expansion of social and cultural domains that fall under its sway, from politics to sport and from music to the news media. However, Kellner seeks to expand Debord's original ideas by distinguishing between different kinds of media spectacle. These would include the megaspectacle (large-scale media events attracting mass audiences such as the war on terror or the funeral of Princess Diana), interactive spectacles (involving different levels of audience participation like eviction night on the UK's reality television programme, *Big Brother*) and more overtly political spectacles, such as elections, which are increasingly run as sensational media events only serving to drain them of any more substantial ethical criteria.

Henry Giroux (2006) has argued that, while these features offer a more detailed analysis than Debord's own, these reflections need to be extended even further in the context of the war on terror. The attack on the Twin Towers was explicitly designed to shock. The events of 9/11 then impressed a new relationship between the power of the image and global politics. This new form of spectacle is quite different from the spectacles of fascism and consumerism that Debord (1988: 8) had previously labelled the concentrated and integrated spectacle. For Giroux, fear and terror have become the central components of the spectacle in a post-9/11 world. In the context of the war on terror, politics explicitly adopts the language and metaphors of war. The society of the spectacle now involves not only the economy and the state but also the considerable power of the media and the rise of political fundamentalism. For Giroux, where Debord was mainly concerned with the dominance of consumer capitalism, in the context of the war on terror: 'the spectacle of terrorism affirms politics (of war, life, sacrifice and death) over the aesthetics of commodification through an appeal to the real over the simulacrum' (Giroux 2006: 49).

Giroux's central point is that control is exercised less through the promise of the good life through consumption than it is through fear. It is therefore through fear of terrorism, the Other, Muslims, asylum seekers, the urban poor and those who would seemingly threaten our way of life that the war on terror is legitimated. Nation-states have been able to exploit the spectacle of terrorism through new legislation that curtails the **rights** of citizens while subjecting them to increasing surveillance and control. The spectacle of terror reproduces a war against an ill-defined enemy and, perhaps just as importantly, against democracy and civic freedoms. Furthermore, fundamentalist groups have exploited the politics of the spectacle using images and video technology to promote representations of suicide bombers, violent deaths and representations of abuse and torture. Just as the media utilizes the spectacle in the search for higher ratings, so terrorist organizations use similar devices to attract potential supporters.

Similarly, Jean **Baudrillard** (2002) argues that the idea of the spectacle in the context of 9/11 evokes the memory of many disaster films and symbolizes the fragility of the American empire. The network society has actually managed to impose 'a single world order', yet this has created its own forms of resistance and sown the seeds of its own destruction (Baudrillard 2002: 12). However, the politics of war and fear are more part of Debord's original reflections than Giroux seems to be aware. For Debord, the society of the spectacle is likely to produce terrorism only if this would itself act as a form of spectacular domination. Terrorism was likely to flourish, as the dominant could be judged 'by its enemies rather than by its results' (Debord 1998: 24). Nevertheless, both Giroux and Debord are in agreement that the spectacle can only be substantially challenged through the recovery of more democratic modes of dialogue. As we shall see, it has been new media's capacity to potentially encourage more democratic and dialogic forms of communication that has so excited some media scholars.

NEW MEDIA AND IDENTITY

The idea of the rebirth of the society of the spectacle would undoubtedly be criticized by other media theorists for neglecting different aspects of technological change. In this setting, Mark Poster (1995) argues that the reflections of the media pessimists indicate the inability of critical theory to understand the significance of new media. Much critical theory is overwhelmingly concerned with whether or not the media limit or foster autonomous social relations rather than investigating the ways in which media might constitute new subject positions. For Poster, what is at stake is not the way new media help to foster domination or resistance, but 'a broad and extensive change in the culture, in the way identities are structured' (1995: 24). That is, virtual reality helps to evoke new possibilities for the imagination given its emphasis on play, simulation and discovery. The development of new media allows citizen/consumers to explore the boundaries of different identity formations while pleasurably entering into different imaginary worlds. It is new media's relatively decentralized structure that potentially turns everyone into a producer and a consumer of information that constitutes subjects as multiple and unstable. These possibilities dispense with the opposition between a 'real' and 'fictitious' community and enable participants to express themselves without the usual visual clues and markers. Such a situation encourages the proliferation of local narratives, the experience of different realities and a diversity of knowledge. According to Poster, such is the prevalence of these features that we are now able to talk confidently of a 'second media age' that has broken with the hierarchical arrangements of the past. For instance, there is currently much excitement about the idea of 'Second Life', which allows web participants to construct imaginary selves while allowing them to interact playfully with virtual others. Such features, according to Poster, abound on the Internet and push the argument beyond questions of liberation and domination.

Certain aspects of Poster's arguments are in evidence in some of the discussion of fan culture. Much of the work in cultural studies has sought to treat the idea of being a 'fan' as a fairly ordinary identity, which often involves the development of virtual or on-line identities. For John Fiske (1992), to be a fan involves a pleasurable reworking of the texts and forms of visual culture that the media of mass communication and, in particular, new media make commonly available. Fans are not so much passive in this process but, by interacting with media cultures, produce new meanings and understandings. The fostering of forms of 'in-group solidarity' among those who participate within a particular fan group acts as a way of marking themselves off from the rest of the world or 'official culture'. To be a fan is to mark your distinction from non-fans or other fan groups and to establish yourself within a wider community. As Fiske is well aware, all communities produce formal and informal rules. Indeed, many fan communities, despite being low in 'official' cultural capital, establish their own hierarchies and alternative forms of capital, employing means not recognized by the wider culture by which fans can increase their esteem and status within a particular fan community. This might be by becoming particularly knowledgeable about a team or celebrity, or by running an unofficial website, or indeed helping to run a fan club by producing an online newsletter. However, of all these different activities, it is the accumulation of fan knowledge that is most important.

Those who have 'expertise' within a fan community are those most likely to gain respect from other fans. In this respect, fans are often 'buffs' and avid collectors of a diverse range of material from videos to magazine articles and from newspaper clippings to 'unofficial' photographs and bootlegs. Fans, then, are highly selective and often collect a wide range of cultural and symbolic forms and objects that, while unique to the fan, are meaningless to outsiders. As Henry Jenkins (1992) argues, anyone who speaks from the position of a fan does so from the position of a lowly and subordinate identity.

The circulation of 'in-group' meanings within a particular fan community is a pleasurable way to make collective identities. This form of community might exist as an on-line Internet discussion group, through face-to-face meetings or by being at a concert or sporting event. As Fiske argues, this form of cultural productivity is produced specifically for circulation among people who share similar passions and tastes. These might include the production of fan web pages or indeed fanzines. During my own small study of on-line fan communities, I found many features similar to those mentioned by Fiske and Jenkins. However, my own reflections sought to balance the productivity evident in virtual fan communities with other, more ambivalent features (Stevenson 2006). Indeed, through in-depth semi-structured interviews with David Bowie fans, I was struck less by their active involvement as 'pro-sumers' (which was, of course, in evidence) than by their reverence for a star who was literally 'up there'. Bowie was not an equal to be interacted with but rather an arresting image produced by the culture industry who had, at various points in his career, offered different forms of cultural and sexual politics. The cultural production of star-images relies not only on wider institutional relations of capitalism and the music industry, but also on active forms of identification by many fans who construct websites and come together in a variety of complex ways to discuss their favourite star.

If an overemphasis on the spectacle revisits some of the features of Adorno and Horkheimer's idea of the culture industry, then perhaps talk of a new media age is a return to the more optimistic language of Marshall McLuhan? Despite Poster's criticism of critical theory, it is noticeable that much of the work on online fan communities is keen to debate the democratizing potential of virtual communications. Indeed, just as Williams argued not to reduce 'audiences' to 'the masses', he was equally critical of attempts to overemphasize the technological playfulness of the media. Yet, what the emphasis on more 'popular' media has done is to disrupt the argument that technological media are simply imposed upon people from above. If fan identities are often (although not always) networked identities that are sustained through complex webs of sociality, then they are never simply reflections of processes related to commodification or the reification of the image. Castells (2001) has usefully argued that, despite widespread fears that new communication technology through the development of home-based entertainment has further balkanized the public, much new media has lead to an enhanced form of on-line sociability. So, despite some evidence of role-playing, most 'netizens' construct identities that are consistent with their off-line identities. Much of the more 'ordinary' uses of new media, such as mobile phones, are concerned with making arrangements with friends or sites such as Facebook that allow families and friends to keep in touch over distances. Castells (2001: 129) argues that the Internet has a crucial role to play in maintaining 'weak ties', which might otherwise have been lost. These arguments seemingly have more than a passing resemblance to those of Maffesoli (1996), who has similarly questioned overly pessimistic forms of analysis with respect to which modern culture can be said to be fragmented or privatized. The development of new technology has led to the 'tribalization' of modernity through the construction of new communities. These new communities are built on a culture of individual choice and can be elected into (or, indeed, out of), providing a fleeting sense of belonging, connection and emotional warmth. At its most positive, then, the new Internet culture helps to sustain less a culture of disconnection (although, of course, many people do not have access to the required cultural capital or technology) but, rather, what could be called 'networked individualism' (Castells *et al.* 2007: 175). These features then, arguably, push the debate about new media beyond talk of either global commodification or postmodern playfulness towards the ongoing struggle for a more democratic and autonomous society.

THE TIME OF TECHNOLOGY

The temporal dimensions of media cultures have strong connections to processes of globalization. For instance, Robert Hassan (2008: 111) reports that many Australians would take a six-week journey by sea in the 1960s if they wished to visit Europe. Today, widely available plane travel and, of course, the World Wide Web, e-mail and YouTube that have pushed us into the age of instantaneous and immediate communication. The displacement of temporal frames, associated with the linear and sequential time frames of modernity, by the speeded up dimensions of modern technological society has important consequences for the way we understand technological media cultures. The time of technology and the time of neoliberal capitalism join together in seeking to emphasize the importance of efficiency, speed and the instantaneous. The speed of transactions in the global economy, the circulation of information, the defeat of deferred gratification by consumerism, the enhanced cycles of fashion and, of course, the disposable society, all point to a world increasingly built on acceleration.

These features have been pessimistically analysed by Paul **Virilio**, for whom the speed of modern media destroys thought and the possibility of democratic deliberation. This has introduced a divide between two distinct temporalities that Virilio (1997: 71) describes as the absolute and the relative. The radical divide is between those who live in 'real' time, whose economic, political and cultural activities are driven by speed, and those who become ever more destitute while living in 'real' spaces. The paradox of the information society is leading to an increase in both virtual mobility and physical inertia; that is, the 'terminal citizen' does not have to actually move about as technology is increasingly modeled to fit the contours of the human body. The new interactive space that is facilitated by the Internet, television and virtual reality means that the home becomes a cockpit that receives the world without the occupant having to move. This reduces the subject to a 'vegetative state' or culturally induced coma, where the search is not so much for the possibility of public action, but the 'intensiveness of sensations' (Virilio 2000: 69). The speeding up of 'reality' in real time has an individualizing effect whereby information becomes increasingly focused in on the self. Replaying the earlier concerns of the Frankfurt School and Guy Debord, the speed culture of the Internet and new media more generally act as a form of distraction from our more immediate surroundings and ecological dependence. If, like these writers before him, Virilio uses polemic as a means of alerting us to technological dangers, the problem remains that the analysis becomes disconnected from other 'political' possibilities. Yet it is not hard to understand Virilio's popularity in an age where many are complaining of overwork, stress and the lack of time. Notably, many ecological writers have been concerned to explore some of the pleasurable and emancipatory alternatives available in a life that moves at a slower pace (Soper 2007). There is, of course, some evidence of small numbers of citizens choosing to live less pressurized lifestyles and spend more time with their families, thereby fostering less consumer-orientated patterns of living. Much of the politics of the anti-globalization and environmental movements have sought to promote a discussion about what a less resource-intensive and at the same time a more leisurely and pleasurable life might look like. While such concerns are too easily dismissed as being confined to small sections of the educated middle-classes, the irony is that such features are unlikely to flourish unless they become networked. In short, Virilio does not pay enough attention to the democratizing potential of new media and thereby rules out more ambivalent frames of reference. In particular, the development of locally based indymedia sites (www.indymedia.com) regularly offers local people information about protests, ethical campaigns and alternative lifestyles. Furthermore, the Internet offers possibilities for the development of alternative and citizen-based media (Downing 2003). There is also, of course, now considerable evidence that the net is a crucial public sphere, actively involved in the development of new and alternative forms of politics and identification (Kahn and Kellner 2004). However, we must be careful that we do not understate the extent to which so-called radical Internet sites remain isolated from more 'official' versions of the public sphere and thereby merely end up preaching to the converted (Fenton 2008). Yet such features point to a more complex appreciation of the different time frames necessary to develop cultural and political alternatives beyond a blanket dismissal of speed. Despite Virilio's anti-technological stance, there is increasing concern among a number of civic actors that accelerated time is an in-human time.

MEDIA AND MORALITY

We have already seen that the interconnectivity of the media can have ambiguous effects with respect to connections between media and politics. A different way of exploring these questions is to ask what effects the visualization of suffering has on our shared moral landscape. We might argue that practices of time/space compression make it increasingly difficult to ignore the plight of the 'Other'. The daily screening of images of suffering on our television sets means that it has become increasingly difficult to shrug off our responsibilities towards others in a shared world (Adam 1996). Through televised appeals on behalf of peoples we will never meet we become aware that a donation 'right now' could have an immediate impact on the well-being of others across the planet's surface. This feeds into a politics of compassion and concern for others who share our fragile planet. Television and new media technologies arguably make cosmopolitan compassion and moral solidarity more possible. This is especially the case when such concerns become connected to the emergence of a cosmopolitan civil society that includes the global spread of human rights, charitable agencies such as Oxfam, and the globalization of communication networks. Roger Silverstone (2007) has argued that the radical plurality of both global and new media has increasing brought 'the stranger' into everyday domestic contexts. While this does not deliver a new civic culture by itself, it does at least offer new civic possibilities beyond the nation-state.

However, there are a number of more sceptical voices on this subject. Keith Tester (1995: 475) argues that television can not actually create moral solidarity, but it can provide a cultural resource for those who have a predisposition towards 'moral leaps of the imagination'. The images and perspectives of the media do not have any automatic moral consequences. That is, the representation of murder, war and suffering on television has no necessary connection to the development of cosmopolitan solidarity. More pessimistically than Roger Silverman, Tester (2001) argues that a world which is awash with images helps to foster a blasé attitude among the audience whereby they repeatedly fail to be shocked by the pictures of horror and distress that are the daily diet of the television news. Television images are too fast and fleeting to leave any lasting moral trace of their presence. In this, the screen is not really a 'window on the world', but can literally be seen as a barrier between the viewer and those whose lives are represented. If the media are a door rather than a bridge we can then keep that door shut in order to maintain our social and moral distance from the sufferings of others (Tester 1997). Indeed, in this scenario, the act of giving is largely a means of maintaining rather than closing social distance. Tester (2001) argues that global news, telethons and documentaries are more often concerned with the cleansing of suffering and the sanitization of the 'Other'.

However, images of suffering still have the capacity to move some people, at least some of the time, into political concern, expressions of sympathy and care. As Stanley Cohen (2001) has argued, it is not so much information overload or a pervasive culture of indifference that affects relatively privileged populations, but demand overload. That people do not respond to every appeal for help does not necessarily mean that the public is indifferent. We might point here to the development of what Ulrich **Beck** (2000) has called 'responsible globalization'. Beck argues that the politicization of global networks seeks to open a new transnational civil society built on consumer boycotts, cross-cultural communication and organizations like Amnesty International, Greenpeace and others who work within a post-national world. Campaigns on the Internet and on the high street against the use of sweat shops by global brand names have utilized the more interconnected world developed by the Internet to politicize everyday forms of consumption. Yet, we might also consider what Luc Boltanski (1999: 5) has called the 'politics of pity', which involves the spectacle of suffering demanding an immediate reaction on the part of the audience. The problem here becomes how to promote feelings of solidarity across what might be huge geographical distances. The media then, unlike the NGOs, are less concerned with justice than they are with pity. This tends to side-step large questions like the justification of war or global inequalities for a politics that highlights the spectacle of suffering rather than more substantive political concerns (Chouliaraki 2006).

The other aspect of new media consumption that continues to attract moral concern is the relationship between children and the Internet. Again, much of the academic debate has moved between a deep concern that the Internet helps to foster a post-literate culture of simulated destruction, consumer orientation and an emphasis on the possibilities for play and imagination. As Sonia Livingstone (2003) points out, however, the evidence base of the research that makes these assumptions is currently quite limited, and yet the material that is currently available suggests a complex and, at times, contradictory picture of children's Internet use. The concern in this area is obvious, given that this is the first generation growing up with the Internet and, perhaps not surprisingly, there seems to be a divide between parents who largely value the Internet for its educational features and children who are more motivated by online entertainment and fandom. However, other work has sought to build a far more complex picture of Internet usage which goes beyond the simple dichotomy of citizenship versus entertainment. Joke Hermes (2006) argues that Internet use and engagement are more contradictory than many assume and this takes on an added meaning in an age where newspaper readership is in decline. It remains, therefore, an open question as to the character of the emergent online civic culture of the young. However, it has been widely reported that young people's comparative lack of civic involvement has less to do with the rise of Internet and is, instead, more intimately connected with the extent to which they feel themselves to be disenfranchised and excluded from democratic spaces and practices (Buckingham 2000). At this point we perhaps need to remember that whether or not the young maintain a sense of commitment and loyalty to democratic ideals is not something that the Internet can resolve. Wider questions of civic commitment and connection need to be rooted in a number of practices and traditions that have a broader set of concerns (Dahlgren 2000).

New media: civic and popular cultures

If the dominant metaphor for new media has been the network, then what is noticeable is that most of the concerns about the so-called new media age can be located in an earlier set of debates. Debates concerning new media have found it hard to break out of a language which contrasts the extent to which new media is caught in cycles of commodification and marketization, and more civic forms of responsibility. If the pessimists reduce the politics of 'new' media to the power of technology and the market, then the optimists speak of the increasing capacity of ordinary people to both make their own culture and live a less regulated and more creative life. As I have argued, these disputes are actually a revision of an earlier set of disputes. If, however, there are genuinely 'new' features to this debate, they are mostly concerned with the significance of: (a) the development of more interactive forms of media, and (b) the relative decline in the ability of the state to impose collective cultures of identification. Both of these features are, arguably, connected to the potential of digital cultures to become democratized cultures under the conditions of a globalized technological capitalism. Yet, while these features are likely to be negotiated differently depending on the context, the extent to which links between new media and the spectacle have made a remarkable return within the social theory of the media is significant. The development of media technologies has seemingly enhanced the already powerful effects of media forms to concentrate upon the visual nature of conflicts. It is, perhaps, not surprising that these features have been enhanced in a technological and consumer-driven society. However, the growth of the complexity of the media has provided citizens and consumers alike not only with opportunities to participate in the official culture of the spectacle but also with spaces in which to explore a range of ethical and political alternatives. There is no culture of the spectacle without a public which is prepared to buy the latest technological gadgets, participate in online discussions, set up personal web pages or seek to domesticate the news of the day. If the network society has indeed led to the increasing commodification of everyday life, it has also seemingly enhanced the possibility for some citizens to become ever more creative within the day-to-day use of media. Amid widespread concerns about the cultures of privatization, consumerism, fundamentalism and a new politics of empire, then it would seem that new media is likely to be a key location in which the struggle for democratic and civic identities is likely to be crucial. Whether these popular movements are 'successful' will, of course, depend less on technology than the agency and engaged horizons of citizens.

References and recommended further reading

Adam, B. (1996) 'Re-vision: the centrality of time for an ecological social science perspective', in Lash, S. Szerszynski, B. and Wynne, B. (eds), *Risk, Environment and Modernity*, London: Sage.

Adorno, T. and Horkheimer, M. (1973) *The Dialectic of the Enlightenment*, London: Allen Lane.

Anderson, B. (1983) *Imagined Communities*, London: Verso.

Baudrillard, J. (2002) *The Spirit of Terrorism and Other Essays*, London: Verso.

Beck, U. (2000) *What is Globalisation?*, Cambridge: Polity Press.

Boltanski, L. (1999) *Distant Suffering: Morality, Media and Politics*, Cambridge: Cambridge University Press.

Buckingham, D. (2000) *The Making of Citizens*, London: Routledge.

Castells, M. (2001) *The Internet Galaxy: Reflections on the Internet, Business, and Society*, Oxford: Oxford University Press.

—— (2006) *The Rise of the Network Society*, Oxford: Blackwell.

—— (2007) 'Communication, power and counter-power in the network society', *International Journal of Communication*, 1: 238–66.

Castells, M., *et al.* (2007) *Mobile Communication and Society: A Global Perspective*, Cambridge, MA: MIT Press.

Chouliaraki, L. (2006) 'The aestheticization of suffering on television', *Visual Communication*, 5(3): 261–85.

Cohen, S. (2001) *States of Denial: Knowing About Atrocities and Suffering*, Cambridge: Polity Press.

Dahlgren, P. (2000) 'The Internet and the democratization of civic culture', *Political Communication*, 17: 335–40.

Debord, G. (1994) *The Society of the Spectacle*, New York: Zone Books.

—— (1998) *Comments on the Society of the Spectacle*, London: Verso.

Downing, J.D.H. (2003) 'Audiences and readers of alternative media: the absent lure of the virtually unknown', *Media, Culture and Society*, 25: 625–45.

Evans, M. (2004) *Killing Thinking: The Death of the Universities*, London: Continuum.

Fenton, N. (2008) 'Mediating hope: new media, politics and resistance', *International Journal of Cultural Studies*, 11(2): 230–48.

Fiske, J. (1992) 'The cultural economy of fandom', in Lisa Lewis (ed.), *The Adoring Audience: Fan Culture and Popular Media*, London: Routledge.

Giroux, H. (2006) *Beyond the Spectacle of Terrorism*, London: Paradigm.

Hardt, M. and Negri, A. (2000) *Empire*, Cambridge, MA: Harvard University Press.

Hassan, R. (2008) *The Information Society*, Cambridge: Polity Press.

Hermes, J. (2006) 'Citizenship in the age of the internet', *European Journal of Communication*, 21(3): 295–309.

Jameson, F. (1991) *Postmodernism, or, The Cultural logic of Late Capitalism*, London: Verso.

Jenkins, H. (1992) *Textual Poaches: Television Fans and Participatory Culture*, London: Routledge.

—— (2005) *Fans, Bloggers and Gamers: Exploring Participatory Culture*, New York: New York University Press.

Kahn, R. and Kellner, D. (2004) 'New media and internet activism: from the "Battle of Seattle" to blogging', *New Media and Society*, 16(1): 87–95.

Kaldor, M. (2003) *Global Civil Society*, Cambridge: Polity Press.

Kellner, D. (2003) *Media Spectacle*, London: Routledge.

—— (2005) 'Globalization, September 11, and the restructuring of education', in G.F. Fishman (ed.), *Critical Theories, Radical Pedagogies, and Global Conflicts*, Lanham, MD: Rowman Littlefield, pp. 87–112.

Livingstone, S. (2003) 'Children's use of the internet: reflections on the emerging research agenda', *New Media and Society*, 5(2): 147–66.

McChesney, R.W. (2000) *Rich Media, Poor Democracy*, New York: New Press.

McLuhan, M. (1994) *Understanding Media: The Extensions of Man*, London: Routledge.

Maffesoli, M. (1996) *The Time of Tribes*, London, Sage.

Melucci, A. (1996) *The Playing Self: Person and Meaning in the Planetary Society*, Cambridge: Cambridge University Press.

Poster, M. (1995) *The Second Media Age*, Cambridge: Polity Press.

Readings, B. (1996) *The University in Ruins*, Cambridge: University Press.

Schiller, D. (2000) *Digital Capitalism*, London: MIT Press.

Silverstone, R. (2007) *Media and Morality: On the Rise of the Mediapolis*, Cambridge: Polity Press.

Soper, K. (2007) 'The other pleasures of post-consumerism', *Soundings: A Journal of Politics and Culture*, 35: 31–40.

Stevenson, N. (2006) *David Bowie: Sound, Vision and Fame*, Cambridge: Polity Press.

Tester, K. (1995) 'Moral solidarity and the technological reproduction of images', *Media, Culture and Society*, 17: 469–82.

—— (1997) *Moral Culture*, London: Sage.

—— (2001) *Compassion, Morality and the Media*, Milton Keynes: Open University Press.

Thompson, E.P. (1968) *The Making of the English Working-Class*, London: Pelican.

Virilio, P. (1997) *Open Sky*, London: Verso.

—— (2000) *The Information Bomb*, London, Verso.

Urry, J. (2000) *Sociology Beyond Societies*, London: Routledge.

Williams, R. (1958) *Culture and Society 1780–1950*, London: Pelican.

—— (1974) *Television: Technology and Cultural Form*, New York: Schoken.

11

CITIZENSHIP, COSMOPOLITANISM AND HUMAN RIGHTS

ENGIN F. ISIN AND BRYAN S. TURNER

While sociology has contributed significantly to the study of social rights in the form of social citizenship, it has, until recently, generally neglected the question of **rights** as such. However, the global growth of human rights in the second half of the twentieth century has begun to attract attention from sociologists (Woodiwiss 2003), especially in the context of debates about **cosmopolitanism**. Human rights are central to the so-called 'juridical revolution' (Ignatieff 2001) and they underpin the notion that cosmopolitanism involves both recognition and respect for other people. Because citizenship is often associated with exclusionary national entitlements, many social theorists have criticized traditional forms of citizenship as national membership, because it, seemingly, cannot provide answers to transnational identities and membership, to growing refugee and asylum problems or to migrant and diasporic communities. In this chapter, while recognizing the merit of much criticism of national citizenship, we offer a modest defence of the tradition of citizenship. It is now widely argued that a global world requires a new set of cosmopolitan values and institutions (Appiah 2006), but what part can national citizenship play in such a context?

Historically, modern citizenship is constructed from a set of contributory rights and duties that are related to work, public service (for example, military or jury service) and parenthood or family formation. It defines belonging to a society through the entitlements associated with service, and is perhaps most clearly evident in a national system of taxation. This model of citizenship as social rights has been closely associated with the legacy of the English social historian and sociologist Thomas H. Marshall (1893–1982). Marshallian citizenship has been subject to extensive criticism over the past two decades and the social model of citizenship has been expanded and deepened by approaches that emphasize the flexibility of social membership, the limitations of citizenship merely as rights, and by perspectives that emphasize **identity** and difference. Citizenship is associated with membership of a nation state and the rights of citizenship tend to be exclusionary, that is they are enjoyed by persons who are members of the sovereign state. One other feature of such citizenship is important in underlining its exclusionary character, namely that it is typically inherited at birth, rather like a property right (Shacher and Hirschl 2007).

By contrast, human rights are those rights that are held by virtue of being human. These are inert and passive rights, without matching duties. Citizenship and human rights are different kinds of rights that should be kept analytically distinct. Yet, the experience of the past 50 years evolved in exactly the opposite direction. The concern to defend human rights has often outmatched the defence of citizenship as entitlement, status and social membership. We stress the crucial compatibility of citizenship and human rights but also emphasize the importance of keeping citizenship and human rights distinct. Citizenship is essential for cultivating civic virtues and democratic values. The notion of duty cannot be separated too widely from rights, and this balance between right and duty, however imperfect, is the essence of citizenship.

Although the origins of the Western institution of citizenship can be sought in the political cultures of ancient Greece and Rome, citizenship rights and duties became significant as an aspect of modern politics only when certain key revolutionary events – the English civil war, the American War of Independence and the French Revolution – had appropriated the political norms of ancient Greece and Rome as their own. These revolutions had much in common; for example, the evolution of citizenship, involving a set of exclusionary rights that established claims to collective resources, and these revolutionary developments eventually contributed to the formation of the modern state and then the nation. There was a shared emphasis on the contributions of the 'common man' in services to the state through taxation and military service. Each revolution, however, appropriated and interpreted citizenship quite differently. The republican French tradition assumed the suppression of differences between citizens, who were to share a common loyalty to the Republic, in which religious identities were excluded from the public domain. French notions about citizenship were the result of the Enlightenment and were expressed radically in the writings of aristocrats like the Marquis de Condorcet (1743–94) who, among other things, championed the rights of women as citizens in his essay of 1790 'On Giving Women the Right of Citizenship' (McLean and Hewitt 1994). The radical theories of Thomas Paine regarding monarchy and 'the rights of man' provided the linking themes between the American struggle for independence and the revolutionary conflicts in France (Nelson 2007). In the United States, citizenship emerged with the characteristics that were described classically by Alexis de Tocqueville (1805–59) in his two volumes on *Democracy in America* (2003) in 1835 and 1840. The citizen was seen to participate in the state through civil society, which was composed of a multitude of voluntary associations such as chapels, denominations and towns. Citizens shared a radical doctrine of egalitarianism, and there was a profound suspicion of the central institutions of government. American citizenship emphasized self-help and the autonomy of the local community. In the British case, citizenship was constituted within the framework of the common law, which safeguarded the privileges of property owners and was a barrier against the power of the state over the individual. Parliament and the rule of law established a system of checks and balances against the rise of an absolutist monarchy. The rights of the citizen were essentially negative freedoms from interference, rather than positive rights to enjoy certain privileges.

Those rights that depend on duties to the state have played an important part in the emergence of two modern movements: nationalism and capitalism. We have observed that much of the research undertaken into modern citizenship has been, implicitly or explicitly, concerned with the tensions and contradictions between citizenship and the state (exclusion versus inclusion, rights versus duties), and between nationalism and capitalism (inward versus outward movements, social cohesion versus accumulation).

While citizenship has been an inherent concern of political thought for centuries (wrapped, as it were, within more illustrious terms such as authority, freedom, state, law, right and duty), it is in the early modern era, at the onset of the revolutionary struggles mentioned earlier, that we see the separation of subjects from citizens. While Thomas Hobbes had difficulties in recognizing the citizen as such, we find Baruch Spinoza bravely declaring in the *Tractatus Politicus* (published posthumously in 1677) that 'I call men citizens in so far as they enjoy all the advantages of the commonwealth by civil right; and subjects in so far as they are bound to obey the ordinances or laws of the commonwealth' (Spinoza 1958 [1677]: 285). Early modern political thought had, therefore, already implicitly concentrated on the rights and duties of citizens in relation to the state. By contrast, modern social thought initially concentrated on the social structures that have distorted and limited the formal rights of citizens, such as social class, gender and race. The debate about citizenship in the United States has concentrated heavily on the issues of slavery, race and immigration, whereas the debate in British social science has been conducted in terms of the tensions between citizenship, capitalism and class structure. Marshall developed the principal theory of citizenship within the context of post-war welfare institutions, drawing from a deeper tradition of social struggles over the distribution of wealth. We shall now turn our attention to those two forms of struggle – redistribution and recognition – that structure claims to and demands of citizenship rights and duties. We shall then question the dominant conception of human rights and proceed to develop a conception of cosmopolitan citizenship to distinguish it from human rights.

STRUGGLES FOR REDISTRIBUTION AND CITIZENSHIP

We need to understand Marshall's contribution to investigating citizenship from the perspective of post-war reconstruction and the dominance of the theories of John Maynard Keynes (1883–1946) with respect to the conditions of full employment and low investment. Marshall saw citizenship as an institution that would guarantee the workers a 'modicum' of civilized life by protecting them from the unpredictable vagaries of industrial accident, sickness and unemployment. Keynesian economic strategies of redistribution were intended to increase employment through state investment in utilities when the business cycle was in a downturn. Marshall's view of social rights was as much about offering the minimum of civilized existence to a depressed, urban working class as it was about giving them protection from unemployment. It was against a background of urban squalor that Marshallian citizenship offered some hope of social reform, drawing from a deeper tradition that extended back to the eighteenth and nineteenth centuries.

The Marshallian understanding of citizenship, which came to dominate socio-logical approaches to social rights in the second half of the twentieth century, hardly needs any elaboration (Barbalet 1988). His argument that citizenship was com-posed of three sets of rights is well-known. Civil rights developed in the seven-teenth and eighteenth centuries and were institutionalized in common law, habeas corpus and the jury system. In English common law, its great spokesman was Sir Edward Coke (1552–1634), whose legal philosophy was expressed in the Petition of Right (1628) against arbitrary taxation and imprisonment. In the second stage, political rights were institutionalized in parliament and an extension of the fran-chise, and social rights in the twentieth century were built into the welfare state.

While Marshall's ideas articulated the basic principles of social policy in Britain, they have come under increasing criticism. There is the obvious criticism that he neglected gender, assuming a conventional sexual division of labour that was increasingly irrelevant as women entered the formal labour market and the traditional family was transformed. He was less concerned with race and ethnicity (but see Marshall 1981), despite Britain's dependence on Commonwealth labour to fuel its post-war recovery. These problems can be summarized by saying that Marshall took the definition of 'citizen' for granted, whereas contemporary theo-ries of citizenship have been primarily concerned with rapidly changing identities: who is the citizen? If contributory rights and duties, relating to work, taxation, mil-itary service and parenthood, defined Marshallian citizenship, what is the status of the unemployed, the disabled, the elderly or the migrant worker? As identity has become a dominant issue of modern social movements, the relevance of Marshall's world appears to have been eclipsed and, with it, his approach to social rights. However, we have argued that identity and citizenship are deeply con-nected (Isin and Wood 1999, Isin and Turner 2002).

Social Keynesianism was resisted in the United States, which retained a stronger notion of individual responsibility for welfare and relied on local com-munity initiatives to address social questions. The social dimension of rights claims has not sat easily with the American emphasis on community action and individual autonomy. De Tocqueville's theory of associational democracy, rather than Marshall's welfare assumptions, dominated American social science. De Tocqueville claimed to demonstrate that the absence of centralized, bureaucratic administration had encouraged individual initiative, and voluntary associations and community groups rather than state agencies had emerged to solve social and political problems. It is commonly argued that Americans are characteristically alienated from formal politics, big government and centralized authority, and hence their political commitments are channelled through local and informal associations (Bellah et al. 1985). Many argue that this active citizenship – partic-ipation in churches, voluntary associations and clubs – has, however, declined throughout the post-war period resulting in an erosion of trust, political participation and interest in politics (Putnam 2000). There is, as we have noted, a powerful ideology of individualism that has been deeply suspicious of state involvement in welfare and therefore often antagonistic to the development of social rights. The contemporary failure of American governments to provide adequate medical coverage for the entire population is simply one consequence of the conservative tradition that places responsibility for health care on the shoulders of the individual. Freedom of conscience is championed, but social rights have been seen as aspects of socialism. The American Bar Association's House of Delegates opposed the Declaration of Human Rights in 1948 because it contained social and economic rights, the Eisenhower Administration attempted to downplay the importance of the two Covenants on rights and, following action by Secretary of State Dulles, the United States did not ratify the Convention on Genocide (Galey 1998). The American political class opposed the Declaration on the grounds that its social provisions smacked of communism and, with the fall of communism, American conservatives have been able to claim that neo-liberal economic policies are the only viable global strategy.

Citizenship and welfare have consequently been profoundly altered by the Anglo-American neo-conservative revolution of the late 1970s, which created a political framework in which governments were no longer committed to the universalistic principles of social rights, a comprehensive welfare state and full employment. Its tenets were either emulated by or, more frequently, imposed on other governments throughout the 1980s and 1990s, thereby becoming a global and allegedly successful strategy to reduce personal taxation, reduce waste and encourage entrepreneurship. These global redistribution strategies, that promoted welfare for work, saw a reduction of state intervention, deregulation of the labour and financial markets, implementation of free trade, reduction in personal taxation and fiscal regulation of state expenditure. These strategies harnessed the doctrines of F.A. Hayek (1899–1992), Karl Popper (1902–94), and Milton Friedman (1912–2006) to the purposes of policy formation. New Right theorists argued that judgements about human needs should be left to the operation of the market, not to governments. Keynesian redistribution policies were replaced by more aggressive neo-conservative regimes in which the enterprising and self-regarding consumer became the driving force of the economy and the existence of the free market was a necessary precondition of freedom. It remains to be seen whether the 'credit crunch' of 2008 will force neo-conservative strategists to argue for the decoupling of the global market and tighter controls over financial markets. Globalization without governance appears to be producing significant social and political instability that is, in part, caused by price inflation of basic commodities such as rice and wheat.

STRUGGLES FOR RECOGNITION AND CITIZENSHIP

Traditional forms of Marshallian citizenship were based on social rights, resulting from the contributions of individuals to the state in the form of work, military service (or similar public duty) and parenting. Contributory and redistributive entitlements presuppose a necessary relationship between right and duty. The entitlements of full-time employment, in which the worker has paid taxes and pension contributions, include unemployment benefit, health care, pensions and education. Taxation and pensions are the two economic institutions that defined Marshallian, post-war citizenship, and the other was wartime service. The hallmark of a democratic modern state composed of citizens is a universal taxation system with few loopholes for avoidance. Tax evasion and corruption are, correspondingly, the hallmarks of failing states, low trust and weak citizenship. Where an adequate taxation system is not functioning effectively, governments may turn to the use of such instruments as a national lottery, such as in Thailand and the United Kingdom, to generate funding for cash-strapped public utilities. The traditional combination of Keynesian welfare economics and Marshallian citizenship has been eroded by broad changes in the labour market, the transformation of modern warfare, the decline of the traditional family, the erosion of pension funds, the changing sexual division of labour and changes in reproduction associated with new reproductive technologies (Turner 2001).

The post-war model of social citizenship is under additional strain because the ageing of the populations of the developed world and the decline in fertility are placing increased financial burdens on state pensions, health care and welfare services. As the active workforce declines in relation to the retired population, there is a reduction in the tax base and an erosion of private income flowing to the state through personal taxation. Because the majority of the population have inadequate savings to support themselves in sickness, retirement and old age, there are few easy solutions to this problem, or at least few solutions that an electorate will happily accept. Middle-class voters have typically welcomed cuts in personal income tax, accepting the argument that left-wing governments are high-spending governments, producing inflation, inefficiency and indebtedness. In recent years in the United States and the United Kingdom, major companies have reneged on final salary pension schemes, leaving even more people without adequate pension coverage for old age.

The economic relationship between house prices, savings, investment and pensions in both countries is indicative of the recent transformation of citizenship by Western governments that have embraced neo-conservative policies. Individuals and their families in the developed world seek to fund retirement by selling their homes on the basis of extraordinary increases in the value of their properties. Personal savings remain low, and young people cannot gain access to the property ladder even when interest rates and mortgage repayments are at historically low levels. The crisis in the American sub-prime market has had global consequences and may well disrupt the relationship between low interest rates, consumerism and cheap mortgages, resulting in economic recession as houses are repossessed by the banks and mortgage companies. Repossession is a significant issue, since homelessness is both a material crisis and a social stigma.

Homelessness is a significant stigmatizing feature in a society dominated by home ownership, not only as an economic asset, but also as a moral criterion (Arnold 2004, Feldman 2004). The defining social principles of Keynesian citizenship – high personal taxation, adequate pensions for retirement and a welfare safety net – are being eroded or eliminated. The institutional framework of a common experience of membership of a political community – taxation, military service, a common framework of national education and a vibrant civil society – is declining, and this development is the real basis of the erosion of social citizenship in modern democratic states. We would suggest that, at least in Europe and the United States, social citizenship is eroded as a consequence of changing government strategies, rather than as an outcome of the social changes analysed by Robert Putnam (2000) in his *Bowling Alone*.

By contrast, in authoritarian regimes, such as contemporary Russia, social citizenship has been squandered, because the government of President Putin suppressed both foreign and domestic non-governmental organizations (NGOs) in the interests of the state's domination of civil society. The result of the damage done to civil society after the collapse of the Soviet Union was, at least initially, a rapid decline in the life expectancy of Russian citizens as they faced an unchecked increase in infectious diseases, alcoholism, prostitution and drug abuse (Turner 2004). This interpretation of recent Russian history since the reforms of Boris Yeltsin is, of course, controversial, but given opposition to large-scale immigration, the country will continue to slide down the hierarchy of populous and thriving societies, in which the Russian state depends heavily on rent from energy resources (Desai 2006). Although the Russian economy has recovered as an outcome of rising commodity prices – especially oil and gas – Russia continues to slide towards authoritarianism, as all forms of legitimate opposition have been silenced.

The argument about state security and the need to defend political borders has turned public opinion in many liberal democracies against outsiders in general, and against Muslim communities in particular. The heightened securitization of the state has therefore typically conflated three categories of persons: migrants, refugees and asylum-seekers. Right-wing parties in Austria, Denmark and Germany have successfully mobilized electorates against liberal policies and towards labour mobility, porous frontiers and foreign workers. The Danish case is a good illustration of a society with a low fertility rate and an ageing population; yet a right-wing media generated the 'cartoon crisis' of 2005–06, which was antagonistic to migrants. Although economic migrants contribute significantly to growth, they are often thought to be parasitic on the welfare system of the host society. These workers do not fit easily into a welfare model of contributory rights in an age of terrorism, when states have turned to the maintenance of security as their principal contribution to the functioning of society. European governments have been reluctant to grant citizenship status to migrants without stringent criteria of membership, and naturalization is often a slow and complex process. Applicants for citizenship are increasingly expected to pass a test to prove that they are knowledgeable about the society they want to join – in fact more knowledgeable than its current citizens. Even more absurdly, certain conservative British politicians have famously expected new citizens, such as Indians and Pakistanis, to support English cricket teams rather than their own national sides (Ameli 2002). There is also a widespread reluctance to accept large numbers of economic migrants – although the causes of discontent vary widely, for example between South Africa and Denmark, or between Malaysia and Australia. The hostility of many American politicians to illegal Mexican migration, even when many Southern states rely heavily on Hispanic communities in the labour market, is further evidence of the new emphasis on security and territory in modern electoral politics. The current US policy to build a wall along the whole length of its Mexican border is illustrative of this new xenophobia. We coin a new term – the enclave society – to express the securitization of liberal societies, the building of physical barriers against foreign immigration and the creation of gated communities to defend citizens against urban incivility (Turner 2008).

Multiculturalism is in crisis, because most liberal governments are retreating from open commitment to cultural diversity, emphasizing instead security, cohesion and integration. In the United States, sociologists like Nathan Glazer (1997 and 2002) are claiming that multiculturalism has failed and, in particular, that the United States is a balkanized community, fragmenting along ethnic divisions. The crisis over Hispanic migration and the ostensibly porous nature of the Mexican border provide further evidence of the retreat from multicultural policies as a method of incorporating migrant communities into the dominant society. These economic and social problems are compounded by the current conflicts between 'political Islam' and the West, which has been epitomized in the notion of 'a clash of civilizations'.

Yet, the combined effects and unintended consequences of neo-conservatism and multiculturalism may well have served to expose the fundamental weakness of modern citizenship based on the nation. This process of the nationalization of citizenship meant that citizenship had become synonymous with nationality. The aspirations to universality of citizenship of the state came up against its national definitions, whether understood as racial, ethnic or even religious. Hannah **Arendt** (1951) pointed out the paradox of what she described as the conquest of the state by the nation. She argued that the rise of the **discourse** on minorities articulated

> in plain language what until then had been only implied in the working system of nation-states, namely, that only nationals could be citizens, only people of the same national origin could enjoy the protection of legal institutions, that persons of different nationality needed some law of exception until or unless they were completely assimilated and divorced from their origin.

> (Arendt 1951: 275)

She described this conquest of the state by the nation as 'the transformation of the state from an instrument of the law into an instrument of the nation' (Arendt 1951: 275). This conquest defined citizens of the state as nationals, whether defined racially, ethnically, culturally or even religiously. This was the real origin of the struggle for recognition on the part of those groups that were ostensibly of the state but which remained out of the nation.

CITIZENSHIP VERSUS HUMAN RIGHTS

These struggles, which are now associated with recognition and citizenship rights for social and cultural minorities, are actually an aspect of a still more complex issue, which is the relationship between the human rights of people *qua* humans and the rights of citizens as members of a nation or the state. Human rights and citizenship, and state sovereignty and rights are often contradictory couplets. The declaration of the National Assembly of France in 1789 claimed that 'the natural and imprescriptible rights of man' were 'liberty, property, security and resistance of oppression'. It went on, however, to assert that 'the nation is essentially the source of all sovereignty' and that no 'individual or body of men' could be entitled to 'any authority, which is not expressly derived from it'. It is therefore inaccurate to consider the declaration as indisputable evidence of human rights. While human rights are regarded as innate and inalienable, the rights of citizens are created by states. These two contrasted ideas – the imprescriptible rights of human beings and the exclusive rights of citizens – have remained an important dilemma in any justification of rights.

It is important to recognize that social rights are entitlements enjoyed by citizens and are upheld by courts within the framework of a sovereign state. These rights can be called 'contributory rights' because effective claims against a society are made possible by the contributions that citizens have made to society, typically through work, war or parenting (Turner 2001). These are duties by virtue of the contributions that citizens are expected to make. In contrast, human rights are rights enjoyed by individuals by virtue of being human and as a consequence of their shared vulnerability. John Rawls (1999: 79) in his *The Law of Peoples* has asserted that 'Human rights are distinct from constitutional rights, or from the rights of liberal democratic citizenship', and he calls human rights 'a special class of urgent rights' that protect people from slavery, mass murder and genocide. We do not entirely follow Rawls's position here since he too readily assumes the legitimacy of the state in bringing relief to distressed groups or regions. Human rights are typically deployed in times of emergency where states have failed to protect their own people or, indeed, have been instrumental in genocide as appears to be the case in the Darfur region of the Sudan. Following a natural disaster, the generals in Myanmar were willing to see their own people suffer in order to defend their power base and to protect their own narrow interests, rather than risk the scrutiny of international welfare agencies, thereby creating a human rights crisis.

Again, Arendt (1951) developed the most devastating criticism of 'the rights of Man'. She complained that these inalienable rights are said to exist independently of any government but, once the rights of citizenship have been removed, there is no authority left to protect people as human beings. Human rights that cannot be enforced by an authority are mere abstractions. They are almost impossible to define and it is difficult to show how they add anything to the specific rights of citizens of states. The 'right to have rights' only makes sense for people who already have membership of a sovereign political community. Arendt recognized the irony that these arguments against abstract human rights were originally put forward by conservatives like Edmund Burke (1729–97), who argued that the rights of an Englishman were more secure and definite than any number of abstract rights of Man.

To put it bluntly, a viable state is important as a guarantee of rights. Human rights abuses are characteristically a consequence of state tyranny, dictatorship and state failure, resulting in civil war and anarchy. There is some validity to Burke's argument: the liberties of citizens are better protected by their own state institutions than by external legal or political intervention. The state is the authority through which human rights legislation is enforced. Perhaps, even more strongly, there is no international authority for human rights and 'the purpose of international concern with human rights is to make national rights effective under national laws and through national institutions' (Henkin 1998: 512). In addition, the chaotic outcome of 'human rights wars' in East Timor, Kosovo, Afghanistan and Iraq should cause us to look with radical scepticism on those governments that claim a right to intervene in the name of protecting citizens from their own states (Chandler 2002). In any case, human rights wars tend to occur selectively when powerful states have a direct interest in the conflict. The governments of the United States and Europe show little interest in intervening militarily in Darfur, in the Horn of Africa or in Myanmar, despite intense lobbying by civil society groups. The United States has, however, committed billions of dollars intervening in Afghanistan and Iraq in its 'war against terror' because it has more pressing and immediate geopolitical interests in the Middle East. The security provided by an authoritarian state might be preferred to fragile democracy that requires foreign armies to sustain it. From a Hobbesian point of view, a strong state is required to enforce agreements between conflicting social groups. Another way of expressing this idea is to argue that we need to maintain a distinction between the rights of citizens that are enforced by states, and the human rights of persons that are protected, but frequently inadequately enforced, by both states and international institutions.

The problem with human rights is that we experience them as important but often remote forms of legal protection against possible or actual threats to our safety and security but, in general, people do not exercise their human rights until they are confronted by a crisis. Human rights are associated with victims not with citizens. In contrast, having an active, dynamic citizenry is a precondition of democracy that upholds rights. There is currently no space within which to have an educational experience of human rights, apart from the somewhat abstract community of humanity. The only genuine opportunity for an experience of human rights as a cosmopolitan citizen would be through an international NGO working at a local level, but such experiences are not open to everybody. The point of a tax on mobility, such as the Tobin Tax, is to create indirectly a sense of cosmopolitan duty, thereby making the notion of a shared cosmopolis less abstract. Citizenship remains important as an active domain of democracy and as the principal expression of being political as belonging. In an age of globalization, it should be regarded as a foundation of human rights and not as a competitor.

GLOBAL CITIZENSHIP VERSUS COSMOPOLITAN CITIZENSHIP

It is doubtful whether citizenship can become global, since it remains a state institution, and it is based on contributions that presuppose a reciprocal relationship between rights and duties, in turn implying a relationship between rights and territory. To employ the notion of citizenship to understand rights claims outside the confines of the state often neglects the effective intellectual domain of the concept. A citizen exists originally within the political confines of a state, and until a genuinely global state exists, which has sovereign powers to impose its will, it is misleading to talk about the 'global citizen'. This criticism suggests that some concepts in social science are based on the state and cannot be redefined arbitrarily. Yet, it does not follow that the concept of citizenship is obsolete, inadequate or must remain contained within the state. Citizenship does extend beyond the state, but through institutions and practices that cannot be captured by the concept of the 'global citizen'. We need to distinguish 'global citizen' from 'cosmopolitan citizen'.

Citizenship is both a legal status that confers an identity on persons and a social status that determines how economic and cultural capital are redistributed and recognized within society. While its existence is confirmed by the provision of an identity card or passport, its practices and virtues also expand beyond the borders that the passport identifies. This expansion happens, not because there is an identical polity that exists at another scale, but because struggles for redistribution and recognition expand beyond and across borders. Such expansion occurs primarily because of mobility, not only of people, but also of ideas, images, products, values and political concerns. Over the past several decades, with the development and deployment of telecommunications, media and transportation technologies, there has been an intensification of social relations – both affinities and hostilities – across borders. While citizens may be contained within state boundaries with their rights and duties, neither their social existence nor the practices of their own states follow such containment. We will consider the impact of the mobility of people below. With regard to the way in which states implicate citizens without their movement, there have been multilateral arrangements and international accords that implicate (or fail to implicate) their citizens in a web of rights and responsibilities concerning the environment (wildlife and pollution), trade (copyright and protection), refugees, crime, minorities, war, children and many other issues. While the enforceability of these accords and compliance are ongoing matters, virtually no state exists in social, political or economic isolation. This implicates citizens of states in an international regime of duties by virtue of their states' involvement. This complex web of rights and responsibilities implicating citizens in various ethical, political and social decisions is an important factor in considering citizenship beyond the state. It does not follow that such thinking should assume citizenship without the state but should investigate the ways in which such overflowing rights and responsibilities can be institutionalized without an appeal to a 'world' or 'global' state. We will now consider citizenship as cosmopolitan rather than as a global institution with a proposal for rights of mobility and to transaction.

RIGHTS OF MOBILITY AND RIGHTS TO TRANSACTION

The underlying rights of a cosmopolis are what we might call 'rights of mobility' and 'rights to transaction'. Many modern rights claims are implicitly or explicitly about crossing or interacting through borders or creating new settlements – rights of migrant labour, rights to hold a passport, rights to enter a country, rights of asylum, rights of refugees and other rights to residence, rights to marry outside one's state, or the right to buy property, goods and services or invest in other states. However, these rights to mobility and transaction do not appear to relate to any duties of mobility and transaction. Let us consider a proposal to develop a Tobin-type tax related to various forms of mobility and transaction. The taxation scheme proposed by James Tobin (1978) was initially designed to stabilize national governments by establishing greater regulation over international financial transactions as opposed to goods and services. The original Tobin proposal was, basically, a stamp duty on foreign exchange trading. This basic idea was later developed and expanded to include other taxation possibilities, such as a global lottery. The Tobin proposal, which was both simple and radical, has the overwhelming merit of being global. However, it does not reach far enough down the social ladder of income and wealth to cover goods and services purchased on the Internet across states. It is, to some extent, a tax on elites and it does not therefore have sufficient social or political depth. Multinational corporations such as Amazon, eBay, Apple and Google mediate global transactions worth billions of dollars and each deals with taxes by setting up state-based subsidiaries with many loopholes and variations. If we add thousands of smaller companies and individuals who sell goods and services via credit card transactions, the global market-place created by e-commerce is vast and largely untaxed. We should look therefore towards a more general and widespread tax on the geographical movements and goods and services transactions of, especially, the middle classes – a tourist tax on petrol consumption or tourist tax on air fuel or aviation, a mobility tax on people entering other countries for tourism by the use of a passport, or a sports tax for people travelling abroad to watch sporting events, a transaction tax on goods and services purchased over the Internet across state boundaries or even internal taxes on crossing internal state boundaries in federal constitutions. These taxes would be modest from the point of view of the individual but they could produce a substantial resource for cosmopolitan agencies in struggles against urban and rural poverty, illiteracy, diseases such as AIDS, environmental degradation, climate change or civil unrest.

There are obvious practical problems with such a cosmopolitan tax. There would, presumably, be considerable political resistance, because arguments would arise over the appropriate balance between contributions and benefits. In the United States, citizens may feel that this is yet another tax on rich societies to support foreign countries that have failed economically or have authoritarian governments. However, a Tobin-like cosmopolitan tax could also generate resources that could be used as relief from losses resulting from flooding and the failure of their own government to protect the residents of Louisiana, or to fund the re-housing of American citizens in Alaska where global warming is making their continuing residence problematic. American citizens of Indonesian descent might approve of human rights relief going to their relatives in Ache after the tsunami. In these terms, it would be more difficult to argue that human rights are only treated as important when they provide a justification for United States' intervention in Iraq and elsewhere. The mobility and transaction tax is conceptualized as a duty that applies, in principle, to everybody and that the resources from this cosmopolitan tax would create funding to meet the needs of rights claimers everywhere. This argument therefore involves a radical overhaul of the original Tobin argument by a creating a tax on global movements and transactions, thereby involving large numbers of people in cosmopolitan citizenship and providing a material foundation for cosmopolitanism as a set of values.

KEEPING CITIZENSHIP AND HUMAN RIGHTS DISTINCT

Citizenship involves, often covertly, an education in civic culture in which, because citizens are patriotically proud of the society to which they belong, they are thereby committed to defending its democratic institutions. In terms of Aristotle's *Nicomachean Ethics*, citizenship creates civic virtues that can only be produced by an education in a particular political and social *habitus*. It is not clear what virtues flow from human rights, which, following Rawls, exist to address urgent and immediate crises such as famines resulting from failed states. By contrast, citizenship virtues emerge from the humdrum politics of everyday life in democratic societies. This is where the significance of cities for both cultivating democratic virtues in everyday politics and linking these virtues to cosmopolitan virtues becomes apparent. It is in cities as democratic spaces that 'acts of citizenship' unfold and constitute links that bind various sites of becoming citizens (Isin and Nielsen 2008).

These important relationships between aesthetics, ethics and politics do not exist with respect to human rights or, if they do exist, then the relationship is vague and fragile. If people started, albeit in a modest way, to pay for their rights and to contribute through taxation to the common good at a global level, human rights would become a more tangible and palpable part of everyday life. The 'ordinary man and woman' would feel involved in global projects to prevent famine and drought, and they would begin to act as cosmopolitan citizens. Without a cosmopolitan taxation system, the UN will continue to be largely dependent on US funding and generosity, both of which have been declining. Without these changes, human rights will be subject to the criticism that they are fake rights because they do not correspond to duties and, more importantly, the prospect of global governance and global citizenship will remain mere political fantasies.

REFERENCES AND RECOMMENDED FURTHER READING

Ameli, S.R. (2002) *Globalization, Americanization and British Muslim Identity*, London: ICAS.

Appiah, K.A. (2006) *Cosmopolitanism: Ethics in a World of Strangeness*, New York: W.W. Norton.

Arendt, H. (1951) *The Origins of Totalitarianism*, New York: Harcourt Brace.

Aristotle (1908) *Nicomachean Ethics*, Oxford: Clarendon Press.

Arnold, K.R. (2004) *Homelessness, Citizenship, Identity: The Uncanniness of Late Modernity*, Albany, NY: SUNY Press.

Barbalet, J.M. (1988) *Citizenship*, Milton Keynes: Open University Press.

Bellah, R.N, Madsen, R., Sullivan, W.M., Swidler, A. and Tipton, S.M. (1985) *Habits of the Heart: Individualism and Commitment in American Life*, Berkeley, CA: University of California Press.

Beveridge, W.H. (1944) *Full Employment in a Free Society*, London: Allen & Unwin.

Chandler, D. (2002) *From Kosovo to Kabul: Human Rights and International Intervention*, London: Pluto.

Desai, P. (2006) *Conversations on Russia: Reform from Yeltsin to Putin*, Oxford: Oxford University Press.

Feldman, L.C. (2004) *Citizens Without Shelter: Homelessness, Democracy and Political Exclusion*, Ithaca, NY: Cornell University Press.

Galey, M.E. (1998) 'The Universal Declaration of Human Rights: the role of Congress', *Political Science*, 31(3): 524–9.

Glazer, N. (1997) *We are All Multiculturalists Now*, Cambridge, MA: Harvard University Press.

Henkin, L. (1998) 'The Universal Declaration and the U.S. Constitution', *Political Science*, 31(3): 512–15.

Hobbes, T. (1991). *Man and Citizen (De Homine [1657] and De Cive [1642])*, Indianapolis, IN: Hackett.

Ignatieff, M. (2001) *Human Rights as Politics and Idolatry*, Princeton, NJ: Princeton University Press.

Isin, E.F. and Nielsen, G. (eds) (2008) *Acts of Citizenship*, London: Zed Books.

Isin, E.F. and Turner, B.S. (eds) (2002) *Handbook of Citizenship Studies*, London: Sage.

Isin, E.F. and Wood, P.K. (1999) *Citizenship & Identity*, London: Sage.

Keynes, J.M. (1936) *The General Theory of Employment, Interest and Money*, London: Macmillan.

Mandeville, B. (1924) [1723] *Fable of the Bees*, Oxford: Oxford University Press.

Mann, M. (1987) 'Ruling class strategies and citizenship', *Sociology*, 21(3): 339–54.

Marshall, T.H. (1950) *Citizenship and Social Class and Other Essays*, Cambridge: Cambridge University Press.

—— (1981) [1969] 'Reflections of power', in *The Right to Welfare and Other Essays*, London: Heinemann.

McLean, I. and Hewitt, F. (eds) (1994) *Condorcet: Foundations of Social Choice and Political Theory*, Aldershot: Edward Elgar.

Nelson, C. (2007) *Thomas Paine: Enlightenment, Revolution, and the Birth of Nations*, Harmondsworth: Penguin.

Putnam, R. (2000) *Bowling Alone: The Collapse and Revival of American Community*, New York: Simon & Schuster.

Rawls, J. (1999) *The Law of Peoples*, Cambridge, MA: Harvard University Press.

Shacher, A. and Hirschl, R. (2007) 'Citizenship as inherited property', *Political Theory*, 35(2): 253–87.

Spinoza, B. (1958) *The Political Works*, Oxford: Clarendon Press.

Titmuss, R. (1958) *Essays in 'the Welfare State'*, London: Allen & Unwin.

Tobin, J. (1978) 'A proposal for international monetary reform', *Eastern Economic Journal*, 4: 153–59.

Tocqueville, A. (1835–40) [2003] *Democracy in America*, London: Penguin Books.

Turner, B.S. (2001) 'The erosion of citizenship', *British Journal of Sociology*, (2)52: 189–209.

—— (2004) *The New Medical Sociology*, New York: W.W. Norton.

—— (2008) *Rights and Virtues: Political Essays on Citizenship and Social Justice*, Oxford: Bardwell Press.

Woodiwiss, A. (2003) *Making Human Rights Work Globally*, London: GlassHouse Press.

12

CULTURAL SOCIAL THEORY

BRAD WEST

The advancement of a cultural paradigm has been one of the most significant developments in contemporary social theory. Despite a burgeoning literature about cultural matters, however, there remains ambiguity about what specifically constitutes a cultural theory. In part, this is explained by the term 'culture' being one of the most used words in the English language and also one of the most complex (Williams 1976). The anthropologists Alfred Kroeber and Clyde Kluckhohn (1952), for example, found there to be over 200 different understandings of the term.

A cultural theory, though, is not defined by mere reference to culture; for example, in the theorizing of popular culture, mass culture or indigenous culture. Instead, a cultural theory is one that gives primacy to the dynamics of culture in its analysis, foregrounding the logics and power of ideas, symbols, myths, discourses and emotions that people use in understanding the world and acting within it. This is illustrated in one of the most widely accepted definitions of culture by the cultural theorist Clifford Geertz, who understands it as a 'historically transmitted pattern of meanings embodied in symbols, a system of inherited conceptions expressed by which men communicate, perpetuate, and develop their knowledge about and their attitudes towards life' (Geertz 1973: 89).

The idea of culture as a symbolic structure, as well as a resource for meaning making, differs from more everyday notions of culture as constituting individual accomplishments or referring broadly to collective ways of life. It is also distinguished from theories that privilege economic, material and other social structural forces. Geertz, for example, contrasts the cultural approach with the competing perspectives of interest theory and strain theory (Geertz 1973: 201). According to Geertz, interest theory provides a reductionist **Marx**ist understanding of culture by closely aligning ideology with social class conflict, where human action is driven by utilitarianism and a superficial notion of rational calculation of personal advantage (Geertz 1973: 202). Strain theories that consider social problems as a consequence of **structural** shifts in society are also limited by their focus on the **functionalist** position of culture in the overall operation of society or the psychosocial health of individuals within it, reducing culture to a 'symptom and a remedy' (Geertz 1973: 200). By contrast, Geertz argues that analytic attention should be squarely focused on the nature and dynamics of cultural variables, with ideology being a system of interacting symbols and patterns of meanings. This is not to say that cultural theorists are uninterested in non-cultural variables but they argue that culture has a 'relative autonomy' from them (Alexander 2003) with it actively shaping, as well as being shaped, by economic, material and other social structural forces.

Despite a general agreement on how cultural theories differ from competing social theories, there is surprisingly little consensus about what might constitute the field of cultural theory. Existing literature in the area is mostly made up of reviews of specific cultural paradigms and surveys of mainstream social theories from a cultural perspective. In particular, cultural theory is often associated with the strengths and limitations of its articulation within the interdisciplinary area of British cultural studies, with its origins in the Centre for Contemporary Cultural Studies (CCCS) at the University of Birmingham. Richard Hoggart (1957) and Raymond Williams (1958, 1977) provided important foundational studies for this particular cultural field. It was Stuart Hall, however, who was most influential in establishing its distinctive critical approach, which defined itself in opposition both the traditional concern of the humanities with literary and artistic merit and the positivistic and structural paradigms in the social sciences. This occurred initially in relation to the development of a 'New Left' analysis of social class (Hall 1985, Hall and Jacques 1983), largely through adapting the work of the Italian Marxist, Antonio **Gramsci** (1971) and, later, in developing a framework for the analysis of new **identities** emerging around youth, race and gender (Hall 1992).

Despite the influence of the Birmingham form of cultural studies, not only in Britain, but in the United States, Australia and elsewhere, cultural theory is constituted by a diversity of cultural perspectives. This includes various sub-disciplines, such as cultural anthropology, cultural sociology, cultural economics, cultural political science and cultural geography. These have often been critical of the unwillingness of British cultural studies to systematically define the principals and methods of its inquiry and frustrated by its intellectual amnesia to cultural themes in classical social theory, for example **Weber**'s (1930, 1921) insights into charismatic authority, **Durkheim**'s (1912) outline of ritual solidarity and **Simmel**'s (1997) observations on interaction and individuality in the metropolis city. **Postmodern** and postcolonial perspectives have also become increasingly influential contributors to the development of cultural theory (Baudrillard 1983, Clifford 1989). These challenge the original neo-Marxist agenda of British cultural studies through an emphasis on the non-class-based logics of global consumption, technological advancement and social status.

So marked has been the collective influence of these various strains of cultural theory, that cultural thought has increasingly been integrated into and combined with mainstream social theory. The shift to more culturally sensitive social theorizing is popularly referred to as the 'cultural turn'. In the social sciences this has had two implications. First, analysis of consumption and lifestyle, such as in the media, art, music and fashion, has become increasingly popular. Where such spheres were once not considered a basis for serious social scientific scholarship, there is now a widespread appreciation of their importance in shaping the economy, politics and the public sphere (Lash and Urry 1994). Second, a cultural approach is increasingly being deployed to analyse other, seemingly more 'serious', areas of social life that were once exclusively analysed in relation to the so-called 'hard' variables of material and economic forces. To take one illustrative case, studies of work and employment were previously dominated by consideration of income distribution, economic competition and elite interests. In coming to terms with new flexible production modes and the global growth of the creative industries, contemporary studies of employment are now just as likely to discuss cultural factors such as identities, images, risk taking, personality and emotions (Hochschild 1997, Vaughan 1996).

The emergence of contemporary cultural theory in the humanities, an area traditionally involved in hermeneutic interpretation, has followed a different trajectory to that of the social sciences. Where social science disciplines have adopted dramaturgical and textual approaches for a better comprehension of post-industrial society, the humanities have increasingly moved from their traditional concern with **aesthetic** refinement to a concern with the analysis of social structure. The integration of **Foucauldian** conceptions of power (Foucault 1973 [1963], 1991 [1975]) and developments in literary criticism have been particularly influential in this paradigm shift.

The widespread influence of Foucault's understanding of power as embedded in **discourse**s provided the humanities with a newfound legitimacy for discussing the social. Foucault states that 'power and knowledge directly imply one another . . . there is no power relation without the correlative constitution of a field of knowledge' (1991: 27). In such works as *The Birth of the Clinic* (1973 [1963]) and *Discipline and Punish* (1991 [1975]), Foucault provided an approach that could locate texts historically within power relationships, for example, in highlighting how professionals in the health and criminal justice systems attained authority through the production of new expert discourses. This conception of knowledge as a force shaping society provided a culturally orientated alternative to the more static Marxist view of dominant ideologies reinforcing the status quo. From the Foucauldian power/knowledge nexus, cultural scholars in the humanities were also able to focus on the counter-discourses and the emergence of new identities, such as those associated with technology and sexuality (Haraway 1991, Butler 1990).

Equally influential in the emergence of cultural theory in the humanities was a movement in literary criticism that saw its intellectual focus move beyond direct concern with textual meanings. The Canadian theorist Northrop Frye (1957) was influential in this development by arguing that the role of the critic should be to make sense out of the text 'not by going to some historical context or by commenting on the immediate experience of reading but by seeing its structure within literature and literature within culture' (Hamilton 1990: 27). In the *Anatomy of Criticism*, this approach allowed Frye (1957) to consider important structural questions regarding the meanings of different genres and narrative trajectories and their popularity in different historical contexts; for example, how the prevalence of realism and ironic despair in contemporary literature relates to new complex forms of social integration.

The Russian critic Mikhail Bakhtin (1981) was also a central figure in the development of a structural poetics with an intellectual concern which goes beyond the immediate text. In contrast to Frye, Bakhtin challenged the idea of meaning being embedded in genre, instead concentrating on the openness of interpretation and its subversive qualities. At the heart of Bakhtin's work is the concept of the 'dialogic' and its relation to the creative and relational aspects of the novel. Rather than literature containing a fixed unitary meaning, Bakhtin argues that, within any single text, there are a number of contending voices that influence interpretation by shifting relations to each other, opening the text up to multiple readings. The idea of dialogic relations has provided an important basis for theorizing the fragmentation of texts in postmodern society. The dialogic has also been influential in developing the concept of intertextuality, which refers to the increasingly common practice of texts making reference to other texts, an act that is thought to challenge the **modernist** ideals of originality, truth and progress (Kristeva 1980).

While awareness of such differences and divisions in cultural theory is important, an overdue focus on these issues has drawn attention away from the common ground to be found among competing cultural paradigms (McLennan 2006). In this chapter, introducing cultural theory, I attempt to focus on what unites, rather than divides, by exploring three key intellectual concerns prominent across various traditions of cultural analysis: symbolic order and ritual, social constructions of time and space and fragmented identities and cultural conflict. Given the blurred line between cultural and social theory, some of the theorists outlined here have been reviewed elsewhere in this Companion. Where possible, however, the chapter has focused on work that is exclusively cultural and often less well-known outside of the intellectual networks of cultural scholars.

SYMBOLIC ORDER AND RITUAL

A dominant characteristic of modern social theory has been an emphasis on the divide between pre-industrial forms of social existence, based on tradition and kinship ties, and the impersonal relations found in modern society. This is evident in such classic binary distinctions as those made by Ferdinand Toennies (1957) between *Gemeinschaft* (community) and *Gesellschaft* (association) and by Max Weber in his influential theorizing of rationality (Weber 1930, 1921). According to Weber, the instrumental logics associated with the **Industrial Revolution** infiltrated other spheres in social life, emptying them of meaning, with humans left to live out a disenchanted existence, trapped in a metaphoric 'iron cage'. From a cultural perspective, such theories are problematic in that they are inattentive to cultural forms, patterns and processes found across different social and historical contexts.

The most important theorist in regard to these 'cultural universals' is the French sociologist Émile Durkheim. Durkheim had a diverse intellectual career, with several of his works being associated with the theoretical perspectives of positivism and functionalism. However, his later scholarship, which culminated in *The Elementary Forms of Religious Life* (1912) provided an important, yet frequently unacknowledged, template for the development of cultural theory, in particular for **semiotic** and ritual analysis. Central to Durkheim's cultural theorizing is an understanding of society as *sui generis* (a Latin term which refers to society having a life of its own and being more than the sum of its parts). In his now classic definition of religion, he argues that society itself is defined by a symbolic differentiation between the sacred and the profane. The sacred are those symbols that demand attention and inspire reverence, in contrast to the more everyday profane. According to Durkheim, whether in traditional Australian Aboriginal clans with totems (the site for his empirical analysis), or in contemporary industrial society with emblems such as national flags, colours and heroes, it is sacred symbols that enable the sharing of collective emotion.

Durkheim posits that the power of sacred symbols comes from their ability to represent collective identity, embodying abstract notions and beliefs that can never be fully conceived of and interacted with in a rational way. This symbolic function is particularly evident in societal rituals, such as commemorations and anniversaries of important historic events. In such cases, the ritual revolves around the adornment of collective symbols which, in turn, allows for a heightened level of emotional energy – which Durkheim refers to as 'collective effervescence'. While symbols are simply ideals, Durkheim argued that their importance to the 'collective conscience', the culmination of shared beliefs and values, means that they affect social life in the same way as if they were real physical forces. Documenting the centrality of ritual to all societies, he writes:

> [T]here can be no society which does not feel the need of upholding and reaffirming at regular intervals the collective ideas which make its unity and personality. Now this moral remaking cannot be achieved except by the means of reunions, assemblies and meetings where the individuals . . . reaffirm in common their common sentiments.
>
> (Durkheim 1912: 427)

Durkheim directly informed the work of various important cultural theorists, including Marcel Mauss (1974 [1924]) on the emotional and diplomatic significance of gift exchange and Maurice Halbwachs (1941) on the constant revising and selective remembering of history. More recently, Jeffrey Alexander (2003) has revived Durkheim's later work in attempting to define the boundaries of cultural sociology. Durkheim's most important legacy, though, is more broadly based, being a template for the general development of semiotic and ritual theories. The originality of Durkheim's theory of symbols, often advanced in public seminars well-attended by other eminent French intellectuals (Smith and

Alexander 2005), for example, positions him as an important precursor to Ferdinand de Saussure and the development of semiotic analysis – the study of sign processes. As will be evident below, central tenets of Durkheim's thought on symbols and rituals also play a prominent role in the work by important contemporary cultural theorists such as Mary Douglas and Victor Turner.

According to **Saussure** (1986 [1916]), language should be understood as a structured sign system in which the relationship between a word and its referent is completely arbitrary. The word 'dog', for example, evokes a mental image of the animal, but does not in any way refer to its look or sound. An important part of this system is the relationship between the 'signifier', the sign or referent, and the 'signified', that to which it refers. This distinction illustrates that language does not have inherent meaning but is rather the outcome of a meaning-making process. Saussure was particularly influential for Roland **Barthes** (1957, 1975) who was one of the early theorists advocating a semiotic approach to understanding contemporary social life. Developing the Saussurian distinction between the signifier and the signified, Barthes pointed to the multiple layers of sign systems, arguing for an interpretive frame that divided between 'denotation', the common or literal meaning of a sign, and 'connotation', involving more abstract and multiple meanings. Using this approach, Barthes was able to deconstruct various *Mythologies* (1957) in French society, illustrating how these were used to naturalize bourgeois ideologies. For example, Barthes illuminated the deep meanings that are central to consumption and contemporary identity, including the religious-like worship of Citroën automobiles and insight into the grandiloquent character of professional wrestling for the working classes.

Pierre **Bourdieu** (1984 [1979]) furthered our understanding of the relationship between symbolic codes and social class beyond textual representations to embodied practices, tastes and dispositions. Where theories of social inequality have traditionally focused on the distribution of resources (economic capital) and the institutional and network ties of elites (social capital), Bourdieu argues that cultural capital is the key to social exclusion. Cultural capital is a form of what Bourdieu refers to as *habitus*, constituted by 'durable, transposable dispositions' (1977 [1972]: 22) that affect the way individuals act socially, present themselves physically and come to establish tastes, aspirations and world-views. In *Distinction* (1984 [1979]), Bourdieu argued that the extent to which an individual holds cultural capital affects their ability to be discriminating in a way consistent with people of high levels of income, education and occupational prestige. Cultural capital as a form of objective and embodied cultural knowledge exists relatively independent of material resources but can be converted into economic capital through facilitating interactions with and access to elite social networks. This conversion is not automatic but contingent, differing in relation to occupational and institutional norms. It is possible, therefore, for someone to hold different degrees of cultural and economic capital.

Where the analytic emphasis of Barthes and Bourdieu is on social class representations, other semiotic traditions in contemporary cultural theory have retained the Durkheimian focus on moral classification. One of the prominent exponents of this school is the anthropologist Mary Douglas, who highlights the importance of symbolic distinctions for collective identity. In her book *Purity and Danger* (1966), she highlights how ideas about symbolic pollution allow for the ordering of society. Her concept of pollution does not refer to the inherent hygienic properties of things but rather to their symbolic properties as 'matter out of place' (Douglas 1966: 36). Notions of dirt and feelings of being disgusted emerge when things are outside of their normal boundary system. Examples include our relation to fingernails, hair and skin removed from the body or cooking utensils being located outside of the domestic zone of the kitchen, such as in a bedroom. For Douglas, symbolic pollution is a cultural universal, and she notes that 'pollution behaviour in one part of the world and another is only a matter of detail' (Douglas 1966: 35).

A large part of Douglas's empirical work involved ethnographies of indigenous societies and analysis of pre-modern texts, such as her classic studies of the Lele people and the linguistic structure of the book of *Leviticus*. At various stages in her career, however, she also elaborated on the relevance of cultural universals for industrial society, including the contemporary symbolism of material goods and acts of consumption (Douglas and Isherwood 1980). Elsewhere, she used the symbolic boundary ideas of grid and group to consider the cultural dimensions of new political movements. In *Risk and Culture* (Douglas and Wildavsky 1982), for example, Douglas and the political scientist Aaron Wildavsky attempted to explain the rise of environmentalism as a consequence of shifts in risk perception. According to Douglas and Wildavsky, environmentalism comes about, not as an objective consequence of increased environmental risks in the second half of the twentieth century, but as part of a social movement in which political entrepreneurs established the environment as a symbol and site to critique the cultural basis of modernity in the era following the Vietnam war.

Where the work of Bourdieu and Douglas has a structural focus on symbolic systems, with meaning established relationally, other contemporary semiotic and ritual approaches emphasize human **agency** and the multiplicity of social outcomes. An important theorist for the development of this perspective is Victor Turner (1969), who argued that cultural analysis has been too concerned with structure, ignoring what he referred to as liminality – periods and cultural characteristics that exist at the margins of society, but which at either particular or regular times and instances are accepted by society. This is despite their literally defying dominant norms and values of the society. Where Durkheim argued that dominant sacred values and norms are reinforced through societal ritual, Turner states that many rituals, such as medieval carnival or Halloween, are characterized by the suspension of everyday rules and order, 'anti-structural' phenomena 'betwixt and between ... custom, convention, and ceremony' (1969: 95). Such liminal periods involve 'threshold' experiences where hierarchies in society are replaced by status ambiguity and role reversal. According to

Turner, the emotional release permitted during ritual times is functional for society in re-establishing a sense of community and acting as a kind of emotional release value for pent-up tensions. Turner, however, avoids **deterministic** thinking about how any particular liminal episode will play itself out, with the spontaneity of liminality opening it up to the 'realm of pure possibility' (1967: 97).

Turner's array of concepts, such as play, flow and social drama, has been particularly influential in the development of the interdisciplinary field of performance studies. The concept 'performativity' has also been an important basis for cultural understandings of the seemingly fundamental (Butler 1990), as well as the unprecedented complexities of contemporary plural society (Roach 1996). Alexander (2004), for example, has used Turner's work to develop a performative framework for an understanding of the September 11 terrorist attacks, accounting for the event in terms of actors, audiences, props, scripts and plots. In the terrorist attack on New York's Twin Towers, for example, Alexander argues that Al Qaeda not only wished to inflict death and destruction but also to create political and social instability in the United States through an act in which American culture would be seen as weak and morally corrupt. While the performance was initially successful in threatening to disrupt social order, this was constructed in the United States public sphere in a way that reinterpreted the event through nationalist mythologies, with the effect of strengthening, not weakening, social solidarity.

Social constructions of time and space

The second key concern of cultural theory outlined in this chapter involves the social construction of time and space. Where social theories have frequently examined society from the standpoint of a belief in absolute values and standard Cartesian notions of time and space, cultural theory is more relativist in highlighting their 'fuzzy' and socially constructed nature (Zerubavel 1981). Here, cultural theories can again be distinguished from social theories emerging from the **Frankfurt School** that invoke a nostalgic crisis metaphor to describe the loss of primordial and authentic social life (Turner 1987). By contrast, Maurice Halbwachs, a seminal figure in theorizing cultural perceptions surrounding time and space, argued that our understanding of the past is always tied to present problems, with the way we remember history being 'essentially a reconstruction of the past [that] adapts the image of ancient facts to the beliefs and spiritual needs of the present' (1941: 7). In recent decades, this approach to the past has provided the theoretical template for a large number of empirical inquiries, including examinations of changes to the portrayal of history in government-sanctioned remembrances and memorials, the presence and interpretation of certain historical events in school textbooks and the new forms of commercial engagements with the past in museums and tourist attractions.

In highlighting the selective nature of historical remembering, such studies point to the socially constructed nature of national consciousness. An important scholar in this area has been the historian Benedict Anderson. In *Imagined Communities*, Anderson notes that 'the nation is "imagined" because its members never know or even hear of most other members, and yet they conceive of themselves as co-members of the same over-riding important unit' (Anderson 1983: 15–16). The idea of nationalism as imagined can be distinguished from other theories of nationalism that have been divided between primordial and instrumental approaches. Primordialists argue that national identity is deeply rooted in cultural and religious beliefs. In contrast, instrumentalists contend that the nation-state is something 'invented' by elites. Anderson provides a more culturally sophisticated account by moving his analysis beyond issues of 'falsity' and 'fabrication', intersecting the two perspectives by appreciating both the community and creative dimensions in the rise of nationalism.

Anderson's theory of imagined communities is closely tied to the development of print capitalism. Here, we have the orthodox Marxist emphasis on class interests and the means of production, accompanied by a culturally sensitive concern with literature and meaning-making. According to Anderson, the rise in technological communication laid the basis for national consciousness by reducing the number of languages, and thus creating larger fields of fixity and belonging. Following **Hegel**, Anderson also observed that newspapers served as a substitute for morning prayer, creating an extraordinary mass ceremony through the process of simultaneous consumption. Thus, in Anderson's theory, agency shifts from the state to individual readers, 'imagining' themselves part of a larger community.

A sub-theme of *Imagined Communities* is that nationalism first developed in the new world rather than in the metropole. Where social theories of nationalism have typically located its origins in Europe, Anderson argued that national consciousness initially grew among colonialists. Where many travelled to the new world to enhance their social standing, upon their return they found that, despite a successful accumulation of economic capital abroad, they were stigmatized by their contact with the colonial frontier. In turn, this created the cultural conditions in the colonies for the development of a new modern form of romantic identification with place, the basis for contemporary national identification.

Where Anderson notes the role of international travel in the formation of national consciousness, contemporary literatures on global mobility have tended to focus on its role in disintegrating national narratives and the possibility of the creation of a new global identity. This is evident in the work of Paul Gilroy (1993), who heralds global travel and other diasporic experiences as a way of dislodging national identities in favour of more hybrid and universal ones. The popular work of the anthropologist James Clifford also argues that travel is 'a figure for different modes of dwelling and displacement, for trajectories and identities, for storytelling and theorizing in a postcolonial world of global contacts' (Clifford 1989: 177).

Central to such thinking about the possibility of global cultures has been the concept of **cosmopolitanism**. While conceived in various ways, cosmopolitanism refers to openness to the world and acceptance of cultural differences within it. Evident in the writings of Kant, its contemporary usage emerges from the post-Cold War debates about the ills of nationalism and the possibilities for a world citizenship. It is currently applied to a variety of international problems, from global justice and human **rights** to global terrorism and global warming. As these are not limited to the boundaries of any particular nation state, scholars such as Ulrich **Beck** (2006) have argued that, to solve them, we must both adopt a cosmopolitan sense of global citizenship and expand international law and governance. A problem with such literature is that it analyses global consciousness as well as being an advocate for it. Recently, important critiques of this literature have emerged from cultural scholars who have raised crucial questions about the cultural desirability of a global political apparatus in the absence of widespread emotional attachment to a global community and the unlikelihood that a strong mythological foundation for such a consciousness would form (Calhoun 2003, Kendall *et al.* 2008).

Where this cosmopolitan literature has advocated the movement away from national consciousness, theorists working within a postmodern paradigm have argued that, in the West, there has already been a break with the meanings associated with modernity. It is argued that these have been replaced by a new sign system underpinned by the global consumption of commodities. According to **Baudrillard**, for example, the 'circulation, purchase, sale, appropriation of differentiated goods and signs/objects today constitute our language, our code, the code by which the entire society communicates and converses' (Baudrillard 1988: 79–80). While Baudrillard considers this code as the new basis for societal integration, it is something that involves a replacing of the real with a simulated or virtual world, 'a hallucinatory resemblance of the real to itself' (1983: 3). It constitutes an environment where the sign loses its traditional reference, the product becoming a simulacrum, where the actor is unable to distinguish between the blurring of the real and the copy. This is particularly the case, it is argued, in urban themed spaces such as shopping malls, housing estates and theme parks, where actors are thought to become lost in a world of commodity fetishism constituted by 'pure and unrelated presents in time' (Jameson 1984: 72).

FRAGMENTED IDENTITIES AND CULTURAL CONFLICT

The final theme of this chapter is fragmented identities and cultural conflict, a grouping of cultural theories that explores changes to collective and individual identity and the associated divisions that have been established in contemporary society as a consequence of the breaking down of traditional attachments to social class, institutional religion and the West. Where Weber (1930, 1968) and other classical social theorists focused on the logics of modernity and its puritan sentiments of constraint, since at least the mid-1960s the emergence of a consumption-based economy has caused a cultural shift towards freedom and impulse. The rapid rise of the media, entertainment and tourist industries, it has been argued, has fundamentally altered the 'spirit of capitalism' (Campbell 1995). Pleasure and play, once seen as a destabilizing force for collective identities now provide an essential basis for individual understanding, the search for authenticity and an important way for new groups to form around generational, ethnic and sexual identities (Taylor 1994).

This new role of pleasure is clearly evident in some of the canonical works of British cultural studies, where consumption practices are theorized as forces of resistance (Hall and Jefferson 1976). In *Subculture: The Meaning of Style*, Dick Hebdige (1979) illustrates the importance of style and image in the creation of such youth groups as mods and rockers, skinheads and punks. Rather than the workplace being the organizing site for social protest, these subcultural groups unite and seek space from the dominant culture through their consumption of goods such as clothing and music, challenging 'the principal of unity and cohesion, which contradicts the myth of consensus' (Hebdige 1979: 18). A problem with these early subcultural studies is that resistance is considered as something that is purely oppositional, typically with its roots in the lived experience of working-class youth. As such, they provided little scope for understanding the role of capitalism in the production of subcultures. As various theorists have subsequently noted, 'alternative' youth cultures are very much part of contemporary capitalism and consumption, such as the post-Fordist search for distinction markers, rather than being inherently rebellious.

For many cultural studies scholars, however, even mass forms of cultural expression have come to be understood as acts of resistance. This reading is possible through cultural products being polysemic, that is, open to various interpretations. For example, in analysing the pop singer Madonna, Fiske (1989) rejected what he considered to be simplistic understandings of popular culture in terms of patriarchal capitalism, arguing that Madonna's displays of sexuality and her use of parody, for example in her Marilyn Monroe imagery, actually encourage resistance to dominant gender norms. According to Fiske, such images that engage in 'mocking the conventional representations of female sexuality while at the same time conforming to them' (Fiske 1989: 104) empower young girls and help them to deal with complex issues of gender by problematizing the binary markers that attempt to pigeonhole women as either saints or sinners.

In a study of women's reading of romantic fiction, Janice Radway (1991) also demonstrates that, from a reception or audience studies perspective, it is problematic to suggest that even the trashiest of popular cultural forms will have a passive ideological effect. From discussions with women readers from a Midwestern town in the United States, she found that, while the text seemed to naturalize the role of the woman in the domestic sphere, women themselves used the escapism of reading as an act of defiance and the stories of ideal love and romance as a way of critically evaluating their own relationships. As Radway states, 'women are reading not out of contentment but out of dissatisfaction, longing and protest' (1991: 214).

Popular cultural forms and styles, though, are not only a site for individual resistance but are also the basis of political groupings. This is particularly evident within new social movements. Traditionally understood, 'social movements' are 'a form of collective action, made up of informal groups of people committed to broad change at the levels of individual behaviour, social institutions and structures' (Jennett and Stewart 1989: 3). They have been subject to various sorts of analysis, including rational choice theories, a paradigm that holds assumptions about people being egoistic and driven to optimize personal gain (cf. Geertz 1973). New social movements, by contrast, have more often attracted cultural analysis, being intimately associated with new identities and lifestyle options such as homosexuality, lesbianism and queer sexuality, environmentalism, spirituality, fundamentalism and anti-globalization movements (Melucci 1994). Given the importance of identity to the involvement of individuals in new social movements, it has been argued that their success should be judged not only by particular political outcomes, but also by their ability to provide a coherent code for an alternative lifestyle, typically established through new forms of global communication associated with the Internet.

Where such studies see society as fragmenting into diverse groupings based on fluctuating coalitions, other cultural theorists have pointed to the emergence of new macro lines of conflict. The so-called 'culture wars' in Western nations, for example, are thought to centre on contemporary social issues such as abortion, gay rights, affirmative action, multiculturalism and censorship. With the great conflicts of the early twentieth century being diminished by increased class mobility, Christian secularism and the rise of third way politics, scholars such as James Davison Hunter (1991) have argued that a meta-divide has appeared between 'the impulse toward orthodoxy' and 'the impulse toward progressivism'. Subscribers to orthodoxy adhere to literal interpretations of values and believe in the unchangeable nature of morality, while those holding the progressive world-view interpret morality relatively, not as a universal truth but as an unfolding reality that reflects the spirit of the age (Hunter 1991). Hunter argues that the culture wars have caused a 'new cultural realignment' with traditional institutions and groups, such as those within established political parties, churches and ethnic collectives, increasingly realizing that they have more in common with those holding their equivalent orthodox or progressive worldviews in other institutions and groups than with many of their fellow members.

THE FUTURE OF CULTURAL THEORY

This chapter has provided an introduction to cultural theory, principally by mapping its rise and by drawing attention to the common themes and intellectual interests that exist across different cultural traditions and perspectives. The theoretical tensions within the field, though, are also highlighted. These principally relate to the existence of cultural universals and debates about cultural patterns and historical continuity. The unprecedented appreciation of cultural variables in academic analysis of social life, though, has also raised new concerns, some by scholars broadly within the field (Rojek and Turner 2000), that cultural analysis is displacing traditional intellectual examinations of the social and accounts of 'real' social action, attitudes and power plays.

At the root of such critiques is a key question regarding the relationship between cultural and other kinds of variables associated with social structures, agency and corporeal experience. Despite the mammoth rise in appreciation of the power of cultural forms over the past several decades, most scholars still understand culture as an abstract force, able to be distinguished from sites where it takes concrete form, such as in material objects and the body, or in its application, for example in Bourdieu's notion of practice (1977). A new direction for cultural theory would be to rethink this dualism, either by increasingly conceiving of material and economic forces in cultural ways or by finding an alternative synthesis (Friedland and Mohr 2004: 4).

REFERENCES

Alexander, J.C. (2003) *The Meanings of Social Life: A Cultural Sociology*, New York: Oxford.
—— (2004) 'From the depths of despair: performance, counterperformance, and "September 11"', *Sociological Theory*, 22(1): 88–105.
Anderson, B. (1983). *Imagined Communities: Reflections on the Origin and Spread of Nationalism*, London: Verso.
Bakhtin, M. (1981) *The Dialogic Imagination*, Austin, TX: University of Texas Press.
Barthes, R. (1957) *Mythologies*, London: Cape.
—— (1975) *The Pleasure of the Text*, London: Cape.
Baudrillard, J. (1983) *Simulations*, New York: Semiotext(e).
—— (1988) *America*, New York: Verso.
Beck, U. (2006) *Cosmopolitan Vision*, Cambridge: Polity Press.
Bourdieu, P. (1984) [1979] *Distinction*, London: Routledge and Kegan Paul.
—— (1977) [1972] *Outline of a Theory of Practice*, Cambridge: Cambridge University Press.
Butler, J. (1990) *Gender Trouble: Feminism and the Subversion of Identity*, New York: Routledge.
Calhoun, C. (2003) '"Belonging" in the cosmopolitan imaginary', *Ethnicities*, 3(4): 531–68.
Campbell, C. (1995) *The Romantic Ethic and the Spirit of Modern Consumerism*, Oxford: Blackwell.
Clifford, J. (1989) 'Notes on travel and theory', *Inscriptions*, 5: 177–88.
Douglas, M. (1966) *Purity and Danger*, London: Routledge and Kegan Paul.
Douglas, M. and Isherwood, B. (1980) *The World of Goods: Towards an Anthropology of Consumption*, Harmondsworth: Penguin.
Douglas, M. and Wildavsky, A. (1982) *Risk and Culture*, Berkeley, CA: University of California Press.
Durkheim, E. (1912) *The Elementary Forms of Religious Life*, London: George Allen and Unwin.
Fiske, J. (1989) *Reading the Popular*, Boston: Unwin Hyman.
Foucault, M. (1973) [1963] *The Birth of the Clinic*, London: Tavistock.
—— (1991) [1975] *Discipline and Punish*, London: Penguin.

Friedland, R. and J. Mohr (2004) 'The cultural turn in American sociology', in R. Friedland and J. Mohr (eds), *Matters of Culture: Cultural Sociology in Practice*, Cambridge: Cambridge University Press.

Frye, N. (1957) *Anatomy of Criticism*, Princeton, NJ: Princeton University Press.

Geertz, C. (1973) *The Interpretation of Cultures*, New York: Basic Books.

Gilroy, P. (1993) *The Black Atlantic*, London: Verso.

Gramsci, Antonio (1971) *Selections from the Prison Notebooks*, London: New Left Books.

Halbwachs, M. (1941) *The Legendary Topography of the Gospels*, Paris: Presses Universitaires de France.

—— (1950) *Collective Memory*, ed. M. Douglas, New York: Harper & Row.

Hall, S. (1985) 'Signification, representation, ideology: Althusser and the post-structuralist debates', *Critical Studies in Mass Communication*, 2: 91–114.

—— (1992) 'Our mongrel selves', *New Statesman and Society*, 19 June, pp. 6–8.

Hall, S. and Jefferson, T. (1976) *Resistance through Rituals*, London: HarperCollins Academic.

Hall, S. and Jacques, M. (1983) *The Politics of Thatcherism*, London: Lawrence & Wishart.

Hamilton, A.C. (1990) *Northrop Frye: Anatomy of His Criticism*, Toronto: University of Toronto Press.

Haraway, D. (1991) *Simians, Cyborgs and Women: The Reinvention of Nature*, New York: Routledge.

Hebdige, Dick (1979) *Subculture*, London: Methuen.

Hochschild, A.R. (1997) *The Time Bind: When Work Becomes Home and Home Becomes Work*, New York: Metropolitan Books.

Hoggart, R. (1957) *The Uses of Literacy*, London: Chatto & Windus.

Hunter, J.D. (1991) *Culture Wars: The Struggle to Define America*, New York: Basic Books.

Jameson, F. (1984) 'Postmodernism, or, the culture of late capitalism', *New Left Review*, 146: 53–92.

Jennet, C. and Stewart, R.G. (eds) (1989) *Politics of the Future: The Role of Social Movements*, South Melbourne: Macmillian.

Kendal, G., Skrbis, Z. and Woodward, I. (2008) 'Cosmopolitanism, the nation-state and imaginative realism', *Journal of Sociology*, 44(4): 401–18.

Kristeva, J. (1980) *Desire in Language: A Semiotic Approach to Literature and Art*, New York: Columbia University Press.

Kroeber, A.L. and Kluckhohn, C. (1952) *Culture: A Critical Review of Concepts and Definitions*, Cambridge, MA: Peabody Museum.

Lash, S. and Urry, J. (1994) *Economies of Signs and Space*, London: Sage.

Mauss, M. (1974 [1924]) *The Gift*, trans. by I. Cunnison, London: Routledge and Kegan Paul.

McLennan, G. (2006) *Sociological Cultural Studies: Reflexivity and Positivity in the Human Sciences*, Basingstoke: Palgrave.

Melucci, A. (1994) 'A strange kind of newness: what's 'new' in new social movements?', in E. Larana, H. Johnston and J.R. Gusfield (eds), *New Social Movements: From Ideology to Identity*, Philadelphia: Temple University Press, pp. 101–32.

Radway, J. (1991) *Reading the Romance*, Chapel Hill, NC: University of North Carolina Press.

Roach, J. (1996) *Cities of the Dead: Circum-Atlantic Performance*, New York: Columbia University Press.

Rojek, C. and Turner, B. (2000) 'Decorative sociology: towards a critique of the cultural turn', *Sociological Review*, 48(4): 629–48.

Saussure, F. (1986) [1916] *Course in General Linguistics*, La Salle, IL: Open Court.

Simmel, G. (1997) *Simmel on Culture*, ed. D. Frisby and M. Featherstone, London: Sage.

Smith, P. and Alexander, J.C. (2005) 'Introduction: the new Durkheim', in J.C. Alexander and P. Smith (eds), *The Cambridge Companion to Durkheim*, Cambridge: Cambridge University Press.

Toennies, F. (1957) *Community and Association*, East Lansing, MI: Michigan State University Press.

Turner, B. (1987) 'A note on nostalgia', *Theory, Culture & Society*, 4: 147–56.

Turner, V. (1967) *Forest of Symbols*, Ithaca, NY: Cornell University Press.

—— (1969) *The Ritual Process*, Chicago: Aldine.

Vaughan, D. (1996) *The Challenger Launch Decision: Risky Technology, Culture and Deviance at NASA*, Chicago, IL: University of Chicago Press.

Weber, M. (1930) *The Protestant Ethic and the Spirit of Capitalism*, London: Allen & Unwin.

—— (1968) [1921] *Economy and Society*, New York: Bedminister.

Williams, R. (1958) *Culture and Society*, London: Chatto & Windus.

—— (1976) *Keywords: A Vocabulary of Culture and Society*, London: Fontana.

—— (1977) *Maxism and Literature*, Oxford: Oxford University Press.

Zerubavel, E. (1981) *Hidden Rhythms: Schedules and Calendars in Social Life*, Chicago: University of Chicago Press.

13

SOCIAL THEORY AND GLOBALIZATION

ERIC L. HSU

Of all the topics of interest in modern social theory, it is decidedly the concept of globalization that still garners the most attention. However, this has not always been the case. Only from the mid-1980s onwards did the term 'global-ization' really begin to take hold within social thought. Before then, the term was used only intermittently and without much fanfare. By contrast, use of the term nowadays has become ubiquitous; it is used by many to explain why and how a whole host of events are taking place.

And yet, despite such talk, what globalization actually involves is not alto-gether settled. As with the terms 'society' and '**feminism**', 'globalization' is a term that carries many different usages and meanings. However, globalization is decidedly not an empty word. Usually, when it is employed, it says something rather specific. David Held and Anthony McGrew, for instance, believe that globalization 'refers to a shift or transformation in the scale of human organiza-tion that links distant communities and expands the reach of power relations across the world's regions and continents' (2002: 1). In their view, globalization is something that affects us all, though in different and disparate ways accord-ing to our unique situation.

This definition, I think, offers us an interesting foray into the matter. As many social theorists would agree, globalization certainly has something to do with the *interconnections* between many different peoples around the world. Similarly, most would also concur that globalization also has something to do with the sense of *interdependency* that has resulted from this interconnectivity, and vice versa. However, how and to what extent these things have occurred and what effects they bring are questions that have not been fully answered.

Accordingly, unpacking these and other views on globalization will be the main focus of this chapter. To be sure, much of the discussion regarding global-ization is guilty of hyperbole and overly simplistic thinking. However, explor-ing issues thematically will hopefully allow us to think more carefully about what globalization involves.

DOES GLOBALIZATION EXIST?

In surveying the numerous debates on globalization, one thing becomes imme-diately apparent: how globalization is defined is of great importance. This is because much of the conceptual disagreement regarding globalization can be traced to a divergence in how the issue is framed.

In this regard, one of the most contentious debates in social theory is whether or not globalization actually exists. For some, this question is best answered economically and, indeed, it is this line of thinking that continues to dominate much of popular debate. Here, what is at issue is the question of whether or not all economies in the world have become more or less global in orientation over the past few decades. While some believe that this *globality* is now the case, others are more dubious of such claims.

One of the, perhaps, more hyperbolic and better known proponents of the globalized economy position is Kenichi Ohmae. In his book, *The Borderless World* (1990), Ohmae contends that the world is quickly becoming a more accessible place. It is accessible in the sense that people all over the world are no longer always confined by the specific localities they find themselves in. For Ohmae, this is because borders of all kinds, especially those of the nation-state, are now being broken and transgressed. As evidence, Ohmae cites the economic trends of the late twentieth century, which suggest that transnational corporations (TNCs) now trump national governments in their running of the world market. Proof of this, in Ohmae's view, can be found in the fact that consumers all over the world are nowadays starting to enjoy goods once only available to certain regions. Globalization has made it possible for consumers all over the world to know of and obtain the things they want, no matter where they or the products originate from. Hence, this is why someone in Brazil can buy a pair of Air Jordan sneakers that are made in China and also why an Australian citizen can enjoy sushi on a business trip to South Africa. More and more, capital, products and even life-styles are no longer determined by national boundaries.

Consequently, for Ohmae, all of this suggests that globalization has greatly re-written the existing world order. Key to this argument is Ohmae's belief that nation-states are no longer the central organizing principle for how people and cultures define themselves. Instead, the world is now caught up in a neoliberal system, whereby borders no longer really matter. Nowadays, what you consume is not necessarily a function of where you are situated. And this, Ohmae says, is why it is necessary to realize that we have entered a new age of global economies. The world, as it stands today, is *truly* global, not just made up of individual units.

There are those, however, who strongly disagree with Ohmae's assessment of the current situation. Globalization, for these thinkers, might very well be a myth. They contend that any indications that more and more of us are living in a borderless world are, at best, exaggerations.

Two of the leading articulators of this view are Paul Hirst and Grahame Thompson, who in their book, *Globalization in Question*, raise many doubts about Ohmae's globalized economy thesis. For Hirst and Thompson, the economic facts simply do not support Ohmae's claim that the world is becoming more economically interdependent or interconnected than ever. They hold that, contrary to some popular viewpoints, we are not actually in a new globalized age. This is buoyed by their belief that international relations now depend, more than ever, on the regulatory power of national governments. As evidence, Hirst and Thompson point to the fact that the worldwide economic market in the Gold Standard period before 1914 was arguably *more* not less open to trade than during the 1980s and 1990s (1996: 2).

This view is underscored by their distinction between an inter-national and a globalized economy. For Hirst and Thompson, an inter-national economy is one in which national entities are still the principal actors in world market relationships. Any interdependence among nations in this regard is of a more 'strategic' nature, whereby international events do not necessarily permeate the domestic policies and processes (1996: 8). In contrast, they define a globalized economy as being much akin to the view posited by Ohmae and his supporters. This is, the view that 'distinct national economies are being subsumed and rearticulated by international processes and transactions' (1996: 10).

Accordingly, for Hirst and Thompson, we are actually closer to living in an inter-national than in a globalized economy. While certain elements of a globalized economy can be detected, they advance the view that the inter-national economic system has not been discarded. This is because the power of supra-national forces to determine the direction of markets has been grossly overstated. Most TNCs, they suggest, are actually tied to the inter-national economy system, and those which are more global in orientation are relatively few in number (1996: 195). Consequently, what Hirst and Thompson ultimately argue is that claims of economic globalization are by no means extensive or unprecedented. All that is really new today is the heightened level of exchange between national economies. And this, they say, is a far cry from living in a globalized economy, as some have claimed we do.

THE TRANSFORMATIONALIST POSITION

In contrast to both those who believe in the globalized economy and those who are more wary, there are those who have been termed by David Held and his associates (1999), the transformationalists. At the core of the transformationalist thesis is the conviction that the believers (hyperglobalists) and naysayers (skeptics) of a globalized economy are both only partly correct; only when we consider and combine both of their perspectives do we get a more accurate picture of globalization.

What the transformationalists propose is that it is not inconsistent to believe that nowadays globalization 'is a central driving force behind the rapid social, political and economic changes that are reshaping modern societies and the world order' (1999: 7), while at the same time to suppose that this by no means implies that prior understandings of world affairs should be completely rewritten. For the transformationalists, globalization does not just replace or leave alone existing forms of social organization, such as the nation-state, as the hyperglobalists and skeptics claim, as much as it *reworks* them. In general terms, this means that globalization does not change everything, but at the same time neither is it inconsequential.

A good example of this transformationalist approach to globalization can be found in the work of Anthony **Giddens**, whose ideas have long been a source of inspiration for the transformationalist position. Giddens argues that globalization is not a departure from **modernity** but a *radicalization* of its precepts. In this formulation, globalization is not so much an entirely new phenomenon that replaces previous modes of social organization, but rather a novel turn in the unfolding of modernity.

Central to this link between modernity and globalization is Giddens's concept of 'time–space distanciation'. What time–space distanciation refers to is the process through which locales are determined by distant events and decisions and vice versa. Accordingly, Giddens believes this to be a key feature of modern life because modernity inaugurates conditions where such a situation is possible. In support of this view, Giddens cites the standardization of time. Before the onset of modernity, 'time was almost always associated with "where" or identified by regular national occurrences' (1990: 17). That is to say, the 'when' of an event was almost entirely controlled by the place where it occurred. Today though, as Giddens notes, things are quite different. With the onset of a post-traditional order – a key aspect of modernity – time now becomes something we take for granted in that it is an independent, abstract measure that is not simply determined by the specific place we find ourselves in. For Giddens, however, one of the main consequences of this is that it makes the idea of place increasingly more 'phantasmagoric'. What happens when locales take on an abstract perception of time is that they thus become 'penetrated by and shaped in terms of social influences quite distant to them' (1990: 19). On a grander scale, Giddens suggests that this process is indicative of another feature of modern settings: the fact that social activity is no longer tied to localities. What time–space distanciation effectively does is to lift out habits and practices from local contexts of interaction so that they can be influenced by distant or spatially absent forces.

By extension, Giddens believes that the same goes for globalization. This is because globalization, in his view, also refers to 'the intensification of worldwide social relations which link distant localities in such a way that local happenings are shaped by events occurring many miles away and vice versa' (1990: 64). However, according to Giddens, it is important to note that globalization is not merely a continuation of the modern project. In fact globalization, by Giddens's account, also refers to the *radicalization* of modern precepts. Such a view is illustrated in the observation that the West (and, by extension, modernity) has lost its privileged hold over certain forms of knowledge (1990: 51–3). Nowadays, as many commentators have noted, the West is no longer so convinced of its own exceptionalism. But this, as Giddens reasons, is not because of modernity's decline around the world as much as it is a consequence of modernity's successful expansion. As support, Giddens cites the fact that Western and non-Western countries can no longer be so easily differentiated by the presence (or absence) of modern institutions (1990: 52). And this in turn, for Giddens, suggests that we have entered a time where modernity has been *radicalized* and transformed by globalization. Whereas once modernity was defined by its ability to know things once and for all, because of globalization it is now more reflexive and aware of its own limitations.

Consequently then, this is why, in the transformationalist account, it is said that globalization does not wholly supersede previous forms of social organization; globalization is not only associated with the blurring of traditional distinctions such as what is international or domestic, but it is also linked to the reiteration of some of those features. Therefore, there are times when things such as the nation-state might be *more* not less influential in determining the interdependency and interconnectivity between nations. And this, as Held and his associates note, makes our view of the contemporary situation much more 'replete with contradictions' that prevent wholesale proclamations about the future (Held *et al.* 1999: 7). Such a nuanced approach is absent from the hyperglobalists and the skeptics, who both tend to approach globalization as an either/or proposition.

CULTURE AS A GLOBAL DIMENSION

Yet another qualm that the transformationalists have with the hyperglobalist and skeptic positions is that these latter groups often accord the economic sector with too much importance (Held *et al.* 1999: 12). The contours of globalization, as Held and his associates maintain, are not something that should be understood mono-causally. For them, it is not enough simply to assume that other social factors follow suit depending on the economic situation. Open or closed markets do not necessarily mean entirely open or closed societies.

Such a view is informed by a number of theorists who have emphasized the importance of *culture* in globalization. One of these in particular is John Tomlinson, who, in *Globalization and Culture* (1999), advances the view that culture plays a critical role in understanding globalization as a multi-form phenomenon. Essentially, Tomlinson's main contention is that culture and globalization dually inform one another; just as globalization offers us new insight into understandings of culture, culture also offers us new ways of looking at globalization.

To explicate, Tomlinson alerts us on the one hand to the fact that '[g]lobalization disturbs the way we conceptualize culture'. This is so because 'culture has long had connotations tying to it the idea of a fixed locality' and, as such, globalization is threatening to such assumptions (1999: 28). In this regard, what globalization does is to recast the frames of analysis. Although it is not the case that locality becomes altogether irrelevant, globalization makes it difficult to cling steadfastly onto cultural assumptions about certain places.

At the same time, Tomlinson informs us that we must also take account of culture as a critical *dimension* in globalization. 'Cultural' here is defined as 'the order of life in which human beings construct meaning through practices of symbolic representations' (1999: 18). However, for Tomlinson, this is not to imply that culture can be somehow disconnected from economic or political activity. He is keen to note that, despite the fact that we often speak of culture as being discrete from other spheres of social life, these spheres all are still nevertheless related. The point for Tomlinson is that culture is significant because it refers to that which cannot be irreducible to either economics or the political. This is because culture is principally about how and what people do to make their lives meaningful, which distilled to its essence is about the ordinary and the everyday (1999: 19). In this regard, culture is significant because it refers to that which is more encompassing and less narrowly instrumental or technical.

Consequently, it is for this reason that culture, as a dimension, should be of great importance to understanding the globalization phenomenon. For Tomlinson, this is especially the case when we consider how discussions about the globalized economy have tended to be rather one-dimensional (1999: 16). Under this paradigm, cultural and political inferences seem to follow solely from the economic conditions. Accordingly, this is why authors from both sides of the globalized economy issue seem to sound so out of touch and hyperbolic; the world in this sense is either becoming globalized or, largely, it is not. In Tomlinson's view, such an approach overlooks the complexity of globalization provided by a more culturally-informed perspective: it is useful to look at culture because it alerts us to the contradictions and transformations that globalization inevitably entails. To this end, Tomlinson looks at the ways in which globalization lifts out and transforms cultural meanings. In effect, what the cultural dimension allows us to do is to explain why **identities** all over the world can change without necessarily the opening or closing up of economic or political markets.

For Tomlinson, this amounts to saying that culture forces us to consider a wider range of issues. For one thing, it raises the possibility of there being a sense of global unicity, without necessarily implying that the world must be so in all regards. Here, Tomlinson points to the work of Roland Robertson (1992: 6), who maintains that globalization has created the feeling of 'the world as a single place' as an influential frame of reference. By this, Robertson means that how people think about their lives is influenced by their increasing awareness of the world as an 'imagined community' (1992: 183). From this perspective, globalization encourages people to take into account 'the world as a whole' while they form decisions and identities (1992: 26). However, as Tomlinson points out, Robertson is not implying here that globalization somehow creates a uniform world culture. Rather, as Tomlinson writes, Robertson directs our attention to the fact that globalization can be understood as a 'complex and social phenomenological condition – the "global human condition" – in which different orders of human life are brought into articulation with one another' (1999: 11).

This means that globalization is not reducible merely to the exchange of goods or political processes. Rather, globalization also involves the negotiation of new identities and conceptual frameworks.

According to those who emphasize the cultural dimension of globalization, a further reason why culture is important is because it reorients how we understand the contours and complexities of global processes. This is particularly salient if we explore the thesis that globalization is, in actuality, a process of worldwide homogenization. What defenders of this position propose is that, more often than not, an effect of globalization is to impose cultural values – especially those that are deemed Western – on people all over the world. Such a view is taken up by Serge Latouche who, in *The Westernization of the World* (1996), contends that non-Western cultures are being destroyed by the West's global pursuit of profit. His contention is that the rise of the West has extended to all aspects of life for most everyone around the world. This is especially so for the 'Third World', which he believes is bearing the brunt of this forced cultural uniformity. According to Latouche, these groups are being seduced by the rather singular mindset of the West's obsession with technology and continual profit. As a result, the rich diversity in cultural practice they once possessed has gradually become eroded.

Cultural theorists like Tomlinson are, however, skeptical of such claims. For them, globalization does not necessarily involve the imposition of Western values on non-Western societies. Globalization is a much more complex phenomenon. While it is tempting to assume, as Latouche does, that the world is trending toward uniformity, such is actually not the case. For Tomlinson, this is evidenced by the ways in which culture does not transfer between social entities in a unilinear fashion. This means that cultural texts, such as television programs and clothes, are not simply assimilated by those on the 'receiving end'. Instead, as Tomlinson writes, 'movement between cultural/geographical areas always involves interpretation, translation, mutation, adaptation, and "indigenization" as the receiving culture brings its own cultural resources to bear, in dialectical fashion, upon "cultural imports"' (1999: 84). Hence, this is why people in different parts of the world interpret the same television show or a movie persona, such as Charlie Chaplin, in quite disparate ways (Tomlinson 1991). These differences suggest that globalization does not necessarily bring about a flattening out or homogenization of culture. Instead, what many like Tomlinson conclude is that more theoretical sophistication is needed to form a clearer picture of what is actually happening. While it is the case that capitalism and other Westernized social forms are implicated in the shaping of global culture(s), it is not so clear that globalization only involves the wholesale proliferation of all things Western.

To this end, some thinkers in this vein have proposed new conceptual images that try to better capture the complexity that globalization actually involves. This is reflected in the recent increase in new terminology. For instance, Ulf Hannerz speaks of globalization as inaugurating a 'creolization' of identities. This is his notion that globalization cultivates the inter-mixing of seemingly different cultures, even despite the fact that some of these cultures are traditionally more powerful politically and economically than others. According to Hannerz, 'creolization' is a useful term because it captures a point that some social commentators have ignored; that the exchange of culture, even between two unequal groups, is hardly ever one-sided. From this view, the colonized can also influence the colonizers, just as the periphery can talk back to the core (1992: 265). Accordingly, this is significant because it presents a more accurate view of how global processes proceed. Cultural flows, he contends, always involve an element of creolization, whereby those with supposedly greater cultural prestige, such as those in the West, are themselves transformed by those that they try to dominate. Played out in global settings, this means that cultures are not simply being lost to homogeneity so much as they are being hybridized. Globalization is just as much about cultural gain as it is about loss.

Similarly, another neologism that has gained currency within social thought is Roland Robertson's usage of the Japanese business term, 'glocalization'. Glocalization encapsulates the idea that global processes are also local in their orientation. That is to say, for Robertson, not only is globalization a macro system oriented affair, it also involves a localized component. From this stance, not only are local discourses remade by overarching global forces, but localized issues are raised to the global level. An example of this can be seen when goods and services that are global or near global in reach are tailored to the localities in which they find themselves (1995: 28); for instance, this is why the menu at McDonald's varies from country to country. The point for Robertson, however, is that this is not just a one-way process. Just as McDonald's must tailor its menu to local preferences, the converse is also true. What is local also becomes a matter of global importance. Thus, conversely, an incident of torture in a US-run prison camp in Iraq can have reverberations around the world, transmitted by the global news media. What this says is that local events have as important an effect on the global stage as global forces have in transforming localities. Here, the emphasis is on how globalization increasingly makes the relationship between the local and the global much more complex, but at the same time increasingly more relevant.

Another concept that has found some traction among social theoretical debates on globalization is the term, 'creative destruction'. This is Tyler Cowen's (2002) application of a Joseph Schumpeter metaphor which suggests that global cultures create as much as they destroy. In fact, according to Cowen's thesis, cultures in the global age are destroyed *because* new ones are created. This is so because cross-cultural exchange does not just lead to a flattening out of cultural tastes and repertoire. In Cowen's view, it is the case that, when cultures come into contact with each other, more not fewer forms of cultural expression are created, at least at the outset. For example, Cowen cites the incorporation of Czechoslovakian beads into the South African Ndebele art-making tradition. Even though these beads were not indigenous to Africa, they have become, since the nineteenth century, an essential material for the adornment of aprons, clothing and textiles (2002: 8). However, as Cowen notes, the trade-off is that, invariably, some cultural aspects are lost because of the cultural blossoming process. The production of new cultural expressions means that older ones can no longer be taken as given. In Cowen's view, this is especially true when we consider what happens to 'poorer' cultures which come into contact with 'richer' ones. Although poorer cultures in this situation find new ways of enhancing and preserving parts of their cultural repertoire when they hybridize with the 'richer culture', they are also forced to leave behind aspects which might previously have been significant. Put differently, Cowen believes that newness begets oldness, just as creativity begets destruction (2002: 55–6). He further contends that this is how we should understand the richness and complexity of the cultural side of globalization.

Taken as a whole, all of this new terminology suggests that globalization is by no means a monolithic phenomenon. And this is especially true if we include a consideration of culture; it would be a mistake to assume that economics and politics can completely determine other dimensions of social experience without some additional cultural input. Thus, those who make extrapolations from economical or political conditions alone often miss the more disparate and varied nature of global processes.

THE HOPES AND DANGERS OF GLOBALIZATION

Along with culture, another prominent debate within social theory about globalization concerns whether or not we should consider it as a drawback or a benefit. Should we view globalization with hope and optimism, or is it something profoundly troubling? Furthermore, does globalization heighten or address global conflicts and inequalities? Ought we to stay the course or is it time to consider new alternatives?

For some, the conclusion is that globalization is, by and large, a favorable phenomenon. This view tends to highlight the benefits and favorable opportunities that globalization has brought about, on both a long- and short-term basis. Often, what is cited is the fact that people appear to be living longer and more varied lives. This, some say, is why we should be optimistic about the direction in which globalization is taking us. Others, however, remain unconvinced by such arguments. From this perspective, globalization has not only exacerbated existing problems, but has also created new ones with which we must now contend. The fact that global inequalities and terrorist attacks appear to be on the rise confirms the validity of this viewpoint.

Among writers who take a rather optimistic stance on globalization, Thomas Friedman's work, *The Lexus and the Olive Tree* (2000), has been highly influential. At the core of Friedman's hopefulness is the belief that the benefits of globalization outweigh its drawbacks. Nowhere is this more apparent than in his concept of the 'golden straitjacket' – a metaphor for the increasing pressure for nation-states to transfer their economic sovereignty to the global market-place. Friedman believes that it is actually advantageous to wear the golden straitjacket because, even though it reduces the degree of control which citizens feel they have, it also makes people all over the world feel more interconnected and inter-dependent. This happens because, in this new paradigm of globalization, wealth is produced mainly when everyone learns to fall in line with what is good for the whole of the system (2000: 106). Hence, waging war with other countries by extension is not something that countries want to do if they seek to further their prosperity. Interestingly enough, what Friedman cites as evidence is the curious observation that war has not been waged between countries that both have a McDonald's. This, which he terms the 'golden arches theory', illustrates how globalization in some senses can be the solution and not the cause of global conflicts (2000: 250).

Moreover, a further reason why we should view globalization favorably is because it not only encourages peace between nations, but it also has the ability to foster more just and accountable forms of intra-societal governance – an idea that Friedman loosely terms, 'globalution'. According to Friedman, globalution happens because globalization allows investors to determine, to some extent, the way in which politics is conducted. Why this is so has largely to do with the increasing influence that global economic markets have over political decisions. In the era of globalization, corrupt and undemocratic governments are compelled to open themselves up to more democratic transparency, as they are left no other option than to concede their political power if they want to benefit from the onset of a new global capitalism. Otherwise, transnational corporations and, in turn, capital will look elsewhere for profit. Globalization then, in Friedman's eyes, is a force that can encourage the world to take up democratic forms of governance. To shy away from the golden straitjacket is to deny the drive for progress.

Along these same lines, another popular sentiment among those who are opti-mistic about globalization is that the drive to globalize is, by and large, the answer to addressing world poverty. That is to say, globalization is the means of improving the general human condition rather than the cause of its downfall. We find this argument in authors like Martin Wolf (2004) and Indur Goklany (2007) who both point to the fact that, even though there are still great inequalities in the world, people appear to be living fuller, longer and more varied lives. In effect, what this position argues is that those who criticize globalization throw the baby out with the bathwater. Globalization has, in fact, improved the plight of the world's poor and this is evidenced by some tangible metrics, like the considerable rise in life expectancy worldwide.

Of course, by contrast, there are those who dispute with the enthusiasts of globalization. For these critics, globalization is something we should find pro-foundly problematic. This stance tends to highlight the dangers and global injus-tices which still persist, despite assurances that globalization can be beneficial.

One of the more notable sources of this skepticism is the popularly termed 'anti-globalization' movement. Proponents of this campaign typically argue that there is little reason to believe that those rose-colored promises about globalization will ever be fulfilled. This is especially true of present-day wealth inequalities. World poverty, they claim, has not only shown little sign of improvement but, in actuality, might indeed be worsening. As evidence, they cite figures (like those from the United Nations Development Program), which suggest that income disparity between the richest and poorest countries has widened significantly since the nineteenth century. This, they say, suggests that economic globalization does not 'lift all boats' as it does 'lift all yachts' (Buckman 2004: 68). Inherent in globalization is the fact that the rich prosper while the less well-off get poorer.

According to Naomi Klein, this happens because globalization is not only concerned with integration, but also with exclusion. At the same time that globalization tries to tear down borders so that capital can become more mobile, new restrictions are imposed so that only a few benefit from this transformation (Klein 2002: 81). In other words, whereas globalization promised us windows, for a large portion of the world, there are only fences. This is true not only of those classes within nations but also and, perhaps especially, between them. For example, when it comes to enjoying the fruits of the expansion of 'free' trade, entire sections of the world, like much of sub-Saharan Africa, seem to be written out of the equation. Ultimately, therefore, what the anti-globalization stance contends is that globalization, as it stands now, is an illusion. The realities on the ground simply do not support the grandiose promises that have been made.

In addition, another line of critique leveled at the optimistic globalist position concerns the issues of terrorism and global security. Here, it is suggested that, as opposed to the views of those who believe that globalization can promote peace and prosperity, global conflicts such as the 9/11 attacks on the World Trade Center are not aberrations of globalization so much as they are its direct products. Such a view is articulated by Stanley Hoffman (2002), who argues that globalization both fosters and facilitates conflicts and resentments all across the globe – to such an extent that we should think of terrorist violence and globalization as going hand in hand. Hoffman reasons this is the case because the same changes that globalization heralds – such as the opening of borders and the spread of global media – are the very things that make terrorism a viable option (2004: 4).

Accordingly, in light of these debates on the benefits and drawbacks of globalization, there is one pertinent question that emerges: what next? If globalization is indeed as deadly and unjust as some claim, what can be done about it? There have been many varied responses to this question. For instance, some claim that we should scrap the impulse to globalize and return to more localized ways of living and governance. This is a sentiment often found in the anti-globalization movement: the answers to the ills of the global are to be found in the local. Globalization must proceed from the ground up so that we can place people over profits.

Conversely, there are those who believe such a response is not an entirely satisfactory solution and that it is naïve to think that locally based action can adequately address global challenges. Such a point is made by David Held, who, as a self-termed transformationalist, is principally concerned with finding a synthesis of the pro- and anti-globalization viewpoints. It is true, Held concedes, that those who expose the shameful inequalities of globalization are partly correct about the new global market system. Indeed, by itself, the system cannot guarantee that it will have only positive effects on the environment, health, welfare and the pursuit of justice (2004: 154). But, by the same token, Held maintains that we should not discount many of the lessons learned from the pro-globalization viewpoint. It would be wrong to think that domestic issues, such as immigration, national security goals and economic prosperity are not intertwined with those that are international. And, as such, this makes locally based solutions inadequate to address all of the issues that people face. We must think bigger and wider.

The way forward then, for Held, is to advocate a 'global social democracy – one that contains clear possibilities of dialogue between different segments of the pro-globalization/anti-globalization spectrum' (2004: 163). To do this, Held appeals to a belief in **cosmopolitanism** principles. What Held and many others like him see in cosmopolitanism is the possibility that issues can be raised and adequately addressed at a global level.

One of the benefits of thinking in this way, according to Kwame Anthony Appiah, a leading scholar on cosmopolitanism, is that we begin to think in wider terms and more creatively about governance. Instead of remaining completely confined by the nation-state to which we each respectively belong, cosmopolitanism appeals to a much broader outlook: that we are also all part of the human community (1998: 91). This, in turn, is what many believe can function as a new ethos to face the challenges that globalization offers us. Cosmopolitanism extends the concern of the citizen beyond his or her own borders, developing the desire to interact with other cultures beyond our own.

Of course, Appiah makes it abundantly clear that this is not to say that cosmopolitanism is coterminous with uniformity. Just because 'cosmopolitans suppose that all cultures have enough overlap in their vocabulary of values to begin a conversation', this does not mean that 'we could all come to agreement if only we had the same vocabulary' (2006: 57). The true appeal of cosmopolitanism is that there is, at one and the same time, a call to recognize our common universality and a call to tolerate our differences. Thus, in Appiah's reckoning, it is not only impossible to have exactly the same values as others, but it is also important that we celebrate diversity. Committing to cosmopolitan principles means that you are both a member of a unique culture or society and part of the larger whole of humanity.

However, as some have noted, trying to actualize cosmopolitan virtues is not something that comes about easily. This is a point articulated by Ulrich **Beck** who, in *World Risk Society* (1999), identifies the deferral of risk as one of the most serious obstacles to cosmopolitanism. Here, Beck refers to the possibility of adopting a 'me first' attitude when it comes to addressing global problems

and conflicts. Despite the fact that managing risk is now something that we realize must be dealt with globally, this does not imply that all risks are shared
equally (1999: 5). As occurred in New Orleans during Hurricane Katrina, those
who have the means and wherewithal can leave those less well off behind when
there is a disaster or crisis. Thus, an obstacle which advocates of cosmopolitanism must face is what Beck calls the condition of 'organized irresponsibility'
(1999: 6). Nowadays, why we should be invested into the fate of others is far
from obvious.

Along these lines, a further reason to doubt that cosmopolitanism can be easily realized is connected to the idea that contemporary globalization does not
seem terribly encouraging of comprehensive and sustained courses of action.
Such a view is taken up by Anthony Elliott and Charles Lemert who, in their
work *The New Individualism* (2006), argue that ours is an age not of long-term
planning but of ceaseless reinvention. Here, Elliott and Lemert focus on the
more personal aspects of social life that are affected by global transformations.
By considering this dimension of social experience, rather than top-heavy
accounts of the global economy as is the norm, Elliott and Lemert postulate that
globalization not only ushers in a new economic system but also profoundly
alters how we understand ourselves. Whereas before we might have been content with consistency and stability, nowadays flexibility is seen to be highly
desirable. From surgical culture (Elliott 2008) to endless corporate downsizings
(Sennett 2006), the message today sounds loud and clear: who you are and what
you do can should be ready to change in a heartbeat. And this, Elliott and Lemert
say, does not bode particularly well for addressing social challenges that involve
more than quick fixes.

GLOBALIZATION AS A USEFUL CONCEPT

Finally, another discourse within social theoretical debates on globalization concerns its utility as a concept. At issue here is whether or not globalization has
any lasting bearing on the social sciences. Why should we be engaging with the
idea of globalization? And also, by extension, what does it tell us?

To these questions, the response for most of recent social theory has been to
affirm the significance of globalization within social thought. Globalization,
from this standpoint, is important because it challenges many of the classical
assumptions about social analysis. It brings to bear the fact that new conceptual
frameworks are necessary to supplement certain erstwhile lines of thought,
which now seem woefully inadequate and/or outdated.

To this end, much has been written about the role that globalization has
played in reformulating a central conceptual system, which has been at the core
of most of the modern social sciences: that of 'the social'. This is a topic elaborated on in the work of John Urry, who postulates that globalization undermines
much of what we traditionally assume constitutes 'society'. Here, what Urry
harps on is the long-held connection between society and the metaphor of

region. If we are to take globalization seriously, this he says is a link which needs to be revisited. This is so because such an account of society is ill-equipped to handle the issue of mobilities, which he believes globalization brings to the fore (Urry 2000: 2). In support of his argument, Urry cites a growing literature, which asserts that many traditional categories such as the territorially bounded nation-state are, to some degree, losing their traditional efficacy as concepts. This has, primarily, to do with the fact that the mobility of people and objects is becoming more complex and varied. The fact that tourism and online shopping are becoming more and more popular all over the world would seem to confirm this point.

Accordingly, to act as a corrective measure, Urry proposes that we replace the link between society and region with the metaphors of networks and fluidity (2000: 33). Doing this, he says, enables us to see how a territorially bounded notion of society ultimately fails to capture the current situation. Ours is a world where people and objects flow in and out of networks, both virtual and literal. To argue otherwise is to focus on the solidity of social **structures** when we should be looking at how bonds and boundaries are now being broken and reformed.

However, in opposition to those who herald globalization as a watershed concept, there are others who are highly skeptical about globalization's enduring relevance within social theory. Such a point is made by John Ralston Saul in his work, *The Collapse of Globalism* (2005). Saul's main contention is that it is wrong to assume that globalization will always be with us; just like other epochs, its time will come and go. And indeed, for Saul, it already has. Globalization, especially in an economic sense, is something we can begin to refer to in the past tense. Saul buttresses this claim by pointing to other issues which have started to supplant globalization's erstwhile prominence: a revival in nationalism, the change in geo-politics and religious transformations. These, he says, are what we should be looking at. The globe is, increasingly, a dated reference.

In much the same way, but on somewhat different grounds, Justin Rosenberg also argues against the conceptual weight accorded to globalization. For Rosenberg, instead of being a valuable site for study, globalization actually says very little. In fact, when compared to classical approaches to historical analysis like those of **Marx** and **Weber**, Rosenberg believes globalization to be intellectually redundant (2005: 65). Another reason why Rosenberg believes globalization to be of little or no use today is his view that there are fundamental flaws in its theoretical underpinnings. What it purports to explain – how relations of space are being reformulated and reconstituted across the world – is something that always requires a whole host of qualifications, which mainly involve non-global references. In turn, Rosenberg questions why it is then useful to employ globalization if it possesses no theoretical weight of its own (2005: 64). Ultimately, what this all says to Rosenberg is that, sooner or later, globalization as a concept will meet its demise. While it has had its time in the spotlight, it will soon make way for other terms and concepts that actually matter.

In the face of such criticisms, it is decidedly not unreasonable to give credence to the notion that globalization might be losing some of its luster, if not its pertinence. But even so, this is juxtaposed with the raging debate that continues over the lasting relevance of globalization to social theory. That scores of commentaries on globalization continue to be produced from almost all corners of the world seems to confirm, in one sense, which group decidedly seems to be holding sway. And yet, so as not to discount the healthy skepticism over globalization, it is important to note that there has been an emerging shift in how some theorists have decided to pursue the topic.

To my mind, something indeed has changed. But *pace* Saul and Rosenberg, I am less certain that the idea of a 'post-global' age is the right conclusion. Rather, if anything, there appears to be a call, not so much for answers to the challenges we face, as for new lines of questioning. In other words, I think the idea of globalization is not so much undergoing a crisis as a *re-imagination*.

And still, much to the anxiety and criticism of some social theorists, where this will lead us is difficult to say. But perhaps, as Charles Lemert suggests in *Social Things*, this might be the very point of taking global matters seriously: 'On and on these global things spin' (2005: 181). And so it is with globalization and social theory. Whence dizzy, it is time to refocus. Whence settled, it is time to keep moving. The difficulty is in keeping straight which is which.

REFERENCES

Appiah, Kwame Anthony (1998) 'Cosmopolitan patriots' in Pheng Cheah and Bruce Robbins (eds), *Cosmopolitics*, Minneapolis: University of Minnesota Press.
—— (2006) *Cosmopolitanism*, New York: W.W. Norton.
Buckman, Greg (2004) *Globalization: Tame It or Scrap It?*, London: Zed Books.
Cowen, Tyler (2002) *Creative Destruction*, Princeton, NJ: Princeton University Press.
Elliott, Anthony (2008) *Making the Cut*, London: Reaktion.
Giddens, Anthony (1990) *The Consequences of Modernity*, Stanford, CA: Stanford University Press.
Friedman, Thomas (2000) *The Lexus and the Olive Tree*, London: HarperCollins.
Hannerz, Ulf (1992) *Cultural Complexity*, New York: Columbia University Press.
Held, David (2004) *The Global Covenant*, Cambridge: Polity Press.
Held, David and McGrew, Anthony (2002) *Globalization/Anti-Globalization*, Cambridge: Polity Press.
Held, David, McGrew, Anthony, Goldblatt, David and Perraton, Jonathan (1999) *Global Transformations*, Stanford, CA: Stanford University Press.
Hoffman, Stanley (2002) 'Clash of globalizations', *Foreign Affairs*, 81(4): 110–15.
Golkany, Indur (2007) *The Improving State of the World*, Washington DC: Cato Institute.
Hirst, Paul and Thompson, Graham (1996) *Globalization in Question*, Cambridge: Polity Press.
Klein, Naomi (2002) *Fences and Windows*, London: HarperCollins.
Latouche, Serge (1996) *The Westernization of the World*, Cambridge: Polity Press.
Lemert, Charles (2005) *Social Things*, New York: Rowman & Littlefield.
Lemert, Charles and Elliott, Anthony (2006) *The New Individualism*, Milton Park, Oxon: Routledge.

Ohmae, Kenichi (1990) *The Borderless World*, New York: HarperBusiness.

Robertson, Roland (1992) *Globalization: Social Theory and Global Culture*, London: Sage.

——(1995) 'Glocalization: time–space and homogeneity–heterogeneity', in Mike Featherstone *et al.* (eds), *Global Modernities*, London: Sage, pp. 25–44.

Rosenberg, Justin (2005) 'Globalization theory: a post mortem', *International Politics*, 42: 2–74.

Saul, John Ralston (2005) *The Collapse of Globalism*, London: Atlantic Books.

Sennett, Richard (2006) *Culture of New Capitalism*, New Haven, CT: Yale University Press.

Tomlinson, John (1991) *Cultural Imperialism*, London: Pinter.

—— (1999) *Globalization and Culture*, Chicago: University of Chicago Press.

Urry, John (2000) *Sociology Beyond Societies*, London: Routledge.

Wolf, Martin (2004) *Why Globalization Works*, New Haven, CT: Yale University Press.

Part II

CENTRAL TERMS AND THINKERS

Terms in **lower-case bold type** cross-refer to separate entries.

Theodor **ADORNO** was born Theodor Ludwig Wiesengrund in 1903 in the city of Frankfurt am Main, the only child of a wealthy wine merchant, Oscar Wiesengrund, and Maria Barbara (née Calvelli Adorno), an accomplished singer. Adorno's father was of Jewish descent and had converted to Protestantism, while his mother was Catholic. Along with Maria, further early musical influence may be attributed to his aunt Agathe, and music remained an abiding passion throughout his life and writings. His later critiques of music within popular culture are better understood in the light of his being an accomplished child pianist. Also a gifted student, Adorno attended the elite Kaiser Wilhelm-Gymnasium, graduating at the top of the class (interestingly, Walter **Benjamin**, a close friend and fellow critical theorist, had been a student a decade before). Rounding off his intellectually stimulating childhood, the famed German composer Bernhard Sekles was his private music teacher, and he read Immanuel Kant's *Critique of Pure Reason* with the influential German journalist and cultural critic Siegfried Kracauer on weekends.

By 1921, Adorno had enrolled at the University of Frankfurt (now known as Johann Wolfgang Goethe Universität), studying music, philosophy, and psychology. Quite quickly he attained a PhD with the neo-Kantian philosopher Hans Cornelius as his supervisor (also the mentor of Max **Horkheimer**). Already, Adorno had met two later colleagues and co-authors, Horkheimer and Benjamin. The following year, in 1925, however, he moved in a different direction, as he left for Vienna to study composition with Alban Berg. Berg had been a student of Arnold Schoenberg, the prominent leader of the Second Viennese School; the influence of Schoenberg has been characterized as a post-Romantic expansion of tonality, and later, atonality. For years, Adorno wrote on music in the journal *Anbruch* (Dawn), yet, on reading Georg Lukás' *History and Class-Consciousness* in the late 1920s, his contact with Benjamin increased, resulting in the 1931 completion of his habilitation (a post-doctorate degree in certain European and Asian countries), *Kierkegaard: Construction of the Aesthetic*.

Although he fled Germany in 1934, working as an advanced student at Merton College, Oxford, Adorno continued to return for visits until 1937. With Hitler's power ever-increasing, in 1938 he was forced completely to flee Europe, moving to America to become an official member of the Institute for Social Research with his friend Horkheimer. This was the point when he adopted Adorno as his surname, and Wiesengrund as his middle name, normally abbreviated to W. Unfortunately, Benjamin did not accompany them, remaining in Paris until his premature death trying to flee Europe in 1940. However, despite this bitter turn of events, Adorno was prodigious in his long decade abroad, writing the seminal **critical theory** texts *Dialectic of Enlightenment* (1947) with Horkheimer and completing *Minima Moralia*, a collection of aphorisms. He also completed *Philosophy of New Music*; clearly the time with Berg was influential, as the work dealt with Schonberg and Stravinsky. Also, while working at the

University of California (he and Horkheimer had moved there after three years in New York), Adorno co-wrote the widely read *Authoritarian Personality*, a psychosocial study of Fascism and authoritarianism.

In 1949, Adorno returned to Frankfurt, gaining his first and only tenured professorship in 1956 at the re-established Institute for Social Research (now known as the **Frankfurt School**). Along with other Frankfurt theorists and his soon to be renowned student Jürgen **Habermas**, he engaged in many public debates, both in writing (major works included *Negative Dialectics* and *Aesthetic Theory*) and on the radio. As he railed against **positivism**, among his renowned opponents were Karl Popper and Hans Albert. In these intellectual disputes and his earlier writings from America, the nature of Adorno is truly encapsulated: a diverse academic, engaged in varied subjects from music and culture to pure philosophy, attempting to navigate the treacherously difficult terrain of a post-**Hegelian** and post-**Marxist** contextualization and historicization of social theory. Affecting many later theorists, the generalized supposition that mass culture and capitalism have totalitarian tendencies has been repeatedly challenged and modified; however, his effort to ground theory in a critical awareness of modern sociality is widely praised. Even his critics acknowledge his work and ideas as enormously influential across cultural and social realms.

As the student uprisings were beginning to gather momentum, with Adorno pronouncing many of the resistances empty of intellectual merit, his lectures became increasingly volatile scenes. Deciding to take a vacation with his wife, he travelled in 1969 to Switzerland and attempted to ascend a 3,000 metre high mountain, resulting in heart palpitations. Brought to the clinic of the nearby town of Visp, he suffered further palpitations and died the following morning of a heart attack.

AESTHETICS covers the wide variety of questions and difficulties that arise from a theoretical investigation of art and beauty. Traditionally considered to be a philosophical discipline, it is in fact inseparable from a broad range of thought and perspectives, including (but not limited to) science and social theory. Requiring the dual abilities of experience with the arts and the capacity to formulate such experiences systematically, it almost seems counterintuitive to artists themselves. For many, especially those that create it, art is not capable of being reduced to such a formulaic characterization; as Eliseo Vivas and Murray Kreiger noted in their edited work *The Problems of Aesthetics* (1955), the difficulty in communicating the language of aesthetics often produces no more than a 'soliloquy', making it hard 'to blame those who find the aesthetician an unpleasant companion'.

For all the plagued intricacy of aesthetics, including questions surrounding the nature of art, the creation of art, the artistic object, the function of art, and, perhaps the most complex, the aesthetic experience, there is a clear impetus for social theorists to maintain interest. Ideally simplified, an interaction occurs between an artist and an aesthetic object; an interaction occurs between the aesthetic object and a spectator; an obvious interaction occurs between the spectator and society; yet, most vitally, society cyclically returns to affect the artist. The intertwining illustrates why any theory of the social must consider aesthetics.

Both **critical theorists** and **postmodernists** have focused strongly on aesthetics; however, the predominant claim has been of continual deterioration in the face of advanced capitalism. In positing the idea of the 'culture industry', Theodor **Adorno** and Max **Horkheimer** posited two important theses; first, aestheticization was a growing phenomenon, and second, that art was progressively becoming standardized and commoditized. Inspired greatly by Walter **Benjamin**, they argued that such trends pointed toward a homogeneity, and hence a constricted diversity of culture, which in turn limited the **agency** of individuals. Many of the same themes, albeit within a different framework, have been taken up recently in works by Fredric **Jameson** and Jean **Baudrillard** as, arguably, the culture industry has intensified with globalized mechanisms of distribution. Yet notably, for all the denunciative focus on the constrictions, the converse is also vital to observe; within aesthetics is a realm of freedom arguably unattainable in any other medium, and the critical thinking that social theorists mandate as necessary for social change will inherently be constituted, at least in part, by artistic expression.

AGENCY encompasses one pole of a fundamental debate within social theory, often juxtaposed with its perceived dialectic opposite, **structure**. Most simply expressed, agency encompasses the actions taken by individuals (social actors). However, as expected from this discussion's status as a perennial debate in sociology, contextual concerns and particular perspectives enact more nuanced approaches with regard to the nature of human agency. Of course, most people would say they generally have a sense of self-determination in their choices, but the extent to which such decisions are determined by grander structures elicits significant divisions among theorists.

Ethnomethodologists and **phenomenological** sociologists are especially of the mind that humans do create the world around them, positing a view that social structures should be demoted in importance relative to individual autonomy. Whether it is the ideal type of charismatic individuals who change history forever, in both positive and horrifying manners, or even at a more common micro level, the everyday choices that constitute our lives, all signs point to autonomy of the self. In arguing against agency, some theorists, especially in the **critical theory** and **Marxist** traditions, have claimed that, while voluntary action is perceived as freely chosen and intentional, the notion of personal choice is a façade. Simple actions may be determinable by the individual, and some social actors effect great changes in society, but for the vast majority our grander choices are prefabricated by larger social structures, especially culture and the economy. A valid point of contention with regard to this philosophy concerns social change. If it is true that choice is illusionary, agency theorists posit the difficult conundrum of how societies change over time. Only with some level of human action would change be possible.

DANIEL MENDELSON

Two social theorists who have arguably transcended this dualistic view of agency and structure are Pierre **Bourdieu** and Anthony **Giddens**. The former's critique of polar positioning within this debate was based on his assertion of the inevitably bounded nature of agency and structure. To separate either from the other would produce no coherent picture of society. Giddens's theory of structuration is also a powerful critique of extreme perspectives on either end of the spectrum.

Louis **ALTHUSSER**, a reviver and renowned interpreter of **Marx**, was born in 1918 in the Algerian town of Birmendreïs, which at the time was under French occupation. After the premature death of his father, a banker whom he saw as a removed, controlling figure, his mother moved the family to Marseilles. In France, Althusser excelled at school in Lyon, gaining entrance to the prestigious École Normale Supérieure. Though his entrance in 1939 was delayed by his placement in a POW camp for French soldiers, as a Catholic he was able to survive, and actually remarked that he enjoyed the comradeship of the imprisoned group. Later known for his, at times, brilliant and highly original interpretation of Marx, Althusser's early work was centred instead on **Hegel**, the subject of his 1948 Master's thesis, and also wrote on Ludwig Feuerbach, a German philosopher and anthropologist, and Montesquieu, a French political philosopher. Yet this period is largely forgotten relative to the later decades devoted to his rereading of Marx, in which Althusser turned the entire traditional interpretation of the seminal thinker on its head, to the delight of some and dismay of other Marxist academics.

The main focus of Althusser's prolific career was an impenitent reinvigoration of Marxism, though he was also shamelessly unorthodox. His first task involved the proclamation of an **epistemological** break within Marx's thinking. Over the 1960s, Althusser's first famous works were published in French, including the later translated titles *Reading 'Capital'* and *For Marx*. Many Marxists had identified with Marx's earlier works in which he espouses the humanist notion of class struggle; the proletariat suffered a loss of dignity under the rules of capitalist organization, and the revolution prescribed by Marx would restore their autonomy and decency. Althusser broke from this tradition, declaring Marx's later work to be not based on 'ethical inspiration' of human life, but instead a conceptually based investigation of the modes of production as produced by the **Industrial Revolution**. Indeed, the notion of the alienated worker was replaced by that of surplus value, and the notion of (human) needs was replaced by a less subjectively based analysis of the economic and social conditions of labour. Therefore, 'man' could not be separately abstracted from economic structures and processes. In this theoretical antihumanist view of Marx, Althusser first illustrated his unique perspective, originating a mode of a more **structuralist** Marxism (though he was critical of pure **structuralism**).

The reception of his critique of humanism within Marxism was follow by a Freudian-influenced investigation of the successes and failures of communist revolution in practice. For Marx, the economic contradiction of capitalism was paramount, whereas Althusser believed there to be many interrelated factors, of which the economy might be the most significant, but on its own was not the sole locus of attention. He theorized a combination of complex structures in synthesis, similar to **Freud**'s conception of 'overdetermination', in which the diverse processes of the unconscious are condensed in dreams, with no ability to assign casual primacy (as the interlinks make such a project implausible). This argument rejected Marx's notion of superstructure and base, instead positing more relationality in society's structural arrangements.

Arguably, Althusser's most popularized work revolves around his rethinking of ideology, most notably in the 1969 essay 'Ideology and Ideological State Apparatuses'. In effect, Marx and Engels had argued that ideology was specific to capitalist societies, its embodiment seen in the acceptance of exploitative economic relations. Althusser audaciously speculated that ideologies went beyond the economy, and were an inherent aspect of all societies, capitalist, communist or other, as their function was to 'equip' individuals to operate in their particular environments. Additionally, Althusser believed ideology to be unfalsifiable based on this reasoning, in that ideology is lived sociality, not knowledge-based. Yet, this abstraction and apparent discursion from class-based consequences of ideology led to his response in the distinction of repressive state apparatuses (RSAs) and ideological state apparatuses (ISAs), the two methods by which the capitalist state ensures stability. RSAs encompassed traditionally violent methods of coercion, including police, army, law, prison, all involving penalties of varying degrees. ISAs, however, were contingent upon ideology, not force, and included arenas outside the orthodox Marxist conception of ideology, namely the family, the church, the media, and, most dominantly for Althusser, the education system. He argues that schools are almost machine-like in their production of suitable citizens for society, in a pejorative and ominous assessment of contemporary subject formation.

Althusser was aptly critiqued for his steadily mounting pessimism, as, despite his occasional identification of revolutionary possibilities, his theory tended toward a **deterministic** view of an already stabilized society. Yet his taking apart of humanism within the later Marx has influenced many disciplines outside Marxism, especially those that have gone beyond their traditional Enlightenment origins. Unfortunately, Althusser was never mentally stable, and was declared unfit to stand trial in the 1980 murder of his wife. Though he wrote much after his productive period in the 1960s, most of these works were not published or read with nearly the same enthusiasm. Althusser spent much of his last decade in French mental hospitals, dying in 1990.

Roland **BARTHES**, the gifted writer, **semiotician** and literary and social theorist who helped to popularize **structuralism** before identifying its inherent weaknesses, was born in 1915 in Cherbourg, Normandy. Barthes's father was killed in a naval battle before Barthes was even a year old, forcing his mother to raise him in impoverished conditions, mostly in Paris. Much of his early life was a struggle; in 1935, he contracted pulmonary tuberculosis, spending the vast majority of his twenties in hospital. Some theorized that this time spent alone and debilitated contributed to a uniquely reflective state of mind, as Barthes seemingly refused to take surface appearances as the whole schema.

As a result of the serious period of illness, it would not be until the age of 32 that he would be able to hold a full-time job, when Barthes left Paris to be a librarian (and later, a teacher) in Bucharest. The communist government expelled the staff two years later, and he moved to Egypt to teach at the University of Alexandria. Soon after, Barthes moved back to France as an assistant in the education office at the CNRS (*Centre National de la Recherche Scientifique*), the largest governmental research agency in France. At this point, his fame began to increase, mostly due to his bimonthly essays for the magazine *Les Lettres Nouvelles*. Collected for *Mythologies* (1957), his first major work, Barthes wrote in an affable but perceptive manner, taking apart diverse 'myths' of culture, from Einstein's brain, to wrestling, to French wine. The instructive aspect of these entertaining pieces was actually quite deep; through cultural symbols, the bourgeois imposed a value system, and therefore created divided factions within society. Three years after arriving at the CNRS, he moved to the sociology section and, within seven more years, he was director of the sociological study of signs, symbols and representations. During the 1960s, several attempts were made to establish a scientific approach to decoding such culturally embedded symbolism, including *On Racine* (1963), *Elements of Semiology* (1964) and *The Fashion System* (1967). His approach was novel and intrigued a generation of thinkers, with his assertion that nothing in culture was what it seemed to be, and yet everything in culture was capable of being decoded.

In a major shift, Barthes published his seminal post-structuralist work *S/Z* (1970), in which he abandoned his pursuit of a scientifically based analysis of literature and culture. Instead, through a rewriting of Balzac's short story *Sarrasine*, he illustrates that meaning does not come from the author, or from the text alone, but rather through an analysis and interpretation by a reader of the text. In this line of thinking, Barthes was closely relatable to Jacques **Derrida**'s notion of deconstruction, in which the claim of symbols acquiring universal meaning is abandoned, exposing an inherent flaw in the structuralist approach. Barthes continued this theme of the relationship between author and text in *Lover's Discourse* (1977), which is organized alphabetically, exemplifying the decentring of the author. These works illustrated his distinction between two types of writing: *écrivain*, or the dense prose of academia, versus his more favoured and utilized *écrivant*, characterized by an idiosyncratic and creative nature. Indeed, Barthes had apparently intended to write more fiction, though he died in 1980 after being struck by a laundry van.

Barthes is certainly celebrated within many realms of academia, yet his critics point mainly to one limitation of his work, that he rarely linked his work within literary theory and aesthetics to politics and the economy. While Barthes was a socialist in personal life, *Mythologies* contained a clear vindication of capitalist meaning and values, yet his post-structuralist work is claimed to lack this character. Despite this valid criticism, Barthes's significant contributions to social and literary theory, especially in structuralist and post-structuralist thought, continue to reverberate as the mythical ordering of texts and media symbolism grows ever larger.

Jean **BAUDRILLARD**, the notoriously controversial **postmodern** and **post-structural** theorist of contemporary culture, who is most well-known for his ideas on simulation and hyperreality, was born in Reims (in north-eastern France) in 1929. His grandparents were peasants, and his parents were civil servants; he was the first of his family to attend university, attending the Sorbonne to study German. Baudrillard henceforth broke from his childhood environment, following a mundane but common path of teaching his specialization at a French lycée. However, his epiphanal and transitionary moment would occur with the combination of two events, namely obtaining a position at the radicalized faculty of the University of Nanterre (the famed *Mouvement du 22 Mars* was popular there, a group that Jean-François **Lyotard** had also recently joined) and, quite obviously, the student uprisings of 1968, in which he later verified his participation. The same year, he would publish his first work, influenced by Roland **Barthes** and the sociologist Henri Lefebvre, *The System of Objects*, whose critique of everyday objects (fashion and gadgets among others) was a **Marxist** interpretation of alienation resulting from consumer desire or, as Baudrillard termed it, the 'codes' of purchase.

With the early 1970s, his Marxist leanings and concrete, more traditionally academic analyses both began to disappear from his writing. *For a Critique of the Political Economy of the Sign* (1973) broke with orthodox Marxism by positing a loss of meaning in both exchange value and use value, as **Marx** believed use value retained significance. Most importantly, this work signalled what would become Baudrillard's theme for much of the rest of his career, namely the simulation of the real, in which reality is without meaning, having been imitated to the point of nearly total nihilistic absence.

With the appearance of *Symbolic Exchange and Death* (1976) and *Simulacra and Simulation* (1981), Baudrillard became a prominent figure, introducing, among many significant notions, the term 'hyperreality'. This thesis argued that in the progression of history there has been an increasing removal of reality, as simulacrum replaced 'symbolic exchange', which for Baudrillard was the only true reality. Symbolic exchange consisted of interactions that involved a loss, including death and sacrifice, whereas in the simulation, there is only the notion of gain and clarity. Importantly, symbolic exchange was seen as more prevalent in premodern times, yet it is not absent in the contemporary epoch; it is, however, quickly subsumed by simulation, the symbolic only ever a fleeting instant.

Much of the following work from the mid-1980s onwards applied this uneven dichotomy of simulacra/symbolic to contemporary events, which has elicited both extremely widely read works and a correlated mountain of criticism. Following, by comparison, a relatively banal look at archetypal American objects and cities in the 1986 work *America* (the road, the desert, New York, Hollywood and so on), Baudrillard's most famed and controversial move was the prediction and the later 'confirmed' declaration that *The Gulf War Did Not Take Place* (1991). Unfortunately, he is often unfairly demonized for apparently forgetting the casualties and injuries of civilians and soldiers in the war. That the war is simulated does not remove the actuality of suffering, but in fact implies a poorer situation in which politicians and generals operate via computer simulations and long-range weapons in the creation of a falsified media reality. The war does indeed take place, individuals do indeed perish, yet the considerable symbolic is easily overwhelmed by an immense simulation.

Baudrillard continued to address controversial issues, notably the attacks of the 11th of September, garnering further criticism. Even his supporters lamented his sporadically formed declarations, which often lacked, according to his main editor Mark Poster, 'sustained, systematic analysis', polarizing opinion in 'refusing to qualify or delimit his claims'. Yet many still find his concept of hyperreality, in the face of a loss of traditional or Marxist politics, a powerful framework within which to judge truth in contemporary society. Though he died of typhoid in 2007 and his well-publicized incorporation in the film *The Matrix* is a distant memory, there is little reason to believe that Baudrillard's influence will wane, given the increasing prevalence of reality television, 24/7 news channels and the seemingly unflinching embrace of new technologies.

Zygmunt **BAUMAN**, the prominent social theorist of modernity whose recent proposition of a 'liquid modernity' has been especially instrumental, was born in the Polish town of Pozna in 1925. Forced to flee the country due to his Jewish heritage and the growing presence of the Nazi regime in 1939, he arrived in Soviet Russia and pursued a university education in which a **Marxist** perspective was touted as the path to freedom and equality. After the war concluded, Bauman returned to Poland, his career beginning with a position at the University of Warsaw; however, he would be forced from his home once again, along with several other Jewish colleagues, due to their critical analysis of an oppressive government. The University of Tel Aviv would be a stepping stone to the University of Leeds, where he was awarded the Chair of Sociology in 1971. This marked the beginning of his work gaining prominence, although the most well-received of his publications were actually written after his retirement, as Emeritus Professor at Leeds.

His early work had a more pronounced Eastern European bent, with greater concern for socialism, democratization and the role of government, but his best-known work began to surface in the late 1980s. *Legislators and Interpreters* (1987) and *Modernity and the Holocaust* (1989) were the start of a distinctive perspective of **modernity**, wrapped in the assumption that an ordering of society was feasible (and necessary); yet Bauman convincingly theorized concerning the failure to contain uncertainty and disorder. Especially in the latter work, he showed the destructive nature of the 'civilizing process', despite its ineptitude in managing inherently chaotic aspects of civilization; further, this predicament showed the dichotomous nature of modern **rationality** and ethics. Within *Modernity and Ambivalence* (1991), the concept of ordering took an intriguing turn, as Bauman argued that some (the 'strangers' of society) will always be considered on the outside of such a project.

A growing awareness of **postmodernity** and consumerism inspired the next set of works, including *Intimations of Postmodernity* (1992), *Postmodern Ethics* (1993) and *Postmodernity and its Discontents* (1997). In essence, a historical transition brought about a situation where actions were not traceable in the same manner as a more reliable and simplified epoch. An unconscious treaty exchanged security for supposed freedom, yet this freedom was imaginary, with its simultaneous creation of ambivalence and fear.

However, it was his considerable shift to the theory of liquid modernity that has catalysed so much current interest in Bauman's work. He has always resisted, in analysing the categorically shifting epochs, the proposition that the current system is a deformation of another period. Rather, in looking through a lens of consumerism, Bauman explicated his metaphor of the 'fluidity' of contemporary society, in which the objects' 'flow of time' becomes more significant than 'the space they happen to occupy'. Across multiple realms, notably in *Liquid Love* (2003) and *Liquid Life* (2005), Bauman further analyses earlier themes of uncertainty and the resulting feelings of trepidation (within the liquid framework), markedly in *Liquid Fear* (2006).

While Bauman's positions on subjects have changed with time, especially his transition from modernity to a postmodern perspective and, finally, to that of liquid modernity, the themes of his career are perhaps clearer than some of his contemporaries. Though Marxism is an obvious influence, Bauman is so highly regarded for his updated rendition of this perspective, encouraging a huge diversity of authors (**Simmel**, **Gramsci** and Levinas, among many less well-known theorists) to take a critical approach to the consequences and possibilities (or lack thereof) within the project of the Enlightenment and modernity (and, indeed, orthodox Marxism itself). In arguing that, rather than repression, forces of seduction are paramount in the structuring of power and culture in society, Bauman builds a unique critique of the consumption-saturated life and intriguingly incorporates ethics and morality within such a schema (in line with the **critical theory** notion of emancipatory thinking). Despite the thought-provoking publications of the last four decades of the twentieth century, the legacy of his work of the past decade on liquid modernity, life and love will surely be the most enduring, as society continues to encounter the problematic consequences of an ironically paralysing, fluid flexibility, and the resulting fearful unease it brings in contemporary life.

Simone de **BEAUVOIR**, the central figure of French feminism and existential philosophy, was born in 1908 in Paris. Her parents held polarizing political views, her father embracing far right-wing politics, her mother a strict Catholic, a situation which she later stated had encouraged her to become a radical thinker. Beauvoir had a precocious late childhood academically, training to teach philosophy at the Sorbonne; at that time, the École Normale Supérieure did not allow women to study at the main branch (instead having a lesser, women-only campus which did not even teach philosophy). After giving a presentation on Leibniz in 1929, she was allowed into the École, and subsequently received the second highest marks on her *agrégation*, behind only her lifelong partner, Jean-Paul Sartre. She was the ninth woman to receive an *agrégation* in any topic, and the youngest ever (male or female), at the age of 21. At this point, Georg **Hegel** and Karl **Marx** were not part of her studies, though they would later play a larger role, as they were not offered as part of the curriculum. Instead, Beauvoir's focus was on diverse thinkers including Plato, Immanuel Kant, Arthur Schopenhauer and Friedrich Nietzsche.

Sartre and Beauvoir would have a complicated relationship from her matriculation on, as the separation of their intellectual influence and their romantic status is at times hard to decipher. Nevertheless, after working in secondary schools as a philosophy teacher for over a decade, Beauvoir published her first work in 1943, a novel entitled *She Came to Stay*. She would leave teaching to write full time and, perhaps more significant for her burgeoning career was the establishment in 1945, along with Sartre, of the left-wing political and literary themed review *Les Temps Modernes*. This publication would be quite influential in the debates of the late 1940s and 1950s, though it must be stressed again that, given the gendered climate of the era, Sartre was the celebrated founder, with Beauvoir less recognized.

This would drastically change, however, with *The Second Sex* (1949), her seminal work of feminist existential social theory. The famous phrase 'one is not born, but rather becomes, a woman' is derived from this work; Beauvoir's essential point was a revolutionary one, only fully realized nearly two decades later with events that shaped rights movements of 1968. Drawing on an analysis of women's oppression, her philosophical background was explicated in a whole new realm. The study of subjectivity within existentialism and phenomenology had been taken up by Søren Kierkegaard, Edmund Husserl and Martin Heidegger, yet Beauvoir's unique framework explicated the differentiated experience of a woman's existence in a patriarchal society. Here, the woman was the 'absolute Other'.

Unfortunately, the first translation of *The Second Sex* into English was hurried and mangled much of the textual meaning, yet subsequent analysis by French-speaking academics, especially after her death in 1986, cemented her status as a forerunner to much of the latter movements of feminism (though they strayed from her ideas, both Luce **Irigaray** and Judith **Butler** have acknowledged its significance). It would be a mistake, though, to speak only of Beauvoir's feminist influence; indeed, this popularized and limiting conception was made prevalent at a time when Sartre was considered the intellectual star of the duo. Her novels and an extensive four-volume memoir, notably *Memoirs of a Dutiful Daughter* (1958) and *Old Age* (1970), contain much of the engaging philosophy of her more famous counterpart, often in less convoluted prose. The tokenizing assessment of Beauvoir as solely a feminist brings forth further the social theory of *The Second Sex*, and is a loss, considering the brilliance of her diverse thought.

Ulrich **BECK**, a key contemporary social theorist of modernization, particularly with regard to the notion of a 'risk society', was born in 1944 in Stolp (then under German rule, now Polish). Through his interest in sociology, psychology, political science and philosophy at Munich University, where he started in 1966 and received his PhD in 1972, one can trace the influential theoretical contentions of his current research. His most well-known work, *Risk Society* (1986) rightfully garnered him significant accolades. After a brief period teaching at the University of Münster and a decade at Bamberg, Beck returned to Munich as director of their Institute for Sociology in 1992.

In *Risk Society*, Beck argues that the perception of risk within contemporary society has had a fundamentally transformative impact. Vitally, risk was apparent in previous eras of history; indeed, natural disasters constantly tested communities across the globe. Yet Beck distinguishes the period before the work's publication as a particularly significant moment in risk acuity, in which institutions are undermined by risk as influenced by human responsibility: what **Giddens** later termed 'manufactured risk' (as opposed to external risk). Hence, the nature of risk, with modernization, has been fundamentally altered, especially in ecological, political and cultural realms. While scarcity and social class are still very relevant, arguably among the paramount aspects of industrial society, risk has grown relative to scarcity, and risk relations have grown relative to class relations. Just as capital was dispersed unequally, so too is risk, with different and potentially more catastrophic implications (as in Chernobyl and other such disasters).

Beck (also as a co-author with **Giddens** and Scott Lash) has argued that a plausible response to a risk society is contained within the notion of a reflexive modernization, in which organizing techniques of society are continually assessed to allow for reform and proper utilization of the knowledge available in a technologically advanced culture. Critiques have reproved this concept, claiming that it affords individuals too much agency, in effect committing the diametric transgression of **structuralism**, whose proponents afford little or no agency. Notwithstanding this valid rebuke, Beck has remained an influential theorist, coining a further influential notion in sociological thought (a 'second

DANIEL MENDELSON

modernity', in which modernity turns on itself, further modernizing the already modernized), and continues to lecture widely, holding simultaneous posts at Munich University and the London School of Economics.

Walter **BENJAMIN** was born in Berlin in 1892, the eldest child of Emil, a wealthy Jewish banker from Paris, who had moved to Berlin to become an antiques trader, where he met his wife, Pauline Schönflies. Benjamin enjoyed a relatively tranquil and comfortable childhood, growing up in the sought-after west end of the city. As he noted in his semi-autobiographical *A Berlin Childhood Around 1900*, there were tedious aspects of middle-class urbaneness: school life was often strict and unimaginative and, despite having two siblings, Benjamin expressed feelings of loneliness. Also, at the age of thirteen, after attending the prestigious Kaiser Friedrich-Wilhelm Gymnasium for three years (coincidently, his Frankfurt colleague Theodor **Adorno** would also attend a decade later), he became sufficiently ill for his parents to send him to a country boarding school in Thüringen. Despite these lesser aspects of his formative years, there were numerous upsides to these somewhat dull and illness-ridden years. Already well-read to keep himself entertained, Benjamin found the country school quite progressive and, fortunately, he happened to study under Gustav Wyneken, an important supporter of a radical youth movement, whose purpose was to regenerate German culture. Despite returning to Kaiser Friedrich after two years, Benjamin stayed in contact with Wyneken and his early work signified the influence of this formative mentor.

At the age of 20, Benjamin began his studies in philosophy at Freiburg University. Clearly still an activist at heart, he contributed a number of pieces to Wyneken's journal *Der Anfang* (The Beginning), advocating radical reform in cultural and educational politics. Continuing this trend of youth activism, in 1914 Benjamin returned to Berlin while still studying and was elected president of the city's 'Free Student Group', where he first met his future wife, Dora Sophie Pollack. Yet, for all the success, there was tumultuousness and tragedy; two close friends and fellow activists, the poet Fritz Heinle and his fiancée Rika Seligson, committed suicide in reaction to the approaching Great War and the resulting split of their movement. Some, including Wyneken, viewed the conflict as a defence (and eventual renewal) of German culture, while others simply feared devastation and ruin. The whole experience deeply affected Benjamin, and in 1915, he stopped all communication with Wyneken and disbanded the group.

Only three months later, he met Gershom Scholem, an influential friend who would help focus him on philosophical questions surrounding Judaic thought and mysticism. Benjamin moved to Munich, excused from military service due to his poor eyesight, and continued to evade authorities by leaving for Switzerland in 1917, the year he married Dora. It was in these times of exile that he completed his doctorate, entitled 'The Concept of Criticism in German Romanticism'. He returned to Frankfurt (his first encounter with Adorno) to pursue his habilitation

232

(a post-doctorate degree in certain European and Asian countries). However, his novel study of seventeenth century German plays of mourning, distinguishing them from classic tragedies and redeeming their scorned reputation, was dismissed (he withdrew it, on advice, to prevent later humiliation). Only after over half a century would this seminal work be acknowledged for its adept insights into the inherent imperfection and weakness of humanity. Despite this later restitution, the pursuit of a secure academic post was not to be for him.

For the next and final 15 years of his life, Benjamin was forced to live precariously as a freelance writer, often suffering from a lack of funds. For all the tribulations of his later life, his work was prolific; in the style of fragmentary asides and quotations, he wrote the influential works *Paris Arcades* (1927), *One-Way Street* (1928) and the renowned *Work of Art in the Age of Mechanical Reproduction* (1935). After remaining too long in Paris, and detained in Spain by guards during his attempt to flee Europe for America, Benjamin is thought to have committed suicide by an overdose of morphine in 1940. Fortunately, Adorno, Hannah Arendt, and Max **Horkheimer** were able to publish many of his works. It was through their efforts that Benjamin was established as a foremost cultural and social observer of the twentieth century. Indeed, *The Work of Art in the Age of Mechanical Reproduction* is still admired for its revealing exposition of modernism, despite his inability to predict the rapid advance of technology in the post-war era. Effortlessly crossing numerous and diverse realms, including Judaic mysticism, German Romanticism, **modernism**, and a quite unique version of **Marx**ism, Benjamin is rightfully considered a paramount social theorist, whose early death at 48 was all the more tragic in view of his seemingly unlimited potential.

Herbert **BLUMER**, a prominent member of the **Chicago School**'s second wave, was born in 1900 in Missouri. The youngest of three children, his father Richard George Blumer, was a cabinetmaker and Margaret Marshall Blumer was a homemaker. Blumer's early years were spent on a five-acre farm outside St. Louis, in a community with only a one-room schoolhouse, where he finished grammar school in 1913. Despite being a successful high-school student, he had to leave halfway through his education to assist in rebuilding the family business, which had burned down.

A devoted reader of socialist literature, Blumer put his first substantive job as a stenographer on hold as he dreamed of being a humanitarian world leader. This would clearly require a more extensive education. Making up the two years of missed high school in seven months, he was admitted to the University of Missouri in 1918. Here he found unbridled success in diverse realms, as, by his graduation, he had been elected captain of both the debating and football teams. This was also the site of Blumer's first sociology class (his professor was Charles Ellwood), although the apparent attraction of the course was a misleading connection to socialism. Despite this mistaken idea, he became a sociology major and, with Ellwood as supervisor, he completed a Master's thesis entitled 'Theory of Social Revolutions'.

Amazingly, in 1924, Blumer enrolled in the doctoral sociology programme at the University of Chicago and, simultaneously, began a career in professional football with the Chicago Cardinals. The 1930s were a tumultuous time for Blumer, as he took over George Herbert **Mead**'s social psychology class in 1931, when the pioneering philosopher fell ill. In 1933, a knee injury cut short his bright future in football; however, he continued as a line coach for three more years. It was in this period that Blumer developed the theory he is most remembered for, as he coined the term **symbolic interactionism** in the journal *Man and Society* in 1937. Drawing on an earlier study in which he analysed the autobiographical writings of children on their movie-going experiences, Blumer altered the perspective of object orientation for many sociologists, positing a (Mead-influenced) theory of social interaction. Essentially, he argued that we view objects differently depending on the meaning we assign, a practice whose progression depends on states of interaction, which are apt to change over time.

Blumer would move from Chicago to the University of California, Berkeley, developing the sociology department there and investigating a broad variety of issues, including industrialization, racism and the use of illicit drugs. However, his influence in these realms is overshadowed by the meticulous approach he applied to quantitative methodology and the theory of symbolic interactionism. Despite Blumer's death in 1987, the one-time president of the American Sociological Association is firmly established as a central twentieth century social theorist.

Pierre **BOURDIEU**, among the most recognized of all post-Second World War French sociologists, was born in 1930 in a small rural region of Béarn in southwestern France. His background was decidedly not elite, his father being the postman of their small village. Despite the academic obstacles inherent in these circumstances, Bourdieu was quite successful, gaining entrance to the famed École Normale Supérieure, where he studied philosophy with Louis **Althusser**. Indeed, as seen through interviews and his work, he never forgot his roots, and continually embraced the outsider status that accompanied his improbably elite education. Following graduation and a short stint as a lycée teacher, he made a move which would radically influence the rest of his career, taking a post in 1958 as lecturer in Algiers. This move, however, must be seen in light of Bourdieu's inquisitive nature, as Algeria was the pre-eminent problem for French society at the time, with the Algerian War beginning that very year. His ethnographic research concerning the clash of peoples in the area, published in America in 1962 as *The Algerians*, was an instant success in France, firmly establishing his reputation as a renowned sociologist.

Yet it was, arguably, issues of power and different forms of capital, beyond the purely economic, which propelled Bourdieu to the intellectual heights he would later reach (he was made Director of Studies at the École Pratique des Hautes Études in 1964 and Chair of Sociology at the illustrious Collége de France in 1981). What distinguished his social theory from that of his peers was a unique perspective on **agency** and **structure**, encapsulated in the ingenious notions of 'habitus' and 'field'. Breaking away from the structuralism and constraint of Althusser's Marxism and Claude **Lévi-Strauss**'s anthropology, Bourdieu sought to account for the genesis of social practice. In so doing, a more nuanced account of everyday life materialized, notably through *habitus*, which referred to the complex process by which social structures are internalized by individuals. Resulting from learning and acting in a particular subset of society, the actor got the 'feel for the game', achieving an understanding of society and one's place in it. Society itself was composed of fields, which were the spaces of social interaction, whose autonomous nature was moderated by other interacting fields. Following **Weber**'s expansion of **Marx**'s concentration on what he might have termed a field of the economy, Bourdieu saw diverse and energetic fields in many arenas; one of his most influential identifications was that of education, the subject of multiple works (notably *The Inheritors*, 1979).

Most important to the notions of *habitus* and field is the accumulation of various forms of capital, another expansion on the work of Marx. Instead of simply positing monetary capital, Bourdieu added 'symbolic' and 'cultural' capital (capital defined as a socially valued good). Symbolic capital referred less to defined objects than to senses of honour, dignity and power. Cultural capital, quite interrelated to symbolic capital, referred to the social groupings and kinships determined for the individual at birth (and reorganized as life went on). For Bourdieu, these non-material forms of accumulated power were not the sole definer of class, but were an integral part of social stratification, their influence often underestimated. These themes were applied in many seminal works, including aesthetic tastes in *Distinction* (1979), elite French education in *The State Nobility* (1989) and the subjective nature of class-based appreciation of the arts in *The Rules of Art* (1992).

In transgressing the traditional debate of agency and structure, Bourdieu acquired many dissenters, who have critiqued his theory from both sides, either claiming he grants too much freedom, or stating that the notion of *habitus* is too closely aligned with structuralism. Yet undeniably, Bourdieu must be championed as (in ways some find analogous to Georg **Simmel**) a tireless defender of the deprived from the perspective of the outsider. This was particularly evident in what would be Bourdieu's last fight (he died of cancer in 2002) against the detrimental consequences of neoliberal policy and globalization on culture and individuals. Perhaps best encapsulated than in 1999, when he addressed a group of leading patrons of the audio-visual arts in Paris querying, 'Masters of the world, do you know what you are doing?', Bourdieu's reactionary and political spirit of cultural critique would never be constrained during his lifetime.

Judith **BUTLER**, the key contemporary social theorist of comparative literature, politics, feminism and psychoanalysis, was born in 1956. She received her PhD from Yale in 1984 and her dissertation was published three years later as

Subjects of Desire: Hegelian Reflections in Twentieth Century France. However, it was her unique synthesis of Simone de **Beauvoir**, Jacques **Derrida**, Sigmund **Freud**, Julia **Kristeva**, Jacques **Lacan** and, perhaps most significantly, Michel **Foucault** in *Gender Trouble* (1990), that firmly established her position internationally as a central figure in social theory. The title plays on the 1974 film *Female Trouble*, an important allusion considering the movie's main character, Divine, plays a drag artist. This seemingly ordinary role, in actuality, brings to the surface many significant questions surrounding gender and sex, especially with regard to the performative role of sexual identity. Indeed, even the fact that *Female Trouble* is a film has meaning within Butler's framework; illustrating her transcendence of earlier feminist writing, the notion of 'performativity' encapsulates the precarious nature of gender, questioning whether it is a kind of 'persistent impersonation' that goes beyond the arguably simplified identity politics of previous feminisms.

For Butler, in some ways like Lacan's metaphor of the mirror stage, the unified sense of sexuality lies, its cohesion a mask which covers inherent divergences and fragmentation. These arguments were previously strongly advanced by women of colour and those of impoverished nations, for whom the idea of a unified female perspective was troubling, given its pronouncement by mostly white women of developed countries. Butler additionally contended, in a similar vein, that the assumption of a unified sexed body, male or female, is a glossing of real differences. For gender to simply be a dichotomous formation is a falsehood, yet of particular note in her work is the formation and maintenance of this discourse.

Building on, but also critiquing, Beauvoir's famous edict, 'one is not born a woman but becomes one', the analysis in *Gender Trouble* is decidedly political, with its Foucauldian concern for discursiveness of the gendered performance and its implications for power struggles. What she terms the 'heterosexual matrix', later updated as 'heterosexual hegemony' in *Bodies That Matter* (1993), is an attempt to describe the normative regulations of sex. Problematically (in some regards especially for heterosexuals), the acting out of the overwhelmingly present cultural representations imbued in 'masculinity' and 'femininity' solidifies an illusion of the self with regard to gender and sex. Heterosexual relations are destructive in their severe limiting of sexual identity as, for Butler, there should exist an entire spectrum of gendered and sexual selves, but they are subsumed by the contemporary sexual discourse.

Though Erving **Goffman**'s notion of performance was not overtly political, and was certainly not projective (or encouraging) of radicalism, vitally present in Butler's theory of performativity is the necessity of transgressing our constraining framework of sexuality. Repeatedly she locates within those that 'gender bend' the potential to break from such an inhibited situation. Yet her concern with the psychic nature of the self also creates a predicament for full embodiment of our gender identification. Essentially, it is doubtful whether we can truly represent our 'phantasmatic' sexual selves. Posed against the assured singularity of biological reductionism, Butler argues for our multiplicitous nature, and can therefore be seen as a precursor to the formation of 'queer theory'. It is, however, unclear whether this might imply an inherent inability to feel right about our sexuality.

Though *Gender Trouble* has been cited by hundreds of publications, the large majority supportive, a valid theme of dissention surrounds her significant underestimation of the refusal to identify with cultural norms. In making the case for performativity so strongly, Butler's account of the discursive formation of sexuality seems dubiously exaggerated. Her social theory is ostensibly incapable of describing the vast diversity (and uncertainty) within the formation of gender. Yet, aside from this problematic characteristic of her work, the outcrop of social theory concerning the self and sexuality has been enormously influential in advancing the understanding of identity in contemporary times. Though her focus has shifted in recent years to Jewish philosophy, Zionism (she has been noted for her anti-Zionist ideals) and Israeli politics, Butler's work of the 1990s has retained much of its initial power, diverging and creating new thought to the benefit of numerous academic disciplines.

Cornelius **CASTORIADIS**, a key innovator of **Marxism** and theoretician of creativity within **psychoanalysis**, was born in Constantinople in 1922. Though he studied traditional political science subjects at the University of Athens, including economics, law and politics, he was also committed to active politics, especially significant given the precarious tension of political divisions during the Second World War. With his life threatened by Stalinists and fascists, due to his having joined the Greek Communist Youth, Castoriadis moved to France in 1945, founding *Socialisme ou Barbarie*, an influential group whose writings over 15 years significantly impacted the environment of the 1968 rebellions. An economist at the Organisation for Economic Co-operation and Development from 1946 until 1970, he later became a practising psychoanalyst, in effect mirroring a similar intellectual shift from Marx to **Freud**, and was director of the École des Hautes Etudes en Science Sociales until close to the time of his death in 1997.

Early in his career, Castoriadis developed an untraditional perspective and critique of Marxism, illustrating fundamental weaknesses of the theory. Orthodox Marxists believed capitalism would lead, inescapably, to collapse, due in part to the progressive diminution of profit. Castoriadis argued, in the early 1950s, that class struggle and technical change were not so amenable to predictions and inherent inevitabilities; rather, people's actions, especially technological innovations, had real effects on capitalism, making it implausible to extrapolate into the future. Further, signalling his later embrace of the diversity within psychoanalytic thought, Castoriadis (an economist by profession) declared the economy to be an insufficient framework for the analysis of capitalism. As was propounded in various ways by numerous neo-Marxists, there was much beyond a reductionist view of the economy as the sole locus of capitalism. Yet, intriguingly for Castoriadis, culture and sexuality were intertwined within society, with no one arena significantly more essential than the others. Culture was common in many new formulations and critiques of Marxism but, in addressing sexual intimacy, there is a sense of prophecy of future considerations in social theory, given the early epoch of his writing. He continued to write on similar themes until the dissolution of *Socialisme ou Barbarie* in 1965 and the events of 1968.

With the 1970s came a new focus in his career, as the intrinsic creativity of the unconscious self became his framework of analysis. Culminating with *The Imaginary Institution of Society* (1975), Castoriadis reclaimed the radical potential of Freudianism, making an important further connection between psychoanalysis and social theory. Critics of Freud had argued that his reduction of the human psyche to specific and similar structures of desires and instincts, across all individuals, was tantamount to the removal of their ingenuity and originality. Castoriadis, however, saw within the constant repositioning of the self in societal and historical trajectories an indeterminacy that necessitated creative input by the individual. As the psyche continually modifies representation and fantasy through input over far-reaching sources (social institutions and cultural norms at the most basic level), there is a sense of creation which transcends the trite formulations of pseudo originality (as characterized within much of the 'reinvent yourself' mainstream media).

Yet, most significant for Castoriadis, as he argued in *Philosophy, Politics, Autonomy* (1991), was the notion that this form of creativity did not inherently imply good outcomes. He made the provocative but logical claim that creativity and indeterminacy of the self trigger worlds both dazzling and horrifying, as 'Auschwitz and the Gulag are creations just as much as the Pantheon and *Principia Mathematica* '. Given his earlier observation that the unpredictability of capitalism prevented assurances of its desirable upheaval, it should come as little surprise that the indeterminacy of action does not imply consistently pleasant results. In this masterful formulation concerning the erratic autonomy of the creative actor, both for the brilliant and the despicable, the thoughtful perspective of Castoriadis has exemplified both the limitations of a determinate Marxism and the endless prospective nature of the Freudian subconscious.

CHIGACO SCHOOL refers to various periods of intellectual prominence exhibited by the department of sociology at the University of Chicago. Established in 1892 (following the creation of the University of Chicago in 1891) by Albion Small, it was the first North American sociology department, and with its formation came the first major North American sociology journal, the *American Journal of Sociology* in 1895. Though it may be considered too vague a term, especially due to the important Chicago School of economics, two specific periods of the sociology department's history were heavily influential and merit the eminent status of Chicago School.

Chicago was a perfect example of the rapid growth that many American cities underwent around the turn of the twentieth century. Only three decades before the University of Chicago came to fore, the total inhabitants numbered 10,000; by the time many of the first Chicago School academics published their classic empirical studies, the populace numbered over two million. It was this environment that stimulated the interest of researchers informed by philosophical pragmatism and the subsequent analysis of urban social processes. Mostly characterized by direct fieldwork and empirical investigation of observations, for this first group of the Chicago School (Nels Anderson, Ernest Burgess, Frederic Thraser, Clifford Shaw, Edwin Sutherland, William Thomas, Louis Wirth, and Florian Znaniecki among others), the intricate and, at times chaotic, city provided much of the inspiration for their work. As Robert Park, an early prominent chair, remarked to his students,

> Go and sit in the lounges of the luxury hotels and on the doorsteps of the flop-houses; sit on the Gold Coast settees and on the slum shakedowns; sit in the Orchestra Hall and in the Star and Garter Burlesque. In short, go get the seat of your pants dirty in real research.

Following this advice, many of the studies that followed showed the dirtiness of living in a fast-growing city, as their focus included crime, immigration, homelessness, poverty, delinquency, and other dynamics of a harsh city life. Novel methods of research resulted, such as case-study and participant observation.

The second wave of the **Chicago School** was arguably more influential in American sociology, especially in the period shortly following the Second World War. While this cohort also had a pragmatic observational lineage, led first by George Herbert **Mead** (though technically a member of the philosophy department, Mead's social psychology class could not help but be intertwined with the sociology department) and later by Herbert **Blumer**, explicit theory was also developed within the department under Everett C. Hughes. In this industrious time, many useful theoretical perspectives and corresponding terms were further explicated in a social realm. Most notable perhaps was Blumer's term 'symbolic interactionism', which, in essence, replaced the social behaviourism framework more popular under Mead. Stressing the interplay of the self and group, with due consideration for personal and collective symbols (and their meanings), Herbert Blumer made a seemingly simple sociological foray, although it in fact spawned an entire discipline. From Émile **Durkheim**'s work on collective consciousness through Anthony **Giddens**'s notion of practical and discursive knowledge, the Chicago School's focus on groups, symbols, and meaning has been of constant significance for much of the history of sociology.

Anna Julia **COOPER**, the nearly forgotten social theorist best known for her phrase 'Black Woman of the South', was born in 1858 in Raleigh, North Carolina. She was the daughter of an enslaved woman, her biological father believed to be a prominent landowner. A precocious child, Cooper won a scholarship to a newly opened school run by the Protestant Episcopal Church, intended as a missionary project to aid the education of recently freed slaves. She thrived there, showing equal aptitude in both the humanities and sciences. Yet the school's focus was undeniably centred on men, training most for the ministry, and the most ambitious for university. Cooper fought to take subjects outside the specific 'Ladies' course', such as Greek, which were reserved only for male students; this early experience exemplified an important later theme in her work, namely the differentiated treatment of White women versus Black women, and Black men versus Black women. She would stay at the school after her graduation as an instructor, and later attend Oberlin College. It was while teaching at the Colored High School of Washington DC, however, that she would write her most influential work.

Before turning 30, and to very little contemporary acclaim, Cooper wrote *The Colored Woman's Office* (1892), a text whose broad applications still resonate in feminist thought. Published by an obscure printing firm, the work was not recognized to nearly the same extent as later works on Blackness within the writing of W.E.B. Du Bois or early **feminism** within the writing of Charlotte Perkins **Gilman**. Essentially, this illustrated the very argument she was making; as a Black Woman (of the South), she occupied a position at the bottom of two social scales in nineteenth-century America. Cooper had a gender predicament, as White feminists ignored her standpoint, while Black men subjugated her (to be fair, just as White men subjugated White women). It was agents of Booker T. Washington, the famed Black figure of the late nineteenth century, who had her fired from her post as a schoolteacher. The tragic position of the Black Woman that Cooper described was present not only in interaction with Whites, but also with Blacks. As Charles Lemert notes, W.E.B. Du Bois's wife 'lies in a plain grave in Massachusetts while he is lavishly entombed in Accra, Ghana'.

Two messages resonate most strongly from Cooper's 105-year life: the optimism surrounding cultural and academic enrichment, and the divisions that concretely structure all social relations. While the latter was made clear above, and stands in opposition to Gilman's (and many later feminists') essentialism, the former is equally noteworthy. Given her illustrious education (at the age of 65, she became the fourth Black woman in American history to receive a PhD), it is not surprising that she might stress the importance of education. What is important, however, is that this was the method by which she proposed that Black women would, and should, feel an obligation to improving the repute of the entire African-American community. Cooper truly embodied her own philosophy, returning to her position in segregated schools after Washington's power waned. While she recognized the painfully differentiated structure of both gender and race (and their combination) decades before any other theorist, her life's commitment was not combative, but rather focused on the betterment of those whose freedom and power had been constrained. As every new American passport quotes from Cooper (pp. 26–7), 'The cause of freedom is not the cause of a race or a sect, a party or a class – it is the cause of humankind, the very birthright of humanity.'

COSMOPOLITANISM, throughout its long history, has been approached from numerous perspectives by a diverse set of thinkers, though it is most often associated with the notion of a worldly citizenry that does not derive membership qualifications based on nationality. Some of the earliest discussions of such a framework come through the thought of Diogenes of Sinope, the famed Greek 'cynic', and later in the political philosophy of Stoics, with Cicero a prime exemplar. During this time, before the Common Era, most Greek males were defined primarily by their city of origin. Based on this designation, they were afforded certain opportunities (and consequently certain limitations), an arrangement that Diogenes and Cicero rejected. Already, two prominent themes of contemporary cosmopolitanism were evident in their writings, namely identity and responsibility. Clearly, the notion of cosmopolitanism has been framed both positively and negatively in each of these realms. Regarding identity, a 'worldly' individual may be valued for their sundry knowledge of cultures, but may also elicit fear as a perceived threat to a nationalist homogeneity. Global responsibility in the era of the information revolution may seem arduous, given the complex organization of intricate international relations, and yet feelings of allegiance that cross cultural boundaries have engendered real benefits in raised morality and humanitarianism.

The lineage of approaches to cosmopolitanism within social theory is illustrious, given the seminal theorists that have touched on the perspective to different degrees. From the eighteenth through to the mid-twentieth century, prominent thinkers such as Immanuel Kant and Georg **Hegel** had discussed the notion of 'universal hospitality', Georg **Simmel** wrote perceptively on the complicated role of the stranger, while Emmanuel Levinas and Jacques **Derrida** approached cosmopolitanism through distinct analyses of the 'Other' (that which is differentiated or not considered). More recently, Zygmunt **Bauman** revisited the Other of Levinas in *Postmodern Ethics* (1993), Ulrich **Beck** proposed a nuanced cosmopolitanism that sought to avoid a hegemonic world order, and Kwame Anthony Appiah's *Cosmopolitanism: Ethics in a World of Strangers* (2006) examined the difficulty (and simultaneous necessity) of speaking across difference in enacting moral duties.

Cosmopolitanism bears significantly on the processes of globalization; arguably, the former has regained, in recent times, the prominence that it lost to the powerful discourse surrounding the latter. For years after its rise in academic circles, globalization was considered mainly in terms of those things that could be reduced to economic implications, namely global corporations, movement of labour forces and the international monetary exchange. However, with time came a deeper appreciation of the cultural and emotional transformations exerted by such developments and, hence, the ethical and multifaceted framework of cosmopolitanism has returned to the fore. Given globalization's massive restructuring of networks and nation-states, the theoretical debates over cosmopolitanism have grown ever-more complex and, consequently, have been reinvigorated as a vital philosophical quandary for social theory.

CRITICAL THEORY has varied meanings depending on the frame of academic analysis in which one engages. Literary critical theory has been characterized by leading social critical theorists (such as Jürgen **Habermas**) as essentially hermeneutical, in that literary critical theorists tend to seek knowledge through interpretation of texts and symbols. There is little that is normative about this process. In contrast, social **critical theory**, popularized by the **Frankfurt School**, is guided by an ideal of emancipation and freedom from entrapment, focusing on increasing personal autonomy and diminishing societal domination. This desire for social transformation is what, for many, most dominantly distinguishes social critical theory, placing it to some degree in a sociological lineage of **Marxism**. Max **Horkheimer**, an initiator of the Frankfurt School, made a similar distinction in his 1937 essay *Traditional and Critical Theory*, stating that critical theory is a social theory oriented toward critiquing and changing society as a whole, in contrast to traditional theory, which seeks merely to understand or explain.

Horkheimer also sought to oppose logical positivism and thought of critical theory as a radical progression of Marxian theory that cut off any strain of positivistic philosophy. This contrasted directly with the dominant empiricist thinking of Auguste Comte, as Horkheimer and Theodor **Adorno** argued in the decade after the Second World War that such a mode of thinking inaccurately represents realistic social processes. To improve society, and to understand the relation between **structure** and **agency**, the founders of the Frankfurt School traversed many disciplines of social science, including (but not limited to) sociology, anthropology, economics, history, political science, **psychoanalysis** and psychology.

Despite their widespread influence, notable critics have derided the Frankfurt School for intellectual elitism and a form of idealism with no tenable political implications. Perhaps the most stinging criticism comes from philosopher Karl Popper, who stated, 'Marx's own condemnation of our society makes sense. For Marx's theory contains the promise of a better future. But the theory becomes vacuous and irresponsible if this promise is withdrawn, as it is by Adorno and Horkheimer.' Caught between a critique of contemporary society and no assurance of a revolution or a more optimal society, critical theorists have found themselves the target of much disdain.

Though there were multiple groups of intellectuals during the prolific decades (1950s to 1970s) of critical theory, some of the most notable theorists in the tradition were Max Horkheimer, Theodor Adorno, Walter **Benjamin**, Erich **Fromm**, Herbert **Marcuse**, and Jürgen Habermas. There were quite significant differences among these theorists; however, their most significant publications have been often classified within the diverse realm of critical theory.

Jacques **DERRIDA**, the inventor of the critical and literary practice of 'deconstruction', was born in Algeria in 1930. Owing to clear and unavoidable obstacles, including his Sephardic Jewish heritage, his education was disrupted in the early 1940s by the war and anti-Semitic measures of the Vichy government, so it was not until 1949 that he would be able to leave for Paris to study at the Lycée Louis le Grand. However, success would quickly follow, as he was accepted into the École Normale Supérieure to study philosophy at a particularly amazing time, with Louis **Althusser** and Michel **Foucault** among his peers. Though Derrida was awarded a scholarship to Harvard to study the unpublished work of Edmund Husserl, the esteemed founder of **phenomenology**, his career was again interrupted, this time by a period of compulsory military service in Algeria (where he taught French and English to the children of troops).

It was not until the late 1950s and early 1960s that Derrida would enter the public eye, though soon after he would take the intellectual community by storm. In 1959, he delivered a now famous paper on genesis and structure within Husserl's writing, critiquing his positioning of consciousness as an unmediated and pure representation of the self, which secured him a position at the Sorbonne in 1960. This year also marked his first publication, a translation of and introduction to Husserl's *Origin of Geometry*, and further publications in major French journals. However, 'The Ends of Man' conference at Johns Hopkins University and his seminal paper 'La Différance' at the Sorbonne in 1966 cemented his prestige. Through these conferences, and the publishing of three books in 1967, including the massively prominent *Of Grammatology*, Derrida began to introduce his most influential concepts of deconstruction and *différance*, which acted as a catalyst in shattering the overwhelmingly uncritical reception of **structuralism**.

Following Heidegger's seminal work *Being and Time*, Derrida introduced deconstruction, as not a destruction, but rather as an analytical disassembling of Western ontology. He insightfully argued that an inherent gap stood between authorial intention and textual meaning. Many thinkers had given primacy to writing, claiming it to be a superior and more reliable form of meaning than speech, which was thought to be the locus of possibly mistaken purpose. Their contention, which Derrida dismantled, was that, with the ability to think, write and rewrite text, it could have a semblance of ultimate symbolism; each reader would know exactly what the text conveyed, in the adopted interpretation of **Saussure**'s signifier–signified being a definitive relationship. Importantly, Derrida does not argue that speech and writing diverge our intentions, but rather that the concept of a pure and original intention is not plausible, given the unstable nature of symbolic communication.

Related to deconstruction is his equally important notion of *différance*, which means both to differ and to defer; as symbols search for meaning, they attempt to find it through more terms, cyclically leading to a self-defeating deferral of central truth. **Lacan,** too, had suggested that terms were linked in such a manner, yet the innovative aspect of Derrida's theory lay in his crushing of the subjectivity that allowed for any sort of centering. He made the claim that true intentions and a real subjectivity are unfeasible: the implications of this are enormous.

Though Derrida turned away from linguistics and later considered **psycho-analysis**, ethics and politics, his reputation for pushing the boundaries of **structuralism** is usually the focus of critique of his approach. Clearly, when challenging the orthodoxy of usually static disciplines, one is bound to elicit some adverse reactions. While Derrida was a politically engaged individual, his early theory is abstracted from social and cultural contexts, with little regard for political implications. The question of non-linguistic communication is not addressed. Additionally, Derrida's obtuse style of writing has been condemned by other philosophers and social theorists as pretentious and intentionally difficult. Nonetheless, his concept of deconstruction, in stressing the necessity of openness in meaning, has been seen by some thinkers as a rallying cry for the marginalized voices of society. Despite his death in 2004, this remains a vital consideration for contemporary social theory.

DETERMINISM is a philosophical position that considers events to be causally decided through links to past events, in a chain reaction. The degree to which a deterministic view permits deviation from a preset order varies significantly; fatalistic determinists believe that social actors have no influence whatsoever on their behaviour and actions, and hence on future circumstances, while less orthodox determinists permit a probabilistic framework of causal determination that allows for some deviation from the chain reaction. Both positions, however, are firmly entrenched within social theory on the **structural** side of the **agency** debate.

Notably, a variety of deterministic themes posit different structures as the dominant paradigm responsible for setting the rest of future events. Scientific determinism refers to the belief that all events have a measurable cause and effect, and while the causes and effects of interacting events are too complex to map out at any point in time, it would be theoretically possible to do so entirely. With all current events mapped, one could conceivably predict the occurrence of future events using the laws of nature. Biological determinism, sometimes associated with the eugenics movement, refers to the belief that a human's biological composition is the determining factor in their behaviour and actions; an accepted contemporary use of biological determinism is within the law, as defendants have successfully argued in court that their brain chemistry overruled any sense of intentionality.

Economic determinism, an outcrop of **Marxism**, is arguably the most debated theme of determinism within sociological theory. Marx believed that modes of production and class structure determined social, political and cultural aspects of life; Friedrich Engels tempered this assertion after Marx's death, claiming that economic relations should not be considered as acting in a closed form of causality, but rather should be seen as a 'decisive influence'. Within this downplaying of constraint, the importance of determinism is fully apparent; at an extreme end (so-called 'hard determinism'), the concept of free will is considered impossible. This position has been rightfully criticized. Perhaps most interesting to consider, and the locus of the debate in recent time, is the compatibility of free will and determinism (so-called 'soft determinism'). As this stance recognizes both the immense difficulty of acting outside structural constraints, and also the possibility of doing so, it is an approach that has been well-received within social theory.

DISCOURSE is an idea fundamentally based within **Saussure**'s (and other semioticians) differentiation between language as it is used (what he termed *parole*), and the systemic and structured underlying rules of language (*langue*). Saussure believed that the former could not provide as worthy an analysis as the latter, as *parole* is inherently individualized, and therefore conditional. The structural rules stayed put; *langue* was therefore the reliable site of investigation. Discourse, contrarily, is positioned within *parole*, focusing on language's patterns with regard to usage. For this reason, those new to linguistics are more likely to pick up on discourse analysis than Saussurian linguistics. Notably, however, the study of discourse aimed to complement and discover new structural rules, all the while providing concrete instances of discursive practices within society. What the notion of discourses supplemented for Saussurian social theorists was a fuller theory of structural linguistics, one which could delve into implied meaning (whereas Saussure had focused on explicitly signified meaning).

Both Roland **Barthes** and Michel **Foucault** contributed greatly to theories of discursive analysis through their participation in **structuralism** and **post-structuralism** debates. In *Mythologies* (1957), Barthes made the vital point that, often, Saussure's signifiers had more to them than a simple dictionary definition; wine might be an alcoholic beverage made from grapes, but this said little of its heralded hierarchal position in French society. Only through discovering these auxiliary implied meanings (Barthes's myths) would a complete representation be possible.

Foucault formalized similar ideas, in a series of works of discursive formations, such as *The Order of Things* (1966) and *The Archaeology of Knowledge* (1969). He posited, like Barthes, that there was more to sequences of signs than simply their individual definitions; Foucault termed the supplementary meaning an *enouncement*, often translated as a statement. These statements produced relations between the subject and the signs and, notably, statements too interacted. Discursive formations, as elucidated in the specific example of medicine in *The Birth of the Clinic* (1963), referred to the regularized production of knowledge through statements. Crucially, such processes are intertwined within relations of power, as Foucault believed all discourses involve struggles over meaning and construction of subjects. Judith **Butler** aptly noted that discourses create a limit to what is acceptable in speech.

It is vital to consider, however, that discourses are nearly always temporary, given a long enough timeframe. They may easily encompass an era, yet the orthodox account of structuralism is insufficient to characterize their eventual demise and replacement by other discourses. Hence, post-structuralists saw within discourses a locus of social change, as analysis might necessarily lead to the challenging of their repressive formations, as Foucault accomplished to some extent with *The History of Sexuality*.

William Edward Burghardt **DU BOIS**, the enormously influential African-American theorist and social activist, was born in 1868 in Great Barrington, Massachusetts. His youth was not marked by overt racism. The town he lived in had a population of nearly fifty Blacks, and Du Bois was allowed (if not wel-comed) into the homes of many White families, playing with neighbourhood children without incident. Yet there was an increasing awareness of his differ-ence, and the resulting negative reactions of other townspeople, as he accounted in the autobiographical work *Darkwater: Voices from Within the Veil* (1920), 'slowly, I realized that some folks, a few, even several, actually considered my brown skin a misfortune; once or twice I became painfully aware that some human beings even thought it was a crime'. One of his first memories of such disapproval occurred during the purportedly joyous exchange of cards among the children of his schoolhouse. At first, everyone seemed to be enjoying the activity, but a female classmate refused his 'peremptorily, with a glance', initi-ating the feeling that he was 'different from the others . . . shut out from their world by a vast veil'. Du Bois, however, was not one to submit to an oppressive society; instead, he claimed that such events 'spurred [him] to tireless effort', and the effort showed, as he attained admirable grades. His family was too poor to afford higher education, however, as his father had abandoned the family at an early age. Assisted by funding from neighbouring Whites, Du Bois enrolled at Fisk University in 1885.

It was at Fisk that his race became a greater factor than before, with two sep-arate (though related) themes emerging. First, there was a sense of embrace-ment, as he remarked in a public speech to his classmates, 'I am a Negro and I glory in the name!' Later in life, he recalled that this marked the end of his ego-centricity, replaced with a greater awareness of community. Second, there was the ominous and sobering observation of more overt racism. Unlike the north-eastern United States, where bigotry occurred mostly behind the scenes, Fisk was located in Nashville, with prominent signs of discrimination, including seg-regated public arenas, blatantly unequal treatment in the legal and education systems, and sporadic (but assured) assaults and murders.

Du Bois would next move to Harvard, entering in 1888 as a junior with his Fisk Bachelor's degree in hand. Though his fellow white students were con-temptuous, he would find solace in brilliant professors, especially William James. His synthesis of history and philosophy placed his approach firmly in the sociological tradition, but sociology was still regarded with some apprehension in the United States, so he pursued a doctoral degree in history. This path took him to Germany for two years, where Du Bois came into contact with Max **Weber** and also had a slight reprieve from the oppressive American south. In 1895, he would submit 'The Suppression of the African Slave-Trade to the

United States of America, 1638–1870', which was published the following year in the *Harvard Historical Studies*, making him the first African-American to attain a PhD from Harvard.

The Philadelphia Negro (1899) was published in between his 1897 magazine article 'Of Our Spiritual Strivings' and the subsequent collection of essays of which it was the lead, the seminal work *The Souls of Black Folk* (1903). The former was arguably more a work of sociology (and highly regarded in its own right for pioneering American urban ethnography), but it is the magazine piece and *Souls* that currently stand out as his most renowned works of social theory. His powerful account of the twoness of his people, the double-consciousness of being both an 'American and a Negro' was at the heart of the notion of *souls* (notably pluralized). Probably influenced in part by the multiple selves theory of James, or the duality of modern rationality in Weber (potential for progress, as opposed to the ensnaring cage), Du Bois employed his literary prowess in composing robust visual metaphors, especially 'the veil'. A concept adapted from African-American folklore, it was a metaphor to describe the way in which the powerful concealed the marginalized along physical, social, economic and political lines. From this perspective, it achieved its purpose for those in control, who did not want a glimpse of those they exploited. Yet Du Bois forcefully noted that the veil was unable to prevent the hidden from seeing their oppressors. From this unique position of secreted perception, he optimistically posited the potential for empowerment. This awareness, the 'gift of second-sight', was a central idea for much of twentieth-century race politics.

With the death in 1915 of Booker T. Washington, the notorious assumed leader of Black America, Du Bois commenced his rise to prominence. He continued to write across many genres and mediums, focusing his attention on more broadly international issues of race; however, nothing eclipsed *Souls*. Rather, it was his political ambitions and activism that distinguished the rest of his career; he played a major part in the Harlem Renaissance of the 1920s and 1930s, and was a catalyst for the civil rights movement, dying in Ghana in 1963, the day before Martin Luther King's famous speech at the Lincoln Memorial. Yet the feeling of admiration was not unanimous, most interestingly among Blacks. One might expect some Whites to despise Du Bois, and indeed they did, but usually due to nonsensical bigotry rather than reasoned dissent. Many African-Americans, on the other hand, believed that Du Bois spoke down to them, treating them as uneducated fools; this condescension was apparent in speeches in which he referred to Blacks as 'you people', and made disparaging remarks concerning their collective accomplishments. **Feminists**, especially those of the Black feminist movement, critiqued his position of double-consciousness for ignoring the distinctive position of the woman (Anna Julia **Cooper**'s *Black Woman of the South* actually predated *Souls* by nearly a decade).

These issues aside, his life's trajectory was a symbol of a changing attitude in America, and one could not find a more fitting representation. From his being physically impeded in 1899 from reporting on a horrifying lynching (in which pieces of the victim's bones and charred internal organs were sold to eager onlookers) to earning the respect of the majority of his fellow citizens (of all races), Du Bois powerfully embodies the potential potency of social theory.

David Émile **DURKHEIM** was born in the French province of Lorraine in 1858, approximately seven months after the death of Auguste Comte, the originator of the term sociology, whose **positivistic** framework is often mistakenly cited in describing Durkheim. For three generations, Durkheim's family were rabbis, culminating with the appointment of his father as Chief Rabbi of their community. Despite this prestige, the honour was social and spiritual, not financial, and Durkheim's mother was forced to supplement her husband's income by working as a seamstress. Indeed, the family led a frugal and austere life, one which would instil in the young man an appreciation for dedication and hard work, and a disdain for whimsicalness in life and thought.

Despite the ostensible destiny of following in the religious path of his elders, Durkheim attended the local school, Collège d'Épinal, a move which confirmed his desire for a secular education. His father agreed to this arrangement, provided that he maintained as studious a lifestyle as one would in rabbinical school, and this he surely accomplished, recognized as an outstanding pupil and finishing two years earlier than was typical with a baccalaureate in Letters (1874) and Sciences (1875).

After matriculation, Durkheim left for Paris to attend the École Normale Supériore, which attracted the best students in the country. It was difficult for him to get in, given his family's financial circumstances; however, after multiple attempts, he was accepted. The institution housed the greatest French minds, yet this environment came at a price–students were locked inside the grounds, except on Thursday and Sunday afternoons and one evening until midnight per month. Durkheim's first year was a near-failure, as the courses were mainly Latin verse and Greek prose; although he was quite academically capable, his preference was clearly for more scientifically based learning, a theme which would dominate his approach to sociology. The final two years were more successful, though even his rising prominence could not dispel personal doubt, as a fellow student remarked, 'I heard him [Durkheim] discuss for hours with a logical fervour which was the marvel of his hearers – he could not have been more strained, more nervous, more eloquent.'

It was within this institution that Durkheim first would embrace a scientific approach to social sciences, following his teacher Émile Boutroux (to whom he later dedicated his dissertation and first major work, *The Division of Labour*) who taught that philosophy should be grounded in the sciences and in touch with nature and reality. Finishing in 1882, the experience in Paris had reinforced Durkheim's views that social theory must be distinctive from other sciences, but that dilettantism in research and thinking must be avoided for its weakness of aloof groundlessness. Further, during this period, Durkheim was heavily influenced by reading Renouvier, the neo-Kantian whose concern with morality and unity directly affected his later works. Renouvier had additionally argued for the role of will and decision-making in reasoning, a path which Durkheim would pursue toward a notion of scientifically studied and socially constructed morality.

Following a five-year stint teaching philosophy in French lycées, during which time one year was spent in Germany studying contemporary social philosophy and psychology (and possibly his first introduction to **Marx**), Durkheim's career began its amazing trajectory to the height of French social sciences. Notably, the very idea of social science had been fiercely attacked in academic circles, with Comte's reputation in disrepute; absolutely no such class or chair was available until the University of Bordeaux made a controversial (and triumphant) move, creating a post in 'social science and education' in 1887 specifically for Durkheim to fill. The 15 years he spent at Bordeaux were enormously prodigious, as he finished *The Division of Labour* (1893), *Rules of Sociological Method* (1895) and *Suicide* (1897). The simplified purpose of these seminal works was to establish sociology as newly born science. Instead of engaging in the imposed debates surrounding the concept of a social science, in which he had performed so admirably that one contemporary reporter remarked that sociology had 'won the right to be mentioned at the Sorbonne', Durkheim sought to establish the discipline with studies of social and philosophical dilemmas from an empirical perspective. *Suicide* was the paramount effort in this regard, in which he convincingly argued that statistical analysis showed cultural and social causes to lie at the heart of an act considered purely subjective. From this argument one can deduce a primary theme of most of Durkheim's published work, that being the inherent presence of social bonds in all realms, no matter how veiled the group mentality or, in his term, the 'collective consciousness' happens to be. Despite *Suicide*'s later critiques (the official statistics he used were suspect), the theoretical perspective would later become massively influential within **structuralism** in France and **functionalism** in America. The year of its release, he also started *L'Année Sociologique*, an important journal for the cause of supporting the social sciences.

Durkheim moved to the University of Sorbonne in 1902, but was not made a full professor in education until 1906. It was not until 1913 that he was made professor of education and sociology, illustrating both the anti-Semitism (following the Dreyfus affair) and anti-sociology views of French academic elites. Despite these setbacks, his classes were extremely successful, and his publication of *Elementary Forms of Religious Life* (1912) was the culmination of his career, cementing his status as the foremost French sociologist. This was an attempt to return to the issues of morals he had first discovered in Renouvier and, interestingly, a return, albeit with a scientific eye, to his religious childhood. It was also the only work translated into English during his life. Tragically, his son Andre died in the Serbian campaign of 1915; Durkheim would never fully recover from the grief. After a stroke in 1916, Durkheim made a partial recovery, but succumbed to his illness in 1917.

EPISTEMOLOGY is, at its most basic, the philosophical investigation of the nature of knowledge. Yet this simplistic definition obscures the monumental influence which its broad application has had in classical and contemporary social theory. Beginning during the Enlightenment, epistemology's inception was signified by the split of two philosophical schools, namely rationalists and empiricists (though one can trace its themes, especially in rationalism, back to the Ancient Greeks). Although both factions attempted to transcend opinion, belief and other biased forms of knowledge, they acquired two distinctive and, during the seventeenth century, oppositional routes. Rationalists (René Descartes and Leibniz were among the most central) believed that knowledge was best synthesized through formal methods of mathematics and logic, without the need to observe the world (hence, Descartes' famous dictum 'I think, therefore I am'). With the discovery of fundamental axioms, they posited that a 'pure' reasoning would follow. Empiricists (Galileo provided a scientific basis for the philosophies of John Locke, George Berkeley and David Hume) dismissed such approaches to knowledge, instead arguing that impression-based experience was vital, and only through interaction with the world was there any possibility of developing substantive knowledge. Debates between rationalists and empiricists centered on these differing models of knowledge acquisition, especially the possibility of innateness for the former and the *tabula rasa* (blank slate) for the latter.

There were, however, attempts to combine perspectives into a more unified form. Isaac Newton, though better known for his scientific than theoretical contributions, embodied aspects of both empiricism and rationalism. In his diverse experiments, especially those concerning the consequences of forces being applied to the objects which developed his renowned laws of physics, he was engaged in both empiricist experience (the observation of objects) and rationalist rule construction (force equal to mass multiplied by acceleration). Immanuel Kant also transcended the empiricism and rationalism divide, incorporating principles of both in his contention that basic logical categories, including time, space and causality among others, were necessary for the utilization of experience at all. While they were therefore prior to experience (rationalism), such conceptions were only valid within the space of possible experience (empiricism).

Debates over epistemology in some ways frame the differences in approaches across social theory to this day. While more nuanced attitudes are common to contemporary movements, many of the same themes exist. Interpretation of meaning has led sociologists to differing methods of finding meaning; some (especially users of the General Social Survey) rely on large statistical databases with their scientific methods of validation, while many social theorists are proponents of interviews and individual expression in the search for a more 'real' experience (as opposed to numerical representations). **Post-structuralists** and **postmodernists** in some ways discard issues of epistemology entirely, arguing (from different perspectives) that meaning is inherently lost. It is no surprise that these theorists are dismissive of Enlightenment philosophy, given their positions on the acquisition of unconstrained and unbiased knowledge.

It would be a mistake to believe, however, that even in the dismissal of epistemology's virtues would one transcend its influence. Arguably, the questions surrounding the acquisition of knowledge, even if one believes such a project to be impossible, have inspired centuries of social thought. With the alteration (or intensification) of some of the characteristics of modernity, it is probable that debates on epistemology will only become ever-more intriguing focal points of insight into our social worlds.

ETHNOMETHODOLOGY is literally made of three separate words, namely 'ethno' (people), 'method' and 'ology' (the study of). Put together, the meaning of the term becomes clear, as the field is composed of the study of people's methods. However, some ambiguities still exist. Most ethnomethodologists are concerned with the habits we commonly take for granted, that which we tend to associate with 'commonsense'. Yet, arguably, these actions are composed of intricately structured routines. Whether it be driving a car, having a conversation with a friend, or carrying out the tasks of our given occupations, ethnomethodologists believe there to be a rich tapestry of basic rules and resources within the very creation of a stable sociality. In particular, the search for the interpretive rules of human action and interaction is given primacy over the construction of grander frameworks of meaning, based on the contention that such a construction in the latter case cyclically determines the original analysis, ending in a meaningless self-referential theory.

This becomes particularly relevant for language and speech, a view that is shared in realms beyond ethnomethodology (indeed, within **postmodernism**, but especially within **structuralism** and **post-structuralism**). In conversation analysis, for example, ethnomethodologists have declared numerous such taken-for-granted and interpretive rules, including the notion that, generally, a single individual speaks at a given time, or if more than one, then for a very short period. However, such approaches were not fully accepted within mainstream sociology, especially in its early stages. Garfinkel, whose coining of the term and explication in *Studies of Ethnomethodology* (1967) garnered much attention, was also the subject of numerous critiques in the 1970s. Though simplified, a common form of dissent was to declare ethnomethodology lacking in substantial importance. Due to its focus on the composition of society's regulations and order, many believed the discipline to be fundamentally incapable of approaching larger social and political issues.

Though there are still chasms in the ethnomethodology versus sociology debate, **Giddens** in his *New Rules of Sociological Method* (1976) and *The Constitution of Society* (1984) employed an integrated and insightful combination of a more conventional social theory and ethnomethodology. In seeking to describe the creation of a social order and go beyond a dichotomous actor against **structure** framework, Giddens used a ethnomethodologically influenced theory, based in part on everyday analysis, to shed light on the organization of societies. While ethnomethodology has not remained the provocative challenger of sociology it once was, its lasting effect has been influential in demanding that social theorists take into account the nature of everyday reality, conversation, talk and sociality.

FEMINISM, like many terms associated with social theory, is often incorrectly assumed to describe a coherently unified and simply applied category, when in fact its present diversity is nearly unparalleled in any other discipline. For all its multiplicity, however, there is a sense of historical lineage, a common heritage from which most of the more specific outcrops can trace their descent. Without delving too deeply into the long history of feminism, a useful start would be eighteenth-century England and the brief but momentous life of Mary Wollstonecraft, whose *Vindication of the Rights of Women* (1792) posited the then revolutionary idea that women were not naturally inferior to men, but rather suffered due to a lack of education. Many Victorian women would continue to fight against prejudicial misconceptions throughout the nineteenth century, epitomized eloquently in a letter between Geraldine Jewsbury (Charles Dickens was an admirer of her writing) and Jane Carlyle (wife of the famous historian Thomas Carlyle), 'still we have looked, and tried, and found that the present rules for women will not hold to us'. This first wave of feminism (of course, only so-named after the second wave of the 1950s to 1970s, and the third wave of the last generation) was concerned initially with equal education, but expanded its focus to other public realms, most notably that of suffrage, where they were eventually successful, with the granting of voting rights to women in 1920 in the United States and 1928 in Britain. Further concurrent reforms transpired within higher education, legal systems, and advanced professions (though one should not mistake reform for equal footing, as this was plainly not the case).

The second wave of feminism initiated a diversification of feminist thought that continues to this day, and was largely influenced by Simone de **Beauvoir**'s *The Second Sex* (1949). This seminal work pioneered an awareness of the social construction of the feminine, immortalized in the famous phrase, 'one is not born, but rather becomes, a woman'. On the cusp of various rights movements, the 1960s saw a proliferation of analysis of the marginalized role of women in less overt forms and public realms. Betty Freidan's bestselling *The Feminine Mystique* (1963) spoke to the hidden oppression surrounding the culturally mandated role of 'housewife', arguing against the unfulfilling position that was unjustly delegated, on the whole, only to women. Second-wave feminists effectively initiated conferences and further developed the philosophy and tenets of the movement, composing recommendations for furthering equality that were submitted to world leaders.

A splintering of ideas did occur from the outset of the second wave, especially for those whose sole focus was abortion and reproductive rights (who may have supported other reforms in theory, but did not actively engage in these issues in practice), yet the decades between 1970 and 1990 saw a much greater diversification of feminism. Juliet **Mitchell** made the case for a psychoanalytic foundation to feminism. Race and geography became vital aspects of feminism for many social theorists, who argued that the essentialist perspective of a unified 'every woman' position was precarious, as it lumped together an upper-middle class white woman from America and an impoverished slum-dweller from Mumbai. Arguably, these issues were already apparent in the late nineteenth century, as seen in Anna Julia **Cooper**'s work. More recently, Judith **Butler** expanded the realm of feminism even further through her performativity thesis of gender; in acting out a limiting role of gendered desire, the multiplicity of sexuality is problematically constrained. Butler's separation and diversification of gender and sexuality initiated an entirely new subset of feminist thought, as would later be embodied in queer studies.

Indeed, the expansion of focal areas within feminism continues to this day, as witnessed in the advent of post-feminism and postmodern feminism. Truly, huge divides may separate two individuals who both call themselves feminists. While some analysts have critiqued this development of immense diversity, claiming that the power of the movement's original ideals was diluted, this dissention fails to consider the historic path of feminism. Given the constriction that dominated the field until a century ago, in which pseudoscience was used by an omnipotent patriarchy to declare women 'lesser beings', it should come as no surprise that the freedom to think and write about feminist ideals would bring about a plethora of perspectives. There never should have been a single definition of feminism but, for a time, this was the only conceivable path to take. Clearly, there is much to be commended in the first wave of feminism, but there remained, nonetheless, a heavily restricted environment. Second- and third-wave feminism were emblematic of an increasingly emancipated culture though, undoubtedly, significant contemporary feminist issues, both philosophical and pragmatic, continue to proliferate in society.

Michel **FOUCAULT**, undoubtedly among the most prominent **structuralist** and **post-structuralist** theorists, was born in 1926 in Poitiers, France. His father was a renowned surgeon and the family was financially secure. Foucault's early education was not marked by immediate distinction; however, he attended the Jesuit Collège Saint-Stanislas, where he enjoyed some success. With the Second World War fully engaging their city (which came under German occupation), there were understandable delays to his burgeoning education. However, after the war, Foucault was admitted to the École Normale Supérieure. This period had a major influence on his life, both intellectually and personally; Foucault met Louis **Althusser** and exhibited his ability to truly embrace a multidisciplinary approach to his work (in 1948 he attained a preliminary degree in philosophy and, one year later, in psychology). Yet he also suffered a bout of acute depression during this period, affecting his later views of psychiatry and psychopathology.

After completing his agrégration in philosophy in 1952, he taught psychology in the philosophy department at Lille until 1955. More importantly, this marked his 'unofficial intern' period at Saint Anne Hospital in Paris, which would hugely impact his writing on medicine and asylums. Despite these prominent themes of critique, it is difficult to trace a unique path for the rest of his illustrious career.

Following his first publication in 1954 (which he later recanted), Foucault left France, taking positions in Uppsala, Warsaw and Hamburg. These years saw the research that would go into the publication of his first major work on his return to France, *Madness and Civilization* (1960). Drawing on research into the historical perspectives of asylums of the eighteenth and nineteenth century, he posited the medicalization of madness, within the framework of the Enlightenment tradition of reason. The critique's real intellectual punch was the controversial argument that the construction of truth, knowledge and power were intertwined in discourses that necessarily exploited and secluded individuals. Though his analysis was placed within the field of medicine, his illuminating insight inspired a grander critique of the development of power relations in contemporary society. Especially influential in the student revolutions over the next decade, Foucault's reputation was very much on the rise. His next work, *Birth of the Clinic* (1963) experimented with structuralist themes, focusing on linguistic systems of signification within French medical practices. This decade saw further publications within the then dominant theoretical paradigm of structuralism, linking Foucault to Jacques **Lacan** and Roland **Barthes**.

After a two-year period spent in Tunisia in the late 1960s, Foucault distanced himself from structuralism and went in a different intellectual direction. In 1968, he was appointed to the University of Vincennes, and soon after to the eminent Collége de France chair in History of Systems of Thought. This marked Foucault's change of focus to criminology, governmentality and sexuality, although he continued to stress the discovery of contingent historical trends that decided discourses and power relations. With a heavy workload, there were essays but no major works until 1975, when the seminal works *Discipline and Punish* (translated to English in 1977) and *The History of Sexuality* (first French volume in 1976, translated to English in 1977) were published. Modern society was argued to be a disciplinary society yet, with a keen eye for what many took as given, Foucault showed how new forms of power subjugated individuals through classification and division. In the former, the idea of the panopticon was elucidated as a metaphor for the surveillance of the populace. This work also introduced the term 'power-knowledge', further solidifying Foucault's notion of their intertwined nature. Though he never finished the proposed six volume *History of Sexuality*, the first three volumes were hugely significant, especially the concept of biopower, which referenced the government's attempt to control groups of people through techniques of technological power. Foucault envisaged a wide range of diverse methods for achieving the subjugation of bodies, arguing a fundamental shift from traditional violent state intimidation.

While Foucault had an enormous impact on contemporary social theory, he is not without his critics, who claim his historical accounts were inaccurate and were not always applicable cross-nationally. Ironically, he spent his last days at the Salpêtrière hospital, which he had condemned as a locus of biopower for the French government. Foucault was the first major French public figure to die of an AIDS-related illness in 1984; the front page article in *Le Monde* did not reference AIDS at all. Though his work was varied and unclassifiable as wholly Marxist, structuralist or post-structuralist, his unique philosophical and historical critiques of contemporary society elevated his status, placing him, rightfully, among the most significant social theorists of the twentieth century.

The **FRANKFURT SCHOOL** is used to refer to what was initially a literal department of **critical theorists**, first headed by Max **Horkheimer**, at the University of Frankfurt am Main; the actual title of their program was the Institut für Sozialforschung (Institute for Social Research). Importantly, those most closely associated with the Frankfurt School did not use this term to describe themselves, and there were significant divergences, both intellectual and geographical. The latter was especially the case with expulsion of the mostly Jewish-born neo-Marxist academics from Germany in the lead-up to the Second World War. Not all of the members made it however; Walter **Benjamin**'s death is the subject of debate, but it is very likely to have occurred due to Nazi influence.

For over a decade after their exile, with Horkheimer, Theodor **Adorno**, Herbert **Marcuse** and Erich **Fromm** eventually finding themselves in America, the clear philosophical question for these theorists was the horrifying magnitude of the Holocaust. This led to *The Authoritarian Personality* (1950), written primarily by Adorno of the Frankfurt School and American psychologists of the University of California, Berkeley. Empirically based, but theoretical at its core (their findings very much relied upon **psychoanalysis**), it epitomized the **epistemological** mediation between **positivism** and social philosophy. A seminal work in social theory, it would establish the Frankfurt School, and Adorno especially, as prominent academics worldwide.

With the end of the war, most members returned to Germany to reform the Institute, while others (Marcuse and Fromm) stayed in the Americas. Their research continued to diverge, however a common spirit in the critical theory tradition and a reliance on **Marx**, **Freud** and **Weber** contributed to a systematic critique of advanced capitalism and the culture industry. Though Jürgen **Habermas** would uphold the prestige of the Institute, studying under Adorno, he had significant disputes and should be considered a Frankfurt School member primarily in name.

With the rise of **structuralism**, and later **post-structuralism** and **postmodernism**, the critical theory of the original members has diminished in influence amongst most current academics. Dissenters decried an overwhelming negativity, especially in Marcuse's *One Dimensional Man* (1964) and Horkheimer's later works, in which society was found to be full of cultural dopes, whose false desire for consumer goods would always obscure the fulfillment of true desires (and hence true happiness). Anthony **Giddens** and Pierre **Bourdieu** exemplify the preferred contemporary perspective of social actors retaining more **agency** than the Frankfurt School ever afforded. However, in their return to classical social theory and their vehemently determined critique of culture, the significance of the Frankfurt School persists in many current strains of social theory.

Sigismund Schlomo **FREUD**, the founder of **psychoanalysis** and a profoundly influential theorist, was born in Freiberg in 1856, the son of a Jewish wool merchant. His mother was the second wife of the elder Freud, and he would be the first of her seven children. Freud's childhood was a triumph, as he was a precocious student and recognized as such at his local Gymnasium, and yet he was immersed in a chaotic environment, shrouded by poverty and tragedy. His father, Jacob, was not able to financially support the large family, his business remaining strangely unsuccessful despite a booming economy, necessitating a move to Leipzig and later to Vienna (leaving behind an extensive extended family in Freiberg); his brother Julius would succumb to an intestinal infection when Freud was two years old, probably dying in the confines of the family's one-room apartment; his nursemaid, who took to the young child (his mother Amalia being preoccupied with the newborns) was caught stealing, arrested, and sent to prison just as Freud began to develop a bond with her. Perhaps due to these dreadful circumstances, he immersed himself in books as a youth (for all his ineptitude as a businessman, Jacob was a loving and nurturing father and taught Freud to read at a young age), reading Shakespeare at eight and simultaneously studying Greek, Latin, French, Hebrew, Spanish and English. In 1873, Freud completed his matura (final examinations) and achieved outstanding marks in all subjects, enabling his entrance to the University of Vienna.

Despite his later preoccupation with sciences, Freud's first year was mainly focused on the humanities, especially philosophy. He obviously cared for the discipline, as indicated in personal letters; however, his ambition was to become famous by contributing to the considerable achievements of science in the late nineteenth century. While still living at home, Freud immersed himself in scientific research, dissecting 400 eels in Carl Claus' Institute of Comparative Anatomy in search of their gonadial structure, leading to his first publications. Building on his research, he went on to work for six years with the leading physiologist Ernst Brücke, whose belief in physical and chemical causes as the only forces in life processes would influence Freud's later divergent views. Although the founding of psychoanalysis would directly oppose such a contention, the language of cause and effect that Brücke and other empiricists espoused was ever-present in Freud's social theory.

His engagement to a family friend of higher socio-economic status necessitated, after years of their partial separation and a trying courtship, a move from research to practising medicine to assure a livelihood for the couple. Indeed, Freud had been accepting a monthly stipend from another mentor, Joseph Breuer, with whom he would later publish *Studies on Hysteria*. After being granted permission by Brücke to study with the renowned neurologist Jean-Martin Charcot in Germany, Freud returned home and established a clinical practice in 1886. He treated mainly upper-middle class women for psychotic illnesses; hysteria had recently been established by Charcot as a respectable field and one worthy of interest (and debate), as these patients showed no physical signs of ailment and yet were clearly distressed. These experiences led to his work with Breuer on the infamous first patient of the 'talking cure', Anna O, and with it the first mention of psychoanalysis in 1896.

To appreciate the massive contribution of Freud, one must emphasize the that for centuries humans had increasingly been placed at the centre their own universe, their sovereignty unchallenged. Copernicus's revelation that the earth revolved around the sun was crushing to this belief, as was Darwin's theory of evolution. Freud must be considered in a similar vein, as he decentred the notion of a cohesive, unified self. He accomplished this by the ingenious separation, still relevant today, of consciousness, preconsciousness and the unconscious. This division was vital, as preconsciousness referred to the relatively banal and temporary forgetting of memories that are easily recalled with reminders – a name, what one had for dinner the night before, and so on. Much more significant to psychoanalysis was the unconscious, whose constitution is based on the denial and suppression of feelings and desires, outlined in Freud's eminent terms: repression, sublimation, and defence, among others. He theorized that these mechanisms were enacted to rid the mind (unsuccessfully) of childhood experiences, often sexual in nature, though they could be accessed through analysis of dreams, fantasies, slips of the tongue, and other visual and linguistic signs that had been previously considered unimportant. This methodology of studying the unconscious and its relation to consciousness has influenced various strands of social theory, with its most noted proponents in **critical theory**, **structuralist**, **post-structuralist** and **feminist** thought, amongst others.

Freud's most famous works outlined the fragmented identity of the self, including his controversial separation of consciousness into id, ego and super-ego and the distinction of repression in the pleasure, reality and death instincts (first outlined in the 1920 essay 'Beyond the Pleasure Principle' and more fully explicated in the 1923 work *The Ego and the Id*). The 'talking cure' is often ridiculed today by a society set on treating psychiatric illness with pharmacological solutions. Additionally, Freud's emphasis on dreams and sexual experiences in *The Interpretation of Dreams* (1899), while extremely original and important for later scholarship, is often considered overstated and borderline fanatical (especially the famous Oedipus complex, explicated in the 1905 work *Three Essays on the Theory of Sexuality*). Yet undeniably, Freud's insistence that we consider our identities as composed of divergent and conflicting emotions and desires beyond the simply physical, many of which we are intriguingly unaware, has resonated ever since, even more than it did at the time of his fleeing Nazi-occupied Austria for London and his death in 1939.

Erich **FROMM**, the renowned social psychologist, psychoanalyst and early member of the **Frankfurt School**, was born in Frankfurt am Main in 1900. He was three years older than his colleague Theodor **Adorno**, and two and five years younger than Herbert **Marcuse** and Max **Horkheimer** respectively; yet while the Holocaust arguably affected each member of the Frankfurt School equally, it was Horkheimer and Fromm that were seemingly most affected by the First World War, as Fromm later stated 'When the war ended in 1918, I was a deeply troubled young man who was obsessed by the question of how war was possible, by the wish to understand the irrationality of human mass behaviour'. Raised by Orthodox Jewish parents and quite learned in the Talmud (a historical record of rabbinic discussion concerning customs, law and ethics), Fromm began studying law in 1918 at the University of Frankfurt am Main, but switched within a year to sociology at the University of Heidelberg under Max **Weber**'s brother, Alfred Weber, and the famed philosopher and psychiatrist Karl Jaspers. It was this duo of influences which catalysed his distinctive perspective of a truly 'social' psychology, yet additionally a growing interest in **psychoanalysis** under Wilhelm Reich in the 1920s greatly influenced Fromm's thinking.

In 1930, Fromm both finished training as a psychoanalyst and, due to his expertise in psychology, was appointed by Horkheimer to the Frankfurt School. Though his religious background remained prominent (in a secularized analytic fashion), a revised psychoanalysis to some extent became his dominant paradigm, along with **Marxism** (due to his associates). His first major work, *Escape From Freedom* (1941), exemplified this synthesis. Essentially, Fromm argued that the human urge for individualism opposed the formation of 'primary ties' (family, society, nature and so forth). However, as social conditions were unable to maintain this opposition, the result was feelings of doubt and insecurity. Freedom became 'an unbearable burden', with the individual forced to submit to authority to regain a sense of certainty about life. The year of publication of this work is critical, not only in that Fromm and the other Frankfurt School academics were forced from Germany, but also that *Escape* was commended for its early and prescient psychological analysis of the Second World War. Indeed, the political underpinnings grew ever-more significant, as would be the case throughout his career.

The theme of an unconscious determined by societal influences, spanning more than simply economic structures, placed Fromm in a unique position in his appropriation of Karl **Marx** and Sigmund **Freud**. Though he critiqued these seminal figures, he also held them in high esteem, as all his work drew significant influence from their writings. Despite his respect for Freud, Horkheimer and Marcuse felt he had broken too much from radical impulse of psychoanalytic theory, leading to a rupture between Fromm and the Frankfurt School. His engagement with Marx was also at odds with other neo-Marxists such as Louis **Althusser**, in that Fromm emphasized the earlier humanist writings; this found its culmination in *The Sane Society* (1955), his clearest statement of social political theory.

Despite these divergences, Fromm's prominence continued to grow, and later translated into political success. *The Art of Loving* (1956) was an international bestseller, exploring different types of love, their development and their problematic constitution. In 1958, Fromm co-founded a movement based on *The Sane Society*, the SANE peace organization, whose goals were the halting of nuclear proliferation and peaceful negotiation of international conflicts; the group currently has around 100,000 members. Publications in the 1960s developed his theme of humanism within Marx, especially *Marx's Concept of Man* (1961) and *Beyond the Chains of Illusion: My Encounter with Marx and Freud* (1962), leading to his being awarded 'Humanist of the Year' by the American Humanist Association in 1966.

Even at the time of Fromm's death in 1980, the divisions between him and the other critical theorists were considerable. One must appreciate these real differences and their consequent separation (Fromm spent much of his time after 1950 in Mexico City, and later Switzerland). Additionally, there is a possibility that Fromm's unique perspective was aided by the geographic and intellectual space. There is little reason to regard his work as lesser than Adorno, Horkheimer and Marcuse; indeed, Fromm should be seen as a precursor to *The Authoritarian Personality* and had much to contribute regarding alienation and political culture. In some ways, like Walter **Benjamin** (albeit for an entirely different reasoning given Benjamin's premature death), a Fromm revival would still inform debates of contemporary social and political theory.

FUNCTIONALISM concerns a powerful tradition in sociological theory, most often associated with **Durkheim** and Talcott Parsons, based broadly on the consideration of society as a system in much the same way as an organic essence; like the human body (a common analogy used by functionalists), whose different components work together to maintain the overall person, society's constituent parts are to be considered from the perspective of their functioning in meeting the requirements of a grander scheme. Just as blood's functions, among many, are to carry food and oxygen to cells, carry waste away from cells and regulate body temperature, so too is religion's function to create and maintain social solidarity, the latter explicated by Durkheim in *The Elementary Forms of Religious Life* (1912). Without blood, the body would be fatally limited; without religion, society would be detrimentally impeded. This approach is distinguished from a historical explanation of phenomena and, notably, Durkheim stressed the need for both. However, in concentrating on the necessary involvement of certain facets of society in the production of a larger, cohesive whole, orthodox functionalists consider chronological accounts as **epistemologically** lacking.

A more nuanced functionalist perspective advocated by Robert Merton discerned two types of function. Manifest functions are those involving intended consequences and outcomes of which observers are aware, while latent functions are distinguished by their seemingly hidden or unintentional consequences. Neo-**Marxists** have identified the growing presence of latent functions in advanced (or postmodern/liquid) modernity; Zygmunt **Bauman** has insightfully commented on the growing distance between our actions and their far-reaching implications. An individual may support a charity by purchasing a sponsored product, with the manifest intention of performing a positive social act. The latent function, however, may range from an insignificant to a horrendous outcome, depending on the sponsor of the promotion. With the complexities of advanced capitalism, it has become increasingly difficult to trace latent webs of transnational consequences.

Functionalism was criticized in the latter half of the twentieth century for its lack of explanatory power and its ontological dilemmas. It was posited by social theorists (Anthony **Giddens** in particular) that the attribution of functions to societies is misplaced, as the focus should fall back on the social actors themselves. This debate, while differently constituted than the original arguments over **structure** and **agency**, retained some familiarities in the valuation of systems or individuals in the construction of society. However, in a revival of the tradition, Jeffery Alexander has argued for functionalism to hold a place as one interpretation among many, used not for providing explanations, but rather as a descriptive framework. In encouraging functionalists to embrace multiple paradigms, a positive conciliation has had the benefit of a richer approach to social theory.

Anthony **GIDDENS**, one of the most prolific of contemporary social theorists, was born in 1938 in Edmonton, north London, his father a clerical worker for the London Transport and his mother a housewife. Giddens's father's job dealt with the refurbishment of carriages on the underground and, from an early age, he was imbued with an awareness of pervasive petty crime in society. He has referred to the suburb he grew up in as 'something of a wasteland', but to this day returns to watch his favourite football team, the Spurs, who play at the nearby Tottenham ground. Although Giddens managed to gain entry to the local grammar school (his brother, now a successful director of television commercials, did not and was limited to a secondary modern education), he did not consider himself a particularly outstanding student. Rejected from two universities due to a lack of qualifications, the University of Hull granted him entry on the basis of a successful interview and he pursued a degree in philosophy. However, the philosophy department was so small that the main lecturer's leave of absence that year forced him to search out other subjects. He was moved to the psychology department and also told to study sociology, a discipline with which he was unacquainted at the time. Fortunately,

his mentor was Peter Worsley, a well-published, left-leaning and inspirational professor, and Giddens was so enamoured that he graduated with a first-class honours
degree in sociology in 1959.

After Hull, Giddens enrolled in an MA sociology programme at the London
School of Economics at the suggestion of Worsley. Though his academic aspirations had clearly developed since Hull, he said he did not take the course 'all
too seriously . . . I wrote about a fun topic'. Indeed, he had only intended to use
the MA to launch a career as a civil servant. However, despite Giddens's modesty and joviality, his near-PhD length dissertation, 'Sport and Society in
Contemporary England', was far from trivial, and can now be seen as a precursor to what would become a popular topic in sociology. Drawing mainly on Max
Weber, he sought to show how a long history of sport had become rationalized
in modern times. On the strength of its completion, and with the support of his
supervisor, Giddens obtained an academic post at the University of Leicester.
Initially sceptical of an academic career, the interview (conducted by Ilya
Neustadt, the head of the department, and Norbert Elias) changed his mind completely; they took his interest in the historical rationalization of sport quite seriously, reassuring and encouraging an apprehensive Giddens.

From this appointment on, Giddens steadily became a force in British sociology, and later in British and world politics. After a brief time in North America
as a lecturer, he returned to England, resigning his post at Leicester for one at
Cambridge University. His first book, *Capitalism and Modern Social Theory*
(1971) is one of the most widely read textbooks on the works of the seminal
social theorists Karl **Marx**, Max **Weber** and Émile **Durkheim**. Giddens wrote
extensively during the 1970s, including his important subsequent publications of
New Rules of Sociological Method (1976–a riff on Durkheim's 1895 *The Rules
of Sociological Method*) and *Central Problems in Social Theory* (1979). These
works established Giddens's status as a major interpreter of classical sociology
and innovator of contemporary issues, but his 1984 book, *The Constitution of
Society*, was even more influential. In detailing what he called 'structuration theory', he proposed a new language for the interpretation of the age of modernization, including the influential terms 'duality of structure', 'double hermeneutic'
and 'reflexivity'. While later work would cover a diverse range of topical issues,
such as social change in *The Consequences of Modernity* (1990), personal life in
Modernity and Self-Identity (1991), politics in the bestselling *The Third Way*
(1998) and globalization in the recent *Runaway World*, Giddens's most important
contribution to social theory lay in moving beyond a dichotomous duality of
agency and **structure**. As he argued in *Constitution of Society*, people's awareness of their surrounding social structures can be seen as a complementary and
reflexively organized blend of personal actions and societal institutions, rather
than the oppositional perspective popular in the works of earlier theorists
(Marxist Louis **Althusser** had little faith in agency, for example).

This is not to imply that 1984 was Giddens's peak; indeed, he is consistently
acknowledged to this day by sociologists and politicians alike. His recent

DANIEL MENDELSON

achievements include: consultant to Prime Minister Tony Blair and President
Clinton, director of the London School of Economics (1997–2003) and honorary
degrees from 15 universities. Despite various criticisms of his structuration theory as overly simplistic and somewhat confounded in assigning no primacy to
structure or agency, Giddens is undeniably among the most respected, prolific
and cited sociologists alive today.

Charlotte Perkins **GILMAN**, the celebrated writer, social theorist and forerunner of American **feminism**, was born in Hartford, Connecticut in 1860. Because
her father, a writer himself, abandoned the family when Gilman was young, she
was forced to relocate often with her brother and mother. Mired in poverty, they
relied for refuge mainly on Gilman's aunts on her father's side, including Harriet
Beecher Stowe, the author of *Uncle Tom's Cabin*. With her mother ill for long
periods of her childhood, Gilman was quite isolated, often visiting public
libraries to occupy her time. Though she was well read, especially considering
her family's finances and the limited opportunity structure for young women in
the nineteenth century, this did not translate into academic success. However,
Gilman was also a talented artist and managed, at the age of 18, to gain entry to
the Rhode Island School of Design. For several years, she supported herself selling hand-painted trade cards.

   In 1884, Gilman, not without reservation, married the artist Charles Stetson,
and had a child a year later. She suffered from post-partum depression, though
the treatment of this illness was then brutally misguided. Her husband and
doctors came up with a diagnosis of 'nervousness' and 'hysteria'. The usual
'cure', at the time, was enforced bed-rest, though this also meant no artistic
outlets; for an individual who had been immersed in a childhood of reading,
had been in the company of famous authors and had painted professionally for
half a decade, this must indeed have been a torturous experience. The strain of
the experience took its toll on the marriage, leading to an unlikely (again, considering the power afforded women in the nineteenth century) separation and
later divorce.

   Additionally, this course of events was the impetus for a much more influential consequence as, in 1890, she wrote and later had published in *The New
England Magazine* her first acclaimed work, *The Yellow Wall-paper* (1892). A
fictionalized tale, though clearly based on her personal experiences of five years
previously, the novel was an account of a woman whose confinement, as treatment for depression, leads to madness. At a primary level, the aesthetic repul-
siveness of the yellow wallpaper is symbolic of the misery of the situation,
especially for an artist of her calibre. Yet, more significant was the broader critique of control and subjugation in a patriarchal society (Gilman used the term
'androcentric-world' to describe the structural suppression of women). Notably,
the repetitive orderliness of the wallpaper's pattern may be interpreted as an
allusion to the expectation that women would perform the mundane household
duties every day of their lives. Gilman's early experience of being raised by a

single mother certainly was not glamorous, but the sense of self-reliance and individuality (reinforced in the years of financially providing for herself before her marriage) helped to form her perspective.

Gilman wrote prodigiously across diverse media and fields, publishing over 2,000 works, mostly in self-published journals. After *The Yellow Wall-paper*, her next most successful publication was *Women and Economics* (1898). Rejecting Marx's conception that class was the single most important division in society, Gilman systematically argued that gender was of even greater importance. Bourgeois women were limited in cultural and intellectual realms in ways that bourgeois men were not; poorer women experienced a doubly suppressed life, forced to contribute financially through hard labour during the day, only to return to domestic duties at home. As Charles Lemert has noted, Arlie Hochschild has continued this lineage of analysis with her notion of the 'second shift' of household responsibilities.

Though there is a clear indebtedness to Gilman's foresight among later feminists, she has also been the subject of criticism, mainly concerning her essentialist perspective. Beyond her consideration of working class women, there is little discussion of other difference in women's standpoints, which is a particularly troubling aspect of her social theory given the conditions of nineteenth century African-Americans. Some social theorists have since referred to the 'double-bind' of being black and female, suffering from oppressive relations in both race and gender, an idea that Anna Julia **Cooper** had recognized as early as the 1890s. Judith **Butler** exemplified the contemporary transcendence of a unitary feminist perspective, initiating the study of queer theory, based on her notion of the unstable performativity of gender. These theoretical weaknesses aside, it is Gilman's personal resolve and strength which are arguably most admirable, for, in the face of a domineering patriarchy, she stood her ground. The formidable constraints of the time did not limit her creative force; rather, it was amplified by a tenacious brand of humanism. An advocate of euthanasia for the terminally ill, Gilman took a lethal dose of chloroform in 1935, three and a half years after her diagnosis of terminal breast cancer.

Erving **GOFFMAN**, the pioneer of the dramaturgical approach to symbolic interactionism, was born in 1922 in the small farming village of Mannville, Alberta, a community far north of the Canadian-American border. His parents, Max and Ann Goffman, were Ukrainian Jews who managed to emigrate from Europe before the First World War. Although his father was a shopkeeper and his mother was a homemaker, with English far from their first language, Goffman demonstrated a strong predilection for academia, despite being affectionately described as a 'prankster' by his sister. He studied chemistry at the University of Manitoba in 1939; a few years later he managed to obtain a position at the National Film Board, located across the country in Ottawa. After a brief stint with the Board, during which he met Dennis H. Wrong (presently among the Faculty Emeriti at New York University Department of Sociology), he decided to enrol at the University of Toronto, where he gained a Bachelor of Arts degree in sociology and anthropology. Fortunately for Goffman, two distinguished social scientists were among his mentors, namely C.W.M. Hart and Ray Birdwhistell. The latter is of particular significance to the development of Goffman's interests, as Birdwhistell was a famed American anthropologist who coined the term 'kinesics', which refers to the interpretation of body language, including gestures and facial expressions.

After completing his BA in 1945, he enrolled at the University of Chicago to pursue graduate study in sociology. As returning American veterans of the Second World War were provided with free education under the G.I. Bill (officially known as the Servicemen's Readjustment Act of 1944), the university was arguably overfilled. Despite the chaos of the post-war years, Goffman was able to complete his Master's degree by 1949, including a thesis that investigated relationships between personality and social class. Unlike most of his later research, this unpublished manuscript made simultaneous use of interviews, surveys and quantitative data. For his doctoral thesis, entitled 'Communication Conduct in an Island Community', Goffman spent a year analysing social interaction in the sole hotel of Unst, a small community off the coast of Scotland at the northern end of the Shetland Isles. From 18 months of research would come his first major and most celebrated work, *The Presentation of Self in Everyday Society*.

Goffman did not immediately return to Chicago, instead spending a year in Paris finishing his dissertation. In 1952, he came back to Chicago and married Angelica Choate, whose family's societal prominence greatly contrasted with Goffman's humble heritage. Soon after the birth of their only child, Tom, in 1953, Erving moved his family Washington DC, where he pursued ethnographic projects at Saint Elizabeths Hospital. This research would lead to one of the more significant sociological studies of the twentieth century, *Asylums*, published in 1961. Following the publication of this work, Goffman was made a Full Professor at the University of California at Berkeley in 1962, achieving this distinction only four years after Herbert **Blumer** had extended him an invitation. Despite the tragic suicide of his wife in 1964, the 1960s were a time of prolific academic success, his most notable publications including: *Stigma: Notes on the Management of Spoiled Identity* (1963), *Interaction Ritual: Essays on Face-to-Face Behavior* (1967) and *Strategic Interaction* (1969).

By the time of the publication of *Strategic Interaction*, Goffman had resigned from Berkeley to accept the prestigious Benjamin Franklin Chair in Anthropology and Sociology at the University of Pennsylvania. He continued with an extremely productive academic career, marked by *Relations in Public* (1971), *Frame Analysis* (1974), *Gender Advertisements* (1979) and, lastly, *Forms of Talk* (1981). Goffman succumbed to stomach cancer in 1982; although more than a quarter century has passed since his death, his work is still widely cited and influential among a diverse set of academics. But, more vitally for Goffman, he remains implicitly significant for the understated presentation of self which we make daily.

Antontio **GRAMSCI**, one of the most central of Western Marxists and arguably only outweighed in influence by **Marx** himself, was born in Ales, a small town on the island of Sardinia, Italy in 1891. His father was a minor public official whose corrupt practices were detrimental to the family, especially during his imprisonment in 1898, when the young Gramsci was forced to leave school and work in lowly jobs to help support his siblings and mother. Despite six years of this hardship, and an accident which stunted his growth and caused him to be hunchbacked, Gramsci would finish secondary school in Cagliari and, against all odds, win a scholarship in 1911 to the University of Turin. He studied literature and linguistics, but ceased to attend in 1915 with a burgeoning reputation as an intellectually gifted journalist for socialist newspapers. Despite never completing a degree, Gramsci arguably left with a greater understanding of history, philosophy and politics than many of his peers, in part due to his involvement with the organization of trade unions among Italy's poor (who were being recruited by the newly established automobile companies of Fiat and Lancia).

A long and complex set of events, well-documented in multiple sources, engaged Gramsci for the next two decades until his death in 1937. Briefly, his politics brought him to the forefront of many different communist and socialist journals and movements in what was a remarkably chaotic time for Italian politics (and indeed, more broadly, for European and Soviet politics too), as Mussolini began to exercise his power. Gramsci formed many different alliances, necessitating trips to Moscow and Vienna; however, the significant outcome was Gramsci's arrest in 1926, after the Mussolini government used an attempted assassination attempt to enact radically drastic laws against political opposition.

As Gramsci had shown before, immense hardship would neither prevent his intellect from shining through, nor would it dampen his compassion for the working classes. Posthumously published as the *Prison Notebooks* (1947), he wrote prodigiously while incarcerated, amassing approximately 30 notebooks and some 3,000 pages of historical analysis and social theory in slightly over a decade of captivity. The themes he elucidated would remain relevant for decades of Marxist thought; of crucial importance were the discussions of cultural hegemony, domination in political and civil society, and critiques of materialism and economic **determinism**.

Cultural hegemony was Gramsci's answer to the question of why social transformation had not materialized as predicted by orthodox Marxist theory. His reasoning focused on the process of consensus building within antagonistic groups towards support of the modern state. Though never fully enactable due to existing communities which predated the state, hegemony acted through a blend of brute force and perceived consent. Individuals eventually saw the norms of the state as the ideal (if only) way to survive and, in cases of increased resistance, a more liberal (democratic) state formed as a compromise. Nevertheless, in each version of the modern state, the elected minds (Gramsci's 'hegemonic intellectuals') authorized reason by way of propositions that were mediated to the point of being far removed from reality. In a cyclical mode, through schooling, religion and other such frameworks, Gramsci goes beyond a simple model of repressed anti-state ideas, forming a nuanced view that inspired much scholarship in the realm of state control and power.

Due to his poor health, the authorities released Gramsci shortly before his death. As he had to spend the last year of his life in hospitals, it is tempting to pity the seminal thinker. Perhaps more than nearly any other theorist, however, he embodied both sides of Marxism, in his intense political involvement (praxis) and immensely influential scholarship (Louis **Althusser**, Michel **Foucault**, Stuart Hall and Zygmunt **Bauman** are among the many indebted to his work). Given the impediments faced throughout his life, even his dissenters must acknowledge his intellect, but undoubtedly as impressive was his personal commitment to the enactment of his own philosophy.

Jürgen **HABERMAS**, a highly influential and unique social theorist of rationality, among other topics, was born in 1929 outside Düsseldorf, Germany. His father was a high-ranking official in the Cologne Chamber of Industry and Commerce, and instilled a conservative Protestant ethos. While little has been recorded on Habermas's childhood, it is quite clear that the influences of the World Wars would have significantly impacted his worldview. His later ideals of democracy and open forums, with a paramount concern for reason in the public sphere undoubtedly stemmed from a repressive upbringing at the height of Nazism.

Despite these grand and overwhelmingly destructive decades for Germany, his education stayed on track and, in his early twenties, he intermittently attended the universities of Göttingen (1949) and Zürich (1950), before staying at the University of Bonn from 1951 until his matriculation with a doctorate in philosophy in 1954. Intriguingly, during this period, Habermas had been interested in the existentialism of Heidegger, but challenged his proclamation of the 'truth and greatness' of National Socialism. This marked a fundamental discord between Habermas and the German philosophical tradition, one which would distinguish him from many of his contemporaries in the following decades, including some of the **Frankfurt School** theorists, whose thoughts are often falsely conflated with his own.

In 1956, after a brief stint as a journalist, Habermas returned to academia as Theodor **Adorno**'s assistant at the newly reformed Johann Wolfgang Goethe University in Frankfurt. This period of studying under Adorno and Max **Horkheimer** mistakenly leads some to believe that Habermas's perspective was sympathetic to the views of the rest of the Frankfurt School; yet, in reality, he disagreed with what he saw as a paralytic vision of society, in which scorn for mass culture and scepticism of politics led to a pessimistic vision of social change. Habermas worked in the broad tradition of critical theory and shared Adorno and Horkheimer's vision of an evaluative, multidisciplinary mode of thought (as opposed to traditional theory, which they considered descriptive and explanation-based), also sharing a concern for the problematic nature of modernity and contemporary rationality, yet his view was undeniably more optimistic, while still judicious.

This fundamental aperture led to the completion of his habilitation in political science at the University of Marburg under Wolfgang Abendroth, published in 1962 (and only translated into English in 1989 under the title *Structural Transformation of the Public Sphere*). In this important early work, many of Habermas's later themes are evident, such as drawing out the historical development of the bourgeois public sphere from the eighteenth until the mid-twentieth century, and it became quite clear that he favoured the political engagement of an earlier epoch. He argued that, although the eighteenth century was clearly not symbolic of equality among groups (with obviously apparent sexism and racism), the uncommodified nature of discussion in salons did represent a closer example of unconstrained open debate than the media-influenced twentieth-century version. This transition was identified within the nineteenth-century shift from small discussions to a mass public sphere. In effect, Habermas was calling for *communicative* rationality, in which true discussion and openly critical debate was feasible, rather than *instrumentive* rationality, which he thought was based on instructed and thereby constricted modes of thought. Since rationality was key to solving the predicaments of modernity, this distinction was paramount.

All of these themes were developed in Habermas's most famous work, *Theory of Communicative Action* (1981). Though he had written much on the epistemological foundation of social sciences in the late 1960s and early 1970s (*Theory and Practice*, *Knowledge and Human Interests* and *On the Logic of the Social Sciences*), this opus solidified his standing among the premier social theorists of rationality. He was attacked by Michel **Foucault**, Jacques **Derrida** and Jean-François **Lyotard** for his defence of the Enlightenment-based notion of dialogue improving our decision-making capacities; yet, so long as the dialogue was separated from a Cartesian philosophy of consciousness and thereby brought about a better understanding of social problems, this argument profoundly influenced the debate.

For all of the praise that Habermas's theory has received, his critics have been quite vocal, with certain noteworthy points of contention. Of particular importance was the popular critique that neutral algorithms to solving social problems were idealized and implausible in many situations. Regardless of the degree of dialogue, there are always cases in which the superior argument will not be agreed upon, as the conclusions become hopelessly subjective. Despite this fundamental flaw in his theory, Habermas has surely contributed an enormous amount to the tradition of critical theory, modernization and concepts of rationality.

Georg **HEGEL**, the paramount social philosopher of the eighteenth century, was born in 1770 in Stuttgart, Swabia, the eldest child of a minor civil servant in the court of the Duke of Württemberg. At this time, Germany was divided into small states (Swabia was in the south) and, throughout his life, Hegel retained a strong Swabian accent and parts of speech distinctive to the Swabian dialect. A prolific reader, his youth was filled by the insights of both classical and modern works, from Homer and Sophocles to Goethe and Schiller. At his local Gymnasium, Hegel studied history, theology and classics, although there is little indication that he was regarded as extraordinarily intelligent. Despite the lack of recognition at this time, Hegel continued to immerse himself in academia; notably, he began a diary in Latin in 1785, and was inspired by Sophocles' *Antigone*, resulting in close care for his younger sister, Christiane.

The first indications of Hegel's true intellectual development began at the University of Türenberg where, in 1788, he enrolled in their theological seminary. At matriculation, his aim was to become a Lutheran pastor, but the influences of more secularly philosophical friends and the significant political events of the late eighteenth century seemingly dictated a different path. Of his contemporaries, the most notable were Friedrich Hölderlin and Friedrich von Schelling. Initially brought together by a mutual admiration for Plato and Rousseau, they also could not help but be taken in by the French Revolution and the recent works of Immanuel Kant. Some scholars have pointed to Kant's practical philosophy within a moral and religious framework as a welcome outlet for Hegel from the more constrictive theological orthodoxy of Türenberg. The three even planted a 'liberty tree' to celebrate the Revolution, despite the certain disapproval of elders at the seminary.

After finishing his studies in 1793, Hegel spent three years as a house-tutor in Berne, Switzerland. Though letters to Schelling confirmed a continued interest in a revolutionary critique of the contemporary society (especially politics and religion), this time was seen as an isolating period. Despite access to a fine library and writings on folk-religion, the experience was clearly not socially amenable. Through the help of Hölderlin, who was a house-tutor in Frankfurt, he was able rejoin his Türenberg friends in 1796 and, once again, be immersed in a suitably stimulating environment. The death of his father in 1799 left Hegel with enough financial support to pursue more formal education, and Schelling helped him to secure a post as an unsalaried lecturer at Jena University on the strength of his 1801 doctoral dissertation, *On the Orbits of the Planets*, in which he had argued for the existence of only seven planets. In the same year, he published his first book, *Difference between the Systems of Fitche and Schelling*; however, it was not until 1807 that Hegel was seen to mature into the enormously influential philosopher and social theorist whose work was essential to European thought for nearly a century and a half. In this year, *Phenomenology of Spirit* was published, in which Hegel began to signify his separation from Schelling (a later critic of his work) who had left Jena in 1803.

From this point until his death from cholera in 1831, Hegel was prolific and enormously successful. Despite a difficult lecturing style (he did not invite questions or comments, and was constantly coughing and clearing his throat), his fame grew, especially during the last 15 years of his life, which he spent in

Berlin. Among his seminal works were the *Encyclopaedia of the Philosophical Sciences* (1817), *Elements of the Philosophy of Right* (1820) and two further editions of the *Encyclopaedia* (1827 and 1830). In these works, the notable Hegelian dialectic came to the fore in the historically minded notion of thesis-antithesis-synthesis: an initial idea generates a counter-position (thesis-antithesis), which resolves into an improved idea (synthesis). Importantly, however, the synthesis is only a partial truth in the totality of ideas, and therefore the process repeats cyclically. This theory was hugely influential in developing a philosophical place for historical development. Though **Marx** found the model too idealistic (he proposed class struggle and economic factors to expand on the initial abstraction), Hegel's legacy is undeniable, especially within Marxist and **critical theory**, and later as an oppositional perspective for the development of the **post-structuralist** and **postmodern** movements.

Max **HORKHEIMER**, the influential critical theorist and leader of the **Frankfurt School** before Theodor **Adorno**, was born in 1895 in Stuttgart, Germany. His family was composed of Orthodox Jews and, while he was not pressured to pursue a rabbinical path, he was coerced into working at his father's factory at the age of 16 and briefly conscripted into the army in 1917. Nonetheless, after the conclusion of the First World War, Horkheimer began his academic career by attending Munich University, studying philosophy and psychology. A fateful move to Frankfurt University resulted in the good fortune of meeting Adorno, his long-standing friend and collaborator, as he completed his habilitation in 1925 on Kant's *Critique of Judgement*. Additionally, other immensely important German intellectuals were his contemporaries, including Edmund Husserl, Martin Heidegger and Georg Lukács. Yet it was his appointment as Director of the Frankfurt Institute that would fuel his academic reputation.

Before Horkheimer's appointment, Frankfurt had been a traditionally orthodox Marxist institute but, under his influence, the focus came to be on more diverse critical positions, as signified by the development of **critical theory**. Though he had written about such a philosophy as early as 1937 in the essay 'Traditional and Critical Theory', the next few years were pivotal and immensely formative. Horkheimer's move (both figuratively and literally, as the school disbanded in Germany under the Nazis, fleeing through Geneva and Paris before settling in New York) was necessitated as a response to the Holocaust, as the relatively optimistic feel of his earlier works dissipated in the face of the horrors of the Second World War. In the seminal work *Dialectic of Enlightenment* (1944, co-authored by Adorno) and *Eclipse of Reason* (1947), he advanced the argument that civilization was plummeting into a state of brutality. Horkheimer believed that concrete thought regarding issues of morality and politics (objective reason) was subsumed by thought regarding technical efficiency and purposefulness (subjective and instrumental reason). The rise of the position that all ethical positions are equally hollow and mere inclinations spelled the transition from the former to the latter. In the tradition of critical theory, Horkheimer posited that a return to true and objective reason would elicit a purer sense of rationality for the betterment of societies.

With Adorno taking the reins of the Frankfurt Institute in 1953, four years after their return to Germany, Horkheimer was to become a less central figure, especially as Herbert **Marcuse** gained influence with the student movements of the 1960s and Walter **Benjamin**'s works were posthumously published. Additionally, his later work was criticized as being overly pessimistic, as Jürgen **Habermas** justifiably remarked that he had ignored the democratic achievements of modernity. Yet, to understand Horkheimer, one must consider the trajectory of a German Jewish academic whose life spanned both World Wars, dying in 1973 in Nuremberg. Though, periodically, his perspective is excessively ominous, his cautious (but unflinching) expectations for a better society are both motivated, and blemished, by witnessing first-hand some of the most horrific atrocities of the twentieth century.

IDENTITY, most simply described, is the sense of self or personhood that both internally and externally characterizes an individual. From this base definition, however, numerous questions arise; once seen as a stable entity, social theory has compellingly challenged this notion, arguing for a more fluid framework of the self. Indeed, certain identities seemed quite durable from a pre-**modern** sensibility, especially those established from a young age, including gender, ethnicity and religion. There was rarely a questioning of these base characteristics of personhood.

However, especially within a **psychoanalytic** paradigm, complexities arose. **Freud**'s initial split of the unconscious from consciousness indicated a not fully unified self, a perspective that was furthered with his later organization of the psyche into the id, ego and superego. Identities had to be managed and controlled, as base instincts (the id) contradicted cultural structures and **discourses** (the superego), as mediated by the ego. Jacques **Lacan** added to the idea of a split identity with his influential essay on the 'mirror stage', a metaphor which involved the recognition by an infant of itself in the mirror. Cohesion of the self was the fallacious message taken from this identification, and yet, paradoxically, this was the moment when the baby's world fractured, as oneness with the mother was forever broken in the positing of a self on its own.

Louis **Althusser** used Lacan's metaphor to illustrate how identities were formed through institutional structures, as explicated in his essay on ideological state apparatuses in *Lenin and Philosophy and Other Essays*. Subjects were created through a process of interpellation, in which ideology 'hails' individuals, with those individuals responding to the hailing, and henceforth acknowledging their subject self. This account was heavily based on **structural** processes of identity formation.

From a less restricted and more contemporary perspective, Anthony **Giddens** extensively argued in *Modernity and Self-Identity* (1991) that the late **modern** era provided an opportunity for active formation of the identity in what he termed 'the trajectory of the self'. Though not always a pleasant process, Giddens believed that the transition from a solid modernity allowed for freedom in actions, due to a reflexive evaluation of one's situation and society, unseen in any prior epoch. From a change of house to a change of partner, disliked arrangements were dispensable, as more suitable aspects of identity were readily available replacements. Contrarily, many theorists have argued that the reflexivity Giddens surmises is structured through discourses, as true formation of identity is entirely constricted by dominant paradigms of language and tradition. As Judith **Butler** and theorists elaborating on her seminal work *Gender Trouble* (1990) posited, gendered relations continued to revolve around heteronormative ideas of the self (as aptly implied in the subtitle, *Feminism and the Subversion of Identity*).

Clearly, the issue of identity has vexed the thoughts of social theorists for all of its history, from the classical approaches (**Marx**'s economic **determinism**, **Weber**'s bureaucratic self and **Durkheim**'s collective consciousness) to the latest work in social theory. Perhaps, however, a theorist from the middle of these periods is suitable to conclude with, namely Erving **Goffman**. Indeed, his writings in *Stigma* (1963) explicated the vital notion that our identity was not necessarily fully within our control. However, his possibly even more intriguing supposition focused on the dramaturgical perspective, which essentially called into question the authenticity of identities altogether.

The **INDUSTRIAL REVOLUTION**, a term whose coinage is often attributed to the economic historian Arnold Toynbee who outlined its tenets in a series of lectures in 1881, was apparent to many in England nearly a century before. Indeed, embedded in the Romanticist writings of William Blake in the late eighteenth century was the notion of social change as caused by industrial transformation. **Marx**'s counterpart, Friedrich Engels, moved to Manchester (a city at the heart of the Revolution) in 1842 to work for a textile firm in which his father was a shareholder; three years later, he had composed *The Condition of the Working Class in England in 1844* (1845), which spoke of 'an industrial revolution, a revolution which . . . changed the whole of civil society'.

The exact dates of the Industrial Revolution are disputed by historians, though often the term is split into two distinct periods. Lewis Mumford, the American historian, has argued that the Revolution extended as far back as the introduction of the printing press in the late fifteenth century. Most historians, however, date the beginnings within the early 1800s, with the period from then until approximately 1850 termed the First Industrial Revolution. The causes are also disputed. Undeniably, however, a larger workforce was essential to the Revolution. A much lowered infant mortality rate and better knowledge of epidemics (including the improved isolation and exclusion of sickly itinerants) contributed to a population explosion; so too did a lowering of the age of marriage. **Weber**, in the *Spirit of Capitalism and the Protestant Ethic* (1905), proposed that religious faith and Puritan ethics contributed to the progression. The Second Industrial Revolution refers to massive changes in technological infrastructure, especially the steam engine, which propelled the Revolution further into the twentieth century; it also refers to the spread of such changes from Britain to other countries in Europe and North America.

Of concern were the incredibly significant social transformations that marked the transition from pre-eighteenth century life to the modern era. Rural areas were consolidated into cities, with a consequent explosion in population density. Transportation, through improved road systems, the development of railway systems and advanced ships made the spread of peoples and products viable at ever-increasing speeds. Capital was invested in amounts never before thought possible, mostly in textiles, metals and coal, fueled partly by colonization and newly imperialized markets.

Yet classical social theorists saw problematic outcomes: labour conditions were dire (especially for the multitude of exploited children in coal mining), inspiring the writing of Engels and Marx; cities, with their immense growth in population density, were the target of Georg **Simmel**'s analysis; Weber wrote of increased bureaucratic operations that allowed for all the progress to take place, but also noted the 'iron cage' of rationality which imprisoned humanity in rule-based orders of life. Academics in colonial studies continue to situate the brutal effects of British imperialism.

Arguably, the Industrial Revolution, combined with the underpinnings of the Scientific Revolution, inaugurated social theory as a discipline. It was these periods of massive social change that led to a divergence between the realm of philosophical inquiry and social theory. Contradictions bulged at society's seams. For all the advances and progress of the Industrial Revolution, the quality of human life also diminished markedly; the discrepant paradox of simultaneous development and deterioration remains paramount to contemporary social theory, particularly given the current proclamations of an 'information revolution'.

Fredric **JAMESON**, among the most celebrated of contemporary American Marxist political and cultural theorists, was born in 1934 in Cleveland, Ohio. Jameson attended Haverford College, then still heavily influenced by its Quaker roots, and did postgraduate work in French at Yale University under the famed German philologist Erich Auerbach. With Auerbach's influence, he was able to travel to Germany and France on a Fullbright fellowship, completing a doctoral thesis on the literary style of Sartre, which would be the basis of his first major work, *Sartre: The Origins of Style* (1961). This was a time of immense relief for the American populace, with the Second World War won and the Great Depression overcome. Communism was despised, barely discussed in political forums as anything but an evil ideology and, unsurprisingly Jameson's early career was not characterized by a close Marxist affiliation. Crucially, however, his time spent away from the stagnant optimism and political conservatism that characterized much of the United States in the 1950s certainly helped to develop his later critique of capitalism.

Upon returning to America, Jameson began to teach at the University of California at San Diego, arguably the commencement of his engagement with the Western Marxist tradition (he engaged first with French theorists, then with broader European Marxists, such as Lukács, as opposed to the Soviet Marxist tradition). Though 1968 did not see him at the front lines of the protests, Jameson did found the Marxist Literary Group, leading to his first Marxist work, *Marxism and Form* (1971). Jameson argued that the conception of culture is dichotomous; there is oppression and servitude under the logic of capitalism, a false consciousness imposed by a ruling class in cultural ideology that has significant implications for economic and political domination, yet, vitally, culture also has a transcendent dimension, with the utopian goal of progressive liberation of consciousness. Additionally, Jameson added a crucial dimension, that of postindustrial capitalism. In updating orthodox Western Marxism, and combining these notions with a **structuralist** perspective in *The Prison-House of Language* (1974), Jameson was able to harness the best analytic aspects of the symbolic critique of consumer capitalism (which he argued was more relevant than the factory capitalism of **Marx**'s time, hence 'postindustrial'), and overcome the static limitation of **structuralism**, invoking a conception of a revolutionary, albeit tempered, **agency** on the part of the marginalized.

After positing literature, especially the role of realism and **modernism**, as central to Marxism in *The Political Unconscious* (1981), Jameson's seminal works on **postmodern** Marxist theory, *Late Marxism* (1990) and *Postmodernism* (1991) appeared. Indeed, he had identified such trends in lectures given as early as 1982, as he argued that, with the 1960s, a new age had crystallized, the influence of literature diminishing in the face of popular art and video. Working from Ernest Mandel's *Late Capitalism*, Jameson believed culture to central in the changes of a postmodern epoch. A number of key themes emerged from his analysis that have become synonymous with debates on the postmodern: 'postindividuals' are seen as affected by a broken sense of narrative, a transformed, abstract space, a difficulty of emotion in complex experience, all contained (whether knowingly or not) by a market system with depthless and meaningless cultural products. Though Jameson did envision a 'cultural politics', reinvigorating a sense of culture as the location for progress and reform, arguably his perspective of the postmodern contains less agency than his earlier work.

While, undoubtedly, his career has been massively influential in picking up the Marxist pieces of the post-Second World War period, critics have lambasted his position, some calling Jameson and others like him 'tenured radicals', a shot at their privileged position and seeming disconnection to public policy. Though there may be mild praise for his embracing of Third World cinema and art, there is some truth to the argument that the academic positioning of Marxist theory, of which Jameson is not the sole culprit, has disengaged the non-university affiliated individual. Yet Jameson is to be commended for his significant contributions to an analysis of a postindustrial/postmodern society and his tireless assault of dominant economic and cultural politics, as he has rejuvenated **Marxism**, renewing its existence in the changing world of contemporary life.

Julia **KRISTEVA**, the highly influential linguist, philosopher, psychoanalyst and forerunner of **post-structuralist** thought, was born in Bulgaria in 1941. She pursued an undergraduate degree in linguistics at the University of Sophia, but it was her move to Paris in 1965 to attain her doctorate that forever altered her life's path. Upon arrival, the fellow Bulgarian linguist Tzvétan Todorov initiated introductions to some of the foremost French intellectuals, notably Roland **Barthes**, Claude **Lévi-Strauss**, and her future husband and co-founder of the avant-garde journal *Tel Quel*, Phillipe Sollers. It was Barthes, however, who invited Kristeva to give a talk on the then obscure Mikhail Bakhtin, whose unique perspective on literary theory would greatly influence much of the rest of her career. Bakhtin's notion of the dynamism of texts would inspire Kristeva, propelling her over time to the central position she currently holds.

Upon her arrival in France, much of the linguistic and social theory community was enthralled by the work of Ferdinand de **Saussure**, whose framework of the symbolic nature of language was wholeheartedly embraced. However, critiques began to surface that called attention to the stagnancy and lack of meaning in such a structured system of meaning. This perspective ran in opposition to the seemingly heterogeneous and malleable nature of poeticism. Kristeva argued that the application of a scientific logic of truth and falsehood to art was flawed in its inability to account for subjectivity. In positing the concept of 'semanalysis', a combination of **semiology** and **psychoanalysis**, she valiantly rethought both disciplines, bringing bodily drives to language and, conversely, communication to the body. In doing so, Kristeva fundamentally altered the tradition of linguistics, integrating the disorderly unconscious of **Freud** into the previously stabilized and structured (yet for this very reason problematic) study of language. Of particular note was her idea of the 'semiotic' as closely aligned with affects of the repressed unconscious, thereby altering Saussurian linguistics to allow for transgressive subjective meaning, going beyond that which is not reducible to the literal symbolism of the subject. The semiotic may not be categorized as traditionally symbolic but, for Kristeva, it is still imbued with meaning. These concepts of the late 1960s and early 1970s culminated in the publication of her massively influential doctoral thesis, *Revolution in Poetic Language* (French publication 1974, abridged English translation 1984).

With her training as a clinical psychoanalyst and the birth of her child, there was a shift in Kristeva's work in the late 1970s and early 1980s. Rather than focusing solely on language, Kristeva comments on subjectivity in a broader sense, especially within the realm of maternity and also psychoanalytic theory. In the essential works *Powers of Horror* (1982) and *Tales of Love* (1987), she argued for motherhood as the locus of a fundamental division of the body and language; the process of pregnancy follows the symbolic-semiotic partition, especially within the mother–child separation. This is the point of introduction of her term 'abject', which refers to that which we find painful and horrible, but is a significant part of our culture (with specific reference to the casting away of the child from their mother). Though we are forced to separate to create our own identity, it is nonetheless an agonizing process. Applied to the marginalization and splitting of minority groups within society, Kristeva's powerful social theory comes to the fore, especially as adopted by some **feminists**.

Though her work has been embraced widely, several critiques have been levelled against her theories. It is unclear in Kristeva's estimation how the individualized notion of the semiotic might extend to larger social structures. While the broadening of her writing may seem workable, she has been accused of abstraction to the point of losing political force, which is ironic given her involvement in many political acts, notably the 1968 student riots. Also, some feminists have accused her of essentializing femininity to maternity. Yet despite these criticisms, Kristeva has remained a force in the intellectual world, influencing diverse modes of thought, as witnessed in the publishing of the successful analysis of melancholia and depression in *Black Sun* (1989) and three novels in the 1990s. Additionally, it is clear in this epoch of forced immigration, relocation and division that the theories of exclusion so prominent in her thinking will remain highly relevant.

Jacques **LACAN**, the most famed psychoanalyst after Sigmund **Freud**, was born in 1901 in Paris. His father was a successful salesman, providing a middle-class lifestyle for the family; his mother was a devoted follower of Catholicism, though this influence did not last significantly into Lacan's adulthood, as it did for his younger brother, who entered a monastery. After being rejected for military service, Lacan would begin his post-secondary education, entering medical school directly at the age of 18, and finishing his degree with a specialization in psychiatry in 1926 at the famed Sainte-Anne Hospital.

The 1930s would see an explosion of opportunities for the young analyst, as he would be accepted into the Paris Psychoanalytic Society and write his seminal psychoanalytic work on the 'mirror stage' in 1936. Catapulting his academic reputation, this article would bring him into contact with many academic circles, which he embraced. Freud had surmised that psychoanalytic theory stood to benefit from a diverse study of art, literature, language, philosophy and society, and this was certainly embodied by Lacan's personal relationships with some of the premier intellectuals of his time, including Martin Heidegger, Maurice

Merleau-Ponty, Claude **Lévi-Strauss**, Michel **Foucault** and Georges Bataille, among others. Lacan's varied interests would be made more prominent in his later annual public seminars, which spanned decades and covered Plato, Aristotle, Descartes, Kant and **Hegel** within the philosophical tradition, Ferdinand de **Saussure** and Charles Peirce within linguistics and semiotics and, additionally, many famed anthropologists and literary figures.

Though the 1960s would mark Lacan's height of popularity with the publication of a 900-page collection of his essays in *Écrits* and the formation of divisions within universities of Lacanian thought, arguably his most influential concepts concerned the interconnection of the imaginary, the symbolic and the real, whose roots were planted as far back as three decades earlier. The 'imaginary' was born from his analysis of a phenomenon which many parents and children with younger siblings have witnessed first hand; a baby, sometime between (usually) six and eighteen months has the experience of seeing themselves in the mirror and recognizing the reflection as their own self. Lacan believed this fundamental realization, termed the 'mirror stage', to be problematic, in that the visual affirmation of bodily unity does not correspond with the fragmented ego of the latter self, resulting in a 'lack', an alienation and gap between the imagined identity and the 'real' identity. Our attempts to stabilize ourselves, as with the identification in the mirror, are inherently flawed and implausible.

Since the imaginary fails to create a stable identity, Lacan posits that linguistic representation is the consequent strategy, as encapsulated in the 'symbolic'. Even before the imaginary of the mirror stage, the baby is immersed in a symbolic environment of the family, as simply seen in the naming of the child (usually discussed prior to birth, if not wholly decided). In a more structured mode, the symbolic still does not achieve the stabilization and filling of the 'lack' that characterizes our identity for Lacan; due to the universality of language, it is incapable of representing the singularity of the individual. This entrapment in the lacking representational symbolic is what Lacan calls the 'Other', as it cannot be identified in the 'other' of the mirror stage. These alienations amount to a flawed sense of the 'real', one that is not obtainable as the imaginary-symbolic-real relation explicates.

Though Lacan has had his virulent critics, it is important to note that he was primarily a clinician and psychoanalyst, his theory coming from his training and practice. Though purposefully obtuse at times, his desire was to challenge the reader and thinker, provoking them to a deeper level of self-understanding. Lacan cannot be categorized as **structuralist** or post-structuralist, although his writings have indications of both; yet what can be said is that his investigations, rooted in the relationship of the analyst and analysand, provide valuable insight into the nature of the social bond and that which lies beneath the surface. While he had issues with mainstream psychoanalysts in his later years, forcing him to form his own organization, undoubtedly Lacan's influence, despite his death in 1981, has been of the utmost degree within various contemporary disciplines, including **feminism, post-structuralism, postmodernism** and literary and film theory.

Claude **LÉVI-STRAUSS**, the unprecedented anthropologist whose focus on the previously ignored structuring underneath the surface of cultures encouraged the linguistic turn in social theory, was born in 1908 in Brussels, Belgium. Born into a Jewish family, he studied philosophy and law at the University of Paris from 1927 until 1932, thereafter seizing the opportunity to teach sociology in São Paulo from 1934 until 1937, simultaneously doing research among Indian tribes of inland Brazil. Though he returned to France in 1939, this move was short-lived as Lévi-Strauss was forced to flee the rise of Nazism in Europe, escaping to New York and teaching at the New School for Social Research from 1941 until 1945. It was during this time in America that he was first influenced by the structural linguistics of Ferdinand de **Saussure**, which would ignite a new perspective that affected his subsequently prolific career.

Very early in his academic life, one can deduce through his unique set of influences in *Tristes Tropiques* (1955) the thinking that made Lévi-Strauss so important, namely a synthesis of **Marx**, **Freud** and, quite intriguingly, geology. Though, at first glance, one may not find much in common between the first two, let alone all three, Lévi-Strauss's insight was based on the notion of reality being truly discoverable below the surface appearance of phenomena. For Marx, underlying economic conditions explained grander ideological arrangements; for Freud, surface mental states were less important to consider than unconscious thoughts in the shaping of the self; and, within geological theory, the past strata of rocks, vegetation and the like were of the utmost importance to fully evaluate present conditions. Mostly based on his field work in the Brazilian rainforests, it was a controversial account. His defiance of the anthropological orthodoxy, in which an intellectual separation from natives was considered paramount to an accurate first-hand study, was shown in his desire to dig deeply into the symbolic nature of actions; for Lévi-Strauss, communication was crucial, and through an analysis of the structured signification of even the most 'uncivilized' cultures, he believed there could be a deeper level of understanding than was previously afforded to anthropologists. Beyond the scientific study of language, the embedded analyst was bounded by their intuitions in a subjective and faulty judgement, no matter how much distance they attempted to create.

The early 1960s saw Lévi-Strauss cement his status as a forward thinker, combining his anthropological background with an innovative interpretation of structural linguistics, as seen in his most read works, *Totemism* and *The Savage Mind* (both published in English in 1962). Importantly, he never claimed a universal structure, as some **structuralists** did, but rather a universal tendency toward structuring. From this perspective, Lévi-Strauss argued against the conservative voices in anthropology that claimed a lack of thought in the 'uncivilized' mind, instead arguing that they too create systems of categorical significance, albeit differently ordered ones.

A four-volume series dedicated to the study of mythology would follow, in which Lévi-Strauss argued that even the most convoluted myth is deducible from logical transformations of one to another. Following one myth from South

America led him all the way north to the Arctic circle; in this regard, he continued the contention of order and structure's visibility in even the most unlikely places. This mode of thought was then a controversial perspective that brought Lévi-Strauss considerable controversy, but his influence, which has since diminished with the rise of **post-structuralism**, was immensely significant for the dissolution of anthropology and social theory. The winner of France's highest academic honour in his 1973 election to the Académie Française, he became its first member to reach the age of 100 in 2008, and, incredibly, continues to write (although less frequently) on the arts.

Jean-François **LYOTARD**, the central leader (or demonized piñata, depending on one's perspective) of **postmodernism**, was born in 1924 in Versailles, France. His youth was especially noteworthy, despite his father being a rather mundane sales representative. Yet these simplistic origins gave little indication of the later combative Lyotard, author of over 30 books and many more articles, some quite controversial. After his lycée education, a degree in philosophy at the Sorbonne and positions at French universities would follow; yet the real move which radicalized the young thinker was a teaching post in an Algerian high school less than a decade before the Algerian war, prominently engaging him in the far-left political sphere. In 1954, he joined *Socialisme ou Barbarie*, a neo-Trotskyite group founded by Cornelius **Castoriadis**, though differences would cause Lyotard to leave for the *Mouvement du 22 Mars*, a group closely associated with the 1968 student uprisings. The events of the late 1960s would radically alter his focus, and indeed his prestige, elevating him to the status of academic celebrity in the 1970s and 1980s.

His first publication in 1954, *Phenomenology*, was a defence of Maurice **Merleau-Ponty**'s argument that perception could not be wholly reduced to the symbolic or language. Lyotard contended that sensations, experiences and feelings could not necessarily be encapsulated within a **Saussurian** framework of signifiers, hence there was more than could be expressed in language. The next major work, *Discourse, Figure* (1971), continued this line of thought, and better connected its philosophy to the political sphere. In essence, there existed a 'figural' layer of expression, which existed prior to symbolization. This proposition ran directly against **structuralism**, but it was Lyotard's hope that, due to this outsider status of the figural (generally embodied in avant-garde art), it might be considered a mode of resistance. His reasoning relied on the notion that **discourse** was helplessly intertwined in the repressive powers, though the symbolic could not be harnessed and controlled as such.

The political atmosphere and revolutions of 1968 altered Lyotard's career, as subsequent analyses brought him stardom. *Libidinal Economy* (1974) and *The Postmodern Condition* (1979) were both widely read (especially the latter) and debated in France (and, later, across the English-speaking world). The former has been declared by Lyotard himself as 'scandalous', with its unique style and a lack of concreteness. Essentially a fusion and critique of **Marxism** and

Freudianism in the context of the previous decade's events, a vision of amalgamated desire and capital amounted to an apolitical and individualistic text. A marked transition came with *The Postmodern Condition* (*PMC*), as a more nuanced view of critique and politics developed. Lyotard believed Marxism to be flawed in its totalization of analysis, a 'grand narrative'; postmodernism incited 'incredulity towards metanarratives' and he not only identified, but also encouraged feelings of incredulity towards proponents of a fully encapsulating discourse. Universality was demoted, no longer a viable position. Importantly, this additionally challenged the Enlightenment tradition of increasing knowledge correlating with greater well-being; *PMC* discarded such notions, as the influence of Ludwig Wittgenstein's language games began to play a role in Lyotard's thinking, and would continue to do so in his later and, arguably, more significant works.

In a synthesis of the best ideas of the previous two decades, the 1980s saw Lyotard address justice in the age of postmodernism, building on Wittgenstein further in *Just Gaming* (1979) and *The Differend* (1983). In the latter work, he continues the idea of language games, in which human activities are 'games' with 'rules of conduct' and, notably, they are filled with disputes. If I were to play the 'game' of discussing sport, I would justify my opinion that a team is great by commenting on their ability to play well with 'chemistry', 'heart', 'drive' and so forth. In opposition, someone might counter with an appropriate verbal retaliation. Though most games exist as such, some disputes question the basis of the dispute itself, termed a 'differend'. In these cases, the disputes cannot be had, with fundamental disagreement being the inevitable outcome, challenging the prospect of ethics. From a political perspective, this was an ominous prediction of irreconcilable differences, as it logically followed from his critique of visions of totality.

Clearly, defenders of the project of **modernity** found a perfect sparring partner in Lyotard, and he happily obliged, engaging himself in many public discussions until his sudden death from leukaemia in 1998. Accused of encouraging the 'postmodern mess' he created, his final two works returned to some of the hopefulness of the pre-1968 writings. Once again, Lyotard finds art to be the mode of relieving the 'postmodern condition' in *The Inhuman* and *Lessons on the Analytic and Sublime*, as the less commodified works incite thought and reflection, even in the cases in which they annoy. His influence is paramount for both his supporters and detractors and, although the debate of the postmodern may have for the moment subsided, the critique of universality and the power of the **aesthetic** continue to be fundamental contemporary concepts.

Herbert **MARCUSE**, a integral and unique member of the **Frankfurt School** who inspired much of the revolutionary fervour of 1960s American politics, was born in 1898 in Berlin, Germany. The son of a prosperous Jewish merchant, Carl

Marcuse, and the grandson (on his mother, Gertrud Kreslawsky's side) of a wealthy Jewish factory owner, Marcuse enjoyed a pleasant childhood, only possible in the early decades of twentieth-century Germany, before the violently overt anti-Semitism of the Nazi party. With this freedom to pursue intellectual thought, Marcuse gained a PhD in literature from the University of Freiburg in 1922. After a brief stint as a bookseller, he returned to academia in 1928 in a glorious but sadly ironic situation: Marcuse studied under the foremost philosopher of his era, Martin Heidegger, whose sympathies for Hitler's Socialism were never renounced, despite later pleas by Marcuse to reconsider the assertions (Hannah Arendt, among many other important former students, also pursued Heidegger on this issue).

This period under Heidegger, cut short in 1934 as the need to flee Germany became clear, was productive and instructive of Marcuse's later work. His focus in various articles was orthodox **Marxism**, yet the distinctive twist was an incorporation of a **phenomenological** perspective. The goal, arguably achieved, was to enlighten Marxist theory, filling in what Marcuse saw as a neglect of social, cultural and psychological analysis (as opposed to a political and especially economic focus). The year before his exile from Europe to America, he had established himself sufficiently in Germany to obtain work with Theodor **Adorno** and the other **critical theorists** in Frankfurt. Their dialogues would continue at Columbia University in the late 1930s.

Though Marcuse left the university life for a decade to work with the United States government analysing media effects and Nazism, 1941 saw the publication of his first major work, *Reason and Revolution*. In it, he argued the case for similarities between Georg **Hegel** and Karl **Marx**, introducing German social theory at an approachable level for an American audience. Though it was well received, *Eros and Civilization* (1955) was notably more successful, possibly due to its anticipation of countercultural themes that, in retrospect, were obviously emerging. This work was later criticized for its use of some of **Freud**'s more biologically reductive concepts, yet the synthesis of a Freudian framework and a Marxist critique of a repressive bourgeois society struck a chord with a large proportion of radicalized students. Of particular note was Marcuse's term 'surplus repression', which claimed that beyond Freud's notion in *Civilization and Its Discontents* of the repression necessary to allow for a functioning society, additional repression was at work within technological and consumerist spheres that limited social actors' potentials. It is important to be aware that, while Marcuse was characterized as solely demonizing technology, in actuality his position was more complex, as he identified its methods of domination but also saw its potential, if correctly harnessed, to allow for a freer society. Despite the discussion of repression, there was a clear note of optimism to the work, as he proclaimed the potentiality and feasibility of a liberated and pleasurable society.

After publishing on Soviet Marxism and an appointment at Brandeis University, Marcuse's most well-known work was published in 1964, entitled *One Dimensional Man*. If his framework in earlier work was cautiously optimistic, this seminal piece of the American student revolutions was criticized for its beleaguered pessimism. Despite this rejection, his illumination of new forms of social control and a one-dimension mode of thinking, in effect dominated to the point of uncritical submission, was heralded by the New Left as their manifesto and gained him a huge following across the world. He argued that, with the creation of false consumer needs, social actors were integrated into a systemic mode of capitalism that eliminated any self-reflection or individualization. Arguably more than any Marxist of his generation, Marcuse brought to light the subjective nature of revolution and, in positing novel forms of domination, he also focused attention on a richer conception of liberation than orthodox Marxism. Moving from Brandeis to the University of California at La Jolla, he continued these themes with a slight retraction of his pessimism in many important works, including *An Essay on Liberation* (1969) and *Counterrevolution and Revolt* (1972).

Despite his death of a heart attack in 1979 and subsequently waning influence with the rise of **post-structuralism** and **postmodernism**, Marcuse remains highly regarded for his prescient eye for cultural criticism and updated Marxism. His nuanced, dichotomous view of the dominating effect and liberating potentialities of technology and culture are still influential across a variety of theoretical fields.

Karl **MARX**, certainly the most renowned of all classical social theorists within sociological thought, was born in Trier (then part of the Kingdom of Prussia) in 1818. Although Marx's father, Heinrich, had a long family history of rabbinical figures, he converted to Lutheranism in order to practise law. Home-schooled until the age of thirteen, Marx's academic career never flourished to the degree of some of the other seminal social theorists of this period; while he entered the University of Bonn at the precocious age of seventeen, studying law at the instigation of his father, Heinrich also compelled him to switch to the University of Berlin, in part due to a lack of academic success. This switch proved to be immeasurably influential on his career, as Marx joined a bohemian and activist intellectual group (later known as the Young Hegelians) and engaged seriously in the study of philosophy and history. Completing his dissertation in 1841, he was forced to submit it to the University of Jena due to his somewhat radical associations.

For two years would Marx be involved, first as a journalist and later as editor, with the politicized newspaper *Rheinische Zeitung*. Unluckily, the Tsar of Russia happened to read a critique that Marx wrote about him and ordered the Prussian government to shut the paper down. Without a job, Marx moved to Paris and relied on friends and family inheritance to support himself and his newly started family. This was indeed a productive time, however, as Marx was involved in public intellectual life, meeting (and debating with) the notable anarchist Bakunin and the romantic poet Heine. It was also at this point that he would meet Friedrich Engels, a key figure throughout his life; Engels would not only be a close friend and collaborator, but also was financially secure and offered Marx considerable assistance.

It is impossible to speak of a singular theme for the rest of Marx's illustrious career, as many Marxist academics have identified. Two strands arguably do carry through all of his writing: a critique of the dispossessing nature of capitalist society, combined with a belief in the inherent contractions of such an economic structure, and an individualist framework of methodology, as he believed that people made history, albeit often unknowingly. However, it is true that contradictions (or refinements) in his work are apparent. Notably, **Althusser** crystallized the differentiation of his early writings from the later ones, describing a transition from abstracted humanist proclamations to a more concrete and analytical dissection of capitalism. In his first seminal collection, *The Economic and Philosophical Manuscripts of 1844*, the humanist notion of alienation was developed. Marx argued that individuals lacked control of their lives in a wage and factory economy, in that, from the original stage of production to the final product, the worker is disconnected and unable to claim any legitimate bond. While a day-to-day account might appear innocuous and perhaps even laudable for its efficient mode of assembly (one must consider his critique in opposition to the popular and formidable British political economists of his era, namely Adam Smith and David Ricardo), Marx passionately turned this optimism on its head, calling for a revolt against such practices. Though this work was only published posthumously and did not develop a strong thesis regarding the causes of such an arrangement, his concept of alienation and the resulting feeling of estrangement propelled his later and more methodological critique of capitalism.

Marx's next major work, *The German Ideology* (1846, also not published until later) further developed his incredibly influential ideas on historical analysis of class and labour division. Indeed, the vital idea of surplus and the struggle over its constitution (and distribution) was explicated, which would be a crucial element of his later work. Probably his most well-known work, *The Communist Manifesto*, followed in 1848, coinciding with a move to England. In this work the evolutionary vision, associated with his distinctive historical materialism, came to the forefront of Marx's thinking; feedback between history and the economy created turbulent situations, which he proposed that the proletariat classes could use to overthrow an inherently contradictory structure run by the bourgeois. Somewhat rhetorical in style, the *Manifesto* has been criticized as naive and problematically idealistic; however, its impact was undeniable.

In a return to the fundamental question of how such arrangements of property, surplus and forces of production and labour came to produce classes, Marx published a lengthy work *The Grundisse* (1858), from which *A Contribution to a Critique of Political Economy* (1859) came. Aside from his illuminating metaphorical discussion of base and superstructure in the preface, the works were perceived as overly complex and verging on the incomprehensible, especially compared to the poetic *Manifesto*. Despite this setback, his opus, *Capital*, was published in 1867 (two later volumes were published posthumously), finally providing a firmer, almost scientific grounding to the earlier humanist proclamations. Especially noteworthy is the concept of human value reduced to economic value; our labours vanish into commodities, whose presence in society ominously dominate in the form of an artificial world. Though a historical account of labour and accumulation is given, *Capital* is more concerned with the theory of capitalism, and less with its progression through time. Idiosyncrasies of the system are not presented, yet his economic theory bears heavily on the broader social theory of life in the early stages of the **Industrial Revolution**.

Marx, for all the canonization of his work, has had fervent critics. Indeed, the proposition of the rise of the proletariat has been completely dismissed; the *Manifesto* taking its place as an eloquent but inaccurate analysis. Of course, his broader thinking continues to be important for labour theory, though blatant dissenters question his relevance beyond an archaic account of factory life. Arguably, Marx has been justly superseded, with the positing of more complex accounts of capitalism. With his death in 1883, the dissemination and fragmentation of Marxism began, with as many varieties of thought as any singular figure could possibly inspire. It is within this immense and disparate cluster of influence that classical social theory truly illustrates its importance. The times necessarily change; there is nothing one can do to prevent such an occurrence, as it inevitably invalidates one's specific predications. Beyond these unavoidable problems, Marx's commitment to theoretical concern for the dispossessed individual in an alienating economy retains its relevance, and unfortunately will probably continue to do so for far longer than he had hoped.

George Herbert **MEAD**, a founder of social psychology and a central figure for later generations of the **Chicago School**, was born in South Hadley, Massachusetts in 1863. His father, Hiram Mead, was a Congregationalist minister and pastor, while his mother, Elizabeth Storrs Billings, was a homemaker at the time of his birth. At the age of seven, Mead was moved (along with his mother and older sister Alice) by his father to Oberlin, Ohio, as Hiram was to become a professor of homiletics at Oberlin College's Theological Seminary. A vibrant educational community, Oberlin College was noteworthy for the early acceptance of female (1833) and African-American (1834) applicants. Hiram taught until his death in 1881, two years after Mead had enrolled at the youthful age of sixteen. Elizabeth took over his post until 1883, the year that Mead graduated with a BA. She later became president of Mount Holyoke College for the decade of 1890–1900.

Mead did not find immediate academic success; after Oberlin, his first job as a grade school teacher only lasted four months. For three and a half years subsequently, he worked as a surveyor for the Wisconsin Central Rail Road Company. However, in 1887 he enrolled in a MA philosophy degree at Harvard University, also studying psychology and four languages. Clearly, Mead was keen to take on difficult academic challenges. The influential pragmatist William James was teaching at Harvard during this time; however, George studied under George Palmer and Josiah Royce (though interestingly, Mead stayed at James's house and tutored his children).

After Harvard, Mead travelled to Germany to study for a PhD in philosophy and physiological psychology at the University of Leipzig. Notably, William Wundt (a founder of experimental psychology) was one of his mentors. However, he never finished his studies, as they were interrupted in 1891 when Mead was offered and accepted a professorship at the University of Michigan. It was during this period back in America that he became a close personal and intellectual friend of John Dewey, the influential philosopher who would soon (1894) become head of the newly founded department of philosophy at the University of Chicago. At the invitation of Dewey, he spent the rest of his academic life in Chicago, continuing in the pragmatist tradition of Harvard philosophers Charles Peirce and William James.

Mead is remembered for his enormous contributions to social theory under the guise of social psychology and philosophy. Like Ferdinand de **Saussure**, the famous Swiss linguist, Mead's most famous work *Mind, Self and Society* was published in 1934, three years after his death, by his former students via lecture notes and unpublished papers. In fact, despite prodigious writing, he never published a book, instead publishing only articles and book reviews. Considering the great influence Mead had as he parted ways with individualized psychology, stressing the social processes and communication pathways inherent to the functioning mind, it is quite remarkable that without the aid of his students, the impact of his work would be much less. Other important posthumous works were *The Philosophy of the Present* (1932), *Movements of Thought in the Nineteenth Century* (1936) and *The Philosophy of Act* (1938).

Mead's wife died on Christmas Day in 1929, less than two months after the devastating stock market crash. Emotionally distraught, for the two years thereafter he became progressively more unwell. Although Dewey arranged a post for him in the philosophy department of Columbia University, Mead never took up the appointment, as he died in Chicago in the spring of 1931.

Maurice **MERLEAU-PONTY**, who, along with his close associate Jean-Paul Sartre, was among the most famed **phenomenologists** of the twentieth century, was born in 1908 in Rochefort-sur-Mer, in western France. His father was killed in the First World War when Merleau-Ponty was quite young. Merleau-Ponty managed to gain entry to the famed École Normale Supérieure, completing his degree in philosophy there in 1930. Many famed thinkers studied and taught at the École over the generations; however, this particular period included Sartre, Simone de **Beauvoir** and Simone Weil. His influence was critical for many later French thinkers, including Michel **Foucault**, Louis **Althusser**, and Claude **Lévi-Strauss**, whose seminal work *The Savage Mind* was dedicated to Merleau-Ponty.

While the Second World War would delay his scholarship, as he served in the French infantry, Merleau-Ponty received his dissertation from the École in 1945, after writing his most noted work, *The Phenomenology of Perception* (published in French in 1945). In developing new relationships between numerous dualisms, including the self and the world, the subject and the object, and the body and the consciousness, Merleau-Ponty was drawing on many philosophers, but particularly the work of Edmund Husserl. His critique of empiricist and idealist notions of the body within the philosophical tradition was influential for its development as a mode of inquiry, rather than a simple object which is solely controlled and used by the mind. From this perspective, Merleau-Ponty is often considered an existentialist, in that his focus was considerably concentrated on the nature of human existence. Within such a framework, the influence of Heidegger's philosophy is also apparent in his work. Merleau-Ponty is additionally known as a proponent of perception, remembered for giving it 'primacy'; in essence, however, he did not dismiss scientific measurement and inquiry, but rather elevated the credibility of observation as a pathway to knowledge.

In the years following, there were numerous politically themed works, including *Humanism and Terror* (1947), the essays of *Sense and Non-Sense* (1948) and *The Adventures of the Dialectic* (1955). The first two titles were concerned with the method by which actions attain meaning though history since, at the time of the actual event, its situational character is unknown and only develops with later reflection. Though there was a notable engagement with **Marx**, in identifying (especially in *Sense and Non-Sense*) the need for a philosophy of praxis, *The Adventures of the Dialectic* moved to a post-Marxist schema. The work was also influenced heavily by a nuanced perspective of structuralism, as would be expected owing Merleau-Ponty's friendship with Claude **Lévi-Strauss** and Jacques **Lacan**. Yet his view was unique, in that he refused to see man wholly subsumed by structural rules. As some scholars have noted, Merleau-Ponty should be considered a loose precursor to theories that surround the agency–structure interplay, such as those of Pierre **Bourdieu** and Anthony **Giddens**.

Though his post-dissertation work was criticized for a lack of systematic coherency and for his inability to suggest an alternative to Marxism, this is an area open to dispute as Merleau-Ponty died suddenly of a stroke at the age of 53; many essays were unfinished and might possibly have achieved some reconciliation of the prolific and diverse themes. Therefore, his supporters draw out conclusions which illustrate an escape from such a stunted position, while detractors claim that no such move is possible. In either case, the diverse range of his thoughts, especially those concerning the body in fields as far-ranging as feminism to cognitive science, exemplifies the continuing influence of the seminal phenomenologist.

Juliet **MITCHELL**, the initiator of a conciliatory move between **feminism** and **psychoanalysis**, was born in Christchurch, New Zealand in 1940. At the age of four, with the war ending, Mitchell moved with her family to England, where she benefited from a progressive, co-educational schooling; she later attended St Anne's College, Oxford for both undergraduate (1958–61) and the start of postgraduate studies. However, Mitchell left for a brief stint at the University of Leeds as an assistant lecturer, followed by a move to the University of Reading, where she was made full lecturer in the English department in 1965. Though the stay in Leeds was short, it was during this period that she began to be involved with the *New Left Review*, an influential journal of the British New Left. Mitchell became the only female member of the editorial board in 1963. An anecdote from this period, recounted in a later work, aptly summarized the isolation and intrigue of the situation, as she noted, 'I remember sitting at a table with all the men of *New Left Review* and . . . people saying, . . . "I will think about Persia", "I will think about Tanganyika", as they were then, and I said, "Well, I'll think about women" – and there was silence.'

Despite these obstacles, Mitchell's prestige rose with the publication of her seminal article in 1966, 'Women: The Longest Revolution'. Though other social theorists before her had expounded on orthodox Marxism's mistaken reductionism of society to the economy, her incorporation of the status of women was influential. As Mitchell argued, the position of women incorporated numerous elements. Drawing on Louis **Althusser**, she posited that this structure was overdetermined, in that each singular aspect was autonomous, but they were not remote, as one sector was capable of strengthening or terminating the others. The four aspects affecting the woman's condition, for Mitchell, were production, reproduction, sexuality and socialization. Her hope was that the transformation of the weakest of the four (which changed through varying historical conditions) could initiate a grander transformation. Her first major book-length publication, *Woman's Estate* (1972), continued the theme of women's liberation, focusing especially on the dynamic of Althusser's familial ideology, and how such a framework of family dynamics would impede emancipatory efforts. This year also marked Mitchell's departure from the Reading teaching post, as she began to lecture on a freelance basis, perhaps allowing her the intellectual space and freedom that would result in her consequential embrace of psychoanalysis.

Mitchell's most cited work would be published two years later, breaking new ground in feminist accounts of Sigmund **Freud**. In *Psychoanalysis and Feminism* (1974), she derided what was then a typical feminist reaction to psychoanalysis: the claim that Freud affirms sexual difference and misogyny, embracing a patriarchal **structure** of society through biological **determinism**. Rather, Mitchell believed that Freud was simply describing and calling attention to this organization; psychoanalysis was an illustrative account, with no intent to sanction such an arrangement. Further, going beyond the apolitical theory of Jacques **Lacan**, Mitchell believed psychoanalysis to be essential not only in understanding the oppression of women, but also in challenging the ideological constraints. Through focusing on the historical unconscious acquirement of cultural gender norms, and their consequences for the psyche (and the consequences of the psyche formation for women), she made it clear that the goal of using psychoanalysis in tandem with feminism was decidedly political. Only through such an approach could the entrenched patriarchy be 'undermined and eroded'.

While it is the case that her synthesis was quite successful, shaping new directions in feminist psychoanalysis, many feminists still had trouble with her wholesale approval of Freudianism. Other dissent was based on the optimistic conclusions that her emancipatory framework of psychoanalysis entailed. Critics of Mitchell believed that her deductions did not follow from the earlier analysis of ideology. Judith **Butler** argued against another perceived weakness in her conflation of gender and desire, as Butler's performativity thesis posited their unnaturally forced cohesion.

For those immersed in social theory, and indeed any critical discipline, though Mitchell's rereading of Freud may have elicited problematic outcomes, her ambitious attempt to revisit a social thinker must be seen as commendable. Intellectuals frequently repeatedly perpetuate an analysis of a particular theory or event. In the era of 24/7 news and increasingly viral Internet journalism, this process has amplified to dangerous levels. Mitchell made a provocative claim regarding psychoanalysis and feminism, which ran counter the intuition of nearly all her colleagues. Yet she did so through the use of original texts, disregarding orthodoxy in an articulate manner. As is the case with many 'post'-disciplines, such an approach will necessarily elicit contrary views; however, the reward of fresh discussions and perspectives far exceeds any level of initial discomfort.

MODERNITY as a period of human history is a term of implausible specificity or exactitude as, for different social theorists, there is debate regarding its actual dates and the processes which define it. Most broadly, modernity is seen as an epoch which began around the time of the democratic and **Industrial Revolution**s, and certainly its foundation was laid by the philosophical and **epistemological** debates of the Enlightenment. For some, this means going back as far as the French Revolution, whereas for others, the revolutions of 1844 are a more appropriate point of departure for its wholesale inception.

Despite this ambiguity, social theory and sociology as disciplines are seen to have sprung into being in response to the changes witnessed in differing social and political relations. From classical social theory, concern for modernity is witnessed in Karl **Marx**'s analysis of alienation within factory labour, Max **Weber**'s focus on rationalization within bureaucracy, Émile **Durkheim**'s discussion of organic versus mechanical solidarity and Georg **Simmel**'s concentration on monetary exchange and the stranger. Contrasted with more traditional forms of society, modernity is constructed in relation to the loss of closely regulated, small and homogeneous communities; the advent of city life, the increased production capability of factories and the necessary division of labour to support these trends diminished the significance of previous organizations of existence. Many of the accounts of modernity in the pre-World War era were encompassed by the degenerate effects of capitalism.

More contemporary analysis of modernity has addressed its possible transition into new forms beyond capitalism, including the notion of risk in Ulrich **Beck**'s risk society, its destructive and genocidal potential, most notably explicated in Zygmunt **Bauman**'s *Modernity and the Holocaust* (1987), and its effect on autonomy and reflexive knowledge within Anthony **Giddens**'s structuration theory, among many other theorists. Yet the previous two decades have brought even more complexity to the status of modernity, as witnessed in the changing nomenclature; now seen as antiquated, modernity has been replaced by the likes of Beck's second modernity, Bauman's liquid modernity, Giddens's and others' late modernity and, possibly the most provocative of all, **postmodernity**. Proponents of these replacements are not in agreement with regard to modernity's status throughout the course these changes. Indeed, late modernity implies an intensification of modernity's attributes, whereas some postmodernists posit modernity's complete dissolution. The debates surrounding the end (or lack thereof) of modernity stand to be the most instructive focal points of current scholarship on the subject.

PHENOMENOLOGY describes an approach to philosophical investigation that is wholly concerned with the nature of consciousness. It was developed by Edmund Husserl, the German philosopher and friend of Georg **Simmel**, who believed consciousness to be the only sure form of knowledge. The phenomeno-logical perspective can be seen as a response to the seventeenth century **episte-mological** debate of rationalism and empiricism. Husserl declared that everything from mathematical law and formulae to sensation and experience could only be grounded through consciousness. As later philosophers of mind have found, such a reduction can lead one to question the existence of every other human being.

From this description alone, the field seems limiting for social theory; yet, as is often the case, innovators and dissenters alike progressed the tradition beyond its initial position, exploring various syntheses and applications. Maurice **Merleau-Ponty** was in the former category, as his work *The Phenomenology of Perception* (published in French in 1945) developed new dualistic relationships, the most relevant in this context being the body and consciousness. In doing so, Merleau-Ponty advanced a critique of empiricism in treating the body objec-tively, dissolving the vital importance of consciousness. Herbert **Marcuse** also could broadly be considered an innovator of phenomenology, applying Husserl's concern for consciousness in his exploration of Sigmund **Freud** and Karl **Marx**. Also, **ethnomethodology** is indebted to Husserl's thought, as consciousness bears heavily on the construction of social worlds.

The most noteworthy critic of Husserl among social theorists was Jacques **Derrida**, whose 1959 paper argued forcefully against Husserl's notion of con-sciousness as an unmediated and pure representation of the self. It was this dis-cussion, early in Derrida's career, of the falsified projection of consciousness that inspired the influential notions of *différance* and deconstruction. Therefore, the phenomenological tradition should be seen as a catalyst, among both its propo-nents and dissenters, into grander debates of epistemology. While it would be problematic to claim that Husserl directly influenced **post-structuralism** and **postmodernism**, a more plausible claim would be that the context of phenome-nology, specifically the concern for acquisition of knowledge and meaning, con-siders many of the issues which are still central within contemporary social theory.

POSITIVISM, in its original sense within a social theory framework, referred to a philosophy of scientific inquiry which borrowed principles from the Scientific Revolution of the Renaissance and attempted to use them to perform studies of the social. Initiated by Auguste Comte, who originated the term 'sociology' (the study of the social), orthodox positivists insisted that only observable entities, as experienced directly, were valid entities **epistemologically**. This philosophy was originally framed in opposition to metaphysical and religious approaches, which dominated philosophical thought throughout the Middle Ages. Today, the social theories that may be considered to run counter to positivism are **psychoanalysis** and **postmodernism**. This is due to the problematic desire of positivists to perform observations of phenomena, correlate trends and attempt to construct social laws that would, ideally, work in much the same way as Newtonian laws of physics or thermodynamic laws of chemistry. Members of the **Frankfurt School**, especially Theodor **Adorno**, condemned such an approach as inherently limited to the production of practically meaningless quantified facts that lacked the deeper understanding of human actions essential to social theory.

Émile **Durkheim**'s *Suicide* (1897) exemplifies both the truths of the critiques and the contributions of positivism that dissenters take for granted in contemporary sociological thought. The latter were clearly evident with the dismantling of the biased and unconfirmed supposition that suicide was wholly an individually influenced resolution. In fact, using quantified data, Durkheim showed suicide to be affected by numerous social and non-social structures, from religious faith to hours of sunlight. However, as anti-positivists are quick to note, much of the 'reliable' data that Durkheim depended on were later shown to be faulty, due to their subjective compilation. Essentially, positivists rely on social facts to be accurate to the same degree as scientific facts, which is, indeed, a precarious starting point (Thomas Kuhn has also argued against the scientific method outside of social spheres). Seemingly, social theory is better modelled on quantum physics, with its inherent unpredictability, than on Newtonian physics's **deterministic** framework.

A mediation between orthodox positivists and anti-positivists has seen fruitful benefits for social theory research. Though caution is required in the use of numerical social inquiry, the embrace of an empirically solid theoretical perspective is championed by many social theorists. Truly, only a fine line exists between purely speculative theory and one suited to empirical testing. Yet the debate surrounding positivism has brought necessary attention to the inherent predicament of the contradictory 'social sciences'.

POSTMODERNISM essentially only assumed its eminent position in social theory circles with Jean-François **Lyotard**'s *The Postmodern Condition* (1979), as he infamously declared his 'incredulity towards metanarratives'; yet, for a century before its publication, postmodern notions had been developing, especially within art and architecture. It was in fact an English painter, John Watkins Chapman, who arguably initiated the term's usage to describe art that went beyond Impressionism. The early twentieth century saw various usages of the term, including theological anti-modernists who avowed the **modern** secular world. They claimed that the 'postmodernist' was an individual who adopted a more religious approach to life, as witnessed in the writings of Bernard Iddings Bell. This was quite a positive application compared to that of the celebrated historian Arnold Toynbee, who, in 1939, applied the notion of the postmodern to the period from 1875 until his day. For Toynbee, the 'post-Modern Age of Western history' was signified by cultural decline and worldwide war, and was to be decried in comparison to the modern age it had replaced (that is, the previous four centuries).

For all the discussion of postmodernism in the humanities, it was architecture that revived the notion of postmodernism leading up to its wide adoption in social theory and popular culture. The architectural theorist Charles Jencks was only born in the year that Toynbee made his postmodern proclamation, yet his *Language of Postmodern Architecture* (1977) undoubtedly did more to resurrect the term than anyone beforehand. Jencks argued that modern architecture (in his words 'International Style') had come to dominate the skylines of major cities, as seen in numerous large projects of straight-lined concrete and glass structures. Lacking a connection to the desire of the public, he posited that such modernist forms were alienating, and promoted a postmodernist eclecticism (the mixing of old and new architectural styles was his most enduring influence) that would be more inviting than the sterile forms which had prevailed previously.

Though Lyotard (two years later) did greatly affect the discussion surrounding postmodernism in social theory, theories of **post-structuralism** had been developing over the previous two decades. Post-structuralism indeed shares some similarities with postmodernism in its scepticism of Universalist proclamations, yet the former focuses on radicalizing a **structuralist** framework, whereas postmodernism in contemporary social theory decries the so-called 'Enlightenment project' of cultural growth and technical progress. In this vein, many eminent thinkers are seen as theorists of postmodernity, including Fredric **Jameson**, Zygmunt **Bauman** (especially his work in the 1990s), Richard Rorty and, perhaps most controversially, Jean **Baudrillard**. Grave doubts regarding modernist discourses are common to all such postmodern theorists, yet the perspectives do range from apprehension in Bauman's work, to almost a celebration in the writing of Lyotard.

In analysing the status of postmodernity, as its prominence has faded to some degree over the past decade, it Is vital to note that most theorists believe in a complex fusion of the modern and the postmodern, as eloquently exemplified in Charles Lemert's *Postmodernism is Not What You Think* (1997). Additionally, the focal points of postmodernity differ; for Lyotard, postmodernism can be seen as a generic social condition, whereas for Julia **Kristeva**, Luce Irigaray and Hélène Cixous, the deconstruction of patriarchal essentialisms is most significant (now referred to by some as a postmodern **feminism**). Despite these nuanced and varied approaches, it is the analysis of disintegrating modernist social orders and representations that is shared by most social theorists of postmodernity. Though globalization and **cosmopolitanism** have taken hold as the paradigms of recent social theory, the temptation to move past a postmodern perspective is less sensible now than ever before, as the radicalization of modernism continues to expand unabatedly.

POST-STRUCTURALISM, paradoxically, exists as both as a pejorative stance on and an extension of **structuralism**, though the augmentation of Ferdinand de **Saussure**'s semiotic structural perspective is quite radical. Essentially, poststructuralists argued that their predecessors had falsely posited a meaningful relationship of signifier and signified, notably in the pioneering work of Claude **Lévi-Strauss**. In this analysis of Saussurian linguistics, meaning had a rather universal quality, due to its relational position. Through differentiation, all such signifiers acquired their significance; a formal science of structured meaning could be attained through such an examination.

However, for post-structuralist theorists, this logic ran into a problematic point in the chain of signification. If a signifier simply refers to another signifier, and that signifier to another (orange as opposed to red, red as opposed to bed), finding an ultimate signifier seemed implausible, as it would once more be referential. Jacques **Derrida** referred to this process as a potentially continuous 'play of signification'. Therefore, the ideal of a stable structuralist system of meaning was dismantled, and the search for a centred origin of language was viewed as a fallacious endeavour. Jacques **Lacan**, though also associated with the structuralist movement, broke away from the stability of Saussure as early as 1957 through arguing against the inherent meaning of an interlocked signifier and signified (so too did Roland **Barthes** in his later publications, most notably the 1970 work *S/Z*).

In certain ways, post-structuralism finds common advances to the **postmodernism** of Jean-François **Lyotard**. Both frameworks dismissed universalizing narratives and centred origins (as seen also in the post-structuralist attack by Michel **Foucault** on the original Subject). From this perspective, post-structuralism addressed the predicament of **determinism** in structuralism, as accounting for social change in the latter proved difficult. Yet issues still remain in the former, as Anthony **Giddens** has critiqued post-structuralism for its inability to explain reference. The radicalization of structuralism enhanced the very problem of elucidating on the connection between the signifier and the signified. This has generated difficulties in applying post-structuralism to more traditional issues of social theory as, arguably, Derrida and Lacan initiated a further 'retreat into the code' of Saussurian linguistics. While there were explicit implications with regard to decentred **identities** and cultural discrepancy, the reality of social things is, to some degree, lost within the myriad of deconstructive (in Derrida's sense of the word) practices.

Perhaps the most crucial contribution of post-structuralist thought was the attention it brought to the deficiencies of deterministic and universalizing notions of the self and society. Truly, the approach prescribed by Derrida is difficult and, at times, unsettling. The justification of this difficulty, however, is witnessed in the novel approach to old problems of **epistemology** and, more broadly, the plausibility of a sociological method. Even if one seeks to dismiss the claims of post-structuralism (and, indeed, Giddens has called both structuralism and post-structuralism 'dead traditions of thought'), it is the consideration of their concerns that exemplifies its continued importance.

PSYCHOANALYSIS, as traditionally characterized, may seem out of place in the context of social theory; for many who possess a surface understanding of Sigmund **Freud**'s life and work, it is a distinctly clinical approach to the treatment of psychological disorders. Often referred to as the 'talking cure' (a term coined by the famed initial patient Anna O), psychoanalysis (built by Freud on the methodology of Josef Breuer) ventured a new approach to curing hysterical patients based on the belief that language has a powerful relationship with emotional agony. Though Breuer was credited with the initial conception, it was Freud who theorized extensively on the relationship between the 'talking cure' and repressed desires. By encouraging subjects to speak freely about their past, repudiated memories were roused and suppressed emotions reclaimed. This 'working through' of past painful experiences, especially those from a young age and of a sexual nature, was thought to alleviate the turmoil that raged subconsciously within the patient.

While a considerable percentage of psychoanalysts still operate on this principle, Freud's later writing and the diverse adaptations of a psychoanalytic framework provide a more complete analysis, politically and culturally, of society. Within these fashions, there is an especially social approach to the theory, as opposed to the purely clinical practice. It is through these perspectives that psychoanalysis has come to be influential in a variety of disciplines, including comparative literature, cultural studies, **feminism** and sociology. To understand these applications, it is necessary to delve into Freud's topological and structural divisions of the psyche.

Topologically, a separation of consciousness, preconsciousness and the unconscious was posited. Consciousness consisted of what philosophies of the Enlightenment had focused on, namely the 'self'. However, the latter two categories, especially the unconscious, significantly defected from the notion of a coherent, unified and rationally conceived **identity**. Preconsciousness described the relatively ordinary memories which we might temporarily forget, but which are easily recalled with reminders – the name of a sporting club, what one did over the weekend, and so on. Vital to Freud's theory was the unconscious, whose constitution was based on the suppression and denial of feelings and desires, outlined in his eminent terms: repression, sublimation and defence, among a myriad of others. He theorized that these mechanisms were enacted to rid the mind of our painful memories, yet they were only successful in temporarily suppressing such experiences from consciousness. Indeed, the unconscious manifested in fantasies, dreams, slips of the tongue and other visual and linguistic signs that had never been considered very relevant to the constitution of the self. *The Interpretation of Dreams* (1900) delved into the analysis of such phenomena.

Freud's later structural organization of the psyche, the renowned division of ego, id and superego, introduced his theory of drives to the framework of psychoanalysis. The ego mediates between the id, whose instinctual drives demand immediate satisfaction, and the super-ego, whose restraining norms (passed through the parents and culture) appositionally counter the id. This notion of the split subject, within both topological and drive theories, is essential to the social theoretical component of psychoanalysis. Also vital is the construction of identity in relation to others and its implications, given the social transformations of **modernity** (and **postmodernity**).

This classical framework of the repression in the unconscious and the formation of a split identity was significant for many social theorists, especially **critical theorists** and feminists. More broadly, the different schools of psychoanalytic thought (including, but not limited to, ego psychology, **Lacan**ian theory, object relations theory and Kleinian theory) have impacted social thinking in diverse ways, from defence mechanisms to film theory, from depression and melancholy to motherhood.

Undoubtedly, psychoanalysis is among the more contentious of all perspectives in social theory, especially given its framework, which necessarily transcends the scientific method. Psychologists especially have critiqued the inability to prove the presence of the unconscious or document the experiences of the infant. Also, there is the claim that Freud was misogynistic, though Juliet **Mitchell** persuasively argued for psychoanalysis to be seen as an explanatory framework, not a dogmatic methodology. Essentially, psychoanalysis has been both blessed and cursed by its novel and polarizing approach to identity; it benefits from an intense elicitation of interest, yet it is hindered by misrepresentations that have succeeded in erroneously tainting the grander theoretical perspective. Despite these misconceptions, the nuanced perspective of the complexly emotionally affected individual is owed to psychoanalysis, a framework that has become increasingly relevant within a prompt and intensively multifarious society.

RIGHTS, as a concept, were resurrected and universalized on a large scale by the inception of the United Nations and the idea of 'human' rights in the post-Second World War era, yet it would be severely mistaken to believe that their history extends only over half a century. The vast majority of major ancient religions, cultures and schools of philosophy debated more primitive notions of rights. The Ancient Greeks posited ideas which later transformed into those of natural rights (those that are universal and not culturally relative), as did early texts of Christianity, Confucianism, Islam and Judaism. Though it must be noted that many of these groups ostracized certain subsets of their own peoples (slaves, women, mentally and physically handicapped, amongst others), often with more prejudicial positions taken towards outsiders, the basic ideals they conveyed were influential in the composition of the seminal rights text of the twentieth century, the Universal Declaration of Human Rights (UDHR, 1948).

Additionally, legal and political rights were formally developed through historic (and more secular) documents. England engaged in such a practice as far back as Magna Carta (1215), later enacting the Bill of Rights (1689); the former aimed to limit the rights of the King of England, while the latter concerned the spread of rights to Englishmen. Nearly concurrently, and following their respective civil wars, France's Declaration of the Rights of Man and of the Citizen (1789), and the United States' Bill of Rights (1789; it was composed of the first ten amendments of the United States Constitution) were formulated, lending greater credence to the notion of rights. It cannot be overstated, however, that progress in the formation of such concepts lagged far behind their actual universal adoption, particularly evident in the case of African-Americans and women in the late eighteenth century. Indeed, this remains one of the most significant criticisms of the UDHR and of codified rights more generally in contemporary debates.

For all the popularization of human rights since the atrocities of the Holocaust, which was arguably the catalyst for the renewed interest in rights as such (and the creation of the term 'genocide', among other distinct analytic moves), there have been considerable challenges. Unlike other 'contributory' rights (those that necessitate participation on the part of the individual, as exemplified in citizenship and legal rights), the 'natural' rights of all humans have been declared illusionary, most famously by the nineteenth-century political philosopher Jeremy Bentham, who claimed they were 'nonsense upon stilts'. He believed legal and political rights to be attributable to the real arena of the *polis*, whereas one could not explicitly show a 'human right'. However, arguably, it would be difficult to exercise one's political rights if basic human rights were not met.

As globalization and **cosmopolitanism** become greater issues within social theory, the constitution and relevance of rights continues to be pertinent. The ostensible 'Asian-values' debate concerns the thinking of many Eastern state leaders, who claim that rights have been derived from a Western tradition and are therefore not applicable to their nations' ways of life. Many philosophical dilemmas follow, as claims of Western paternalism are juxtaposed with critiques concerning gross maltreatment (especially of women). This is especially significant in Western Asia, North Africa and parts of South Asia, where both 'honour killings' and female genital mutilation are prevalent. In the former example, males have murdered their female family members for bringing 'dishonour' upon the family; honour killings have even occurred when a female has been raped or seeks a divorce from an abusive husband. The United Nations estimates that over 130 million women have been subjected to female genital mutilation (mostly in Africa), which comprises another source of debate, as most Western countries condemn the act for its brutality, while defenders claim that its cultural heritage dates back to pre-Common Era Egypt.

The academic scrutiny of rights continues to be paramount, especially for those social theorists who are concerned with a potential separation between prescription and action. A predicament follows codification, as rights experts are in consensus that enforcement has been only modestly effective. Social theory undoubtedly plays a significant role in the analysis of the language of legislation versus its embodied praxis. Indeed, the controversies that rage on in rights **discourse**s are prevalent in comparable debates within **Marxism**, **post-structuralism** and **postmodernism**.

Ferdinand de **SAUSSURE**, the pioneer of the structuralist turn in linguistics, was born in Geneva in 1857, one year before Emilé **Durkheim** and one year after Sigmund **Freud**. His father was an eminent naturalist, and this theme resonated throughout his family, as there was a tradition of successes in the fields of the natural sciences. A clearly intelligent child, by the age of 15 Saussure had mastered his fifth language, Greek, in addition to Latin and the more commonly taught languages in Switzerland, namely French, German and English (in addition to studying Sanskrit). A family friend and philologist, Adolphe Pictet, was a significant influence in these early years, and it was for Pictet that the youthful Saussure wrote 'Essay on Languages', in which he attempted to argue from an extreme reductionist perspective that all languages were commonly based in a system of two or three basic consonants.

Though he showed such promise in linguistics, due to his family's preferences Saussure enrolled in 1875 at the University of Geneva to study physics and chemistry. However, the philology could not be so easily wrestled from him, and after a year (in which he managed to follow courses on Greek and Latin grammar in addition to his natural science courses), he finally convinced his parents to allow him to study Indo-European languages at the University of Leipzig. This was a fortuitous move, as Pictet could never have matched the intellectual environment that had developed around linguistics at Leipzig. Yet Saussure was surely not out of place; indeed, a professor there discovered what has been termed the 'law of *nasal sonans*', which Saussure himself had postulated years earlier, although he had rejected the idea since it conflicted with eminent theories of the time. In 1878, while spending time in Berlin, he finished his thesis entitled *Memoir on the Primitive System of Vowels in Indo-European Languages*, an acclaimed work among contemporary linguists. In focusing on methodological problems, Saussure showed his prowess for tackling fundamental issues in philology, and received considerable and warranted admiration.

After Germany, Saussure moved to Paris to teach Sanskrit, Gothic and Old High German, later expanding to a more general course on Indo-European philology. Despite being nominated by his older colleagues and receiving a prestigious teaching award, in 1891 he was offered a professorship at the University of Geneva and returned there. Though he married and started a family in Switzerland, Saussure became more reserved and wrote less, publishing no further works. Feeling frustrated by a need to change the terminology to describe the thought process of linguists, he posited a solution to combat this problem in a letter to an editor. Unfortunately, the book would not be written in his lifetime, and his most influential work, *Course in General Linguistics* (1916, henceforth *CGL*), was published by former students three years after his death.

Unlike Herbert **Mead**, whose posthumous collections were based on meticulous notes, Saussure kept sparse records and his courses morphed considerably over the years; *CGL* is actually a synthesis of these diverse and meagre sources. Despite the precariousness of this synthesis, *CGL* made Saussure the most renowned linguist of his time, as many refer to him as the father of twentieth-century linguistics. Additionally, his ideas had an influence far beyond linguistics: many social theorists found inspiration in a framework of language that displaced individuals from the focus, instead concentrating on signs as the product of structures and systems of difference,. From this radical conjecture, a substantial lineage is evident, most formally embodied in **structuralism** (see Roland **Barthes** and Claude **Lévi-Strauss**), **post-structuralism** (see Jacques **Derrida** and Julia **Kristeva**) and, more broadly, in cultural theory.

SEMIOTICS, while originally used to refer specifically to a branch of medical science involving interpretation of signs, broadened within **modernity** to constitute a more general study of signs and their relations to systemic processes. Yet by no means was the investigation of sign systems limited to the modern epoch, as indeed a more basic semiology (as later termed by Ferdinand de **Saussure**) was a focal point for much of Western philosophy, especially evidenced in the writings of Plato and Aristotle; Umberto Eco has even argued that a concern for sign systems is perceptible in the work of the vast majority of major theorists. As far as social theorists are concerned, however, Saussure's formalization of structural linguistics was the vital analytic move that catapulted an intrigue into the sign as a focal point of scholarship.

For Saussure, the sign is composed of two distinct elements, namely the signifier and the signified. The former refers to the object of concern (writing, an object, a sound), while the latter refers to the concept attached to a given object. He stated that, though distinct, the signifier and signified could be metaphorically envisioned as two sides of a piece of paper, inextricably attached. Importantly for Saussure, this attachment was arbitrary; only through relations to other signs was any sense of reference built. The meaning of 'hot' may only be understood in its relation to 'cold' as, without the latter, the former would not be conceivable. Nearly simultaneously (though independently), Charles Peirce, the founder of pragmatism, developed a separate semiology. He posited a triadic relation of an object, its sign and an interpreter of this relation. Both Saussure and Peirce's theories were inherently **structural** and inspired new modes of interpreting social theory, notably the **structuralist** movement in the case of Saussure.

Roland **Barthes**'s *Mythologies* (1957) was a popularized illustration of the importance of a semiological investigation, as the implications of his analysis bore significant findings for society as a whole. Though some Saussurian sign systems are quite clear and simple (a lemon, in most cultures, would signify little more than a sour fruit), other signifiers are grandly complex (language as a prime example) and are therefore apt to have different levels of signification. This was the basis of the myths Barthes identified, whose connotations were often ominous for certain groups, as was the case in his analysis of a magazine cover with a Black solider hoisting a French flag.

Though **postmodernity** and **post-structuralism** have significantly challenged traditional semiology, to some extent, their focus remains the same. As was the case before Saussure, social theory continues to concentrate on communication, especially less overt forms. Though signification has been muddled in contemporary society, the necessity to study sign systems continues unabated.

Georg **SIMMEL**, the least well-known of the canonical social theorists and originators of sociology (**Marx**, **Weber** and **Durkheim**), was born in the heart of Berlin in 1858, the youngest of seven children. His father was a convert to Christianity from Judaism and ran a successful business, though he died when Simmel was quite young. A family friend, who owned a music publishing house, became his guardian; the man's wealth guaranteed Simmel the opportunity of an academic life and, after graduation from the local Gymnasium, he attended the University of Berlin to study history and philosophy. In 1881, he was awarded a doctorate for an essay on Kant's theory of matter, and in 1885 he became a lecturer, though it was a position in which the salary was solely contingent on student fees, with no remuneration from the university (*Privatdozent*). It would be 15 years before he would be made an associate professor, and another 14 before finally being instated as a full professor at the University of Strasbourg, only four years before his death. Though he never practised Judaism, it is highly likely that a lingering anti-Semitism played a role in the rejection of Simmel from academic culture, as his career progression did not mirror the fulsome praise he received as a lecturer and writer. Luckily, many important individuals of his time did warmly regard his company, including Weber and Edmund Husserl, and a few particularly bright students came from his classes, including Georg Lukács and Ernst Block.

Simmel's work is more difficult to systemize and find commonalities in than many of his contemporaries, although this is a notion he himself rejected. In part this had to do with the nature of his work; he wrote prodigiously so, while he published over 20 books, they were dwarfed by the hundreds of articles and short essays that have brought him as much, if not more fame. One of the most widely read today was his paper entitled 'The Metropolis and Mental Life' (1903), which greatly influenced Robert Park and the **Chicago School**, though it was not well-received on its publication. It was delivered at the Dresden city exhibition, and the organizers were upset by Simmel's unenthusiastic view of cities. He was not commenting negatively, but provided a cautionary analysis of the fundamental changes of mechanization and their effects on mindsets of individuals.

In his many other works, Simmel wrote on culture and **modernity**, as well as method, forms and **epistemology**. His perspective was distinctive in moving away from the purely macro towards a more nuanced view of the individual as part of the larger totality. He was quite intrigued by the 'impulse of sociability', especially as it encouraged a mediated level of individuality (too much individuality, he believed, ruined the nature of the social). Simmel proposed it was impossible to understand the full scope of an entity in itself, instead preferring to analyse a fully detailed fragment to shed light on its grander portion. This was particularly evident in two concepts of his better known works: those of the stranger and of money. In both cases, the outsider academic, whose prominence and intellect were ignored time and time again by administrators at Berlin, illustrates the precariousness of our co-operation; we must trust the stranger and do business with them in order to go about our own lives, and yet the taint of the monetary transaction devalues the individual self (especially in the case of the middling stranger). This seemingly minor aspect of the social for Simmel told a much greater story of the tragedy of culture, and its pathological nature.

Simmel died in 1918 of liver cancer, having only attained his place in academic culture four years previously. This is not to say that he did not participate in the intellectual community of Berlin, as he attended many events, had important friends and was quite a popular lecturer himself. Yet this lack of formal recognition bears a particular perspective on his work; at times, his writings presented an idyllic view of human relationships. Though, if one seeks the cautionary and demoralizing perspective of culture and society within modernity, there are plenty of instances of this in his social theory as well. This balance of grand potential and an unkind reality was a lesson Simmel learned firsthand, and one which remains relevant for contemporary social theory.

STRUCTURALISM encompasses a wide and complex stream of ideas that began to dominate many circles of social theory in the late 1950s and 1960s, primarily concentrated in France. Its origins can be found in an attempt to extend the radicalized principles of linguistics that had come about at the turn of the twentieth century. For most philological thought, the focus tended to be on a historical description of languages, including vocabulary and syntax, and the development of phonemes, or elementary sounds of language, across different areas. Linguists began to focus on the **structure** of those elementary sounds, instead of tracing their progress, positing fundamental systems to the framework of communication. Though phonemes can have many different combinations, speakers tend to focus on a select few rather than the maximum possible, creating a structure of acceptable groupings; hence, language is seen as carrying fundamental rules that can be studied and analysed. A clear relation to **Saussure** is evident, with his notion of signifier and signified structuring meaning.

These concepts were extended to the study of social institutions, thereafter claimed to be social structures. The combinations that constitute the rules of family, politics, education and other fundamental arrangers of life are seen to be part of the rules of society, and not randomly constituted. Though social reality may vary, and indeed its appearance seems to change significantly, the argument that structuralists make is that these are surface variations, while deeper structural institutions remain.

From this starting point, structuralism saw many different applications, from the structural anthropology of Claude **Lévi-Strauss**'s binary oppositions, to the structural Marxism of Louis **Althusser**'s modes of production, to Michel **Foucault**'s earlier historical structuralism and, among many more, Jacques **Lacan**'s structural approach to **psychoanalysis**. In all of these varied applications, the focus is shifted from distinct entities to the larger structured relationships between institutions. Another commonality is the notion that the 'givens' of society, what seems normal and natural, are really the result of an underlying structure that can be identified, as Roland **Barthes** perfectly illustrated in *Mythologies*. Finally, most structuralists tend to identify individuals as subject to these structures, not affording them much intentional **agency** beyond what the solidified structures allow.

While structuralism had many adherents, a number of its originators found the theory to contain severe limitations, specifically its claim of universal meaning of structures as implied by the symbolism of Saussurian linguistics. Contextual meaning and more focus on relational structures triggered a backlash against structuralism, resulting in the **post-structuralist** movement, as exemplified especially in the work of Jacques **Derrida**.

STRUCTURE may be differentiated from **structuralism** in its origins and broader encapsulation of the recurring patterning of behaviour and action; this delineation is often clarified by the inclusion of 'social' structure. While the focus of structuralists tended to be on language, at first within a **Saussurian** framework of linguistics and later within Michel **Foucault**'s notion of **discourse**, social structures include all institutions that organize individuals into larger social facts (in the **Durkheimian** sense). From this perspective, schools, political parties, religious organizations and workplaces are seen, among other similar (though usually less influential) groupings as social structures, in that their very organization structures those that are imbued with their practices.

The idea of structure was heavily influenced by the **functionalist** sociology of the late nineteenth century, especially sociobiological metaphors. The application of organic theories to society invoked a framework from which the cell is structured by its various components (mitochondria, cytoplasm, nucleus and so on) that follow direct instructions in order to interact and allow for a functioning whole. Instead of DNA, however, society prescribed norms through culture, though the effect was similar; human actors were seen as conditioned by their functional arrangement, institutionalized by virtue of overwhelming expectations. though vitally, this metaphor was limited in its full application, as social structures are posited as not directly observable; the actions and behaviours of the individual institutionalized actors are visible, but these are a consequence, and should not be equated as directly reducible to the structures themselves.

Both social structure and structuralism are usually posited as dichotomously juxtaposed with **agency**, though social theorists in the late twentieth century, notably Anthony **Giddens** and Pierre **Bourdieu**, worked to explicate the nuanced relation between structure and agency. Both Giddens's theory of structuration, in which social practices mediate between structures and actions, and Bourdieu's theory of fields and *habitus*, in which reproduction of social approaches is constituted through an embodiment of acquired dispositions, illustrated how the orthodox view of social structures is quite deficient, from both an ontological and a practical perspective. The experience of society seemingly involves choice on the part of the individual, which is quite clearly constricted to some degree, but is choice, nonetheless. Additionally, the observation of rapid social change seemingly contradicts the functionalist accounts of embedded social structures. Yet, quite clearly, institutions still structure society to a larger degree than many care to believe. The **Marxist** and **Freudian** influenced notion of false consciousness (and false needs, as Herbert **Marcuse** argued) explicate the process by which our seemingly in-control psyches might be subtly manipulated, to the point where our most private thoughts are dictated by structural processes. In an age of **postmodern** consumption, where Zygmunt **Bauman** has convincingly posited rampant consumerism as a fundamental (and detrimental) aspect of society, the themes of functional structure have arguably intensified under late capitalism.

Paul **VIRILIO**, a provoking and important contemporary social and cultural theorist of technology, space and subjectivity, was born in Paris in 1932. He was raised in Brittany and had an unavoidable confrontation with the Second World War; indeed, he has been noted for keeping a rock from Hiroshima on his desk. In an interview, he stated, 'War was my university. Everything has proceeded from there', and this certainly did not end with the 1940s, as he was conscripted during the Algerian war of independence. Afterwards, Virilio conducted an inquiry into the military organization of space, particularly the Atlantic Wall (the line of bunkers developed along the coast of France by the Nazis to combat the Allied forces). Influenced by Maurice **Merleau-Ponty**, with whom he studied at the Sorbonne in the 1950s, Virilio had diverse interests, from Einstein's theory of relativity to his personal working relationships with renowned French painters and artists.

However, it was the events of 1968 which would alter his career most significantly, in common with so many other French academics of this period. His involvement in the protests would lead to a position as professor in 1969 and director in 1975 with the Paris based École Special d'Architecture. Though he wrote prodigiously from this period on, Virilio's work was recognized outside France primarily only in the 1990s. His influence has been significant since translations became available, especially the earlier writings, whose themes are claimed by some critics to have been reused in his later works.

In *Speed and Politics* (translated into English in 1986), Virilio explicates the argument that technology, specifically with regard to communications and transportation, profoundly and detrimentally affects culture and politics. Using what he termed the 'dromological' analysis (*dromos* were ancient Greek racecourses, but also refers to a journey generally), Virilio proclaimed speed to be a primary aspect of sociality. While others had made similar pronouncements decades before (such as Filipo Marinetti, founder of the 'Futurist' movement, and, more contemporary to Virilio, Marshall McLuhan, who coined the phrases 'global village' and 'the medium is the message'), what differentiated Virilio was his gloominess; instead of seeing greater freedom in such advances, he saw a loss of reference for the subject in the complexity and rapidness of **modernity**. Ever affected by his childhood experience of war, the metaphors of speed found a firm foundation in Virilio's perspective, as he declared, 'today, speed is war, the last war'.

In numerous subsequent works, most significantly *War and Cinema* (translated into English in 1989), *The Lost Dimension* (translated into English in 1991) and *The Vision Machine* (translated into English in 1994), these themes are further developed, although arguably not significantly elaborated on. Critics of his apocalyptic visions of technocratic disasters aside, more sympathetic analytical readers have suggested that the most significant problem with Virilio's work may be its repetitiveness. Arguably, some of the same contentions regarding increased speed and its ominous possibilities have been rehashed over the past three decades. Nevertheless, theories revolving around the transformation of time and space, as technology brings its force to bear on subjectivity, are indeed topics worthy of any amount of attention.

Karl Emil Maximilian **WEBER**, an essential member of classical sociological thought, was born in 1864 in the town of Erfurt, Thuringia, the eldest of eight children. His father, Max Weber Snr, a lawyer and later a German politician, was from a family of early capitalist tradespeople in textiles. His mother, Helene Fallenstein-Weber, was highly educated in comparison to other women of her era, mainly due to the benefit of coming from a family of teachers (she was taught by her father). They were both Protestant, but of quite different persuasions, a conflict which would be intensified by tragedy and later greatly affect Weber's life.

Early childhood was a struggle for Weber as, at two years old, he suffered from meningitis. It is hypothesized that this bout of illness had adverse effects on his health throughout the following decades. Despite his obviously precocious nature (he read vastly, including Spinoza, Kant and an entire 40-volume set of Goethe), primary education did not see him flourish. There was also the unfortunate death of his younger sister in 1876 which caused a rift between his parents – Max Weber Snr was by now a member of parliament and seemed to recover more quickly than the distraught Helene, who was more reserved.

Weber was clearly bored with the rudimentary level of his academic situation. This had two distinct results. First, for a time in his teens, he left Berlin to attend boarding school in Heidelberg, where the shy boy attempted to negotiate the transition into a more confident man; this was exemplified by a slight rebelliousness and, consequently, an uninterested Weber did not sincerely engage with his studies. Afterwards, however (probably due to his mother's austere influence), Weber settled down to what would be prolific career. His boredom was no longer channelled into childish activities, but rather focused on immense projects and incredibly significant publications. These works helped to form, along with those of **Durkheim** and **Marx**, the canon of early sociology.

Still living at home, in 1889 Weber completed his dissertation under Levin Goldschmidt on the theory of the state (*Staatswissenshaft*), focusing primarily on economic and legal history-based work of Italian trade communities. Within three years, he had completed his habilitation and had attained a law degree, achieving a position as lecturer in Roman and commercial law. However, within the same time frame, his nearly 900-page study of agricultural workers in Prussian provinces and its legislative implications signalled a switch in focus from jurisprudence to political economy. Praised lavishly by agrarian historians, the work and a later follow-up vaulted Weber to much more significant standing in German academic life.

Despite these successes, 1897 was a crucially difficult year in his life. Tensions grew between Weber and his father culminating in an argument following which the two would never be reconciled, as Max Snr died a month later. Weber had been genuinely upset with his father, who was clearly quite authoritarian and, at times, preposterously controlling of his wife, Helene; however, the failure to resolve the situation resulted in a mixture of grief and guilt that was extremely hard for Weber to bear. Although many accounts of the two decades following attribute a subsequent mental illness to these events, the actual circumstances are more complex. It is true that Weber had numerous nervous and mental breakdowns, due in part to an enormous workload, a complicated marriage and other health-related problems. Nevertheless, it should be noted that he published yearly from 1889 to 1920 (except 1901). The twentieth century saw Weber formally declare himself a sociologist, while he expanded from law and the economy to cover a wide range of topics, producing numerous seminal works and terms that have ever since had a profound influence on social theory.

Of these works, the most enduring and controversial was his investigation into the roots of capitalism, *The Protestant Ethic and the Spirit of Capitalism* (1905). His thesis of supposing Protestantism as a potential catalyst was based on both economic numerical analysis and more theoretical arguments concerning spiritual dispositions. Travelling to the United States in 1903 had provided him with the opportunity to observe both Protestant sects and the American political process at first hand, which stimulated Weber to think about the **modernizing** effects of capitalism. His later multi-volume epic *Economy and Society* would continue along similar themes in a more robust manner, a division he probably first identified within his own family (Weber categorized his grandfather as an old-world capitalist and his uncle as a new-world capitalist). Religion also was not only of economic interest, as in 1916 and 1917 he published studies of Hinduism, Buddhism and Judaism.

However, arguably his greatest contribution to contemporary social theory can be seen in the terms which we today espouse frequently: rationality, bureaucracy, work ethic, charisma and ideal type, among numerous others, were all extensively addressed, utilized and popularized by Weber. While no political movement began in Weber's name (unlike Marxism with Marx), Weber was thoroughly political and had an immense influence on state politics. Intriguingly, he did so while simultaneously identifying the power of individualism within such a structure (as opposed to Marx and Durkheim). Despite his premature death of pneumonia in 1920, Weber must be considered among the most prodigious social theorists of all time.

BIBLIOGRAPHY

Adam, B. (1996) 'Re-vision: the centrality of time for an ecological social science perspective', in S. Lash, B. Szerszynski and B. Wynne (eds), *Risk, Environment and Modernity*, London: Sage.

Adams, M. (2007) *Self and Social Change*, London: Sage.

Adkins, L. (2002) *Revisions: Gender and Sexuality in Late Modernity*, Philadelphia: Open University Press.

Adorno, T. and Bernstein, J.M. (2001) *The Culture Industry: Selected Essays on Mass Culture*, London: Routledge.

Adorno, T. and Horkheimer, M. (2002) [1944] *Dialectic of Enlightenment: Philosophical Fragments*, Stanford, CA: Stanford University Press.

Agger, B. (1992) *The Discourse of Domination: From the Frankfurt School to Postmodernism*, Evanston, IL: Northwestern University Press.

Alcoff, L. (2006) *Visible Identities: Race, Gender, and the Self*, New York: Oxford University Press.

Alcoff, L., Hames-García, M., Mohanty, P. and Moya, P. (eds) (2006) [2000] *Identity Politics Reconsidered*, New York: Palgrave Macmillan.

Alexander, J. (ed.) (1990) *Durkheimian Sociology: Cultural Studies*, Cambridge: Cambridge University Press

—— (2003) *The Meanings of Social Life: A Cultural Sociology*, New York: Oxford.

—— (2004) 'From the Depths of Despair: Performance, Counterperformance, and "September 11"', *Sociological Theory*, 22(1): 88–105.

Althusser, L. (1971) *Lenin and Philosophy and Other Essays*, London: New Left Books.

Ameli, S.R. (2002) *Globalization, Americanization and British Muslim Identity*, London: ICAS.

Anderson, B. (1983) *Imagined Communities: Reflections on the Origin and Spread of Nationalism*, London: Verso.

Anzaldúa, G. (1987) *Borderlands: The New Mestiza = La Frontera*, San Francisco, CA: Spinsters/Aunt Lute.

Appiah, K.A. (1998) 'Cosmopolitan patriots', in P. Cheah and B. Robbins (eds), *Cosmopolitics*, Minneapolis: University of Minnesota Press.

—— (2006) *Cosmopolitanism: Ethics in a World of Strangers*, New York: W.W. Norton.

Archer, M. (1982) 'Morphogenesis vs. structuration', *British Journal of Sociology*, 33: 455–83.

—— (1990) 'Human agency and social structure', in J. Clark, C. Modgil and S. Modgil (eds), *Anthony Giddens: Consensus and Controversy*, New York: Falmer.

Arendt, H. (1951) *The Origins of Totalitarianism*, New York: Harcourt Brace.

Ariès, P. (1983) *The Hour of our Death*, trans. by H. Weaver, Harmondsworth: Penguin.

Aristotle (1908) *Nicomachean Ethics*, Oxford: Clarendon Press.

Arnold, K.R. (2004) *Homelessness, Citizenship, Identity: The Uncanniness of Late Modernity*, Albany, NY: SUNY Press.

Bakhtin, M. (1981) *The Dialogic Imagination*, Austin: University of Texas Press.
Barbalet, J.M. (1988) *Citizenship*, Milton Keynes: Open University Press.
Barthes, R. (1968) [1953] *Elements of Semiology*, New York: Hill and Wang.
—— (1972) [1957] *Mythologies*, New York: Hill and Wang.
—— (1975) *The Pleasure of the Text*, London: Cape.
Bartky, S.L. (1990) *Femininity and Domination: Studies in the Phenomenology of Oppression*, New York: Routledge.
Baudrillard, J. (1983) *Simulations*, New York: Semiotext(e).
—— (1988) *America*, New York: Verso.
—— (1988) *Jean Baudrillard: Selected Writings*, M. Poster (ed.), Stanford, CA: Stanford University Press.
—— (1988) 'Simulacra and simulation', in Mark Poster (ed.), *Jean Baudrillard: Selected Writings*, Stanford, CA: Stanford University Press.
—— (1990) *Fatal Strategies*, London: Pluto.
—— (1990) *Seduction*, New York: St Martin's Press.
—— (1994) *Simulacra and Simulation*, Ann Arbor, MI: University of Michigan Press.
—— (1998) 'Ecstasy of communication', in H. Foster (ed.), *The Anti-Aesthetic: Essays on Postmodern Culture*, New York: The New Press.
—— (2002) *The Spirit of Terrorism and Other Essays*, London: Verso.
—— (2007) *In the Shadow of the Silent Majorities, or, the End of the Social*, Cambridge, MA: MIT Press.
Bauman, Z. (2000) *Liquid Modernity*, Cambridge: Polity Press.
—— (2001) *The Individualized Society*, Cambridge: Polity Press.
—— (2003) *Wasted Lives: Modernity and Its Outcasts*, Cambridge: Polity Press.
—— (2005) *Liquid Life*, Cambridge: Polity Press.
Beasley, C. (2005) *Gender and Sexuality: Critical Theories, Critical Thinkers*, London: Sage.
Beauvoir, S. de (1989) [1949] *The Second Sex*, New York: Vintage.
Beck, U. (2000) 'The cosmopolitan perspective: the sociology of the second modernity', *Sociology*, 51(1): 79–106.
—— (2000) *What is Globalisation?*, Cambridge: Polity Press.
—— (2006) *Cosmopolitan Vision*, Cambridge: Polity Press.
Beck, U. and Beck-Gernsheim, E. (2002) *Individualization: Institutionalized Individualism and Its Social and Political Consequences*, London: Sage.
Beck, U., Giddens, A. and Lash, S. (1994) *Reflexive Modernisation: Politics, Tradition and Aesthetics in the Modern Social Order*, Stanford, CA: Stanford University Press.
Bell, D. (1973) *The Coming of Post-Industrial Society*, New York: Basic Books.
Bellah, R.N., Madsen, R., Sullivan, W.M., Swidler, A. and Tipton, S.M. (1985) *Habits of the Heart: Individualism and Commitment in American Life*, Berkeley, CA: University of California Press.
Bendelow, G. and Williams, S. (1995) 'Pain and mind–body dualism: a sociological approach', *Body and Society*, 1(2): 83–103.
Benhabib, S. (1992) *Situating the Self: Gender, Community, and Postmodernism in Contemporary Ethics*, New York: Routledge.
—— (1995) *Feminist Contentions: A Philosophical Exchange*, New York: Routledge.
Benjamin, J. (1988) *The Bonds of Love: Psychoanalysis, Feminism, and the Problem of Domination*, New York: Pantheon Books.
Best, S. and Kellner, D. (1991) *Postmodern Theory: Critical Interrogations*, Basingstoke: Macmillan.
Beveridge, W.H. (1944) *Full Employment in a Free Society*, London: Allen & Unwin.
Bhabha, H.K. (2004) *The Location of Culture*, New York: Routledge.

Black, P. (2004) *The Beauty Industry: Gender, Culture, Pleasure*, New York: Routledge.

Blaikie, A., Hepworth, M., Holmes, M., Howson, A. and Inglis, D. (2003) 'The sociology of the body: genesis, development and futures', in A. Blaikie, M. Hepworth, M. Holmes, A. Howson, D. Inglis and S. Sartain (eds), *The Body: Critical Concepts in Sociology*, London: Routledge.

Blumer, H. (1986) [1969] *Symbolic Interactionism*, Berkeley, CA: University of California Press.

Boltanski, L. (1999) *Distant Suffering: Morality, Media and Politics*, Cambridge: Cambridge University Press.

Bordo, S. (1987) 'The Cartesian masculinization of thought', in S. Harding and J. O'Barr (eds), *Sex and Scientific Inquiry*, Chicago, IL: University of Chicago Press.

—— (1993) *Unbearable Weight: Feminism, Western Culture and the Body*, Berkeley, CA: University of California Press.

Borges, J., in Alexander Coleman (ed.) (1999) [1964] *Selected Poems*, New York: Viking.

Boudon, R. (1971) *Uses of Structuralism*, trans. by Michalina Vaughan, London: Heinemann.

Bourdieu, P. (1977) [1972] *Outline of a Theory of Practice*, Cambridge: Cambridge University Press.

—— (1984) *Distinction: A Social Critique of the Judgment of Taste*, London: Routledge.

—— (1988) [1984] *Homo Academicus*, Cambridge: Polity Press.

—— (1990 [1987]) *In Other Words: Essays Toward a Reflective Sociology*, Stanford, CA: Stanford University Press.

—— (1991) *Language and Symbolic Power*, Cambridge: Polity Press.

—— (1993) *The Field of Cultural Production*, Cambridge: Polity Press.

—— (1995) *The Rules of Art: Genesis and Structure of the Literary Field*, Stanford, CA: Stanford University Press.

—— (1996a) *On Television and Journalism*, London: Pluto Press.

—— (1996b) *The State Nobility: Elite Schools in the Field of Power*, Cambridge: Polity Press.

—— (2000) *Weight of the World: Social Suffering in Contemporary Society*, Stanford, CA: Stanford University Press.

Bourdieu, P. and Wacquant, L.J.D. (1992) *An Invitation to Reflexive Sociology*, Chicago, IL: University of Chicago Press.

Braidotti, R. (2001) *Metamorphoses: Towards a Materialist Theory of Becoming*, Cambridge: Polity.

Buckingham, D. (2000) *The Making of Citizens*, London: Routledge.

Buckman, G. (2004) *Globalization: Tame It or Scrap It?*, London: Zed Books.

Burkitt, I. (1997) 'Social relationships and emotions', *Sociology*, 31(1): 37–55.

—— (2008) *Social Selves: Theories of Self and Society*, Thousand Oaks, CA: Sage.

Butler, J. (1990) *Gender Trouble: Feminism and the Subversion of Identity*, London: Routledge.

—— (2004) *Undoing Gender*, London: Routledge.

Butler, J. and Scott, J.W. (1992) *Feminists Theorize the Political*, New York: Routledge.

Calhoun, C. (2003) '"Belonging" in the cosmopolitan imaginary', *Ethnicities*, 3(4): 531–68.

Campbell, C. (1995) *The Romantic Ethic and the Spirit of Modern Consumerism*, Oxford: Blackwell.

Castells, M. (2001) *The Internet Galaxy: Reflections on the Internet, Business, and Society*, Oxford: Oxford University Press.

—— (2006) *The Rise of the Network Society*, Oxford: Blackwell.

—— (2007) 'Communication, power and counter-power in the network society', *International Journal of Communication*, 1: 238–66.

Castells, M., Fernandez-Ardevol, M., Linchuan Qiu, J. and Sey, A. (2007) *Mobile Communication and Society: A Global Perspective*, Cambridge, MA: MIT Press.

Césaire, A. (1972) *Discourse on Colonialism*, New York: MR.

Chandler, D. (2002) *From Kosovo to Kabul: Human Rights and International Intervention*, London: Pluto.

Charlesworth, S.J. (2000) *A Phenomenology of Working Class Experience*, Cambridge: Cambridge University Press.

Chodorow, N. (1978) *The Reproduction of Mothering: Psychoanalysis and the Sociology of Gender*, Berkeley, CA: University of California Press.

Chouliaraki, L. (2006) 'The aestheticization of suffering on television', *Visual Communication*, 5(3): 261–85.

Clarke, S. (1981) *The Foundations of Structuralism*, Brighton Sussex: Harvester.

Clifford, J. (1989) 'Notes on travel and theory', *Inscriptions*, 5: 177–88.

Cohen, S. (2001) *States of Denial: Knowing About Atrocities and Suffering*, Cambridge: Polity Press.

Coleman, J. (1995) [1990] *Foundations of Social Theory*, Cambridge, MA: Belknap Press.

Connell, R.W. (1995) *Masculinities*, Sydney: Allen & Unwin.

Cook, G. (1993) *George Herbert Mead*, Champaign, IL: University of Illinois Press.

Cooley, C. (1964) [1902] *Human Nature and Social Order*, New York: Schocken Books.

Cooper, A.J. (1988) [1892] *A Voice from the South*, New York: Oxford University Press.

Coser, L. (1977) *Masters of Sociological Thought*, New York: Harcourt Brace.

Cowen, T. (2002) *Creative Destruction*, Princeton, NJ: Princeton University Press.

Cremin, C.S. (2005) 'Profiling the personal: configuration of teenage biographies to employ-ment norms', *Sociology*, 39(2): 315–32.

Crook, S. (1991) *Modernist Radicalism and Its Aftermath: Foundationalism and Anti-foundationalism in Radical Social Theory*, London: Routledge.

Crossley N. (2004) 'Fat is a sociological issue: obesity rates in late modern, "body-conscious" societies', *Social Theory & Health*, 2(3): 222–53.

Dahlgren, P. (2000) 'The internet and the democratization of civic culture', *Political Communication*, 17: 335–40.

Dallmayr, F.R. (1981) *Twilight of Subjectivity: Contributions to a Post-Individualist Theory of Politics*, Amherst, MA: University of Massachusetts Press.

Darwin, C. (2001 [1859]) *On the Origin of Species*, Cambridge, MA: Harvard University Press.

Davis, K. (2002) '"A dubious equality": men, women and cosmetic surgery', *Body and Society*, 8(1): 49–65.

Dean, M. (1999) *Governmentality: Power and Rule in Modern Society*, London: Sage.

Debord, G. (1994) *The Society of the Spectacle*, New York: Zone Books.

—— (1998) *Comments on the Society of the Spectacle*, London: Verso.

Derrida, J. (1973) [1967] *Speech and Phenomena and Other Essays on Husserl's Theory of Signs*, trans. by D.B. Allison, Evanston, IL: Northwestern University Press.

—— (1976) [1967] *Of Grammatology*, trans. by G.C. Spivak, Baltimore, MD: Johns Hopkins University Press.

—— (1978) 'Structure, sign and play in the discourse of human sciences', in *Writing and Difference*, trans. by A. Bass, London: Routledge.

—— (1978) *Writing and Difference*, trans. by Alan Bass, London: Routledge.

—— (1981) [1972] *Positions*, trans. by A. Bass, Chicago, IL: University of Chicago Press.

Desai, P. (2006) *Conversations on Russia: Reform from Yeltsin to Putin*, Oxford: Oxford University Press.

307

Devine, F. (2005) *Rethinking Class: Culture, Identities and Lifestyles*, New York: Palgrave Macmillan.

Dews, P. (1987) *Logics of Disintegration*, London: Verso.

Diamond, I. and Quinby, L. (1988) *Feminism & Foucault: Reflections on Resistance*, Boston, MA: Northeastern University Press.

Dinnerstein, D. (1976) *The Mermaid and the Minotaur: Sexual Arrangements and Human Malaise*, New York: Harper & Row.

Douglas, M. (1966) *Purity and Danger*, London: Routledge and Kegan Paul.

Douglas, M. and Isherwood, B. (1980) *The World of Goods: Towards an Anthropology of Consumption*, Harmondsworth: Penguin.

Douglas, M. and Wildavsky, A. (1982) *Risk and Culture*, Berkeley, CA: University of California Press.

Downing, J.D.H. (2003) 'Audiences and readers of alternative media: the absent lure of the virtually unknown', *Media, Culture and Society*, 25: 625–45.

Du Bois, W.E.B. (1989) [1903] *The Souls of Black Folk*, New York: Bantam.

Du Gay, P. (1996) *Consumption and Identity at Work*, London: Sage.

Durkheim, E. (1951) *Suicide: A Study in Sociology*, Glencoe, IL: Free Press.

—— (1964) *The Division of Labour in Society*, trans. by W.D. Halls, London: Macmillan.

—— (1969a) 'Individualism and the intellectuals', *Political Studies*, 17: 14–30.

—— (1969b) 'Deux lois de "évolution pénale"', *Journal Sociologique*, 244–73.

—— (1969c) 'La prohibition de l'inceste et ses origines', *Journal Sociologique*, 37–101.

—— (1973) *On Morality and Society: Selected Writings*, Chicago, IL: University of Chicago Press.

—— (1976) [1912] *The Elementary Forms of Religious Life*, trans. by J.W. Swain (2nd edition), London: Routledge.

—— (1984) [1893] *The Division of Labour in Society*, trans. by W.D. Halls, New York: Macmillan.

Elias, N. (1985) *The Loneliness of the Dying*, Oxford: Basil Blackwell.

—— (2000) [1939] *The Civilizing Process: Sociogenetic and Psychogenetic Investigations*, Oxford: Blackwell.

Elliott, A. (1992) *Social Theory and Psychoanalysis in Transition: Self and Society from Freud to Kristeva*, Oxford: Blackwell.

—— (2001) *Concepts of the Self*, Cambridge: Polity.

—— (2008) *Making the Cut*, London: Reaktion.

Ellis, H. (1898–1928) *Studies in the Psychology of Sex* (7 vols), Philadelphia: F.A. Davis.

Engels, F. (1958) [1845] *The Condition of the Working Class in England*, Stanford, CA: Stanford University Press.

Evans, M. (2004) *Killing Thinking: The Death of the Universities*, London: Continuum.

Fanon, F. (1965) *The Wretched of the Earth*, New York: Grove Press.

—— (1967) *Black Skin, White Masks*, New York: Grove Press.

Featherstone, M. (1991) 'The body in consumer culture', in M. Featherstone, M. Hepworth and B. Turner (eds), *The Body: Social Process and Cultural Theory*, London: Sage.

Featherstone, M., Hepworth, M. and Turner, B. (eds) (1991) *The Body: Social Process and Cultural Theory*, London: Sage.

Feldman, L.C. (2004) *Citizens Without Shelter: Homelessness, Democracy and Political Exclusion*, Ithaca, NY: Cornell University Press.

Fenton, N. (2008) 'Mediating hope: new media, politics and resistance', *International Journal of Cultural Studies*, 11(2): 230–48.

Findlen, B. (1995) *Listen Up: Voices from the Next Feminist Generation*, Seattle, WA: Seal Press.

Fine, G. (ed.) (1995) *A Second Chicago School?*, Chicago, IL: University of Chicago Press.

Fine, G. and Martin, D. (1990) 'A partisan view: sarcasm, satire and irony as voices in Erving Goffman's asylums', *Journal of Contemporary Ethnography*, 19(1): 89–115.

Fiske, J. (1989) *Reading the Popular*, Boston, MA: Unwin Hyman.

—— (1992) 'The cultural economy of fandom', in L. Lewis (ed.), *The Adoring Audience: Fan Culture and Popular Media*, London: Routledge.

Flax, J. (1990) *Thinking Fragments: Psychoanalysis, Feminism, and Postmodernism in the Contemporary West*, Berkeley, CA: University of California Press.

Flory, J., Young-Xu, Y., Gurol, I., Levinsky, N., Ash, A. and Emanuel, E. (2004) 'Place of death: US trends since 1980', *Health Affairs*, 23(3): 194–200.

Foster, H. (ed.) (1998) *The Anti-Aesthetic: Essays on Postmodern Culture*, New York: The New Press.

Foucault, M. (1966) *The Order of Things: An Archaeology of the Human Sciences*, London: Tavistock.

—— (1967) [1961] *Madness and Civilization: A History of Insanity in the Age of Reason*, trans. by R. Howard, London: Tavistock.

—— (1972) [1969] *The Archaeology of Knowledge*, trans. by A.M. Sheridan, London: Tavistock.

—— (1973) [1963] *The Birth of the Clinic: An Archeology of Medical Perception*, trans. by A.M. Sheridan, London: Tavistock.

—— (1979) [1975] *Discipline and Punish: The Birth of the Prison*, trans. by A.S. Smith, Harmondsworth: Penguin.

—— (1981) [1976] *The History of Sexuality* (vol. 1), trans. by R. Hurley, Harmondsworth: Penguin.

—— (1982) 'The subject and power', in H.L. Dreyfus and P. Rabinow (eds), *Michel Foucault: Beyond Structuralism and Hermeneutics*, Brighton, Sussex: Harvester.

—— (1988) 'The ethic of care for the self as a practice of freedom', in J.W. Bernauer and D.M. Rasmussen (eds), *The Final Foucault*, Cambridge: MIT Press.

Foucault, M., G. Burchell, *et al.* (1991) *The Foucault Effect: Studies in Governmentality: With Two Lectures by and an Interview with Michel Foucault*, Chicago: University of Chicago Press.

Fraser, N. (1997) *Justice Interruptus: Critical Reflections on the 'Postsocialist' Condition*, New York: Routledge.

Fraser, N. and Honneth, A. (2003) *Redistribution or Recognition?: A Political–Philosophical Exchange*, London: Verso.

Freedman, E.B. (2002) *No Turning Back: The History of Feminism and the Future of Women*, New York: Ballantine Books.

Friedman, T. (2000) *The Lexus and the Olive Tree*, London: HarperCollins.

Freud, S. (1961) [1900] 'The Interpretation of Dreams', in J. Strachey (ed.) *The Standard Edition of the Complete Psychological Works of Sigmund Freud* (vol. 4), London: Hogarth Press.

—— (1961) [1930] 'Civilization and its discontents', in J. Strachey (ed.), *The Standard Edition of the Complete Psychological Works of Sigmund Freud* (vol. 21), London: Hogarth Press.

Friedland, R. and Mohr, J. (2004) 'The cultural turn in American sociology', in R. Friedland and J. Mohr (eds), *Matters of Culture: Cultural Sociology in Practice*, Cambridge: Cambridge University Press.

Fromm, E. (1941) *Escape From Freedom*, New York: Farrar & Rinehart.

—— (1955) *The Sane Society*, New York: Farrar & Rinehart.

Frye, N. (1957) *Anatomy of Criticism*, Princeton, NJ: Princeton University Press.

Füredi, F. (2004) *Therapy Culture: Cultivating Vulnerability in an Uncertain Age*, London: Routledge.

Galey, M.E. (1998) 'The universal declaration of human rights: the role of congress', *Political Science*, 31(3): 524–9.

Geertz, C. (1973) *The Interpretation of Cultures*, New York: Basic Books.

Giddens, A. (1971) *Capitalism and Modern Social Theory: An Analysis of the Writings of Marx, Durkheim and Max Weber*, Cambridge: Cambridge University Press.

—— (1976) *New Rules of Sociological Method*, Cambridge: Cambridge University Press.

—— (1979) *Central Problems in Social Theory: Action, Structure, and Contradiction in Social Analysis*, London: Macmillan.

—— (1984) *The Constitution of Society: Outline of the Theory of Structuration*, Cambridge: Polity Press.

—— (1987) *Social Theory and Modern Sociology*, Cambridge: Polity Press.

—— (1987) [1985] *The Nation-State and Violence*, Berkeley, CA: University of California Press.

—— (1990) *The Consequences of Modernity*, Stanford, CA: Stanford University Press.

—— (1991) *Modernity and Self-identity: Self and Society in the Late Modern Age*, Stanford, CA: Stanford University Press.

—— (1992) *The Transformation of Intimacy: Sexuality, Love, and Eroticism in Modern Societies*, Stanford, CA: Stanford University Press.

—— (1995) *Politics, Sociology and Social Theory*, Cambridge: Polity Press.

—— (2000) *Runaway World: How Globalization is Reshaping Our Lives*, New York: Routledge.

Gilroy, P. (1993) *The Black Atlantic*, London: Verso.

Giroux, H. (2006) *Beyond the Spectacle of Terrorism*, London: Paradigm.

Glass, J.M. (1993) *Shattered Selves: Multiple Personality in a Postmodern World*, Ithaca, NY: Cornell University Press.

Glazer, N. (1997) *We are All Multiculturalists Now*, Cambridge, MA: Harvard University Press.

Glazer, N. and Montgomery, J. (eds) (2002) *Sovereignty Under Challenge: How Governments Respond*, Piscataway, NJ: Transaction.

Goffman, E. (1959) *The Presentation of Self in Everyday Life*, New York: Doubleday.

—— (1961) *Asylums*, Harmondsworth: Penguin.

—— (1963a) *Behavior in Public Places: Notes on the Social Organization of Gatherings*, New York: The Free Press.

—— (1963b) *Stigma: Notes on the Management of Spoiled Identity*, Englewood Cliffs, NJ: Prentice-Hall.

—— (1967) *Interaction Ritual: Essays on Face-to-Face Behavior*, New York: Anchor.

—— (1969) *Strategic Interaction*, Philadelphia, PA: University of Pennsylvania Press.

—— (1971) *Relations in Public: Microstudies of the Public Order*, New York: Basic Books.

—— (1974) *Frame Analysis: An Essay on the Organization of Experience*, New York: Harper & Row.

—— (1977) 'The arrangement between the sexes', *Theory and Society*, 4(3): 301–31.

—— (1979) *Gender Advertisements*, Basingstoke: Macmillan.

—— (1981) *Forms of Talk*, Oxford: Blackwell.

—— (1983) 'The interaction order', *American Sociological Review*, 48: 1–17.

Goldberg, J. (2007) 'Obama, the postmodernist', *USA Today*, 5 August.

Golkany, I. (2007) *The Improving State of the World*, Washington DC: Cato Institute.

Goodman, D. and Ritzer, G. (2008) *Sociological Theory*, Columbus, OH: McGraw-Hill.

Gramsci, A. (1971) *Selections from the Prison Notebooks*, London: New Left Books.

Habermas, J. (1981) 'Psychic thermidor and the rebirth of rebellious subjectivity', *Praxis International*, 1(1): 79–86.

—— (1998) 'Modernity – an incomplete project', in H. Foster (ed.), *The Anti-Aesthetic: Essays on Postmodern Culture*, New York: The New Press.

Halbwachs, M. (1941) *The Legendary Topography of the Gospels*, Paris: Presses Universitaires de France.

—— (1950) *Collective Memory*, M. Douglas (ed.), New York: Harper & Row.

Hall, S. (1985) 'Signification, representation, ideology: Althusser and the post-structuralist debates', *Critical Studies in Mass Communication*, 2: 91–114.

—— (1992) 'Our mongrel selves', *New Statesman and Society*, 19 June, 6–8.

Hall, S. and Jefferson, T. (1976) *Resistance Through Rituals*, London: HarperCollins Academic.

Hall, S. and Jacques, M. (1983) *The Politics of Thatcherism*, London: Lawrence & Wishart.

Hall, S. and Du Gay, P. (1996) *Questions of Cultural Identity*, London: Sage.

Hamilton, A.C. (1990) *Northrop Frye: Anatomy of his Criticism*, Toronto: University of Toronto Press.

Han, S. (2007) *Navigating Technomedia: Caught in the Web*, Lanham, MD: Rowman & Littlefield.

Hannerz, U. (1992) *Cultural Complexity*, New York: Columbia University Press.

Haraway D.J. (1985) 'A manifesto for cyborgs: science, technology and socialist feminism', *Socialist Review*, 80: 65–108.

—— (1991) *Simians, Cyborgs, and Women: The Reinvention of Nature*, New York: Routledge.

—— (2004) *The Haraway Reader*, New York: Routledge.

Harding, S.G. (1986) *The Science Question in Feminism*, Ithaca, NY: Cornell University Press.

Hardt, M. and Negri, A. (2000) *Empire*, Cambridge, MA: Harvard University Press.

Hartsock, N.C.M. (1998) *The Feminist Standpoint Revisited and Other Essays*, Boulder, CO: Westview Press.

Harvey, D. (1994) *The Condition of Postmodernity*, Oxford: Blackwell.

Hassan, I.H. (1987) *The Postmodern Turn: Essays in Postmodern Theory and Culture*, Columbus, OH: Ohio State University Press.

Hassan, R. (2008) *The Information Society*, Cambridge: Polity Press.

Hazard, P. (1965) *European Social Thought in the Eighteenth Century*, Harmondsworth: Penguin.

Hazleden, R. (2003) 'Love yourself: the relationship of the self with itself in popular self-help texts', *Journal of Sociology*, 39(4): 413–28.

Hebdige, D. (1979) *Subculture*, London: Methuen.

Held, D. (2004) *The Global Covenant*, Cambridge: Polity Press

Held, D. and McGrew, A. (2002) *Globalization/Anti-Globalization*, Cambridge: Polity Press.

Held, D., McGrew, A., Goldblatt, A. and Perraton, J. (1999) *Global Transformations*, Stanford, CA: Stanford University Press.

Henkin, L. (1998) 'The Universal Declaration and the U.S. Constitution', *Political Science*, 31(3): 512–15.

Hepworth, M. (1995) 'Positive ageing: what is the message?', in R. Bunton, S. Nettleton and R. Burrows (eds), *The Sociology of Health Promotion: Critical Analyses of Consumption, Lifestyle and Risk*, London: Routledge.

Hermes, J. (2006) 'Citizenship in the age of the internet', *European Journal of Communication*, 21(3): 295–309.

Hey, V. (2005) 'The contrasting social logics of sociality and survival: cultures of classed be/longing in late modernity', *Sociology*, 39(5): 855–72.

Heywood, L. and Drake, J. (1997) *Third Wave Agenda: Being Feminist, Doing Feminism*, Minneapolis: University of Minnesota Press.

Hill Collins, P. (1990) *Black Feminist Thought: Knowledge, Consciousness, and the Politics of Empowerment*, Boston, MA: Unwin Hyman.

—— (1998) *Fighting Words: Black Women and the Search for Justice*, Minneapolis: University of Minnesota Press.

Hirst, P. and Thompson, G. (1996) *Globalization in Question*, Cambridge: Polity Press.

Hobbes, T. (1991) *Man and Citizen (*De Homine *[1657] and* De Cive *[1642])*, Indianapolis, IN: Hackett.

Hochschild, A.R. (1997) *The Time Bind: When Work Becomes Home and Home Becomes Work*, New York: Metropolitan Books.

Hoffman, S. (2002) 'Clash of globalizations', *Foreign Affairs*, 81(4): 110–15.

Hoggart, R. (1957) *The Uses of Literacy*, London: Chatto & Windus.

Holmes, M. (2007) *What is Gender?: Sociological Approaches*, London: Sage.

hooks, B. (1981) *Ain't I a Woman: Black Women and Feminism*, Boston, MA: South End Press.

—— (2000) *Feminist Theory: From Margin to Center*, Cambridge, MA: South End Press.

Horkheimer, M. (1947) *Eclipse of Reason*, New York: Oxford University Press.

Howson, A. (2001) '"Watching you – watching me": visualising techniques and the cervix', *Women's Studies International Forum*, 24(1): 97–109.

—— (2004) *The Body in Society: An Introduction*, Cambridge: Polity.

—— (2005) *Embodying Gender*, London: Sage.

Howson, A. and Inglis, D. (2001) 'The body in sociology: tensions inside and outside sociological thought', *Sociological Review*, 49: 297–317.

Hunter, J.D. (1991) *Culture Wars: The Struggle to Define America*, New York: Basic Books.

Ignatieff, M. (2001) *Human Rights as Politics and Idolatry*, Princeton, NJ: Princeton University Press.

Illich, I. (1976) *Medical Nemesis: The Expropriation of Health*, Harmondsworth: Penguin.

Irigaray, L. (1985) *This Sex Which Is Not One*, Ithaca, NY: Cornell University Press.

—— (1993) *An Ethics of Sexual Difference*, Ithaca, NY: Cornell University Press.

—— (2000) *To Be Two*, London: Athlone.

Isin, E.F. and Wood, P.K. (1999) *Citizenship & Identity*, London: Sage.

Isin, E.F. and Turner, B.S. (eds) (2002) *Handbook of Citizenship Studies*, London: Sage.

Isin, E.F. and Nielsen, G. (eds) (2008) *Acts of Citizenship*, London: Zed Books.

Jameson, F. (1984) 'Postmodernism, or the cultural logic of late capitalism', *New Left Review*, 146: July–August.

—— (1998) 'Postmodernism and consumer society', in H. Foster (ed.), *The Anti-Aesthetic: Essays on Postmodern Culture*, The New Press: New York.

Jenkins, H. (1992) *Textual Poaches: Television Fans and Participatory Culture*, London: Routledge.

—— (2005) *Fans, Bloggers and Gamers: Exploring Participatory Culture*, New York: New York University Press.

Jennet, C. and Stewart, R.G. (eds) (1989) *Politics of the Future: The Role of Social Movements*, South Melbourne: Macmillan.

Kahn, R. and Kellner, D. (2004) 'New media and internet activism: from the "Battle of Seattle" to blogging', *New Media and Society*, 6(1): 87–95.

Kaldor, M. (2003) *Global Civil Society*, Cambridge: Polity Press.

Kasulis, T.P., Ames, R.T. and Dissanayake, W. (eds) (1993) *Self as Body in Asian Theory and Practice*, New York: State University of New York Press.

Kellner, D. (1989a) *Critical Theory, Marxism, and Modernity*, Baltimore, MD: Johns Hopkins University Press.

—— (1989b) *Jean Baudrillard: From Marxism to Postmodernism and Beyond*, Stanford, CA: Stanford University Press.

—— (2003) *Media Spectacle*, London: Routledge.

—— (2005) 'Globalization, September 11, and the restructuring of education', in G.F. Fishman (ed.), *Critical Theories, Radical Pedagogies, and Global Conflicts*, Lanham, MD: Rowman & Littlefield.

Kendal, G., Skrbis, Z. and Woodward, I. (2008) 'Cosmopolitanism, the nation-state and imaginative realism', *Journal of Sociology*, 44(4): 401–18.

Kessler, S.J. and McKenna, W. (1985) [1978] *Gender: An Ethnomethodological Approach*, Chicago, IL: University of Chicago Press.

Keynes, J.M. (1936) *The General Theory of Employment, Interest and Money*, London: Macmillan.

King, M., Smith, G. and Bartlett, A. (2004) 'Treatments of homosexuality since the 1950s – an oral history: the experience of professionals', *British Medical Journal*, 328, 429.

Klein, N. (2002) *Fences and Windows*, London: HarperCollins.

Kraft-Ebing, R. (1951) [1886] Psychopathia Sexualis *English*, London: Staples Press.

Kristeva, J. (1980) *Desire in Language: A Semiotic Approach to Literature and Art*, New York: Columbia University Press

—— (1982) *Powers of Horror: An Essay on Abjection*, New York: Columbia University Press.

—— (1984) [1974] *Revolution in Poetic Language*, New York: Columbia University Press.

—— (1987) *Tales of Love*, New York: Columbia University Press.

—— (1989) *Black Sun: Depression and Melancholia*, New York: Columbia University Press.

—— (1991) *Strangers to Ourselves*, New York: Columbia University Press.

Kristeva, J. and T. Moi (1986) *The Kristeva Reader*, New York: Columbia University Press.

Kroeber, A.L. and Kluckhohn, C. (1952) *Culture: A Critical Review of Concepts and Definitions*, Cambridge, MA: Peabody Museum.

Lacan, J. (1977) *Ecrits: A Selection*, New York: W.W. Norton.

—— (1979) *The Four Fundamental Concepts of Psychoanalysis*, Harmondsworth: Penguin.

—— (1988) *The Seminar of Jacques Lacan, Vol. 1: Freud's Paper on Technique 1953–54*, Cambridge: Cambridge University Press.

—— (1992) *The Ethics of Psychoanalysis 1959–60: The Seminar of Jacques Lacan*, London: Routledge.

—— (1998a) *The Seminar of Jacques Lacan, Vol. 2: The Ego in Freud's Theory and in the Technique of Psychoanalysis 1954–5*, Cambridge: Cambridge University Press.

—— (1998b) *The Seminar, Book XX: Encore, on Feminine Sexuality*, London: Tavistock.

Laqueur, T. (1990) *Making Sex: Body and Gender from the Greeks to Freud*, Cambridge, MA: Harvard University Press.

Lash, S. (1994) 'Reflexivity and its doubles: structure, aesthetics, community', in U. Beck, A. Giddens and S. Lash, *Reflexive Modernization*, Cambridge: Polity Press.

Lash, S. and Urry, J. (1994) *Economies of Signs and Space*, London: Sage.

Latouche, S. (1996) *The Westernization of the World*, Cambridge: Polity Press.

Latour, B. (2008) *We have Never been Modern*, Cambridge, MA: Harvard University Press.

Lawton J. (1998) 'Contemporary hospice care: the sequestration of the unbounded body and "dirty dying"', *Sociology of Health and Illness*, 20(2): 121–43.

Leder, D. (1990) *The Absent Body*, Chicago, IL: University of Chicago Press.

Lemert, C. (2005) *Social Things*, New York: Rowman & Littlefield.

Lemert, C. and Elliott, A. (2006) *The New Individualism: The Emotional Costs of Globalization*, London: Routledge.

Lévi-Strauss, C. (1963) [1958] *Structural Anthropology*, trans. by C. Jacobson and B. Grundfest, London: Penguin Press.

—— (1969) [1949] *The Elementary Structures of Kinship*, trans. by J.H. Bell, J.R. von Sturmer and R. Needham (eds), London: Eyre & Spottiswoode.

—— (1970) 'Overture to *le cru et le cuit*', in J. Ehrmann (ed.), *Structuralism*, New York: Anchor Books.

—— (1975) [1964] *The Raw and the Cooked*, New York: Harper & Row.

—— (1977) [1957] *Écrits: A Selection*, trans. by Alan Sheridan, New York: W.W. Norton.

Lewis, J.D. (1979) 'A social behaviorist interpretation of the Meadian "I"', *American Journal of Sociology*, 85: 261–87.

Livingstone, S. (2003) 'Children's use of the internet: reflections on the emerging research agenda', *New Media and Society*, 5(2): 147–66.

Lloyd, G. (1984) *The Man of Reason: 'Male' and 'Female' in Western Philosophy*, Minneapolis, MN: University of Minnesota Press.

Lorde, A. (1984) *Sister Outsider: Essays and Speeches*, Trumansburg, NY: Crossing Press.

Lukes, S. (1974) *Power: A Radical View*, London: Macmillan.

Lupton, D. (1998) *The Emotional Self: A Sociocultural Exploration*, London: Sage.

Lyotard, J.-F. (1984) *The Postmodern Condition: A Report on Knowledge*, trans. by G. Bennington and B. Massumi, Minneapolis, MN: University of Minnesota Press.

McCall, L. (2005) 'The complexity of intersectionality', *Signs: Journal of Women in Culture & Society*, 30(3): 1771–800.

McChesney, R.W. (2000) *Rich Media, Poor Democracy*, New York: New Press.

MacDonald, H.P. (2005) *Human Remains: Episodes in Human Dissection*, Carlton, VIC: Melbourne University Press.

McLaren, M.A. (2002) *Feminism, Foucault, and Embodied Subjectivity*, Albany, NY: State University of New York Press.

McLean, I. and Hewitt, F. (eds) (1994) *Condorcet: Foundations of Social Choice and Political Theory*, Aldershot: Edward Elgar.

McLennan, G. (2006) *Sociological Cultural Studies: Reflexivity and Positivity in the Human Sciences*, Basingstoke: Palgrave.

McLuhan, M. (1994) *Understanding Media: The Extensions of Man*, London: Routledge.

McNay, L. (1993) *Foucault and Feminism: Power, Gender, and the Self*, Boston, MA: Northeastern University Press.

—— (2000) *Gender and Agency: Reconfiguring the Subject in Feminist and Social Theory*, Cambridge: Blackwell.

Maffesoli, M. (1996) *The Time of Tribes*, London: Sage.

Maines, D. (2001) *The Faultline of Consciousness: A View of Interactionism in Sociology*, Chicago, IL: Aldine.

Mandeville, B. (1924) [1723] *Fable of the Bees*, Oxford: Oxford University Press.

Mann, M. (1987) 'Ruling class strategies and citizenship', *Sociology*, 21(3): 339–54.

Manning, P. (1992) *Erving Goffman and Modern Sociology*, Stanford, CA: Stanford University Press.

—— (1999) 'Ethnographic coats and tents', in Greg Smith (ed.), *Goffman and Social Organization: Studies in a Sociological Legacy*, London: Routledge.

—— (2000) 'Credibility, agency and the interaction order', *Symbolic Interaction* 23(3): 283–97.

—— (2005) *Freud and American Sociology*, Cambridge: Polity.

Månson, P. (2000) 'Karl Marx', in H. Anderson and L.B. Kaspersen (eds), *Classical and Modern Social Theory*, Oxford: Blackwell.

Marcuse, H. (1956) *Eros and Civilization*, New York: Vintage Books.

—— (1964) *One-Dimensional Man*, Boston, MA: Beacon Press.

—— (1970) *Five Lectures: Psychoanalysis, Politics and Utopia*, trans. by Jeremy J. Shapiro and Shierry M. Weber, Boston, MA: Beacon Press.

—— (1974) [1955] *Eros and Civilization*, Boston, MA: Beacon Press.

Marshall, T.H. (1950) *Citizenship and Social Class and Other Essays*, Cambridge: Cambridge University Press.

—— (1981) [1969] *The Right to Welfare and Other Essays*, London: Heinemann.

Marx, K. (1976) *Capital: A Critique of Political Economy* (vol. 1), Moscow: Progress Publishers.

—— (1978a) 'Economic and philosophic manuscripts of 1844', in R.C. Tucker (ed.), *The Mark–Engels Reader*, New York: W.W. Norton.

—— (1978b) 'Estranged labour', in R.C. Tucker (ed.), *The Mark–Engels Reader*, New York: W.W. Norton.

—— (1978c) '*Capital*, Vol. I', in R.C. Tucker (ed.), *The Mark–Engels Reader*, New York: W.W. Norton.

Marx, K. and Engels, F. (1967) [1848] *Manifesto of the Communist Party*, Moscow: Progress Publishers.

Marx, K. and Engels, F., in R.C. Tucker (ed.) (1978) [1848] *The Marx–Engels Reader*, 2nd edn, New York: W.W. Norton.

Mauss, M. (1973) 'Techniques of the body', *Economy and Society*, 2 (1): 70–88.

—— (1990) [1924] *The Gift: Forms and Functions of Exchange in Archaic Societies*, London: Routledge.

Mead, G.H. (1936) *Movements of Thought in the Nineteenth Century*, C.W. Morris (ed.), Chicago, IL: Chicago University Press.

Mead, G.H. and C.W. Morris (1934) *Mind, Self and Society: From the Standpoint of a Social Behaviorist*, Chicago, IL: The University of Chicago Press.

Melucci, A. (1994) 'A strange kind of newness: what's "new" in new social movements?', in E. Larana, H. Johnston and J.R. Gusfield (eds), *New Social Movements: From Ideology to Identity*, Philadelphia, PA: Temple University Press.

—— (1996) *The Playing Self: Person and Meaning in the Planetary Society*, Cambridge, Cambridge University Press.

Memmi, A. (1965) *The Colonizer and the Colonized*, New York: Orion Press.

Merleau-Ponty, M. (2001) [1962] *Phenomenology of Perception*, trans. by C. Smith, London: Sage.

Miller, J.B. (1986) *Toward a New Psychology of Women*, Boston, MA: Beacon Press.

Millet, K. (1972) *Sexual Politics*, London: Abacus.

Mitchell, J. (1974) *Psychoanalysis and Feminism*, London: Penguin Books.

—— (1984) *Women: The Longest Revolution*, New York: Pantheon Books.

Moi, T. (1987) *French Feminist Thought: A Reader*, New York: Blackwell.

Mommsen, W. (1987) 'Personal conduct and societal change', in S. Lash and S. Whimster (eds), *Max Weber, Rationality and Modernity*, London: Allen & Unwin.

Moraga, C. and Anzaldúa, G. (1981) *This Bridge Called My Back: Writings by Radical Women of Color*, Watertown, MA: Persephone Press.

Morgan, D. (1993) 'You too can have a body like mine: reflections on the male body and masculinities', in S. Scott and D. Morgan (eds), *Body Matters: Essays on the Sociology of the Body*, London: Falmer.

315

Morrione, T. (ed.) (2004) *George Herbert Mead and Human Conduct*, Walnut Creek, CA: AltaMira Press.

Mort, F. (1988) 'Boys' own? Masculinity, style and popular culture', in R. Rutherford and J. Chapman (eds), *Male Order: Unwrapping Masculinity*, London: Lawrence & Wishart.

Mouzelis, N. (1995) *Sociological Theory: What Went Wrong?*, London: Routledge.

Moya, P.M.L. and Hames-Garcia, M.R. (2000) *Reclaiming Identity: Realist Theory and the Predicament of Postmodernism*, Berkeley, CA: University of California Press.

Nandy, A. (1983) *The Intimate Enemy: Loss and Recovery of Self under Colonialism*, Delhi: Oxford.

Nelson, C. (2007) *Thomas Paine: Enlightenment, Revolution, and the Birth of Nations*, Harmondsworth: Penguin.

Nicholson, L.J. (1990) *Feminism/Postmodernism*, New York: Routledge.

Nicholson, L.J. and S. Seidman (1995) *Social Postmodernism: Beyond Identity Politics*, New York: Cambridge University Press.

Oakley, A. (1980) *Women Confined: Towards a Sociology of Childbirth*, Oxford: Martin Robertson.

Ohmae, K. (1990) *The Borderless World*, New York: HarperBusiness.

Oliver, M. (1996) *Understanding Disability*, London: Macmillan.

Parsons, T. (1965) [1961] *Theories of Society: Foundations of Modern Sociological Theory*, New York: Free Press.

Pateman, C. (1988) *The Sexual Contract*, Stanford, CA: Stanford University Press.

—— (1989) *The Disorder of Women: Democracy, Feminism and Political Theory*, Cambridge: Polity Press.

Poster, M. (1995) *The Second Media Age*, Cambridge: Polity Press.

Probyn, E. (2000) 'Sporting bodies: dynamics of shame and pride', *Body and Society*, 6(1): 13–28.

Putnam, R. (2000) *Bowling Alone: The Collapse and Revival of American Community*, New York: Simon & Schuster.

Radway, J. (1991) *Reading the Romance*, Chapel Hill, NC: University of North Carolina Press.

Ramazanoglu, C. (1993) *Up Against Foucault: Explorations of Some Tensions Between Foucault and Feminism*, London: Routledge.

Rawls, J. (1999) *The Law of Peoples*, Cambridge, MA: Harvard University Press.

Ray, L.J. (1999) *Theorizing Classical Sociology*, Milton Keynes: Open University Press.

Readings, B. (1996) *The University in Ruins*, Cambridge: Cambridge University Press.

Reed, M. (2005) 'Beyond the iron cage: bureaucracy and democracy in the knowledge economy and society', in P. Du Gay (ed.), *The Values of Bureaucracy*, Oxford: Oxford University Press.

Ritzer, G. (2000) *Classical Sociological Theory*, Boston, MA: McGraw Hill.

Roach, J. (1996) *Cities of the Dead: Circum-Atlantic Performance*, New York: Columbia University Press.

Robertson, R. (1992) *Globalization: Social Theory and Global Culture*, London: Sage.

—— (1995) 'Glocalization: time–space and homogeneity–heterogeneity', in M. Featherstone (ed.) *et al.*, *Global Modernities*, London: Sage.

Rojek, C. and Turner, B. (2000) 'Decorative sociology: towards a critique of the cultural turn', *Sociological Review*, 48(4): 629–48.

Rorty, R. (1979) *Philosophy and the Mirror of Nature*, Princeton, NJ: Princeton University Press.

—— (1985) 'Habermas and Lyotard on postmodernity', in R.J. Bernstein (ed.), *Habermas and Modernity*, Cambridge, MA: MIT Press.

—— (1989) *Contingency, Irony, and Solidarity*, New York: Cambridge University Press.

Rose, N.S. (1990) *Governing the Soul: The Shaping of the Private Self*, London: Routledge.
—— (1996) *Inventing Our Selves: Psychology, Power, and Personhood*, Cambridge: Cambridge University Press.
Rosenau, P. (1992) *Post-Modernism and the Social Sciences: Insights, Inroads and Intrusions*, Princeton, NJ: Princeton University Press.
Rosenberg, J. (2005) 'Globalization theory: a postmortem', *International Politics*, 42: 2–74.
Runciman, W.G. (1970) 'What is structuralism?', in *Sociology in Its Place and Other Essays*, Cambridge: Cambridge University Press.
Said, E.W. (1978) *Orientalism*, New York: Pantheon Books.
Saint-Simon, H. (1975) *Selected Writings on Science, Industry and Social Organization*, ed. and trans. by K. Taylor, London: Croom Helm.
Saul, J.R. (2005) *The Collapse of Globalism*, London: Atlantic Books.
Saussure, F. de (1974) [1916] *Course in General Linguistics*, C. Bally and A. Sechehaye (eds) in collaboration with A. Riedlinger, trans. by W. Baskin, London: Fontana.
Sawicki, J. (1991) *Disciplining Foucault: Feminism, Power, and the Body*, New York: Routledge.
Scarry, E. (1985) *The Body in Pain: The Making and the Unmaking of the World*, Oxford: Oxford University Press.
Schiller, D. (2000) *Digital Capitalism*, London: MIT Press.
Sedgwick, E.K. (1990) *Epistemology of the Closet*, Berkeley, CA: University of California Press.
Seidman, S. (1994) *Contested Knowledge: Social Theory in the Postmodern Era*, Malden, MA: Blackwell.
Sennett, R. (1998) *The Corrosion of Character: The Personal Consequences of Work in the New Capitalism*, New York: W.W. Norton.
—— (2006) *Culture of New Capitalism*, New Haven, CT: Yale University Press.
Shacher, A. and Hirschl, R. (2007) 'Citizenship as inherited property', *Political Theory* 35(2): 253–87.
Shilling, C. (1993) *The Body and Social Theory*, London: Sage.
Silverstone, R. (2007) *Media and Morality: On the Rise of the Mediapolis*, Cambridge: Polity Press.
Simmel, G. (1950) [1908] 'The metropolis and mental life', in K. Wolff, *The Sociology of Georg Simmel*, New York: Free Press, 409–24.
—— (1971) [1908] in Donald N. Levine (ed.), *On Individuality and Social Forms: Selected Writings*, Chicago, IL: University of Chicago Press.
—— (1990) *The Philosophy of Money*, ed. T. Bottomore and D. Frisby, London: Routledge.
—— (1997) *Simmel on Culture*, ed. D. Frisby and M. Featherstone, London: Sage.
Skeggs, B. (1997) *Formations of Class and Gender: Becoming Respectable*, London: Sage.
—— (2005) 'The making of class and gender through visualizing moral subject formation', *Sociology*, 39(5): 965–82.
Smith, D.E. (1990) *The Conceptual Practices of Power: A Feminist Sociology of Knowledge*, Boston, MA: Northeastern University Press.
Smith, G. (ed.) (1999) *Goffman and Social Organization: Studies in a Sociological Legacy*, London: Routledge.
Smith, P. and Alexander, J.C. (eds) (2005) *The Cambridge Companion to Durkheim*, Cambridge: Cambridge University Press.
Soper, K. (2007) 'The other pleasures of post-consumerism', *Soundings: A Journal of Politics and Culture*, 35: 31–40.
Spinoza, B. (1958) *The Political Works*, Oxford: Clarendon Press.
Spivak, G.C., Landry, D. and Mclean, G. (1996) *The Spivak Reader: Selected Works of Gayatri Chakravorty Spivak*, New York: Routledge.

Stevenson, N. (2006) *David Bowie: Sound, Vision and Fame*, Cambridge: Polity Press.

Stiegler, B. (1998) [1994] *Technics and Time, 1: The Fault of Epimetheus*, trans. by George Collins and Richard Beardsworth, Stanford, CA: Stanford University Press.

Sturrock, J. (1979) *Structuralism and Since*, Oxford: Oxford University Press.

Taylor, C., Appiah, K.A., Habermas, J., Rockefeller, S.C., Walzer, M. and Wolf, S. (1994) 'The politics of recognition', in Amy Gutmann (ed.), *Multiculturalism: Examining the Politics of Recognition*, Princeton, NJ: Princeton University Press.

Tester, K. (1995) 'Moral solidarity and the technological reproduction of images', *Media, Culture and Society*, 17: 469–82.

—— (1997) *Moral Culture*, London: Sage.

—— (2001) *Compassion, Morality and the Media*, Miltan Keynes: Open University Press.

Thayer, H.S. (1968) *Meaning and Action: A Critical History of Pragmatism*, New York: Bobbs-Merrill.

Thompson, E.P. (1968) *The Making of the English Working-Class*, London: Pelican.

Thompson, J.B. (1989) 'The theory of structuration', in D. Held and J. B. Thompson (eds), *Social Theory of Modern Societies: Giddens and his Critics*, Cambridge: Cambridge University Press.

Titmuss, R. (1958) *Essays in 'the Welfare State'*, London: Allen & Unwin.

Tobin, J. (1978) 'A proposal for international monetary reform', *Eastern Economic Journal*, 4: 153–59.

Tocqueville, A. (2003) [1835–1840] *Democracy in America*, London: Penguin Books.

Toennies, F. (1957) *Community and Association*, East Lansing, MI: Michigan State University Press.

Tomlinson, J. (1991) *Cultural Imperialism*, London: Pinter.

—— (1999) *Globalization and Culture*, Chicago, IL: University of Chicago Press.

Touraine, A. (1988) *Return of the Actor: A Social Theory in Postindustrial Society*, Minnesota, MN: University of Minnesota.

Turkle, S. (1995) *Life on the Screen: Identity in the Age of the Internet*, New York: Simon & Schuster.

Turner, B.S. (1984) *The Body in Society*, Oxford: Basil Blackwell.

—— (1987) 'A note on nostalgia', *Theory, Culture & Society*, 4: 147–56.

—— (1992) *Regulating Bodies*, London: Routledge.

—— (2001) 'The erosion of citizenship', *British Journal of Sociology*, 52(2): 189–209.

—— (2004) *The New Medical Sociology*, New York: W.W. Norton.

—— (2008) *Rights and Virtues: Political Essays on Citizenship and Social Justice*, Oxford: Bardwell Press.

Turner, V. (1967) *Forest of Symbols*, Ithaca, NY: Cornell University Press.

—— (1969) *The Ritual Process*, Chicago, IL: Aldine.

Urry, J. (2000) *Sociology Beyond Societies*, London: Routledge.

Vattimo, G. (1991) *The End of Modernity: Nihilism and Hermeneutics in Postmodern Culture*, Baltimore, MD: Johns Hopkins University Press.

Vaughan, D. (1996) *The Challenger Launch Decision: Risky Technology, Culture and Deviance at NASA*, Chicago, IL: University of Chicago Press.

Verhoeven, J. (1993) 'An interview with Erving Goffman, 1980', *Research on Language and Social Interaction*, 26(3): 317–48.

Virilio, P. (1997) *Open Sky*, London: Verso.

—— (2000) *The Information Bomb*, London: Verso.

Vucht Tijssen, van L. (1991) 'Women and objective culture: Georg Simmel and Marianne Weber', *Theory, Culture and Society*, 8(3): 203–18.

Wacquant, L. (1995) 'Pugs at work: bodily capital and bodily labour among professional boxers', *Body and Society*, 1: 65–93.

Walker, R. (1995) *To Be Real: Telling the Truth and Changing the Face of Feminism*, New York: Anchor Books.

Wartenberg, T.E. (1992) *Rethinking Power*, Albany, NY: State University of New York Press.

Weber, M. (1968) [1905] *Protestant Ethic and the Spirit of Capitalism*, Upper Saddle River, NJ: Prentice-Hall.

—— (1968) [1921] *Economy and Society* (3 vols.), Totowa, NJ: Bedminster Press.

—— (1981) [1927] *General Economic History*, New Brunswick, NJ: Transaction Books.

—— (1993) *Sociology of Religion*, trans. by Ephraim Fischoff, Boston, MA: Beacon Press.

Weber, M., Gerth, H.H. and Wright Mills, C. (1946) *From Max Weber: Essays in Sociology*, New York: Oxford University Press.

Weeks J. (1985) *Sexuality and Its Discontents*, London: Routledge.

Whitehead, A.N. (1925) *Science and the Modern World*, New York: Free Press.

Williams, R. (1958) *Culture and Society*, London: Chatto & Windus.

—— (1974) *Television: Technology and Cultural Form*, New York: Schoken Books.

—— (1976) *Keywords: A Vocabulary of Culture and Society*, London: Fontana.

—— (1977) *Marxism and Literature*, Oxford: Oxford University Press.

Wilson, D.M., Northcott, H.C., Truman, C.D., Smith, S.L., Anderson, M.C., Fainsinger, R.L. and Stingl, M.J. (2001) 'Location of death in Canada', *Evaluation & the Health Professions*, 24(4): 385–403.

Winkin, Y. (1988) *Erving Goffman: Les Moments et Leurs Hommes*, Paris: Minuit.

Wolf, M. (2004) *Why Globalization Works*, New Haven, CT: Yale University Press.

Wollstonecraft, M. (1985) [1792] *Vindication of the Rights of Woman*, Harmondsworth: Penguin.

Woodiwiss, A. (2003) *Making Human Rights Work Globally*, London: GlassHouse Press.

Wouters, C. (2004) 'Changing regimes of manners and emotions: from disciplining to informalizing', in S. Loyal and S. Quilley (eds), *The Sociology of Norbert Elias*, Cambridge: Cambridge University Press.

Young, I.M. (1990) 'Throwing like a girl: a phenomenology of feminine body comportment, motility, and spatiality', in *Throwing Like a Girl and Other Essays in Feminist Philosophy and Social Theory*, Bloomington, IN: Indiana University Press.

Zerubavel, E. (1981) *Hidden Rhythms: Schedules and Calendars in Social Life*, Chicago, IL: University of Chicago Press.

INDEX

Note: page numbers in **bold type** refer to main entries in Part II.

9/11 attacks 162–3, 195, 213, 228

abstraction 131–2
Adams, M. 142
Adorno, Theodor 59, 138, 158, **221–2**, 223, 232, 233, 242, 255, 258, 266, 269–70, 289
advertising images 52, 108–9
aesthetics **222–3**
Afghanistan 182
Africa, female genital mutilation 294
agency **223–4**, 235, 242, 256, 273; Giddens 89–90
AIDS 255
Albert, Hans 222
Alexander, Jeffrey 192, 195
alienation 161, 282; resulting from consumer desire 227; of workers 224
alternative lifestyles 199
Althusser, Louis **224–5**, 234, 243, 253, 259, 270, 282, 299; andpsychoanalysis 66–7; and structuralism 78–9
American Journal of Sociology 238
anthropology 277
anti-globalization movement 167, 199, 212–13
Appiah, Kwame Anthony 214, 241
Archer, Margaret 94–5
architecture 290
Arendt, Hannah 180–1, 233
asylum-seekers 179–80
Auerbach, Erich 272

Bakhtin, Mikhail 191, 274
Barthes, Roland 196–7, **225–7**, 245, 254, 274, 291, 299; and cultural theory 193; and structuralism 78
basic repression 61–2
Baudrillard, Jean 131–3, 140, 163, 197, 223, **227–8**, 290

Bauman, Zygmunt **228–30**, 241, 260, 287, 290, 300; and identity 141–2
Beauvoir, Simone de 106, **230–1**, 236, 252
Beck, Ulrich 19, 141, 169, 197, 214–15, **231–2**, 241, 287
Beck-Gernsheim, E. 141
Bell, Daniel 128–9
Benjamin, Walter 221, 223, **232–3**, 242, 255, 259, 270
Berg, Alban 221
Berkeley, George 250
biological determinism 244
biopower 254–5
Black feminism 247
Black Woman of the South *see* Cooper, Anna Julia
Blackness 240
Blumer, Herbert **233–4**, 239, 264; formulation of symbolic interactionism 37–42
body idiom 49
body language 263
body theory 102–3, 112–13; bodies in contemporary society 111–12; medicalization of bodies 103–5; social bodies 105–11
body-consciousness 111
Boltanski, Luc 169
Bonald, Louis de 22–3
Borges, Jorge Luis 6, 7
Bourdieu, Pierre 110, 224, **234–5**, 256, 300; criticisms of 99–100; and cultural theory 193; and structuration theory 97–9
bourgeoisie 24, 226
Boutroux, Émile 248
Britain: citizenship 174; cultural studies 189; rights 176
Brücke, Ernst 256, 257

bureaucracy 32
Burke, Edmund 182
Butler, Judith 17–18, 52, 82, 231, **235–7**, 245, 253, 263, 271, 287

Calvinism 33
capital 235; global 142
capitalism 24–6, 32, 74–5, 282; crisis of 120–2; and repression 61, 137–8; totalitarian tendencies of 222
Castells, Manuel 156–7, 165, 166
Castoriadis, Cornelius **237–8**, 278
castration 68
CCCS (Centre for Contemporary Cultural Studies) 189
Charcot, Jean-Martin 257
charisma 34
Chicago School 233, **238–9**, 283, 297
child development 45
childbirth 103
citizenship 173–5; distinction from human rights 185–6; global vs. cosmopolitan 183–4; and human rights 181–3; mobility rights 184–5; and recognition 177–81; and redistribution 175–7; transaction rights 184–5
civil death 50
civil inattention 49
civil rights 176, 247
civilizing process 106
Cixous, Hélène 69, 290
class 111
class conflict 23, 24
Clifford, James 196
co-presence 48–9
Coke, Sir Edward 176
Coleman, James S. 14
Collins, Patricia Hill 150
commodities 74
communist revolution 224–5
community 21
computer literacy 160
Comte, Auguste 23–4, 242, 248, 289
Concordet, Marquis de 174
conflict, cultural 197–9
Connell, R.W. 109–10
conscious 57
consciousness 288; false 300
constructionism 106

consumerism 111–12, 159, 229, 300; and alienation 227; global 197
conversation analysis 251
Cooley, Charles 38
Cooper, Anna Julia 25, **239–40**, 247, 263
Cornelius, Hans 221
cosmopolitanism 168, 173, 196–7, 214, **241**, 291, 294; cosmopolitan citizenship 183–4
Cowen, Tyler 210–11
creative destruction 210
credit crunch 177
critical theory 221, 223, 229, **242**, 255, 257, 266–7, 268; and identity 146–51
cultural capital 99, 110–11, 193, 235
cultural hegemony 265–6
cultural recognition 15
cultural symbols 226
cultural theory 188–91; fragmented identities and cultural conflict 197–9; future of 199–200; semiotic traditions 193–4; social constructions of time and space 195–7; symbolic order and ritual 191–5
cultural turn 189
culture 238; fan 164–5; German 232; and globalization 207–11; industry 158, 223; mass 121, 222; popular 156–70, 198–9; wars 199

Darfur 181, 182
Darwin, Charles 6, 7
de Tocqueville, Alexis 174, 176
death 104
Debord, G. 161
deconstruction 80, 226, 242–3, 288
depression 70–1
Derrida, Jacques 226, 236, 241, **242–4**, 267, 288, 291; and post-structuralism 79–81, 83
Descartes, René 102, 250
determinism **244–5**
Dewey, John 42, 284
différence 80–1, 243, 288
differend 279
digital media *see* new media
disability 104–5
discourse **245–6**, 299
discurs 126–7
discursive consciousness 89–90

division of labour 27, 32
divorce 93–4
double hermeneutic 91, 261
Douglas, Mary 194
dramaturgy 52, 108
dromological analysis 301
Du Bois, William Edward Burghardt 240,
  246–8
duality of structure 88, 261
Durkheim, Émile 13, 23, 26–9, 77, 239,
  248–9, 259, 261, 289; and cultural theory
  192–3; and gender relations 20; and
  identity 136–7
duty 173–4, 175, 178, 181

e-commerce 184
economic determinism 244
economics: globalized economy 205;
  inter-national economy 205; Keynesian
  175–7
education 225, 235
ego 257, 270, 293
Elias, Norbert 106
Elliott, Anthony 215
Ellwood, Charles 233
emancipatory thinking 229
embodiment *see* body theory
empiricism 250
employment studies 190
enclave society 180
Engels, Friedrich 105, 244, 281
Enlightenment 8–9, 22–3, 129, 138–9, 144,
  229, 251, 287
environmentalism 167, 194, 199
epistemology **250–1**, 288
ethnography 47, 50–1, 77
ethnomethodology 223, **251–2**, 288
eugenics 244
exchange values 74
eye, the 31

face 53
false consciousness 300
families 93–4
fan culture 164–5
female genital mutilation 294
feminism 107, 230, 240, 247, **252–3**, 257,
  275; and identity 143–4; post-feminism
  253; post-Lacanian 69; postmodern
  144–5, 253, 290; and post-structuralism

82; and psychoanalysis 67–71, 143–4,
  285–7; *see also* gender, women
Feuerbach, Ludwig 224
field theory 99, 235, 300
Fine, Gary 41
First Gulf War 131, 228
Fiske, John 164, 165, 198
focused interaction 49
Foucault, Michel 190, 243, 245, 246, **253–5**,
  267, 291, 299; and identity 138–9, 147,
  148, 149; and post-structuralism 81–2,
  83; and sociology of medicine 103–5
frame analysis 53
Frankfurt School 222, 242, **255–8**, 258, 266,
  269, 289; and identity 137–8; and
  psychoanalysis 58–9
free association 57
Freidan, Betty 252
French Revolution 8–9, 43, 174, 181
French structuralism 76–9
Freud, Sigmund 56–8, 225, 236, 238, 255,
  256–8, 270; feminist accounts of 286, *see*
  also psychoanalysis
Friedman, Milton 177
Friedman, Thomas 211–12
Fromm, Erich 242, 255, **258–9**; and
  psychoanalysis 60–1
Frye, Northrop 190–1
functionalism 249, **259–60**, 299
fundamentalism 199

game stage 45
Gatens, Moira 107–8
gay theory 82, 148
Geertz, Clifford 188
gender 20, 32, 92–4, 108–9, 236, 253, 263,
  271; and bodily restraint 106; and rights
  176; studies 52, *see also* feminism
Germany, culture 232
Giddens, Anthony 23, 84, 206–7, 224, 239,
  251–2, 255, **260–2**, 271, 287, 291–2, 300;
  criticism of 94–7; and identity 140–1; and
  modernity 91–4; and structuration theory
  87–91
Gilman, Charlotte Perkins 240, **262–3**
Gilroy, Paul 196
Giroux, Henry 162–3
global warming 92
globalization 19, 142, 177, 203, 215–17,
  235, 241, 291, 294; anti-globalization

movement 167, 199, 212–13; and culture
207–11; definitions 203–5; hopes and
fears about 211–15; transformationalist
position 205–7, 214; utility as a concept
215–17
globulation 212
glocalization 210
goal-rational action 33
Goffman, Erving 46–54, 108–9, 236, **263–4**,
271
golden straightjacket 211–12
Gramsci, Antonio 189, 229, **265–6**
Grosz, Elizabeth 107–8
Gulf War, First 131, 228

Habermas, Jürgen 126–9, 133, 222, 242,
255, **266–7**, 270; Rorty's critique of
130–1
habitus 97–100, 110, 193, 235, 300
Halbwachs, Maurice 192, 195
Hall, Stuart 146, 189
Hannerz, Ulk 209–10
hard determinism 244–5
Hayek, F.A. 177
Hebdige, Dick 198
Hegel, Georg 224, 241, **267–9**
Heidegger, Martin 230, 243
Held, David 205, 214
Hermes, Joke 169
heterosexual hegemony 236
Hirst, Paul 204–5
Hispanic migration 180
history: historical knowledge 162; historical
remembering 195
Hoffman, Stanley 213
Hoggart, Richard 189
Hölderlin, Friedrich 268
Holocaust 255, 258, 269
homelessness 178–9
homosexuality 104, 148, 199
honour killings 294
Horkheimer, Max 158, 221, 222, 223, 233,
242, 255, 256, 258, 266–7, **269–70**
house purchase 178
Hughes, Everett C. 239
human rights 27–8, 173–4, **293–5**; and
citizenship 181–3, 185–6; Universal
Declaration of Human Rights
177, 294
humanities, and cultural theory 190–1

Hume, David 250
Hunter, James Davison 199
Husserl, Edmund 230, 243, 285,
288
hyperreality 131–2, 227–8
hysteria 109, 257

I 44, 45, 46
id 257, 270, 293
ideal types 33
identity 135–6, **270–1**; in classical social
theory 136–7; contemporary theories
139–43; and critical social theory
146–51; critical identity 148–9;
critical-self strategy 149; and feminism
143–4; fragmented 197–9; and the
Frankfurt School 137–8; and new media
163–6; and postcolonial theory 143; and
post-structuralism 138–9, 144–6; realist
theories of 149, 150–1; standpoint
theories 149–50; subversion 148
identity politics 51
ideological state apparatuses (ISAs) 66–7,
225
ideology 66–7, 225; Marx 25
Ilich, Ivan 104
Imaginary 63, 64, 276
individualism 177
individualization 106, 142
Industrial Revolution 105, **271–2**
informationalism 156
Institute for Social Research *see* Frankfurt
School
inter-national economies 205
interaction order 48–9
interest theory 188
Internet 156; e-commerce 184
interpellation 66
intersectionality theory 145
intimacy 31
Iraq 182
Irigaray, Luce 69–70, 231, 290

Jakobson, Roman 76
James, William 43, 246
Jameson, Fredric 118–19, 120–2, 132, 162,
223, **272–4**, 290
Jaspers, Karl 258
Jencks, Charles 290
juridical revolution 173

Kaldor, Mary 161
Kant, Immanuel 230, 241, 250, 268
Kellner, Douglas 161, 162
Keynes, John Maynard 175–7
Kierkegaard, Søren 230
kinesics 263
King, Martin Luther 247
kinship 77
Klein, Naomi 213
knowledge: historical 162; narrative 125–6;
    scientific 103, 124–5, 131
knowledge economy 160
Kristeva, Julia 70, 144, 236, **274–5**, 290
Kuhn, Manfred 41

Lacan, Jacques 236, 243, 254, 270, **275–6**,
    285, 291, 299; and feminism 68; and
    psychoanalysis 63–7; and structuralism
    78–9
language 75–6, 88, 124, 251; games 279;
    and gender relations 68; symbolic order
    of 64
langue 76, 245
L'Année Sociologique 249
Laqueur, Thomas 105
Lash, Scott 231
latent functions 260
Latouche, Serge 209
Latour, Bruno 133
Lefebvre, Henri 227
Lemert, Charles 213, 290
Les Temps Modernes 230
lesbianism 148, 199
Lévi-Strauss, Claude 235, 274, **277–8**, 285,
    291, 299; and structuralism 76–8, 83
Levinas, Emmanuel 229, 241
linguistics 64–5, 78, 88, 245, 275, 291, 295,
    298; linguistic turn 124
liquid modernity 141, 228, 229–30
literary criticism 242; and cultural theory
    190–1
Livingstone, Sonia 169
Locke, John 250
loss 63, 68, 70–1
Luhmann, Niklas 126
Lyotard, Jean-François 122–7, 227, 267,
    278–9, 289, 291; Rorty's critique of
    130–1

McLuhan, Marshall 158–9
madness, medicalization of 254

Madonna 198
Maines, David 41
manifest functions 260
Marcuse, Herbert 242, 255, 256, 258, 270,
    279–81, 288; critique of Fromm 60–1;
    and identity 138; and psychoanalysis
    61–3
marriage 31, 77–8, 93–4
Marshall, Thomas H. 173, 175–6
Marx, Karl 12, 16–17, 23–6, 224, 255, 258,
    261, **281–3**; and identity 136; and
    structuralism 74–5, 82–3
Marxism 120–2, 223, 227, 237, 244, 255,
    265, 273, 280
mass culture 121; totalitarian tendencies of
    222, see also popular culture
Mauss, Marcel 77, 110, 192
me 44, 45–6
Mead, George Herbert 37–8, 234, 239,
    283–4; and symbolic interactionism 42–6
media see new media
medicine, sociology of 103–5
men: embodiment 109–10; sexuality 70
mental illness: medicalization of 254;
    sociology of 47, 50–1
Merleau-Ponty, Maurice 110, 278, **284–5**,
    288, 300
Merton, Robert 260
metanarratives 122, 123, 130
Methodenstreit 21, 32
methodology of social theory 16–18
Mexican migration 180
migrants 179–80
Millet, Kate 107
mirror stage 64, 78, 270, 275, 276
Mitchell, Juliet 68–9, 253, **285–7**, 293
mobility rights 184–5
modernity 17–23, 103, 128–9, 206–7, 229,
    279, 287–8; and Giddens 91–4; liquid
    141, 228, 229–30; psychic costs of 62
modernization 321–2
money 31–2
Montesquieu 22, 224
morality, and new media 168–9
mortgages 178
mother–infant bond 63, 68, 70
motherhood 90, 275
Mouzelis, Nicos 95
multiculturalism 180
multiple selves theory 247
Muslim communities 179

Myanmar 181, 182
mythology 78, 277–8, 296–7

narcissism 64
narratives 123–4; metanarratives 122, 123, 130; narrative knowledge 125–6
national consciousness 195–6
neo-Marxism 260
neoconservatism 128–9, 177, 178
neoliberalism 235
networks 156–7
new media 156–7, 170; and identity 163–6; and morality 168–9; and the spectacle 161–3; technology and cultural form 158; and time 166–7
New Right *see* neoconservatism
new social movements 199
Newton, Isaac 250
Nietzsche, Friedrich 230

Obama, Barack 118
object relations theory 67
Oedipus complex 58, 64
Oedipus myth 78
Ohmae, Kenechi 204
ontological security 90, 96, 97
Organisation for Economic Co-operation and Development 237
Other 63, 69, 230, 241, 276
overdetermination 225

pacification 106
Paine, Thomas 174
panopticon 254
parole 76, 245
Parsons, Talcott 14, 40–1, 259
participant observation 239
patriarchal cultures 67
pensions 178
performance 62, 236
performativity theory 52, 82, 195, 253, 287
personal relationships 92–4
phallus 67, 93
phenomenology 110, 223, 243, 280, 284–5, **288**
philology 295, 298
philosophy, Western 80
physical capital 111
pity, politics of 169
plastic sexuality 93
Plato 230

play stage 45
poetry 3, 4–7
political rights 176
pollution 194
Popper, Karl 177, 222, 242
popular culture 156–70, 198–9, *see also* mass culture
positive philosophy 23
positivism 222, 255, 289
post-feminism 253
post-Lacanian feminism 69
postcolonial theory, and identity 143
Poster, Mark 163–4
postmodern feminism 144–5, 253, 290
postmodernism 117–19, 273, 278, **289–91**; and identity 139–40
postmodernity 229, 250–1, 288
post-structuralism: criticisms of 82–4; and Derrida 79–81, 83; and feminism 82; and Foucault 81–2, 83; and identity 138–9, 144–6; and queer theory 82
poverty 11–12, 212, 213
power relationships 81–2, 107, 190
power-knowledge 254
practical consciousness 89–90
preconscious 57
premises, in symbolic interactionism 38, 40
proletariat 24, 25–6
psychoanalysis 237, 238, 255, 256, 257, 270, 274, 289, **292–3**; and Althusser 66–7; Blumer's critique of 41; and feminism 67–71, 285–7; Frankfurt School 58–9; Freudian legacy 56–8; and Fromm 60–1; and Lacan 63–7; and Marcuse 61–3, *see also* Freud

quantification 40
queer sexuality 148, 199, 253; and post-structuralism 82

racism 246
Radway, Janice 198
rationalism 250
rationality 9–10, 266
rationalization 33–4, 106
Rawls, John 181
Readings, Bill 160
real 276
realist theories of identity 149, 150–1
reality 61, 131–2
recognition, and citizenship 177–81

redistribution, and citizenship 175–7
reflex arc 43
reflexive modernization 231
reflexivity 91–2, 261
refugees 179–80
Reich, Wilhelm 258
religion 22, 28–9
Renouvier 248–9
repression 60–1, 60–2, 105–6, 137–8
repressive desublimation 59, 62
repressive state apparatuses (RSAs) 225
reproductive rights 253
resistance 147, 198
rights 27–8, 176, **293–5**; mobility rights
    184–5; reproductive rights 253;
    transaction rights 184–5
risk 214–15
risk society 231, 287
ritual sacrifice 23
rituals 29, 53
Robertson, Roland 208, 210
root images, in symbolic interactionism
    38–9, 40
Rorty, Richard 130–1
Rosenberg, Justin 216
routinization 96–7
rule 89
Russia 179

sacrifice, ritual 23
Saint Elizabeths hospital research
    (Goffman) 47, 50–1
Saint-Simon, Henri 23–4
Sartre, Jean-Paul 230
Saul, John Ralston 216
Saussure, Ferdinand de 64, 243, 245, 274,
    277, 291, **295–6**, 298; and cultural theory
    193; and structuralism 75–6, 80, 83
Schoenberg, Arnold 221
Scholem, Gershom 232
Schopenhauer, Arthur 230
scientific determinism 244
scientific knowledge 103, 124–5, 131
scientific method, in sociology 20
Scientific Revolution 272, 289
second modernity 231–2
Sedgwick, Eve Kosofsky 82, 148
self *see* identity
semanalysis 274
semiology 75, 274, 296, 297, *see also* signs
semiotics 70, **296–7**

sexuality 69–70, 81–2, 92–4, 139, 253;
    Freud 58; male 70; queer 148, 199, 253;
    women's 69–70, 109, 198
Shetland Islands, ethnographic research
    (Goffman) 47–8
Sica, Alan 95–6
signification 64–5, 81, 291, 296–7
signs 193, 296–7, *see also* semiology
Silverstone, Roger 168
Simmel, Georg 29–32, 105, 229, 235, 241,
    272, 288, **297–8**; and gender relations 20;
    and identity 137
simulation 227–8
social behaviorism 37, 239
social bodies 105–11
social capital 110–11
social citizenship 179
social critical theory 242
social interaction 234, 235
social philosophy 255
social rights 176
social stratification 235
social theory: classical 19–35; method
    16–18; and trouble 14–16
socialization 98, 106
sociological theory 14–15
sociology: emergence of 18–22; of medicine
    103–5; scientific method 20
soft determinism 245
space: social constructions of 195–7;
    time–space distanciation 206
spectacle, the 161–3
speech 80, 88, 251
speed 166–7, 301, *see also* time
Spinoza, Baruch 175
sport 261
standpoint theories 149–50
state apparatuses: ideological 66–7;
    repressive 225
stigma 51, 108
strain theory 188
structural functionalism 40–1
structuralism 73–4, 224, 227, 231, 243, 244,
    245–6, 249, 253, 255, 257, **298–9**; and
    Althusser 78–9; and Barthes 78;
    criticisms of 82–4; and Lacan 78–9; and
    Levi-Strauss 76–8, 83; and Marx 74–5,
    82–3; and Saussure 75–6, 83
structuration theory 86–7, 100–1, 261, 262,
    287, 300; and Bourdieu 97–100; and
    Giddens 87–97

structure 73–4, 88–9, 223, 235, 242, **299–300**
subcultures 198
subjectivity 147
suicide 27
superego 257, 270, 293
surplus repression 61, 62
surplus value 24–5, 74–5, 224
surveillance 104, 107, 163
symbolic capital 235
symbolic exchange 227–8
symbolic interactionism 234, 239, 263; and Erving Goffman 46–54, 108–9; and George Herbert Mead 42–6; Herbert Blumer's formulation of 37–42
Symbolic order 63
symbols: cultural 226; sacred 192
systems reproduction 89

taboos 29
talk 54
talking cure (psychoanalysis) 57, 257, 292
taste 111
taxation 178
technology 301; and cultural form 158; and time 166–7
television 157, 158, 159
terrorism 179–80, 213; war on terror 163, 182
Tester, Keith 168
Thompson, Grahame 204–5
Thompson, John B. 95
time: social constructions of 195–7; and technology 166–7; time–space distanciation 206, *see also* speed
TNCs (transnational corporations) 204, 205
Tobin, James (Tobin Tax) 183, 184–5
Toennies, Ferdinand 191
Tomlinson, John 207–9
total institutions 50
totems 29, 192
Toynbee, Arnold 290
traditional action 33
transaction rights 184–5
transformationalism 205–7, 214
transnational corporations (TNCs) 204, 205
trouble, and social theory 14–16
trust relations 92
Turner, Bryan 95, 109

Turner, Victor 194–5
typification 30

unconscious 57, 257, 270, 292; Giddens 89–90
unfocused interaction 49
United Nations 293–4
United States: American Revolution 9; American War of Independence 174; citizenship 174, 176–7; Mexican migration to 180
Universal Declaration of Human Rights 177, 294
universities 160
uprisings (1968) 227, 237, 300
urbanization 105
Urry, John 215–16

value system, bourgeois 226
value-rational action 33
veil, the 247
Virilio, Paul 166–7, **300–1**
von Schelling, Friedrich 268

war on terror 163, 182
warfare 161
Washington, Booker T. 240, 247
Watson, John 44
Weber, Alfred 258
Weber, Max 12, 32–4, 103, 235, 246, 255, 261, 272, **301–3**; and cultural theory 191; and identity 137
Wildavsky, Aaron 194
Williams, Raymond 158–61, 165, 189
Wittgenstein, Ludwig 124
Wollstonecraft, Mary 252
women: embodiment 106, 108–9; exchange of 77; maltreatment of 294; medicalization of 103–4; and romantic fiction 198; sexuality 69–70, 109, 198, *see also* feminism, gender
workers, alienation of 224
Worsley, Peter 261
writing 80
Wyneken, Gustav 232

youth cultures 198

zombie categories 19

Also available from Routledge

Globalization: A Reader

Edited by **Charles Lemert, Anthony Elliott, Daniel Chaffee**
and **Eric Hsu**

Globalization is a clear, comprehensive, critical reader which offers a unique compilation of the major statements – drawn from a variety of historical periods, political contexts, intellectual perspectives and academic disciplines – on the globalization debate. Charles Lemert and Anthony Elliott expertly guide the reader through the complex terrain of globalization – its engaging histories, transnational economies, multiple cultures and cosmopolitan politics.

Encompassing the full range of salient human history, this book's remit spans the Babylonian and Persian empires in Mesopotamia, through ancient Greece and imperial Rome to the long sixteenth century of European world exploration and colonization, to the present day. Represented in the contemporary debates on globalization are leading figures such as: Samuel Huntington, Francis Fukayama, Anthony Giddens, Noam Chomsky, Joseph Nye, Osama bin Laden, Arjun Appadurai, Zygmunt Bauman, Timothy Garton-Ash, Saskia Sassen, Naomi Klein, Kwame Anthony Appiah, James N. Rosenau, David Held, and Amartya Sen.

Selected Table of Contents: Part I – The Age of Empires, 3000 BCE– 1500 CE; Part II – The Modern World System and Industrial Capitalism, 1500–1914; Part III – The Short Twentieth Century: Global Uncertainty and Restructuring; Part IV – The Great Globalization Debate; Part V – Globalization Since 2001–Present; Part VI – Global Futures: Time and Tense

ISBN: 978-0-415-46477-2 (hbk)
ISBN: 978-0-415-46478-9 (pbk)

For more information and online ordering visit:
www.routledge.com

Also available from Routledge

**Ethnographies Revisited:
Constructing theory in the field**

Edited by **Antony J. Puddephatt, William Shaffir and
Steven W. Kleinknecht**

Ethnographies Revisited provides first-hand accounts of how leading
qualitative researchers crafted key theoretical concepts found in their
major book-length ethnographies. Great ethnographic research relies not
on the rigid execution of prescribed methodological procedures, but on
the unrelenting cultivation of theoretical ideas. These contributors focus
squarely on this neglected topic, providing reflexive accounts of how
research decisions were made in light of emerging theoretical questions.

Selected Table of Contents: Part 1 – Generating Grounded Theory;
Part 2 – Working with Sensitizing Concepts; Part 3 – Extending Theoretical
Frames; Part 4 – Conceptualizing Community and Social Organization;
Part 5 – Challenging Established Wisdom; Part 6 – Theorizing from
Alternative Data: Documentary, Historical and Autobiographical Sources

ISBN: 978-0-415-45220-5 (hbk)
ISBN: 978-0-415-45221-2 (pbk)
ISBN: 978-0-203-87650-3 (ebk)

For more information and online ordering visit:
www.routledge.com

Also available from Routledge

The Routledge Companion to Semiotics

Edited by Paul Cobley

"**Paul Cobley has gathered a dream team to cover the essentials of semiotics as it stands at the dawn of the twenty-first century. In a field that is often obscured by verbiage and jargon, this is a much needed volume, written with clarity of purpose and exposition.**"
Paul Bouissac, *University of Toronto, Canada*

The Routledge Companion to Semiotics provides the ideal introduction to semiotics, containing engaging essays from an impressive range of international leaders in the field.

Topics covered include:

- the history, development and uses of semiotics
- key theorists, including Saussure, Peirce and Sebeok
- crucial and contemporary topics such as biosemiotics, sociosemiotics and semioethics
- the semiotics of media and culture, nature and cognition

Featuring an extended glossary of key terms and thinkers as well as suggestions for further reading, this is an invaluable reference guide for students of semiotics at all levels.

ISBN: 978-0-415-44072-1 (hbk)
ISBN: 978-0-415-44073-8 (pbk)
ISBN: 978-0-203-87415-8 (ebk)

For more information and online ordering visit:
www.routledge.com

Also available from Routledge

The Routledge Companion to English Language Studies

Edited by Janet Maybin and Joan Swann

The Routledge Companion to English Language Studies is an accessible guide to the major topics, debates and issues in English Language Studies. The collection includes entries written by a team of well-known language specialists from a diverse range of backgrounds who clearly examine and explain established knowledge and recent developments in the field. Covering a wide range of topics such as globalization, gender and sexuality, and food packaging, this volume provides critical overviews of:

- approaches to researching, describing and analysing English
- the position of English as a global language
- the use of English in texts, practices and discourses
- variation and diversity throughout the English-speaking world

Fully cross-referenced throughout and featuring useful definitions of key terms and concepts, this authoritative volume also includes helpful suggestions for further reading.

The Routledge Companion to English Language Studies will be of interest to those teaching English or wishing to check, consolidate or update their knowledge, and is essential reading for all students of English Language Studies.

ISBN: 978-0-415-40173-9 (hbk)
ISBN: 978-0-415-40338-2 (pbk)
ISBN: 978-0-203-87895-8 (ebk)

For more information and online ordering visit:
www.routledge.com